A-Level
Business
Exam Board: AQA

Revising for Business exams is stressful, that's for sure — even just getting your notes sorted out can leave you needing a lie down. But help is at hand...

This brilliant CGP book explains **everything you'll need to learn** for **both years** of the course, all in a straightforward style that's easy to get your head around.

We've also included **exam-style questions** to test how ready you are for the real thing, along with a section of advice on how to pick up as many marks as possible!

A-Level revision? It has to be CGP!

Editors:
Rob Harrison, Shaun Harrogate, Sharon Keeley-Holden, Ali Palin, Caley Simpson and Ben Train.

Contributors:
Paul Brockbank, Angela Duffy, John Evans-Pritchard, Peter Gray, Jeff Harris, Alison Hazell, Carla Little, Adrian Murray, Nagu Rao, Tom Reilly, Mike Tappenden, Lynda Turner and Keith Williamson.

ISBN: 978 1 78294 351 8

With thanks to Victoria Skelton and Karen Wells for the proofreading.
With thanks to Jan Greenway and Laura Jakubowski for the copyright research.

Cover photo © iStockphoto.com/Pinkypills

Clipart from Corel®
Printed by Elanders Ltd, Newcastle upon Tyne.

Based on the classic CGP style created by Richard Parsons.

Contents

If you're revising for the **AS exams**, you'll need Sections 1-6 and Section 15.
If you're revising for the **A-Level exams**, you'll need the whole book.

Section One — What is Business? (AS)

Why Businesses Exist 2
Mission, Aims and Objectives 3
Revenue, Costs and Profit 6
Different Forms of Business 8
The Role of Shareholders 12
Businesses and the External Environment 14

Section Two — Management and Decision Making (AS)

Management and Leadership 18
Management Decision Making 20
Decision Trees 22
Stakeholders and Decision Making 24

Section Three — Marketing Decisions (AS)

Marketing Objectives 26
Market Analysis 28
Market Research 30
Interpreting Marketing Data 32
Interpreting Elasticity of Demand 36
Marketing Decisions — STP 38
Marketing Decisions — The Marketing Mix 40
Marketing Mix — Product 42
Marketing Mix — Pricing 46
Marketing Mix — Promotion 48
Marketing Mix — Place 50
People, Process and Physical Environment 52

Section Four — Operational Decisions (AS)

Operational Objectives 54
Capacity Utilisation 56
Increasing Efficiency and Productivity 58
Improving Quality 62
Managing Inventory 64
Managing Supply Chains 65

Section Five — Financial Decisions (AS)

Financial Objectives 68
Measuring and Increasing Profit 70
Cash Flow Forecasting 72
Setting Budgets 74
Analysing Budgets 76
Break-Even Analysis 78
Choosing Sources of Finance 80

Section Six — Human Resource Decisions (AS)

Human Resource Objectives 82
Interpreting Human Resource Data 84
Improving Organisational Design 86
Managing the Human Resource Flow 88
Motivation and Job Design 90
Improving Motivation 92
Improving Employer-Employee Relations 94
Employee Representation 96

Section Seven — Mission, Corporate Objectives and Strategy

Mission, Objectives and Strategy 98

Section Eight — Internal Analysis

Financial Analysis — Balance Sheets 100
Financial Analysis — Income Statements 105
Financial Analysis — Value and Limitations ...107
Financial Analysis — Ratios 108
Financial Analysis — Gearing 111
Value and Limitations of Ratios......................113
Analysing Overall Performance 114
Methods of Assessing Performance 116

Section Nine — Analysing the External Environment

Business and the Legal Environment 118
Employment Law 120
Business and the Political Environment..........122
Business and the Economy 124
Inflation and Exchange Rates 126
Government Policy and the Economy 128
The Global Economy 130
Business and the Social Environment............132
Business and the Technological Environment 135
Business and the Competitive Environment 136

Section Ten — Investment Appraisal

Assessing Investments....................................138
Investment Decisions.....................................142

Section Eleven — Choosing Strategic Direction

Marketing Strategies 144
Positioning Strategies 146

Section Twelve — Strategic Methods

Business Growth... 148
Business Growth — Organic 150
Business Growth — External......................... 152
Innovation 154
Entering International Markets 158
Locating Abroad 160
Multinationals 162
International Business Strategies 164
Use of Digital Technology............................. 166

Section Thirteen — Managing Change

Causes of Change 168
Managing Change 170
Overcoming Barriers to Change.................... 172
Managing Organisational Culture................ 174

Section Fourteen — Implementing Strategy

Planning Strategy.. 178
Implementing Strategy 180
Network Analysis.. 182
Difficulties with Implementing Strategy 186
Evaluating Strategy 189

Section Fifteen — Maths Skills

Maths Skills 190

Do Well in Your Exams

The A-Level Exams 193
Get Marks in Your A-Level Exams................. 194
Worked Exam Questions 196

We deliberately haven't included answers to most of the questions — that's because there are lots of valid ways to give your answers. Instead, we've put in a section on how to write answers and do well. Answers to numerical questions are included though, on pages 199-202.

Answers to Numerical Questions................. 199
Glossary 203
Index.. 207

Why Businesses Exist

Here's a bit of background for you. You'd be hard-pushed to get as far as your A-levels and not have some idea about why businesses exist, but there's still quite a lot to learn. Here's the basics to get you started.

Businesses Supply **Goods** or **Services**

1) Businesses sell **products** to customers who are willing to **pay** for them. Products can be **goods** or **services**. Goods are **physical items** like books or furniture, whereas services are actions performed by other **people** to aid the customer, e.g. hairdressers and plumbers provide services.
2) Some businesses sell **necessities** — goods or services that you **need** (like gas and electricity). Others provide **luxury** goods or services — things you **want** but don't need (like holidays and jewellery).

There are **Advantages** to owning a **Business**

A person who starts their own business is called an entrepreneur. Entrepreneurs have to find resources and organise activities needed to start the business.

1) People set up businesses mainly to make a **profit**. This means the business **makes** more money than it **spends**. Starting a business is risky, but many people take the risk because of the possibility of big **financial rewards**.
2) People usually only set up their own business if they expect to make **more** than they could earn working as an **employee** of another company.
3) People may set up their own business so that they can be **their own boss** and make their own decisions — they don't have to answer to anyone else.
4) Setting up your own business also gives you the opportunity to do a job you're really **interested** in.

Most Businesses **Need** to make a **Profit**

Public sector = government-owned
Private sector = privately owned

1) Businesses have to **make a profit** or **break even** (see p.78) to survive.
2) This is especially true in the **private sector** — if a business doesn't make enough money to survive it could go **bankrupt** and have to **close down**.
3) In the **public sector**, it's not as clear-cut. Organisations like the army, the police, hospitals and state schools aren't there to **make money** — they provide a service to the community.
4) **Non-profit** businesses, e.g. charities, have **social** or **ethical aims**, rather than financial ones.

For more on these different forms of business, see p.8.

Businesses can have **Other Aims**

As well as making a profit, businesses may have **other aims**, such as:

- To offer the **highest quality** goods and services possible.
- To give excellent **customer service**.
- To have a great **image** and **reputation**.
- To **develop new products** ahead of competitors.
- To offer a **diverse** range of goods or services.
- To become fully **sustainable** or minimise **environmental impact**.
- To invest in the **local community** or **social projects**.

Geraldine was taking this whole 'aims' thing a bit too literally.

Businesses set specific **objectives** to help them meet their aims, as you'll see over the next few pages.

Don't make all your private sector thoughts too public...

There aren't any questions on this page, but don't let that fool you — there are plenty on the next topic. The most important thing to remember is that, usually, the main aim of a business is to make a profit. However, this isn't always the case. How businesses go about achieving their aims... well, that's a story for the next few pages...

Mission, Aims and Objectives

The mission, aims and objectives of a business are really important — they're what the business wants to achieve. They're so important that you've got three pages on them.

Mission Statements *tell you about a Business's* ***Intentions***

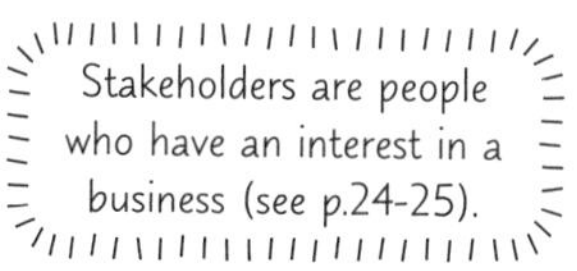

1) The **mission** of a business is its **overall purpose** or **main corporate aims**. The **mission statement** is a written **description** of these aims. Mission statements are intended to make all **stakeholders** aware of what the business does and why, and to **encourage** all employees to **work towards** its aims.
2) Mission statements tell you the **purpose** of the business and include other information, such as its **values**, its **standards**, its **strategy**, who the **customers** are and what makes the business **unique**.
3) Mission statements give clues about the company's **beliefs**. For example, a mission statement that mentions **ethics** and **principles** gives a big hint that **ethical practice** is important as well as **profitability**.
4) Mission statements can give staff a sense of **shared purpose**, and encourage them to work towards **common goals** — having the **cooperation** of all the staff makes it more likely that a business will achieve its aims.
5) On the other hand, companies **don't** have to prove that what they say in their mission statement is **accurate**, so they can say what they think consumers want to hear, without having to do anything about it. However, this is **bad practice**, and a business's **reputation** will be **damaged** if customers find that its actions don't reflect its stated values.

Businesses set ***Objectives*** *at* ***Different Levels***

Mission Statement and Corporate Aims
↓
Corporate Objectives
↓
Functional Objectives

1) Businesses set **objectives** to enable them to achieve their mission. Objectives turn the overall aims of a business into **specific goals** that must be met.
2) The diagram on the right shows the hierarchy of objectives. They can be set at the **corporate** or **functional** level.

Corporate objectives

Corporate objectives are the goals of the business as a **whole**. The corporate objectives will depend on the **size** of the business. A new shop owner might focus on trying to **survive**, while a big international company will want to **grow bigger** and **diversify** its product range.

Functional objectives

Functional objectives (sometimes called **departmental objectives**) are the objectives of each **department**. They're more **detailed** than corporate objectives, and they are **specific** to each department. Businesses need to set **functional objectives** that will help them **achieve** their **corporate objectives**. Whenever a corporate objective is set, **all** the managers in the business have to look at how their department can help to achieve the objective, and set **functional objectives** that will **contribute** to achieving the corporate objective.

3) Businesses set objectives for lots of reasons. If an objective is agreed upon, managers can make sure that **everyone** is working towards a **goal**, and **coordination** between departments should improve. Working towards an objective can also be **motivating** for employees. Objectives are really useful in **decision-making**, as they make it easier to see what the business is trying to achieve.
4) Managers can **compare performance** with their objectives to **measure** the success of the business and **review** their decisions.

Employees *may have their own* ***Personal Objectives***

1) Functional objectives **aren't** the last stage of setting objectives — **team managers** within a department might set objectives for their **team** based on the functional objectives of the whole department and **individual staff members** might even have their own **personal objectives**.
2) E.g. if the sales department has a functional objective to increase sales by 10% over 12 months, the telesales team might have an objective to increase sales from 500 to 550 a week. A telesales operative's objective might be to increase their sales from 20 to 25 a day.

Mission, Aims and Objectives

Objectives should be Specific, Measurable, Agreed, Realistic and Timely

To be effective, a functional objective should be '**SMART**' — specific, measurable, agreed, realistic and timely.

Specific — **Vague objectives** like "to improve quality" **don't** really tell staff what they're supposed to be aiming for. Making them more **specific**, e.g. "to reduce the number of items produced that have defects", means that the business is more likely to **achieve** them.

Measurable — If the objective **isn't measurable**, the business **won't know** if it's achieved it or not. E.g. "to increase profit by 5%" is a measurable objective, but "to improve the business" isn't.

Agreed — Everyone who's going to be involved in **achieving** the objective needs to **know** about it and **agree** to it. E.g. if the objective is to increase sales, the sales manager and salespeople will all need to agree to it.

Realistic — There's no point setting objectives that are **too ambitious**, e.g. tripling sales within 12 months, or achieving a 95% market share. **Impossible objectives** just **demotivate** staff.

Timely — There should be a **specific timeframe** that the objective has to be achieved in. E.g. the objective might be to increase revenue by 5% within 12 months. If there's **no time limit**, staff won't see the objective as **urgent** — they might think they don't need to worry about achieving it because as long as it gets done at some time in the future then it doesn't matter.

Buying a magical thinking cap won't make you SMART.

There are Different Types of Objectives

Businesses will have different objectives, but here are some common ones:

Profit Objectives

See pages 6-7 for more information on profit.

1) **Businesses** that are currently making a loss might aim to become **profitable**. Established businesses that are already profitable might want to **increase** their profits, e.g. by 10% within three years.
2) To achieve its overall profit objective, a business may set **functional** objectives to **minimise costs**, which could be an objective for all departments, or to **increase sales**, which could be an objective for the sales and marketing departments.

Growth Objectives

1) Many businesses aim to grow. The larger a business grows, the more it is able to use its position in the market to earn higher profits.
2) Growth objectives can be based on increasing **revenue**, **market share**, or **expanding** a business.

Survival Objectives

1) Survival just means that a business can continue to trade, rather than running out of **money** or being forced to exit the market for another reason.
2) Survival is often the main objective for **new** businesses, and it becomes a **key objective** during periods of strong competition from other companies, or when the economy is declining or in a recession.

Cash Flow Objectives

1) Cash flow is the money that moves **in** and **out** of a business over a set period of **time**.
2) Businesses set cash flow objectives in order to **improve** their cash flow — i.e. to make sure they always have enough money to make the payments that are due.
3) **Increasing cash flow** gives the company a greater chance of **survival**.
4) There's more on cash flow objectives on p.68 and methods of improving cash flow on p.72-73.

Mission, Aims and Objectives

Social and Ethical Objectives are Important too

1) **Social** objectives relate to benefiting society or people in need. **Ethical** objectives are based on **moral principles** about how businesses treat people and the environment. E.g. principles of fair trade and minimising environmental damage.

2) **Non-profit** organisations, like charities or social enterprises, are set up to achieve social or ethical objectives. E.g. housing associations provide affordable housing for people on low incomes.

3) **For-profit** businesses usually focus on making a **profit**. However, social and ethical objectives are becoming increasingly important, especially as information on how businesses operate is becoming more widely **available**. Businesses might set objectives to provide **facilities** for the local community, or to only buy from suppliers who pay a **fair** wage. People are more likely to buy from a business with good ethical practices, which can help achieve other aims too.

Marks & Spencer successfully made their UK business carbon neutral by setting a number of ethical objectives.

Businesses can have Short-term and Long-term Objectives

1) **Long-term** objectives include things like long-term growth. **Long-term objectives** tend to set the **direction** of a business. They affect the **big decisions** that senior managers make.
2) **Short-term** objectives include things like short-term **survival** and making short-term **profit**, but they often require a business to cut back on its long-term objectives.
3) For example, a business trying to increase on last year's profits might **cut** its **advertising** budget, stop its **training** programme, and cut back on its **product development** budget. At the end of the year it'd have **more profit** because of cutting all those **costs**, but it would have lost out on its other objectives.
4) Businesses are often **criticised** for being too concerned with **short-term gain**. Shareholders often want a **quick return** on their investment, or they'll take their money and go elsewhere. Businesses have to go for short-term profits or risk losing investors.
5) There needs to be a good **balance** between long-term and short-term objectives.

There's more on mission and objectives on p.98-99.

Practice Questions

Q1 Give three examples of information that could be included in a mission statement.

Q2 What is the difference between a corporate objective and a functional objective?

Q3 Give two examples of corporate objectives. For each corporate objective, write down two functional objectives that would help the business to achieve it.

Q4 What does SMART stand for in the term 'SMART objectives'?

Exam Questions

Q1 Explain what a mission statement is, and discuss why businesses see mission statements as valuable. [4 marks]

Q2 Explain the importance of the SMART criteria for setting objectives. [6 marks]

Mission Statement Impossible — I think I saw that at the cinema...

Ok, so it might not be the most exciting part of Business, but this is really important stuff. The stuff about mission statements is quite good anyway — you can just imagine the scene in the boardroom: "Your mission, if you choose to accept it, is to provide quality sofas and dining furniture." Anyway, your mission is to learn these three pages.

Revenue, Costs and Profit

Profit is the most important objective for many businesses. To measure profit, you'll need to understand revenue and costs, and know how they're calculated. Here's a couple of pages to fill you in on the details.

Revenue is the **Money** a business makes from **Sales**

1) Revenue is the **value of sales** — it's sometimes just called **sales** and can also be called **turnover**. It's the amount of money generated by sales of a product, **before** any deductions are made.

Sales include payments for services, not just for physical goods.

2) You can work out the revenue by multiplying the **price** that the customer pays for each unit by the **number of units** that the business sells:

Revenue = selling price per unit × quantity of units sold

E.g. if a business sells 2000 teapots for £8 each, the revenue is **£8** × **2000** = **£16 000**.

3) **Revenue** is affected by both **sales volume** and **price**. If sales volume increases by 50%, revenue will increase by 50%. Increasing the selling price may increase the revenue, but it depends on what effect the higher price will have on the number of sales — see **price elasticity of demand** on p.36-37.

Costs can be **Fixed** or **Variable**

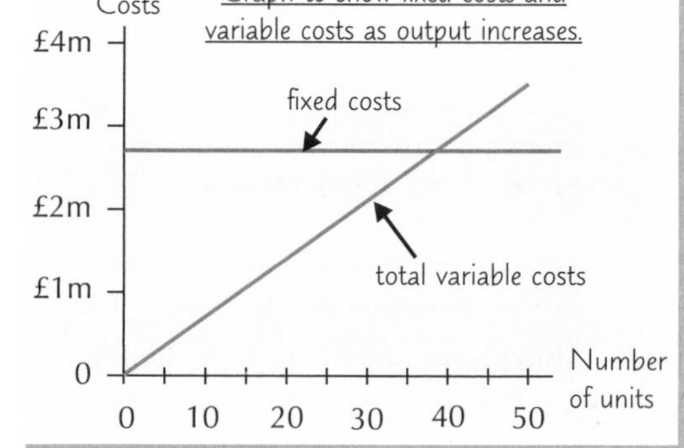

1) **Fixed costs** don't change with output. **Rent** on a factory, business **rates**, **senior managers' basic salaries** and the cost of **new machinery** are fixed costs. When output increases, a business makes more use of the facilities it's already got. The **cost** of those facilities **doesn't change**.

2) **Variable costs** rise and fall as output changes. Hourly **wages**, **raw material costs** and the **packaging costs** for each product are all variable costs.

Total variable costs = variable cost per unit × number of units sold

3) **Semi-variable costs** have fixed and variable parts. **Telephone bills** are a good example of **semi-variable** costs. Businesses have to pay a **fixed** amount for their phone line plus a **variable** amount depending on the phone calls they've made.

4) The **total costs** are just the fixed costs plus the variable costs: **Total costs = fixed costs + variable costs**

Profit is the **Difference** between **Revenue** and **Costs**

Revenue, Costs and Profit were all related.

1) When you deduct the total costs from the total revenue, you're left with the **profit**.

Profit = total revenue – total costs

2) If a business's **total revenue** is **greater** than its total costs, then it will make a **profit**. If the **total costs** are **greater** than the total revenue, then the business will make a **loss**.

E.g. a teapot business has fixed costs of **£4000** pcm and variable costs of **£4** per teapot.
It sells **2000** teapots in one month for **£8** each, so its revenue is **£16 000**.
Its total variable costs that month are 2000 × £4 = **£8000**, so its total costs are £4000 + £8000 = **£12 000**.
So the profit is: £16 000 – £12 000 = **£4000**

3) Businesses can do different things with profit. Most businesses **give it to the shareholders** as dividend payments or **re-invest** the profit in new activities. But they could also pay staff bonuses, invest it in a bank, give it to charity, or use it to fund projects in the local community.

4) **Shareholders** often want a **short-term** reward for supporting the business. In the long term, it's often better for the business to hold on to the profit and **re-invest** it in future projects.

There's more on shareholders on p.12-13.

Revenue, Costs and Profit

Large-Scale Production helps keep costs Low

The more a business produces, the **lower** the **cost per unit** produced. This is because the **fixed costs** are **shared out** between **more items**. The best way to show this is with an example:

1) MicroDave make microwave ovens. The **fixed costs** of running MicroDave are £200 000 per year. The **variable costs** of materials and labour are £15 per microwave.
2) If MicroDave make **5000 microwaves a year**, the total production costs are... £200 000 + (£15 × 5000) = **£275 000**. The **cost per microwave** is £275 000 ÷ 5000 = **£55.**
3) If MicroDave make **20 000 microwaves a year**, the total production costs are... £200 000 + (£15 × 20 000) = **£500 000**. The **cost per microwave** is £500 000 ÷ 20 000 = **£25.**

Businesses use information on Product Costs to Make Decisions

1) Businesses use **costs** information to set the **selling price** of their products and services. They set the price to make sure they'll make a **profit**. (Number of sales × price) – costs = profit.
2) If a business is a "**price taker**" in a very competitive market, it **doesn't have control** of the **selling price** of its products — it takes whatever price the market will pay. Businesses in this situation need accurate **costing** information to work out if it's **profitable** to make and sell a product at all. E.g. farmers have to sell milk, carrots, potatoes, etc. to supermarkets for whatever price the supermarkets are willing to pay — if they try to put their prices up, supermarkets will just buy from other farmers instead.
3) Businesses set **budgets** (see p.74-77) which forecast how much costs are going to be over a year. Managers need to monitor costs so that they know whether they're **meeting** the budget.

Profit is Important for Many Reasons

1) **Profit can motivate people** — People in the business who own shares will receive a portion of the profit as a dividend payment (see p.10). Some businesses offer a profit-sharing scheme, where employees are given bonuses from a share of the total profits.
2) **Profit is a good source of finance** — Profit can be retained in the business and used for investments. This can help the business grow and increase profits. Businesses do not need to pay interest on retained profit, like they do with loans, nor does it need to be paid back in the future.
3) **Profit can be used to attract investors** — Potential investors look at profit levels when deciding whether to buy shares in a company. People are more likely to invest if a business is making a large profit, as they'll expect a good dividend payment.

For more on profits, go to p.70-71.

Practice Questions

Q1 What is the formula for calculating revenue?

Q2 Give three examples of fixed costs.

Q3 Why is profit important? Give three reasons.

Exam Questions

Q1 Bricks 'n' More Tar Co. has a revenue of £650 000 in one year. Their fixed costs are 23% of the revenue, and their total variable costs are 54% of the revenue. Calculate the profit made by Bricks 'n' More Tar Co. [3 marks]

Q2 Beth Brook Hats employs two hat-makers, each at £280/week. Beth, as Managing Director, pays herself £400/week. The other fixed costs are £300/week. The variable costs of raw materials are £14 per hat. Hats sell for £50.

a) Draw a graph to show fixed, variable and total costs for outputs from 0 hats/week to 100 hats/week. [6 marks]

b) Calculate the profit that Beth is making at her current output level of 60 hats per week, assuming weekly sales match output. [4 marks]

If you don't learn this, it'll cost you...

Costs, revenue and profit are pretty simple concepts, but very important ones. They'll crop up in other topics, so make sure you get them straight in your head. You need to be able to calculate revenue and profit, so learn the formulas well, and make sure you're clear on the difference between fixed and variable costs too. Oh joy...

Different Forms of Business

There are loads of different forms of business, and each form has different aims, benefits and drawbacks. Unfortunately there's only one thing for it — get stuck into these pages and learn them all.

Organisations can be in the *Public Sector* or the *Private Sector*

Public sector organisations are owned and run by the **Government**. They aim to provide services to the public, rather than make a profit. NHS hospitals are one example — their aim is to provide health care that's available to everyone. Organisations like the NHS, UK police forces and the fire service are run in a similar way to other businesses, but they don't charge for their services so don't make a profit — they are funded by the UK **tax system**.

Private sector organisations are owned and run by **private individuals**. They range from small sole traders to huge organisations such as John Lewis and ASDA. Most private sector businesses aim to make a **profit**, however this is not always the case — **non-profit** organisations such as **charities** are also part of the private sector.

Non-Profit businesses have different *Aims* and *Objectives*

1) As their name suggests, non-profit businesses are **not** set up to make a **profit**. Instead, they have other aims, often to **help** people in need or benefit the community. Like other businesses, they usually have money coming **into** and going **out** of the business — the main **difference** is that the money generated by the business **doesn't** go to the owners or shareholders as **profit**.
2) **Charities** like the British Red Cross, Oxfam and Amnesty International make money from **donations** and business activities (like charity shops). This money is used to fund charitable activities, e.g. setting up hospitals in developing countries. Charities get **tax reductions** because of their non-profit structure.
3) **Social enterprises** are normal businesses with a **social objective**. The business **trades** and **makes profit** like any other business, but its profits are used to pay for its **social activities**. E.g. the profits from sales of One® Water bottled water are used to fund clean water projects in villages in Africa.
4) **Mutual organisations** like building societies aim to offer their customers the best possible value on products and services. **Profits** are **reinvested** into the business in order to **reduce prices** — that means that building societies can often offer higher savings rates and lower loan rates than banks, because they don't have to pay any of their profits to shareholders.

Liability to pay off *Business Debts* can be *Limited* or *Unlimited*

Responsibility for **business debts** works differently for different forms of business.

Unlimited liability

1) If a business has unlimited liability, the **business** and the **owner** are **seen as one** under the **law**. This is the case for **sole traders** (see p.9).
2) This means **business debts** become the **personal debts** of the owner. Sole traders can be forced to **sell personal assets** like their **house** to pay off business debts.
3) Unlimited liability is a **huge financial risk** — it's an important factor to consider when deciding on the type of ownership for a new business.

Limited liability

1) Limited liability means that the owners **aren't personally responsible** for the debts of the business.
2) The **shareholders** (owners) of both **private** and **public limited companies** (see p.10) have limited liability, because a limited company has a **separate legal identity** from its owners. The **most** the shareholders in a limited company can lose is the money they have **invested** in the company.

The difference between limited liability and unlimited liability is **really important**. E.g. a builder puts **£1500** into their own business and the business hits bad times, then goes bankrupt, owing **£20 000**. If the owner is a **sole trader**, he or she is liable to pay the **full debt** of **£20 000** (on top of the original £1500 they invested). If they're a **shareholder** of a limited company, they only lose the **£1500** they put in.

Different Forms of Business

Sole Trader Businesses are run by an *Individual*

1) A sole trader is an **individual** trading in his or her own name, or under a suitable trading name. Sole traders are **self-employed**, for example as shopkeepers, plumbers, electricians, hairdressers or consultants.
2) The essential feature of this type of business is that the sole trader has **full responsibility** for the **financial control** of his or her own business and for meeting **running costs** and **capital requirements**. Having full responsibility for all the **debts** of the business is called **unlimited liability** (see p.8).

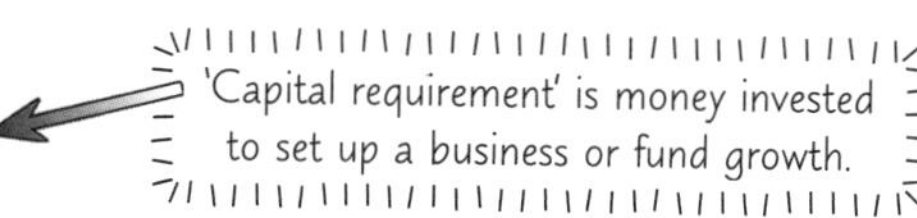
'Capital requirement' is money invested to set up a business or fund growth.

3) There are **minimal legal formalities** — the trader simply has to start trading. However, if the business isn't run under the **proprietor's** (owner's) name, the trader has to **comply** with certain rules under the Business Names Act (1985).

Being a *Sole Trader* has *Advantages* and *Disadvantages*

There are several **advantages** of being a sole trader:

- **Freedom** — the sole trader is his or her **own boss** and has complete **control** over decisions.
- **Profit** — the sole trader is entitled to **all the profit** made by the business.
- **Simplicity** — there's **less form-filling** than for a limited company. Bookkeeping is less complex.
- **Savings on fees** — there aren't any legal costs for drawing up an ownership agreement.

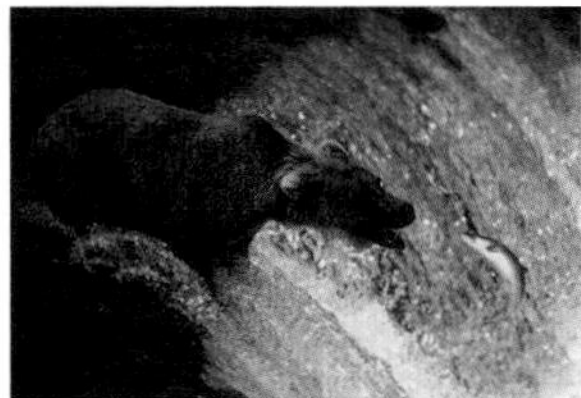
Bears — just another hiccup in Sally's plan to become a sole trader.

There are **disadvantages** too:

- **Risk** — there's **no one** to **share the responsibilities** of running the business with.
- **Time** — sole traders often need to **work long hours** to meet tight deadlines.
- **Expertise** — the sole trader may have **limited skills** in areas such as finance.
- **Finance** — finance is limited to the money that the owner has, or can borrow.
- **Vulnerability** — there's **no cover** if the trader **gets ill** and can't work.
- **Unlimited liability** — the sole trader is **responsible** for all the debts of the business.

Practice Questions

Q1 What is the aim of public sector organisations? How are they funded?

Q2 What do social enterprises use their profits for?

Q3 What's the difference between limited liability and unlimited liability?

Q4 What are the advantages and disadvantages of being a sole trader?

Exam Question

Q1 Peter is a sole trader. Over the last three years he has been making a loss. If this continues, the business may face bankruptcy. Explain the advantages and disadvantages to Peter of being a sole trader as he attempts to turn the business around. [6 marks]

Sole traders — they're not just shoemakers...

...They can also be plumbers, greengrocers... You get the idea. The important thing to remember here is that sole traders have unlimited liability. If you're going to set up as one, you need to be pretty sure that your business isn't going to fail or you'll be in big trouble... cos debts don't mind getting personal.

Different Forms of Business

Companies are different from sole traders. They have limited liability for a start.

There are two kinds of **Limited Liability Companies — Ltds** and **PLCs**

1) There are **private limited companies (Ltds)** and **public limited companies (PLCs)**.
2) Public and private limited companies have **limited liability** (see p.8).
3) They're owned by **shareholders** and run by **directors**.
4) The **capital value** (or the monetary value) of the company is divided into **shares** — these can be **bought** and **sold** by shareholders. Shareholders have part ownership of a company.

There's more on shareholders on pages 12-13.

Private Limited Companies	Public Limited Companies
Can't sell shares to the public. People in the company own all the shares.	Can sell shares to the **public**. They usually issue a **prospectus** to inform people about the company before they buy.
Don't have share prices quoted on **stock exchanges**.	Their share prices can be quoted on **stock exchanges**.
Shareholders may not be able to sell their shares without the **agreement** of the **other shareholders**.	Shares are **freely transferable** and can be bought and sold through stockbrokers, banks and share shops.
They're often **small** family businesses.	They usually start as private companies and then **go public** later to raise more capital.
There's **no minimum share capital** requirement.	They need **over £50 000** of share capital, and if they're listed on a stock exchange, **at least 25%** of this must be publicly available. People in the company can own the rest of the shares.
They end their name with the word "limited" or **Ltd**.	They always end their name with the initials **PLC**.

5) The Companies Act (2006) says that several important documents must be drawn up **before** a company can start trading, including the **memorandum of association** and the **articles of association**.
6) These documents must be sent to **Companies House** — where records of all UK companies are kept. The Registrar of Companies issues a **certificate of incorporation** so that the company can start trading. Once it's up and running, the company is legally obliged to produce **annual reports** of its financial activities.

Companies are **Run** by **Directors**

1) In a **small** private limited company, the **directors** are usually the **shareholders** (owners) of the business.
2) In **larger** private limited companies, **directors** are **elected** to the **board** by shareholders. The board makes the important decisions.
3) Shares in a PLC can be owned by **anyone**. The people who **own** the company **don't** necessarily **control** the company — it's controlled by the **directors**. This is called the "divorce of ownership and control".

Ordinary Share Capital is **Money** raised by **Selling Shares**

1) Shares are sold by companies to raise money. Money raised in this way is called **ordinary share capital**. Ordinary share capital is usually used for **long-term investment**.
2) In return for their investment, shareholders are paid a **dividend**. Dividends are a **proportion** of the **profits** earned by the company which are split and paid out to the shareholders. Dividends are given as a **fixed amount per share** — the more shares an individual holds, the larger the payout.
3) Dividends aren't always paid out. Loans must be repaid first and a company may choose to re-invest their profits into the business.
4) **Market capitalisation** is the **total value** of all of the ordinary shares **issued** by a company. It is found by multiplying the number of shares issued by the current market price of one share.

Market capitalisation = Number of issued shares × Current share price

E.g. In January 2014 a company issues 25 000 shares for £1 each, so its **ordinary share capital** is **£25 000**. By September 2014, the price of its shares on the Stock Exchange has risen to £4. If all shares are fully paid for, the company's share capital remains at £25 000, but its **market capitalisation** will be 25 000 × £4 = **£100 000**.

Different Forms of Business

*Entrepreneurs have to **Choose** a **Legal Structure** for their business*

1) When someone sets up a business, they have to **decide** what legal structure to set up as. Each structure has **advantages** and **disadvantages** — the entrepreneur has to decide which is most **suitable** for their needs.
2) Setting up a **sole trader** business gives the owner **control** over the business, but **unlimited liability** is a drawback. It's a **simple** way to set up a small business, but there's a lot of **risk** involved for the owner.
3) A **private limited company** has **limited liability** and the shareholders keep **control** over who the other shares are sold to, but it's much more **complicated** to set up than a sole trader business. A new business that needs to invest heavily in equipment, land etc. might need to set up as a Ltd to raise finance.
4) **Public limited companies** aren't usually a suitable option for new businesses because they need at least **£50 000** of share capital to start with, and most new businesses can't raise that much money.
5) Businesses can **change** their structure — sole traders can become a private limited company if the business is successful and they want to expand. This will bring more money and ideas into the business. Lots of private limited companies become PLCs when they want to raise more money to **expand** the business. It's much less common, but PLCs can also become private limited companies if they are taken over by a private limited company or if the managers **buy out** the **shareholders**. For example, in 2002, Arcadia Group PLC was taken over by Philip Green's private limited company Taveta Investments Ltd. and is now Arcadia Group Ltd. PLCs can be changed into Ltds if the original owners want to take more control, or to run things more privately.

*Different **Forms** of **Ownership** affect the **Mission**, **Objectives** and **Decisions***

1) The **missions** and **objectives** of **non-profit** organisations are usually to help people or communities in need. They will set objectives to generate enough profit to achieve these aims.

2) **Private sector** for-profit organisations often have **objectives** which focus on **maximising** profits, although they will also pursue other objectives (see p.3-5). **Public sector** organisations tend to have missions aimed towards benefiting **society**. This can mean that **social benefits** are put before costs when making decisions.

3) **Sole traders** and owners of small **private limited companies** have **control** over objectives and decision making. They may change ownership if the business is expanding. For sole traders in particular, changing the business to a Ltd company may mean gaining **expertise** from shareholders, however they may not share the same **values** as the original owner, leading to different **objectives** and difficulties when making **decisions**. Shareholders may also buy a large proportion of the shares, meaning the original owner(s) may **lose control** of the business, which may lead to a change in the mission or objectives.

4) For **public limited companies**, the majority of shareholders are not involved in the management of the business. This can lead to a conflict of interests. E.g. management may wish to pursue objectives designed to achieve long-term gains, but which may cause short-term **reductions** in profits. However, they may need to take into account shareholders' wishes for short-term **boosts** to profits.

Practice Questions

Q1 State two differences between private and public limited companies.

Q2 How do you work out the market capitalisation of a business?

Q3 Why are new businesses not usually set up as PLCs?

Exam Question

Q1 Made-Up Organics, a company selling organic make-up and toiletries, is owned by Isabelle Greenberg, a sole trader. The business has been growing over the past few years and she is thinking of becoming a private limited company instead. Explain the advantages and disadvantages of doing this. [6 marks]

Market capitalisation doesn't mean "MARKET"...

This is all pretty important stuff, so keep reading through until you're confident with all the pros and cons of each form of business. Remember that a Ltd is a private limited company, and a PLC is a public limited company. You should also know how to calculate market capitalisation — number of issued shares × current share price.

The Role of Shareholders

Shareholders invest capital into companies in return for a share of that company. It may sound weird, but that's just the way businesses work. Have a good look at this spread and you'll be a shareholding whizz in no time.

Shareholders are the **Owners** of Companies

1) A shareholder is anyone who owns at least one share in a company. Shares in a **public limited** company can be bought by **individuals**, **companies** or **institutions** (such as pension funds). Shares in **private limited** companies are usually bought by **family** and **friends** of the original owners.
2) For companies, the main **role** of shareholders is to **provide funds**. In small Ltds, the shareholders are often also the directors of the company — the shareholders with the most shares have the most power. In PLCs, most shareholders are **not** involved in running the business, but they have certain rights.
3) Companies hold an **Annual General Meeting** (AGM). Ordinary shareholders have the right to **vote** on key decisions and the performance of the company. Each share that a person holds entitles them to one vote. If a shareholder owns **more than 50%** of the shares, they're called the **majority shareholder**. The majority shareholder has the most **power** in decision-making.
4) Shareholders have the right to receive a **dividend** (a portion of the business's profit), **if** the profit is being used in this way.
5) Shareholders have **limited liability**. If the company can't repay its debts, a shareholder can only lose the money they invested — the amount they spent on shares.

The Bear Truth PLC's annual general meeting was getting way out of control. Again.

Shareholders **Invest** in companies for **Different Reasons**

1) Some shareholders invest in businesses in order to achieve a **capital gain**. They may **buy** shares in a business when the share price is **low** and **sell** them if the share price **rises** to make a profit. E.g. an investor purchases 100 shares at £3 each. The share price then rises to £5 each, so the investor sells them at a profit of £2 per share — they gain £2 × 100 = £200.

2) Shareholders may be paid a **dividend** in return for their investment. Dividends are paid on a **per-share** basis, so the **more** shares a shareholder owns, the **bigger** the dividend.

3) Some people become shareholders because they want to be **involved** in the **running** of a business. People may invest in a **small private limited** company for this reason. A shareholder could influence decision-making in a **PLC** by buying enough shares to make them the **majority shareholder**.

4) Some shareholders will invest in a company because they believe in the **aims** and **objectives** of the company and want to see it succeed, e.g. companies with **social**, **ethical** or **environmental** objectives.

5) A shareholder might invest in a **private limited company** in order to help the company **survive** or **grow**, e.g. to support a family or friend's company.

6) **Venture capitalists** are a particular type of shareholder. They will invest in businesses that they think have the potential to be successful (see p.81). This can be a big financial **risk** but can lead to large financial **rewards**.

The TV show "Dragons' Den" is a good example of venture capital investment. The "Dragons" are professional investors hoping to invest in businesses that will be successful in the future.

The Role of Shareholders

Share Prices** change **Constantly

1) **Private limited companies** have **control** over their share price because shares are **privately** traded between friends and family. A price per share will be agreed between the current owner and the potential investor, based on the current performance of the business.
2) Shares in **public limited companies** are sold on the stock market. The price of a company's shares will be determined by **demand and supply**. If more people want to **buy** a share than sell it (demand is higher than supply), the share price goes **up**. If more people want to **sell** a share than buy it (supply is higher than demand), the share price goes **down**.

Factors influencing demand and supply

1) The **performance** of the company — **better performance** should mean bigger dividend payments. This leads to an **increase in demand** for the company's shares, increasing the share price. If a company reports **low profits**, shareholders may **sell** their shares, increasing supply and reducing share price.
2) **Speculation** and rumour of **new product launches** or **cost saving initiatives** might generate investor **interest**. If the rumoured activity is likely to increase the company's profits, this will encourage people to buy shares in the company. As a result, the share price is likely to increase.
3) **Current share price** — if the share price is **low**, investors might think they can get a bargain if they buy now, hoping that the price will increase in the future. If the share price is **high**, shareholders may decide to sell their shares to make a **capital gain**.
4) **Interest rates** — when interest rates are **low**, the reward for saving money in a bank is reduced. This can increase the **demand** for shares because the financial rewards are likely to be **greater** than the **interest** that would be earned on a **bank account**.
5) The **economy** has a strong influence on demand and supply — when the economy is **strong**, people have more money to invest, and **confidence** that they will get a good return. This **increases** demand and share price. In a **weak** economy, people are **less** likely to risk their money on an investment, **decreasing** demand and share price. Businesses may offer **more shares** in order to try and raise share capital, **increasing** supply.

Share Price Changes** have **Short** and **Long-Term Effects

1) Changing share prices can have a big effect on shareholders who want to **buy** and **sell** shares for **short-term capital gain**. If the share price **increases**, the shareholder will **make money** when they sell the shares. **Decreasing** share prices may mean a shareholder makes a **loss** when selling shares, or they may decide to hold onto the shares and hope the price **increases** again.
2) Shareholders who buy shares as a **long-term** investment are less affected by **short-term price changes**. However, price changes may reflect an increase or decrease in **company profits**, which could mean **higher** or **lower** dividend payments.
3) A **decrease** in share price can reduce the **overall value** of a company, but in the **short-term** this may not cause too many problems as the business already has the **share capital** — they don't lose it. However, if the share price continues to decrease in the **long-term**, this is likely to **reduce confidence** in the company, making it more difficult to attract **new investors**.

Practice Questions

Q1 Explain who shareholders are.

Q2 Give three possible reasons for buying shares in a business.

Q3 Give two reasons why the share price for a company may decrease.

Exam Questions

Q1 Analyse the effects of a sudden decrease in share price on the shareholders of a company. [6 marks]

Q2 Business Books PLC is a company in the private sector. In 2012 it issued 10 000 shares at a cost of £5.00 each. Between 2012 and 2014, Business Books PLC's profits rose by 35%, and the demand for shares was high. Based on this information, do you think that buying shares in Business Books PLC when they were first issued would have been a good investment? Justify your answer. [12 marks]

Your brain's gonna be in high demand to learn this...

It's not easy stuff, but you will need to learn it all. Read through the pages, then cover them up and scribble down everything you can remember until you know it all. Make sure you understand how demand and supply affect share price — big demand or small supply = prices increase, small demand or big supply = prices decrease.

Businesses and the External Environment

Businesses want demand (the amount of their product that people want to buy) to be high and costs to be low. But this depends on external factors — everything from outside the business that affects it.

Market Conditions affect Costs and Demand

Market conditions is a term that describes a wide range of factors affecting the market. These factors influence the **costs** faced by businesses and the **demand** for their products. They include:

Today's market conditions — mostly sunny, with light showers in the afternoon.

Political Factors

1) If **demand** in the economy is too **low**, governments try to **increase** it. They **cut taxes** so people have **more** to **spend**, and **increase** their **spending** in the economy, for example by raising **benefits**. Central banks (e.g. the Bank of England) **reduce interest rates** to cut mortgage payments and **increase disposable income**.
2) Governments try to **reduce demand** if it's too **high**. They **raise taxes** so people have **less money** to spend, and cut government spending. Central banks **increase interest rates** to raise the cost of **borrowing**, **reduce disposable income** and **reduce demand**.
3) The government can also influence demand for **particular** products by using **taxes**. For example, to reduce **carbon emissions**, road tax on **low-emission** and **fuel-efficient cars** has been **reduced**, and road tax on **high-emission** vehicles has been **increased**. **Increased** taxes on products leads to **reduced demand**, as people will try to find cheaper alternatives.

Disposable income is your earnings after tax, National Insurance and pension payment have been deducted.

Labour Supply

1) **Labour supply** has an effect on business **costs**.
2) When unemployment rates are **high**, there's a good **supply** of labour. Businesses can hire staff easily and won't have to pay **high wages**, which means costs can be kept low. People in work will be extra **productive** to protect their job.
3) A **low rate** of unemployment could mean that there is a **shortage** of labour. The people available for employment might not have the **skills** needed for the role, so will need **training**. This can **increase costs** for a business.

Incomes and Economic Factors

1) The state of the economy affects **demand** and **costs**. In a **recession**, businesses need to reduce costs, e.g. with **wage cuts** or **redundancies** to decrease labour costs. **Lower incomes** mean people have **less** money to **spend** on products, so **demand decreases**.
2) In an economic **boom**, wages rise and more people are employed. This may lead to **greater costs**, due to the increased wages. On the other hand, **higher incomes** mean that people have more money to spend, **increasing demand** for products. The increased demand leads to **increased production costs** in supplying more products.
3) **Changing incomes** affect demand for **some** products more than others, i.e. depending on whether they are necessities or luxury products. See **income elasticity of demand** on page 37.

Seasonal Demand and Supply

1) There are **variations** in **demand** and **supply** throughout the year. This is called **seasonality**.
2) **Weather** and **holidays** such as Christmas produce variations in **demand**. For example, Christmas creates high demand for toys. Hot weather creates demand for ice lollies, paddling pools and air conditioning units.
3) They can also cause variations in **supply** — for example, more strawberries are available in summer, which would **reduce costs** for a shop selling strawberries.
4) It's impossible to avoid seasonality. Businesses must have **strategies** to deal with it. After Christmas, demand for retail goods drops, so shops **cut prices** (the **January sales**) to boost demand, and get rid of stock.
5) Food producers can cope with seasonality in supply by **preserving food** — e.g. by canning or freeze-drying. This **meets demand** even when the food is not in season.

Competition is another big factor in market conditions. This is covered in more detail on the next page.

Businesses and the External Environment

Competition can *Reduce Demand* and *Increase Costs*

When a **competitor** enters the market or launches a new product, the **demand** for a rival business's product is likely to **decrease** as people will buy the competitor's product. The rival business is likely to **increase** its **marketing costs** or spend more on **improving** or **diversifying** its products in response to the competition. Alternatively, the rival might try to **cut** its costs to keep the price of its product lower than the competitor's to **increase demand**.

Different markets have different types of competition between businesses:

1) **Perfect competition** is where all firms compete on an **equal** basis — their **products** are pretty much **identical**, and they all charge a similar price. Businesses need to **keep costs low** to keep prices low, otherwise demand will be taken by the competition. However, they also need to keep a **high quality** of product to keep a good level of demand.

2) In an **oligopoly**, a small number of large firms **dominate** the market and charge similar prices. For a business to get ahead, they will focus on **marketing** and **brand image** to increase demand, so **marketing costs** will be **high**.

3) A **monopoly** is where one business has **complete control** over its market. There's **no** competition. A business with a monopoly can **increase** its **prices** without much concern of the demand decreasing, and they are able to keep **marketing costs low**.

Competition amongst a business's **suppliers** can **reduce costs** for the business. E.g. if the price of its raw materials decreases.

Interest Rates Determine the *Cost* of *Borrowing Money*

1) **Interest rates** affect the **cost of borrowing** and the **return on savings**. The interest rate is the **fee** paid for borrowing — it's calculated as a **percentage** of the amount borrowed. For example, if you borrow £100 with a 10% interest rate, you'll actually pay back £110. A **fall** in interest rates means a **decrease** in the **cost of borrowing** for businesses. A **rise** in interest rates leads to an **increase** in the cost of borrowing.
2) Interest rates affect **consumer spending**. **High interest** rates mean most consumers have **less money** to spend — people with existing **borrowing** (like mortgages) have to pay more money back in **interest**, so they have less **disposable income** (the money left over after essential payments like tax), and so market **demand** goes **down**. People might also decide to **save more** to take advantage of the interest earned on their savings, **reducing demand**. **Low interest** rates mean consumers have more disposable income and there is less reward for saving, so **demand** goes **up**.
3) The effect of interest rates on demand depends on the **product**. Products that require **borrowing** (e.g. cars, houses, kitchens and high-end consumer electronics) are more **sensitive** to interest rate changes. When interest rates go up significantly, firms change strategy to diversify away from these goods and into cheaper ones.

Practice Questions

Q1 Give three factors of market conditions that can affect demand for a product.

Q2 How can high unemployment rates affect a business's costs and demand for its products?

Q3 Why could a new competitor entering the market increase the costs of an existing business?

Q4 How does perfect competition affect business costs and demand for a product?

Exam Questions

Q1 Which of the following could reduce demand for a perfume manufacturer's products? [1 mark]
A It is December B High unemployment C Low interest rates D A shortage of perfume on the market

Q2 Riteo Ltd. is an established company in the technology market. Gyreo Ltd. is a new company that directly competes with Riteo. To what extent will this affect the business costs of Riteo? [25 marks]

I was only showing an interest, now you're trying to charge me for it...

There's heaps of info on these pages, so get your head down and get it learned. You may be asked which factors affect demand and costs and why, so try covering up each chunk and scribble down as many points as you can for each.

Businesses and the External Environment

... But wait, there's more — here we've got demographics, environmental and social factors and technology. Cast your eyes across these pages. There's lots to learn, but it'll look impressive if you can remember it in your exams.

Businesses have to Respond to Demographic Changes

1) The **structure** of a **population** changes over time in terms of **age**, **sex** and **race** — this is **demographic change**.
2) Demographic change is important to businesses because it has an **impact** on the **demand** for **products**. Different **demographics** of consumers tend to buy **different things**, so businesses need to adapt the **amount** and **type** of products they are **producing**.
3) Demographic changes can mean that **certain types** of business are more **in demand**. This might allow existing businesses to **expand**, or **new businesses** to be set up.

- The UK has an **ageing population** so businesses have started to target the growing elderly market in order to increase demand for their products. E.g. banks have started offering special rates on **retirement accounts** and software developers are making **brain-training games** directed at older people.
- The **ageing population** in the UK has also led to an increased demand for **doctors** and **nurses**, which has increased the **costs** of the NHS (through more treatments and more staff).
- The number of **working parents** is increasing which creates a greater demand for **childcare services**.
- The UK's population is also becoming more **ethnically diverse** as **immigration** levels rise. This has increased demand for certain products, e.g. for food not traditionally available in the UK. Supermarkets have started to stock more **exotic ingredients** and independent 'international' supermarkets have been set up within certain communities.

4) **Consumer tastes** also change over time — in recent years lots more **men** have started using **cosmetic** and **personal grooming** products. Businesses making cosmetic products may adapt them to be more suitable for **different genders** or create a whole **new product range** targeted at men.

The supply of workers affects business costs

1) An ageing population means that a **smaller percentage** of the population are of **working age** — this may result in the **supply** of workers **decreasing**. Businesses might have to **increase** wages to attract workers, which will result in **increased costs**.
2) **Immigration levels** also impact the **supply** of workers. If lots of **working aged** people are **migrating** into the country, then the supply of workers will **increase**. This can drive **wages down** and **decrease** business **costs**.

Environmental Factors can Increase Business Costs

Nowadays, consumers are **increasingly concerned** with the effect that their purchasing has on the **environment**. This has forced businesses to consider their **impact** on the environment and to do something about it.

1) Businesses pollute the environment through **production** processes, through **traffic pollution** caused by **transporting** raw materials and finished goods, through **dumping waste** in waterways and seas, and through **burying** or **burning waste**. **Packaging** creates a large amount of **landfill** waste and many businesses use up resources in an **unsustainable** way.
2) **Government legislation** forces businesses to deal with some environmental issues (e.g. levels of pollution). Businesses may need to put in place **controls** and **measures** to make sure they are meeting **pollution targets**, which costs the business money. However, if they don't put controls in place and fail to meet government targets, they will incur **large fines**.
3) Some businesses try to **minimise** the **impact** they have on the environment. For example, businesses can try to be more **sustainable** by **replacing resources** as they use them or using **sustainable** or **recycled materials**. A business can adapt its **production process** to make it cleaner, or use renewable energy sources. Product **packaging** is a major issue for retailers — **suppliers** can **adapt** the packaging of their products in order to make them more **appealing** to retailers. E.g. a supplier of tinned vegetables might start to package their products in **cardboard boxes** instead of **metal tins**. However, implementing these things often **increases business costs**.
4) Being **environmentally friendly** can give a company an advantage over competitors and increase **demand**. E.g. Innocent® Drinks strive to be as **sustainable** as possible, which is great for their **public image**. Also, environmental measures can **save** a business money in the long term. **Organisations** have been set up (e.g. Carbon Trust) that aim to help businesses **increase** their **competitiveness** through the changes they make.

Businesses and the External Environment

Ethical businesses have Great Reputations with Consumers

1) **Consumers** are becoming **increasingly concerned** with the ethical and unethical **behaviour** of firms. Not everyone **agrees** on what's ethical and what's not. For example, most people **agree** that **child labour** is **unethical**, but **opinions differ** on whether it's **unethical** to **sell cigarettes** even though they cause cancer.

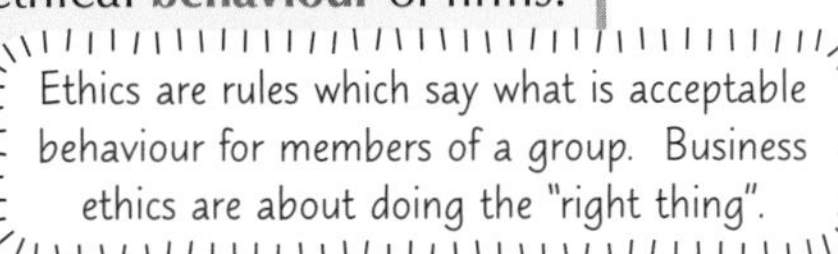

Gus swapped his clothes with a friend. It was not a fair trade.

2) Some businesses have started to implement **fair trade policies** when **purchasing** from suppliers. This means that the business pays **higher** and **fairer prices** for products (especially those from less-developed countries) with the aim of **improving** the **living standards** of their **supplier's** employees. Obviously this will increase the costs of the business, however it also gives them a **unique selling point** (e.g. The Body Shop® products, The Co-operative's Fairtrade chocolate etc.), which can **increase demand**, allowing them to still be **profitable**.

A sweatshop is a factory (usually overseas) where workers are forced to work long hours in poor conditions for low pay.

3) Consumers also care about how a company **treats its workers** — if a company is seen to treat its workers poorly, **demand can drop**. For example, **companies** used to utilise sweatshops to manufacture cheap products, however many have **stopped** following **pressure** (e.g. boycotting) from **customers**.

4) A company that is seen to be **ethical** will have a **great reputation** with customers, so **demand** for the products can be **high** even if they're more **expensive** than rival products. E.g. the shoe company TOMS® gives a lot to children in less-developed countries, so customers don't mind paying extra for the shoes.

Technological Advances can influence Demand and Costs

1) Companies aim to **increase demand** for their products by using **technology** to improve their **marketing**.
2) Many companies now use **technology** to gather **information** about the **lifestyles** of their **customers** and the **products** that they **buy** or are likely to buy (see p.34). This helps them to make sure that **promotions** are **targeting** the right people and stand the best chance of **increasing demand** for products.
3) **Social networking websites** are another way that businesses can use technology to find out more about customer likes and dislikes. People who use these sites often list information about themselves, including the type of **music** they like, where they go on **holiday**, what **car** they drive etc.
   Companies can **target** their **advertising** specifically at the people who are **likely** to **buy** their product — this is **cheaper** than advertising to **everyone** and is just as likely to **increase demand**.
4) New technology can also improve **production efficiency**, which can **reduce** business **costs** in the **long-term** (see p.60). However, new technology is **expensive** to set up in the first place. It can also take the jobs of workers, leading to redundancies — this is an **ethical issue** that could impact **negatively** on the **reputation** of the company, which may **affect demand**.

Practice Questions

Q1 What effect would an ageing population have on the demand for products?

Q2 Give two ways in which environmental factors can affect business costs.

Q3 What does it mean for a company to have fair trade policies?

Q4 Write down three effects that ethical behaviour can have on a company.

Exam Question

Q1 A paper company is thinking of pursuing objectives to reduce waste, pollution and deforestation. Analyse the effects this may have on the company in terms of demand for its paper and its costs. [12 marks]

You demand more amazing business know-how? It's gonna cost ya...

You're at the end of the section, but that's not the end of this stuff — not by a long shot. There's loads more on the external environment on p.118-137. But first, make sure you can remember all the different effects that demographics, environmental factors, ethical factors and technology can have on business costs and demand. Then relax.

Management and Leadership

If you thought management was just telling people what to do, you'd be mistaken — there's a lot more to it than that.

You need to know what **Managers** do

1) Managers **set objectives** for their department, and for the people under them. They decide what **work** needs to be done to **meet** the objectives, and what **resources** they need.
2) Managers **analyse** and **interpret data** — e.g. data on employee performance, sales, production costs, etc.
3) Managers **make decisions** — they'll use data analysis and interpretation to do this. For example, if they know that a store is **busiest** between 11 am and 2 pm, they'll **increase** the number of staff during these times.
4) Managers **review** the effectiveness of their decisions, and make **further decisions** based on their **conclusions**. So if a marketing manager had decided to spend more of her budget advertising **one product**, but this had **no impact** on sales, she might decide to spend the money on promoting a **different product** instead.
5) Managers **appraise** their employees' **strengths** and **weaknesses** and **develop** their **talents**.
6) Managers need to be able to **lead** their staff.

There's a difference between managing and leading. **Managing** means **telling** people what to do and **organising resources** to get the job done. **Leading** means **motivating** people and **inspiring** them to do things. Managers with good leadership skills can **persuade** their staff that their decisions are the **right ones**.

There are different **Management** and **Leadership Styles**

1) **Authoritarian** or **autocratic** style — the **leader** (or **manager**) **makes decisions** on their own. They identify the objectives of the business or department and say **exactly** how they're going to be achieved. It's useful when dealing with lots of **unskilled** workers and in **crisis management**. This method requires lots of **supervision** and monitoring — workers can't make their own decisions. This style can **demotivate** able and intelligent workers.
2) **Paternalistic** (fatherly) style is a softer form of the autocratic style. The leader **consults** the workers before making decisions, then **explains** the decisions to them to **persuade** them that the decisions are in their interest. Paternalistic leaders think that getting **involved** and caring about human relations is a **positive motivator**.
3) **Democratic** style — the leader encourages the workforce to **participate** in the decision-making process. Leaders **discuss** issues with workers, **delegate responsibility** and **listen** to advice. Democratic leaders have to be good communicators. This style shows leaders have a lot of confidence in the workforce — which leads to increased employee **motivation**. It also takes some of the **weight** of decision making off the leader.
4) **Laissez-faire** style is a **weak** form of leadership. **Leaders** might offer employees coaching and support, but they **rarely interfere** in the running of the business. This **hands off** style of leadership would only be appropriate for a small, highly motivated team of **able** workers.

Internal and **External Factors** influence **Management** and **Leadership Styles**

A manager's or leader's **behaviour** is influenced by factors inside and outside the business. Ideally, they need to **adapt** their style to suit the situation.

Internal Factors

1) **Urgent** tasks need different leadership from **routine** tasks. Urgent tasks, like an **unexpected** large order coming in, may need an **authoritarian** leader to **tell** employees what to do and how to do it.
2) A **large**, **unskilled** workforce suits **authoritarian** leadership, whereas a **small**, **educated** workforce suits a **democratic** approach much better.

External Factors

1) In a **recession**, a business needs strong leadership to **guide** it through **difficult economic times**. **Authoritarian** or **paternalistic** leaders can be efficient in times of crisis — they can issue **clear, quick commands** because they don't have to consult others.
2) When the economy is **growing**, managers don't always need such a strong leadership approach. **Democratic** leaders can take the time to **communicate** with employees.
3) **Increased competition** requires **democratic** leaders who can **motivate** their employees to **adapt** to change or expansion. **Laissez-faire** leaders are more **complacent** and don't always provide enough **leadership** to guide their workforce in this situation.

Management and Leadership

The Tannenbaum Schmidt Continuum puts Leadership Styles on a Scale

The **Tannenbaum Schmidt Continuum** places managers on a scale ranging from **autocratic management** through increasing levels of **participation** in decision-making by the workforce. It identifies **seven key types** of management style.

1) **Tells**: **Authoritarian** management style. **Zero involvement** of the workforce in decision making — they're **not** trusted with decisions, so this style can be **divisive** between management and the workforce.
2) **Sells**: The **manager** makes the decision but tries to present it to the workforce as having a **sound rationale**. The workforce are allowed to **ask questions** but they **do not influence** the decision being made.
3) **Suggests**: A decision is **outlined** to the workforce and they are allowed to **discuss** and **ask questions**. This helps them feel that their **opinions** are being **considered**.
4) **Consults**: The manager **proposes** a **tentative decision** and invites **discussion**. The decision is open to being **modified**. This recognizes the **insight** and **value** of workforce participation in decision making.
5) **Joins**: The manager **proposes** a problem and the workforce **work together** to discuss solutions. Ultimately the **manager** will make the **final decision**. This style is useful if the workforce team have **specific knowledge** that helps the manager to make the best decision.

100%
Authority by Manager
Team Participation
0%
1) Tells
2) Sells
3) Suggests
4) Consults
5) Joins
6) Delegates
7) Abdicates

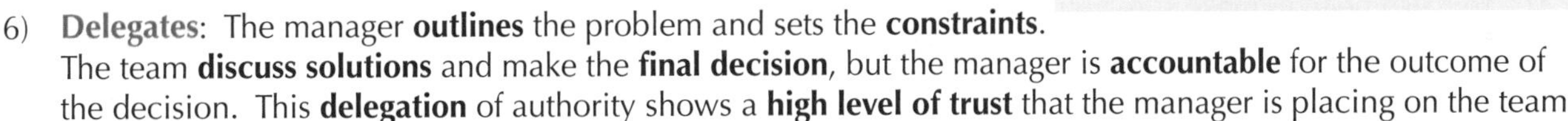

6) **Delegates**: The manager **outlines** the problem and sets the **constraints**. The team **discuss solutions** and make the **final decision**, but the manager is **accountable** for the outcome of the decision. This **delegation** of authority shows a **high level of trust** that the manager is placing on the team.
7) **Abdicates**: The team **define** and **solve** the problem. This is the ultimate level of **freedom** for the workforce . The team are **trusted** to use their **expertise** to make decisions, which should be **highly motivating** for the team. The manager is still **accountable** for the decision, so must be sure the team can handle the **responsibility**.

The Blake Mouton Grid lets managers Assess their Leadership Style

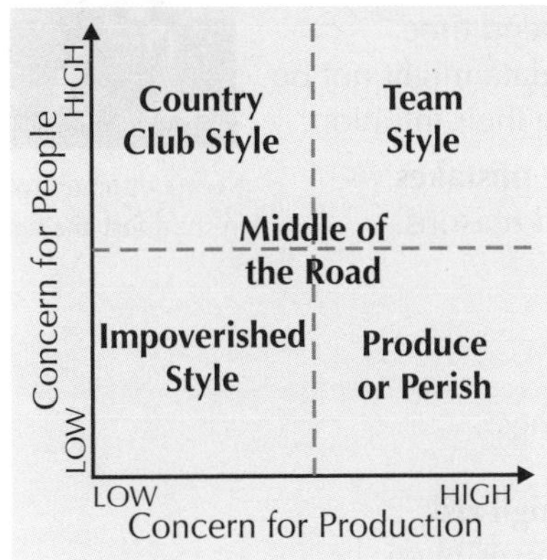

The **Blake Mouton grid** assesses managers based on how much they care about their **employees** and how much they care about **production**.

1) **Impoverished Style**: **Low concern** for **people** and **low concern** for **production**. This is **poor management** of both human and production resources. This results in **low levels of motivation** in the workforce and **low levels of productivity** or **failing quality**.
2) **Produce or Perish Style**: An **authoritarian** focus on the work with strict rules that leads to a **neglect** of workers' **needs** and a **demotivated** workforce. This may result in **high levels** of **absenteeism** and **staff turnover**.
3) **Country Club Style**: An **over-concern** with **worker welfare** and harmony leads to a **happy** but **not very productive** workplace. This leadership style doesn't **motivate** the workers to **increase** their output.
4) **Middle of the Road**: **Average** concern for **worker needs** and **average** focus on **production** leads to **mediocre** results. Although productive output is higher than in the Impoverished or Country Club style, it could be better.
5) **Team Style**: This is seen as the **ideal** leadership style. **High** concern for **people** and **production** creates a **happy**, **motivated** and **productive** workforce. It often uses **non-financial methods of motivation** (see p.93).

Practice Questions

Q1 Give one advantage and one disadvantage of: a) a manager who abdicates responsibility for decision-making, b) the Produce or Perish style of leadership.

Exam Question

Q1 Analyse the effects of a Blake Mouton 'Middle of the Road' leadership style in a car dealership. [9 marks]

The space time continuum would be much more exciting...

Fun fact: Tannenbaum Schmidt translates as Christmas tree Smith. OK, that probably won't come up in your exams, but the continuum might, so make sure you know all the different leadership styles. Then sing 'O Tannenbaum'.

Management Decision Making

Managers can either make scientific decisions (based on data) or decisions based on intuition. All decisions come with risks — it's up to the manager to decide whether the risk is worth it.

Decision Making can be Scientific...

1) Decisions made **scientifically** are based on **data**, and their **outcomes** are compared to the **initial objectives**. This **model** shows how the scientific decision making process works:

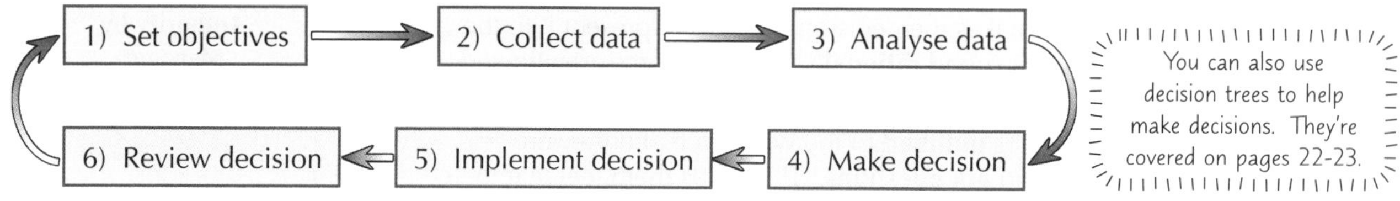

You can also use decision trees to help make decisions. They're covered on pages 22-23.

You can see that this model is a **cycle** — if you **review** your decision and realise that it **isn't working**, you go back to **step 1** and start again.

2) Making decisions based on data **reduces** the risk of making **expensive mistakes**. It is a **logical** and **structured** approach which can be **adapted** if necessary — for example, having analysed the data, you might **review** the objectives, and **change** them if needed.
3) However, it can be **costly** and **time-consuming** because it involves **collecting** and **analysing** a lot of data. It also takes away the '**human element**' so may be **less creative** or **original** than a decision based on intuition.
4) You also need to make sure you have **reliable**, **up-to-date** data. Decisions based on **biased** or **out-of-date** data will be **unreliable**.

... or Intuitive

1) **Intuitive** decision making means making decisions based on a **hunch** or **gut instinct**.
2) Some managers have **good intuition** — they can **sense** when a decision is the right one based on **past experience**. When their intuition is right, it can lead to great business decisions and keep the company ahead of its competition.
3) Decisions based on intuition can be made **quickly** — you **don't** have to spend time collecting and analysing data. If the situation is **new** or **unfamiliar**, using data might not be **helpful** (or there might not be any data available), so managers have to use their intuition.
4) It's **risky** to rely on intuition all the time though, because people can make **mistakes**. Decisions made using gut instinct can be **irrational** or not based on logical reasons.

Kevin's intuition told him he'd lost the fight.

Risk, Reward and Uncertainty influence decisions

When making decisions, managers have to take into account the following things:

RISK — All businesses have to take some **risks**. Some decisions can be **high risk**, but if they are successful bring **high rewards** (see below). Businesses often try to **reduce** risk — **scientific decision making** can help with this.

REWARD — Managers expect decisions to bring **rewards** (otherwise there'd be no point implementing that decision). Rewards can be **financial** (e.g. **higher sales** or **profits**) or **beneficial** in other ways (e.g. **higher productivity** or **lower staff turnover**).

UNCERTAINTY — All business decisions involve some degree of **uncertainty** — no one knows for sure what the outcome of a decision will be. **Scientific decision making** can help **reduce** uncertainty, but you **can't predict** everything, so there will always be some uncertainty.

Managers have to consider all these things when making decisions — for example **borrowing** large amounts of capital in order to **grow quickly** in an **emerging market** could be considered a **high-risk**, **high-reward** decision. However, if there is a **high** level of **uncertainty**, the manager might decide it's not worth the risk. When there's a lot of uncertainty, managers are **more likely** to make **low-risk**, **low-reward** decisions — they won't **gain** much, but they won't **lose** much either if it goes wrong.

Management Decision Making

Opportunity Cost is taken into account

1) **Opportunity cost** is the **benefit** that's **given up** in order to do something else — it's the **cost** of the choice that's made.
2) It's the idea that **money** or **time** spent doing one thing is likely to mean **missing out** on doing something else.
3) It puts a **value** on the product or business decision in terms of what the business had to **give up** to make it.
4) Businesses must **choose** where to use their **limited resources**. Managers **compare** opportunity costs when making decisions. For example, the opportunity cost of an advert halfway through the X Factor final might be screenings of the same advert in five episodes of Hollyoaks.
5) In more formal terms, opportunity cost is the **value** of the **next best alternative** that's been **given up**.

Managers have to consider **Other Factors** as well

There are a number of other factors that affect a manager's decision making — these things have to be taken into consideration too.

MISSION — A business's **mission** (its **main purpose**) will influence the decisions made. All decisions will take the mission into account.

There's more on mission and objectives on p.3.

OBJECTIVES — The **objectives** are the medium- to long-term **targets** that help a business achieve its mission. Decisions will be made with the aim of **achieving** the objectives, and are **reviewed** against the objectives to measure their success.

ETHICS — The firm's **ethics** (moral and social values) have an effect too. E.g. a business might decide **not** to switch to a **cheaper** supplier if that supplier is **less environmentally responsible** than their current one.

EXTERNAL ENVIRONMENT — The **external environment** is all the **outside factors** that affect a business. It includes things like **competition**, **trends** (e.g. **seasonal** demand and supply), the **economy** of the area or whole country and **environmental** concerns. E.g. if a bakery **lowers** the price of their bread, the marketing manager in a rival bakery might decide to do the same to stay **competitive**.

RESOURCE CONSTRAINTS — **Resource availability** is also a factor. Resources include **money**, **people**, **time** and **raw materials** — a business might not plan to grow if there's a **shortage** of local **labour**, or might not advertise if they don't have much **money**.

Practice Questions

Q1 Describe the six-step model used for scientific decision making.

Q2 Give one advantage and one disadvantage of a) scientific decision making and b) intuitive decision making.

Q3 How might uncertainty affect a manager's decision?

Q4 What is opportunity cost?

Q5 Give three external factors that could influence a decision.

Exam Questions

Q1 Explain one way in which a clothing company's ethical objectives could affect its decision making. [4 marks]

Q2 Which option is a manager most likely to choose when making a decision? [1 mark]
A high-risk, low reward B high-risk, high reward C low-risk, high reward D low-risk, low reward.

My patience for revision is definitely a limited resource...

Opportunity cost is a bit of a tricky one to get your head around. For example, the opportunity cost of staying up late to watch your favourite TV programme is going to bed early so you're fresh as a daisy in class the next day. You have to decide if the cost of being tired is worth the enjoyment you'd get out of watching the programme.

Decision Trees

Decision trees are a bit like Magic 8-Balls® — they help with decision making.

Decision Tree Analysis combines **Probability** and **Expected Pay-Off**

1) When businesses make decisions (e.g. whether to open a new outlet, whether to develop a new product to add to their range), they **know** what the **cost** will be, but often the **outcome isn't certain**.
2) **Probability** is the **likelihood** of an event occurring. Managers often **don't know** how likely it is that an outcome will happen, so they make a **subjective estimate** based on **experience** or **past data**.
3) Probability is usually expressed as a **decimal** in decision trees — e.g. 0.6 for a 60% probability. The probability of an event **happening** and the probability of it **not happening** have to add up to **1** (certainty).
4) The **expected value (EV)** of an outcome is the **probability** of the outcome occurring, **multiplied** by the **pay-off** the business can expect to get. To work out the EV of a **course of action**, you **add** the EVs of the **different outcomes** together.
5) **Net gain** is the financial gain after **initial costs** of the decision have been **subtracted**. **Net gain = EV – initial costs**.

Learn these **Features** *of* **Decision Trees**

1) A **square** represents a **decision point**. The **lines** coming from a square show the possible **courses of action** and the **costs** of each action.
2) A **circle** shows there are **alternative outcomes** for a course of action, which are shown by **lines** coming out of the circle.
3) The **decimals** on the lines are the **probabilities** of each outcome occurring.
4) The **values in £s** represent the **pay-off** for the business if that outcome happens.

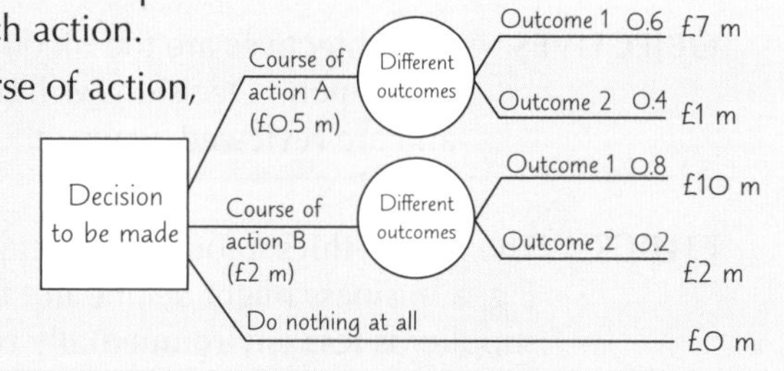

Decision Trees show which **Course Of Action** is probably **Best**

1) When creating a decision tree, managers first identify which **courses of action** are open to the business.
2) They outline the **possible outcomes** of each course of action and assign **probabilities** to them, estimating the probabilities they don't know.
3) The next step is to **calculate** the **expected value** (EV) and **net gain** of each course of action.
4) Managers should usually choose the course of action with the **highest net gain**.

Example — decision tree for launching a new chocolate bar

A confectionery business is about to launch a new chocolate bar.

1) With a **marketing** budget of **£15K** the chance of a **successful launch** is estimated at **0.75**. **Without** marketing, the chance is estimated at **0.5**. The basic launch costs are **£1K**.
2) A **successful** launch would earn a revenue of **£100K** — but if it **failed**, revenue would be **£20K** at best.

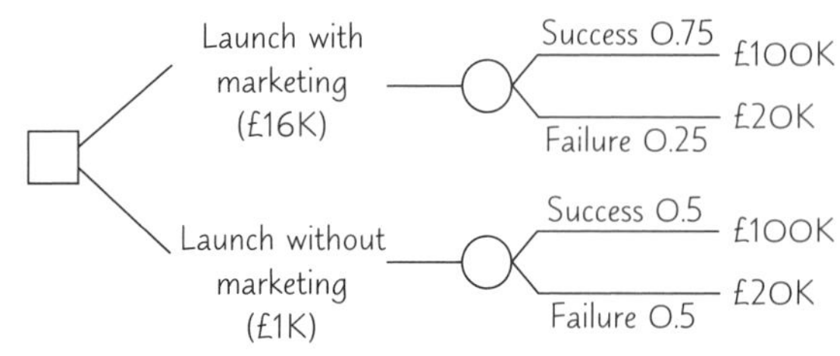

Calculate the **net gain** for each course of action. **Add** the **EVs** for each outcome together, then **subtract** the **initial costs** (here, it's the **launch costs**):

With marketing:
EV = (£100K × 0.75) + (£20K × 0.25) = £75K + £5K = £80K
Net gain = £80K – £16K = **£64K**

Without marketing:
EV = (£100K × 0.5) + (£20K × 0.5) = £50K + £10K = £60K
Net gain = £60K – £1K = **£59K**

Compare the net gain of launching **with** marketing (**£64K**) with the net gain of launching **without** marketing (**£59K**). This shows that spending £15K on marketing is **worthwhile**, so the best course of action is to launch the new chocolate bar after carrying out **marketing**.

Decision Trees

Decision Trees have Advantages...

1) Decision-tree analysis makes managers **work out** and **think about** the **probability** and the **potential pay-off** of each outcome of their chosen action. Managers have to come up with real numerical values for these — much better than vague statements like "this will increase sales".
2) Decision trees are a nice **visual representation** of the potential outcomes of a decision.
3) Decision trees allow managers to compare options **quantitatively** and **objectively**, rather than going for the fashionable option or the option they thought of first.
4) Decision trees are useful in **familiar situations** where the business has enough experience to make **accurate** estimates of **probabilities** and **benefits**.

...and Disadvantages

1) Decision trees are **quantitative** — i.e. they're based on numbers and ignore non-numerical **qualitative data**. **Qualitative data** includes things like the **employees' opinions** about business decisions, and businesses should take qualitative data into account before deciding on a course of action.
2) **Probabilities** are very hard to **predict accurately**. **Estimated pay-offs** are also assumed to be accurate — in real life things may work out differently. If either of these estimates are based on **dodgy** information, the decision is **flawed** too.
3) In reality there's a **wider range** of potential **outcomes** than the decision tree suggests. For example, a new marketing campaign might increase sales for a shorter period than predicted — the decision tree might only allow for success or failure, not for short-term success versus long-term success.

Practice Questions

Q1 Define expected value and net gain and say how each value is calculated.

Q2 Explain the difference between the circles and the squares on a decision tree.

Q3 Outline the stages used in decision tree construction.

Q4 Give one disadvantage of decision-tree analysis.

Exam Question

Q1 Chuse PLC is a multinational business that maintains electronic defence systems. It has won a contract to update the electronics on a submarine. Chuse does not currently have the capacity to complete this contract in the time available. To complete the work in time, Chuse has two options: increase their capacity, or subcontract two-thirds of the work. Expected outcomes are as follows:

Option (cost)	Outcomes	Probability	Profit (£m)
Increase existing capacity (£25 million)	Success Failure	0.6 0.4	500 –100
Subcontract (£50 million)	Success	1	300

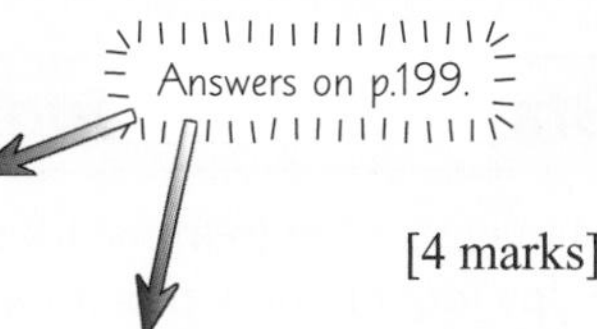

a) On the basis of the information given, construct a decision tree for this problem and label it showing probabilities and forecast pay-offs. [4 marks]

b) Calculate the expected value and net gain for each option. Advise Chuse as to the best option. [8 marks]

c) Analyse the advantages and disadvantages of using a decision tree in this situation. [9 marks]

Decision tree, decision tree, your branches green delight us...

Decision tree analysis is a nifty way for a manager to work out the best option when faced with an important decision. It's based on the potential benefit if things work out well, and the likelihood of it working out well or badly. Work your way through a few decision trees to get the hang of it — don't leave it all until the day of the exam.

Stakeholders and Decision Making

Businesses have to take into account their stakeholders when making decisions. Decisions will affect different stakeholders in different ways — so businesses can try to satisfy all their stakeholders, or just the most important ones.

Businesses have to meet the Needs of Stakeholders

Everyone who is affected by a business is called a **stakeholder**. There are two types: **internal** and **external**.

INTERNAL STAKEHOLDERS — People inside the business

1) The **owners** are the most important stakeholders. They make a profit if the business is successful and decide what happens to the business. In a limited company, the **shareholders** are the owners (see p.12). **Shareholders** usually want high **dividends** and a high **share price**.
2) **Employees** are interested in their **job security** and **promotion** prospects. They also want to earn a **decent wage** and have **pleasant working conditions**. **Managers** have **extra concerns** — they'll probably get some of the blame if the company does badly, and some of the credit if things go well.

EXTERNAL STAKEHOLDERS — People outside the business

1) **Customers** want **high quality** products and services at **low prices**.
2) **Suppliers** are the people and businesses who sell **raw materials** to the business. The business provides them with their **income** — if it can't pay quickly enough, the suppliers can have **cash flow** problems. **Suppliers** want to be paid a **fair price**, and be paid **on time**.
3) The **local community** will **gain** if the business provides **local employment** and **sponsors** local activities. The community will **suffer** if the business causes noise and pollution, or if the business has to **cut jobs**.
4) The **Government** gets more in **taxes** when the business makes good profits.
5) **Creditors** are those who the business owes money to. E.g. a **bank** will want **loans** paid back on time.

Different Stakeholders have Different Objectives

1) Stakeholders all have their own **objectives**, which are often **conflicting**.
2) Businesses have to strike a **balance** to try and keep all their stakeholders as happy as possible. E.g. a business might **cut costs** in order to **increase its profit** if it's trying to keep its **shareholders** happy. But if this reduces the **quality** of the products, **customers** won't be happy and will **stop buying** products — so the plan will backfire.
3) An important balance when making big decisions is between **short-term profit** and **social responsibility**.
    - **Profit** is important — it keeps **different groups** of stakeholders happy. It means **employees** can be **paid well**, **suppliers** have **reliable business**, **shareholders** can expect **dividend payments**, etc.
    - One way to increase profit is to **cut labour costs**. A firm might be able to do this by **relocating** production **abroad**, where labour is cheaper. This decision might satisfy **shareholders** if profit increases, but the **loss of UK jobs** would obviously be **bad news** for **employees** and probably **suppliers** too. The negative impact on the **local community** could damage the **image** of the company with its **customers**.
4) The company must try to satisfy as **many** groups as possible and **still survive financially**. If it can't keep **everyone** happy, the company needs to decide which group to **prioritise** (see below).
5) Stakeholders **don't always disagree** though — sometimes their interests **overlap**. For example, making workers happy can actually help productivity and raise profits.

Stakeholder Mapping considers Power and Interest

Managers have to think about which stakeholder group is most **important** to them. **Stakeholder mapping** helps identify how much **interest** in and **power** (or **influence**) over the business different stakeholders have.

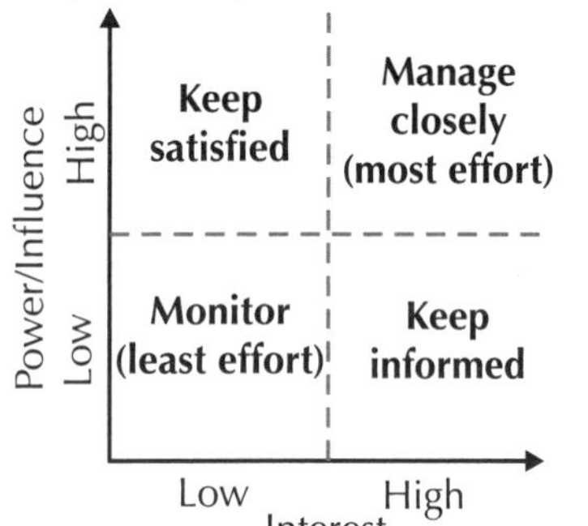

1) A **stakeholder map** helps a business decide how to best **manage** its stakeholders. Each group is mapped to one of four **quadrants**, which determines how much **communication** is needed and how much **attention** is paid to their views when making decisions.
2) Stakeholders with **high levels of power** and **high levels of interest** in the business need to be managed most **closely**, as their satisfaction is **vital** to the business. This group requires the **most effort**.
3) Stakeholders with **little power** and **little interest** in the business require **monitoring** but are **less important** to the business.

Stakeholders and Decision Making

Stakeholder Mapping for a small Italian Restaurant

If you were thinking this whole **stakeholder mapping** thing would make more sense with a **real-life example**, you're in luck. Here's a stakeholder map for a **small Italian restaurant** (i.e. not a chain).

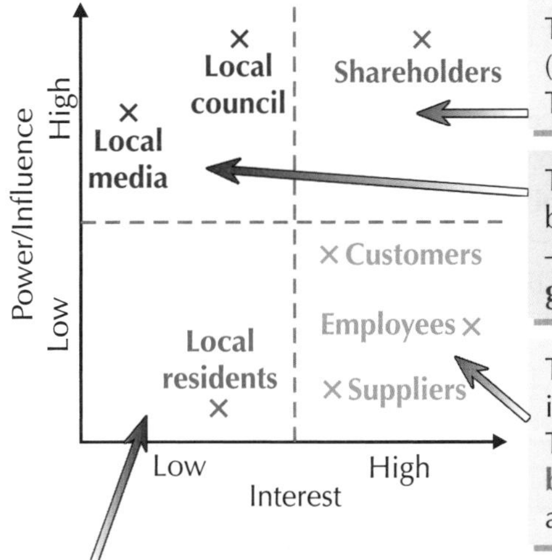

The **shareholders** need to be kept **informed** about new developments (e.g. plans for an outside eating area) and their **opinions** taken into account. They are a **key group** as their investment is **vital** to the restaurant's **future**.

The **local council's environmental health department** has **a lot of power**, but **less** interest in the restaurant. **Local media** can have a **big influence** — if the restaurant is **reviewed** in the local press, it needs to make a **good impression**. These groups mustn't be allowed to become dissatisfied.

The **employees**, **suppliers** and **customers** all have a **strong interest** in the business, but not as much **power** as the **shareholders**. They need to be **informed** about **small changes** and **consulted** on **bigger** ones (e.g. customers should be informed about a new menu and employees should be consulted about changes to opening hours).

Local residents need to be **monitored** to make sure that they are not experiencing any **disturbance** (e.g. from any late night events). This stakeholder group should require the **least communication effort**.

Relationships with Stakeholders are important

1) As well as power and interest, other factors can **influence** a business's **relationships** with its stakeholders. For example, during a **recession**, the business is focusing on **not going bankrupt** so may not be able to fund projects in the **local community**. They may have to **cut wages** and not pay **dividends** as well.
2) Businesses need to **manage** their relationships with stakeholders. If they focus on satisfying **one** stakeholder (e.g. the shareholders) at the **expense** of another (e.g. the employees), it could result in staff **leaving** or **going on strike**, which will **damage** the business. Managing these relationships can **prevent** this from happening.
3) One way of managing relationships is by **consulting** key stakeholders before making any major decisions. Stakeholders are more likely to feel **valued** if their **opinions** are considered. If the stakeholders have **specialist knowledge**, this will benefit the business as well.
4) Good **communication** is vital in managing relationships with stakeholders. For example, keeping **employees** informed about any changes to the business will make them feel included. Businesses can use **social media** and their **website** to communicate with **customers**.

Practice Questions

Q1 Decide whether the following groups are internal or external stakeholders:
a) part time staff, b) pressure groups, c) a bank that loans the business money.

Q2 Give one example where two different stakeholders have conflicting interests.

Q3 Who are the least important stakeholders in the Italian restaurant above?

Q4 Describe one factor that could influence a business's relationship with its suppliers.

Exam Questions

Q1 a) Construct a stakeholder map for a local leisure centre. You should include at least 4 stakeholders. [6 marks]

b) To what extent may the stakeholders influence business decisions made by the local leisure centre? [25 marks]

Employees and vampire slayers — both stakeholders...

Don't get confused between stakeholders and shareholders. Shareholders are stakeholders, but not all stakeholders are shareholders, which is a little befuddling. Anyway, you have to think about how important each group of stakeholders are, and how to keep the most important ones happy (you could write them a poem, that would be nice).

Marketing Objectives

Before a marketing department does anything, it needs to decide what it's aiming for. Then everyone can work as a team towards the common goal. Much better than random chaos.

Marketing identifies customer **Needs** and **Wants**

1) Marketing finds out what customers **need** and **want**. Marketing also tries to **anticipate** what they'll want in the future so that the business can get **one step ahead** of the market.
2) Marketing tries to ensure that the business supplies **goods** and **services** that customers **want** in order to **make a profit**. It's mutually beneficial — the customer gets something they want, the business makes a profit.
3) Marketing covers **research**, **analysis**, **planning** and the "**marketing mix**". The "marketing mix" is all the **decisions** a business makes about promoting and selling a product — see p.40-53.
4) Most larger businesses have a specialised **marketing department** — but marketing affects all departments.
5) Once a company has a **customer base**, marketing helps make sure that customers stay **loyal to that brand** (see p.48 for more on branding).

Marketing Objectives are the Marketing Department's **Aims**

1) **Marketing objectives** are **targets** that a company's **marketing department** sets itself. They are **valuable** in helping the company to achieve its **overall objectives** (see pages 3-5) and should be **SMART** (see page 4).
2) They tend to **focus** on **sales**, but it's not usually as simple as just "increase sales". Marketing objectives are often based on:

Sales Volume and Sales Value

An objective might be to reach a certain **sales volume** (number of units sold) over a certain period of time, e.g. to sell 2 million sewing machines over a year. A sales volume is easy to **visualise**, but it doesn't tell you anything about the amount of money coming in from sales. Businesses that sell a lot of **differently priced** items (e.g. supermarkets) usually base objectives on **sales value** instead, e.g. achieve £500 million in sales over a year.

Sales Growth

A business might aim for a **growth** in sales of a certain **volume** or a certain **value** over a year, e.g. to sell 50 000 **more** sewing machines, or to increase their sales revenue by £50 000 compared to the previous period. Alternatively, they might aim for a certain **percentage growth** in sales, e.g. a 15% increase in the number of sewing machines sold.

Formulas for sales growth, market share and market growth are given on page 28.

Market Share — the percentage of sales in a market made by one firm or brand

A common marketing objective for a business is to **increase their market share** by a certain amount, say 10%. It's useful because it tells a business how well it's doing **compared to its competitors**. To increase market share a business needs to either **entice customers** away from competitors, or **attract brand new customers** in a growing market.

Market Size and Market Growth

The **market size** is the **total number of sales** (or **total value** of sales revenue) in the market over a **period of time**. If the market size increases from one period of time to another (e.g. from one year to the next) then the market is **growing**. A company might set objectives to **stimulate market growth** — as long as the company's **market share** stays the same or grows, they will see an **increase in sales**.

3) The marketing objectives above are **quantitative** — there are **specific figures** to aim for. Marketing objectives usually take **more than one** of these figures into account. For example, a sales growth target will be decided after looking at the market size and growth — a sales target of £2 million is unrealistic if the market size is only £1.5 million.
4) Marketing objectives can also be **qualitative** (**non-numeric**). E.g. improving product **quality**, making sure a particular product **survives** when a rival product enters the market, and creating and maintaining **brand loyalty**.

Brand Loyalty

A business might try to improve its **brand loyalty**, i.e. holding on to **existing customers**, rather than just attracting new ones. **Social media** is a good way of doing this, as it allows **customers** and **businesses** to **interact**.

Marketing Objectives

Marketing Objectives are *Influenced* by *Internal* and *External Factors*

INTERNAL FACTORS

CORPORATE OBJECTIVES — The marketing department has to make sure its objectives are aligned with the company's **overall goals**. For example, if the business wants to **increase profits** in the **short term**, there's no point in the marketing department focusing on a **new product** that's still **two years** away from being **launched**.

FINANCE — The finance department allocates the marketing department's **budget**. This affects what the marketing department is able to do. If the budget is **cut** then marketing objectives may need to be **scaled down**.

HUMAN RESOURCES — **HR planning** (p.88-89) identifies how many **staff** the company needs. If the business has decided to **reduce/increase** staffing levels, marketing will have to adjust its objectives to match what is achievable with these staff levels. E.g. if there are fewer operations staff, the **capacity** (see p.56) will **decrease** so there will be a **limit** to how much marketing can increase **sales volume**.

EXTERNAL FACTORS

MARKET — The **state** of the **economy** has a big impact on marketing objectives. An economic **boom** is a good time to try to increase **sales volumes** since **income levels** are generally higher. In a **recession**, the marketing department is more likely to set an objective of maintaining **market share**.

TECHNOLOGY — In markets where technology changes **rapidly**, marketing objectives tend to be focused on **sales** and **price**, because new technology causes prices to rise or fall very fast. E.g. the price of **regular TVs** has **fallen** rapidly since the introduction of **smart TVs**. Regular TVs might still have a **high market share** because they're so **cheap** — however, it does mean that the marketing department of a regular TV manufacturer will have to **reassess sales objectives** and **pricing strategies** to ensure that they aren't left with **unsold stocks**.

COMPETITORS — The actions of competitors affect marketing objectives, particularly in a highly **competitive** market. If a competitor is focused on **low prices**, then the marketing department may alter their objectives so customers see them as **price competitive**. For example, Microsoft® dropped the price of the Xbox One™ soon after it launched in order to compete on price with the cheaper PlayStation®4.

ETHICS AND ENVIRONMENTAL FACTORS — Ethical and environmental awareness is **increasing** amongst consumers, and behaving in a harmful way can damage a company's **brand image**. For example, some people disapprove of companies that use an **unnecessary amount of packaging**. So a business might change their marketing objectives to include communicating how **ethically and environmentally conscious** they are.

*The **Law** directly affects the **Marketing Objectives***

Government regulations have a direct impact on the objectives of the marketing department:

- **Predatory pricing** (cutting prices to force a competitor out of business) is illegal in the EU and in the US.
- The **Trade Descriptions Act** regulates promotion. Businesses can't lie about their products.
- Advertising of some products is **restricted**. **Prescription medicines** can't be advertised to the public at all and there are very few places where **tobacco** products can be advertised. Advertising of **alcoholic drinks** is also restricted.

Practice Questions

Q1 Give four quantitative measures that marketing objectives can be based on.

Q2 What is brand loyalty?

Q3 Name two internal and two external factors that influence marketing objectives.

Exam Questions

Q1 If new technology is developed that allows toasters to instantly toast bread, analyse the effects on the marketing objectives of a regular toaster manufacturer. [9 marks]

Q2 Jo Porter has just opened a pub in her local village. Analyse the external and internal influences on the marketing objectives she sets. [12 marks]

No, brand loyalty isn't just for fans of a certain comedian...

Marketing objectives aren't just made up — they're based on market research and marketing data for the product in question. Market analysis and research are covered on the next few pages, then interpreting marketing data on p.32-5.

Market Analysis

A market is just a place where people buy and sell things (whether virtually or physically). There are different markets for different products (e.g. the electronics market, the cosmetics market, etc.). Businesses try to get ahead of their competitors by analysing the markets that affect them.

Businesses need to Understand their Market

1) Before a company can try to **sell their product**, they need to **understand** the market they're **operating in**.
2) They need to work out if they're working in a **local**, **national** or **international** market, whether they're selling things **online** or **physically**, and who their **target audience** is.
3) There are **different ways** that a market can be **classified**:

- **Geography** (local, national, international)
- **Nature** of the product (e.g. agricultural, technological)
- **Seasonality** (seasonal or year-round)
- **Development** level (new, growing, saturated)
- Product **destination** (trade, private consumers)

4) Once they've identified their market, the marketing department can carry out **market analysis** — looking at **sales growth**, **market growth**, **market share** and **market mapping**. They can use this analysis to decide how to market their products.

Firms that sell to other companies are called "business-to-business" (B2B). Ones that sell to consumers are called "business-to-consumer" (B2C).

Market Analysis gives firms information about Market Size and Growth

1) Businesses need to know if the market is **growing** (demand is increasing) or **shrinking** (demand is decreasing). The formula for **market growth** is:

$$\text{Market growth (\%)} = \frac{\text{New market size} - \text{old market size}}{\text{Old market size}} \times 100$$

If market growth is negative then the market is shrinking.

2) In a **growing** market, **several** firms can **grow easily**. In a **shrinking** market, **competition** can be **heavy** — there are fewer customers to go around. Firms can **diversify** or they may want to **get out** of the market altogether.

Market Analysis tells firms about their Market Share

1) Market share is the **percentage** of sales in a market that is made by **one firm**, or by **one brand**. It's calculated using this **formula**:

$$\text{Market share (\%)} = \frac{\text{Sales}}{\text{Total market size}} \times 100$$

2) E.g. if **40 000** PCs were sold in a given period and **10 000** were made by Dell, this would give Dell a 10 000 ÷ 40 000 × 100 = **25% market share** (in terms of volume). If **£5m** was spent on fast-food and **£1m** of this was at KFC®, this would give KFC® a 1m ÷ 5m × 100 = **20% market share** (in terms of value).
3) It's important to look at **trends in market share** as well as trends in sales revenue. Letting your market share go down is not good — it means that **competitors** are **gaining an advantage** over you.

Sales Growth can be used to Analyse Market Trends

1) The marketing department will **continuously monitor** the company's **sales growth** in certain markets to see where it is **gaining sales** and where it is **losing sales**. The **percentage change** in sales is calculated using the following formula:

$$\text{Sales growth (\%)} = \frac{\text{Sales this year} - \text{Sales last year}}{\text{Sales last year}} \times 100$$

Sales growth doesn't have to be yearly — it can be measured over any time period.

2) If sales growth is **positive** then the company is **gaining sales**, if sales growth is **negative** then the company is **losing sales**.
3) The marketing department **combines** its analysis of these **figures** in order to see if they are meeting objectives.

Example A software company reporting an annual increase of **5%** in their game **sales** might seem like a good thing. However if the computer game **market** has **grown** by **15%** in the same year then they're failing to grow at the **same rate** as the market, so their **market share** has gone down.

Market Analysis

Market Mapping compares Two Features of products or brands

1) A market map shows **extremes** for **two measures** that are important to customers, e.g. low price vs. high price, low quality vs. high quality, basic vs. luxurious, young customer appeal vs. mature customer appeal.
2) It's laid out as a **matrix**, and the products or brands are **positioned** on it according to where they are judged to lie between each pair of extremes.
3) This market map shows how customers ranked 8 **supermarkets**, labelled A to H, in terms of **price** and **quality**.

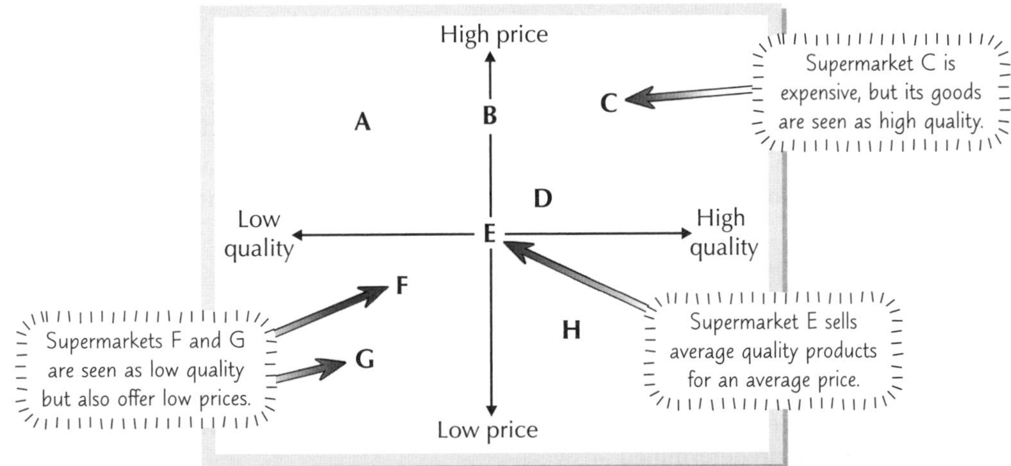

Businesses can get lots of information from Analysing Market Maps

1) Market maps can help a business spot a **gap in the market**. It can try to fill it with a new product or brand, knowing that there won't be any close competitors. Other **market research** will be needed to find out if there is actually **demand** for a product in that gap. E.g. is there a market for high-quality shirts for children?
2) Market maps can show a business who its **closest competitors** are. They can then plan the best **marketing strategy** to persuade customers away from them.
3) If the sales of a product are **declining**, the company might use a **market map** to find out how customers view their product and then try to **reposition** it on the map. Market maps can show the features provided by the most popular brands, which can indicate the **benefits** considered most desirable by the target market.
4) Market maps can show how much customers expect to **pay**, e.g. for cameras of varying quality. This can help a company with its **pricing strategy**.
5) However, market mapping can **simplify** things too much. E.g. in the map above, supermarket A manages to successfully sell **lower quality** goods for **high prices** — this could be due to its **location**, e.g. if it is **conveniently** located within walking distance it means you don't have to drive or use public transport.
6) The positions of products and brands on a market map is usually a **matter of opinion**, and may be **biased**. For example, different people might have **different views** on whether a product is high or low quality.

Practice Questions

Q1 What are the formulas for working out market growth, market share and sales growth?

Q2 What is meant by 'market share'?

Q3 Give an advantage and a disadvantage of market mapping.

Exam Questions

Answer on p.199.

Q1 Henry's Dresses set a 2014 objective to 'increase sales by 10%'. Its sales for 2013 and 2014 are shown in the table on the right.

a) Determine whether it has met its sales objective. [2 marks]

b) Evaluate whether the business has performed well. [9 marks]

Year	Sales	Market size
2013	250 units	600 units
2014	290 units	900 units

Q2 A manufacturer is planning to launch a new range of cupcakes. Analyse how the manufacturer might use a market map in marketing decision making. [9 marks]

I wish market analysis involved actually going to the market...

Market analysis involves handling data and looking at lots of numbers in order to set the correct objectives and make the right decisions for the company. Make sure you can interpret market maps too and you won't get lost in your exam.

Market Research

Market research is the collection and analysis of market information such as customer likes and dislikes. It's especially important before launching a new product — it helps prevent disastrous errors.

Market Research is done for Three Main Reasons

1) It helps businesses **spot opportunities** — businesses research **customer buying patterns** to aid them in predicting what people will be buying in the future. A business might use **research** to help them spot **growing markets** to get into, and **declining markets** to get out of.
2) It helps them decide **what to do next** — businesses can do some market research before **launching a product** or an **advertising campaign**.
3) It helps them see if their **plans are working**. A business that keeps a keen eye on **sales figures** will notice if their marketing strategy is having the **right effect**.
4) However, market research can be **expensive** and **bad market research** can lead to **disastrous business decisions**. So businesses need to **plan carefully** to make sure they get the **maximum benefit** from market research.

Market Research can be Quantitative or Qualitative

1) Quantitative research produces **numerical statistics** — facts and figures. It often uses multiple-choice **questionnaires** that ask questions like: "When did you last buy this product? A: within the last day, B: within the last week, C: within the last month, D: within the last year, E: longer ago, F: have never bought this product." These are called **closed questions** because they have **fixed**, **predetermined** answers.
2) Qualitative research looks into the **feelings** and **motivations** of consumers. It uses **focus groups** that have in-depth discussions on a product, and asks questions like: "How does this product make you feel?" These are called **open questions**. The answer isn't restricted to multiple-choice options.

Closed questions make analysis easier, but sometimes open questions give more informative data.

Market Research can be Primary or Secondary

Primary market research is where a business **gathers new data** (or employs someone to do it on their behalf). **Secondary market research** is done by **analysing data** that's already available.

Primary Research

1) Primary data is gathered with things like **questionnaires**, **interviews**, post / phone / internet **surveys** and **focus groups** (e.g. a group of well-informed people).
2) Businesses do **test marketing** — e.g. they launch a product in one **region** and measure **sales** and **customer response** before launching it across the country.
3) Primary research uses **sampling** to make predictions about the **whole market** based on a sample (see p.31).
4) Primary data is needed to find out what consumers think of a **new product** or **advert**. You can't use secondary data because, erm, there won't be any secondary data on a brand new product.
5) Primary data is **specific** to the purpose it's needed for. This is great for **niche markets** (see p.39) — secondary data might be too broad or too mainstream to tell you anything useful.
6) Primary data is **exclusive** to the business who researched it, so **competitors can't benefit** from it.
7) However, primary research is **labour-intensive**, **expensive** and **slow**.

Secondary Research

1) **Internal sources** of secondary data include information from loyalty cards, feedback from company salesmen and analysis of company sales reports, financial accounts, and stock records.
2) **External sources** include Government publications like the Social Trends report, marketing agency reports, pressure groups and trade magazines.
3) **Secondary data** is much **easier**, **faster** and **cheaper** to get hold of than primary data.
4) However, secondary data that was gathered for a different purpose might be **unsuitable**. It may contain **errors** and it may be **out of date**.
5) Secondary data is often used to get an **initial understanding** of a market. A business may then do more specific primary research to investigate any **issues** or problems that are shown up by the secondary data.

Market Research

Market Researchers need a **Representative Sample**

1) Market researchers survey **samples** of people rather than the **whole market** — this is valuable as it keeps their **costs down** and saves them a lot of **time** and **resources**.
2) The sample should try to **represent** the market. It must have **similar proportions** of people in terms of things like age, income, class, ethnicity and gender. If the sample isn't representative, you've got **problems**. However, it isn't always easy to get a representative sample.
3) A **big sample** has a better **chance** of being representative than a **small sample** — but even a big sample won't necessarily be 100% representative. There's always a **margin of error**.
4) The **size** of the **sample** may depend on how many people a company can **afford** to ask. If the **cash** available for research is **limited**, the **risk** of the information being **inaccurate** increases.
5) The **size** of the **sample** and the **sampling method** is also affected by the **type** of product or business, the **risk** involved and the **target market**. E.g. a company producing wedding dresses won't use random sampling (see below) as men don't form part of their target market. They're more likely to use quota sampling instead.

There are **three** main types of sample:

- **Simple Random Sample** — Names are picked **randomly** from a list (usually from the electoral register).
- **Stratified Sample** — The population is divided into groups and people are selected randomly from each group. The number of people picked from each group is **proportional** to the size of the group.
- **Quota Sample** — People are picked who fit into a **category** (e.g. mums between 30 and 40). Businesses use quota sampling to get opinions from the people the product is directly targeted at.

Market Research needs to **Avoid Bias**

The **quality** of decisions made using market research is only as good as the **accuracy** of the research.

1) Researchers have to be careful to avoid any possible **bias**.
2) Questionnaires and interviews should avoid **leading questions** — questions that are phrased in a way that **leads** the respondent to give a particular answer, e.g "You do like chocolate, don't you?"
3) Interviews suffer from "**interviewer effects**". This is when the **response** isn't what the interviewee **really thinks**. This can be caused by the **personality** of the interviewer — their **opinions** can **influence** the interviewee.
4) The more **representative** a sample is, the more **confidence** a business can have in the results of the research.

Not Spending enough on market research increases the **Risk**

1) **Market research** can be very expensive, but not doing enough market research before starting a business **increases the risk** that it will **fail** — businesses don't stand much chance of getting the product right if they **don't know** whether it's really what the market **wants**.
2) It's much less risky to do market research **before** finalising the details of a product. Research may tell a firm that they have to seriously **adapt** and **develop** their original idea to make it **fit in** with what the market **needs**.

Practice Questions

Q1 Give three reasons why firms carry out market research.

Q2 A toy company is researching the market for a new board game.
Write three open and three closed questions that they could use in a consumer survey.

Q3 List two internal and two external sources of secondary data.

Q4 What are the three main types of sample, and what are the differences between them?

Exam Question

Q1 Discuss why a new business might pay a market research company to gather primary research for them. [6 marks]

Surveys show that most people lie in surveys...

Research takes time and costs money — businesses must make sure the data's accurate or it'll be as much use as a chocolate fireguard. They also have to actually use the findings to provide what their customers want. If a business can use market research to increase their sales and profits, the market research will pay for itself. Everyone's a winner.

Interpreting Marketing Data

Businesses have a lot of mathsy techniques for analysing data, and you need to know how they work.

Time Series Analysis** looks at data over **Time

1) **Time series analysis** is used to reveal **underlying patterns** by recording and plotting data over time. For example, the recording of **sales** over a year.
2) **Trends** are the long-term movement of a variable, for example the sales of a particular product over a number of years. Trends may be **upward**, **constant** or **downward**, but there are usually **fluctuations** around the trend.
3) **Seasonal** fluctuations repeat on a **regular** basis — such as daily, quarterly or yearly, e.g. the use of electricity over a 24-hour period, or the sales of ice lollies over a year.
4) **Random** fluctuations have **no pattern** to them. They also include the results of **major disturbances** like **war**, changes of **government, natural disasters** and sudden **unpredictable events,** e.g. the 2013 "horse meat" scandal.
5) Time series analysis can also be used to look for **links** between **sales** and **marketing** activity. For example, the marketing department might look at trends in sales to see if their **marketing campaigns** are working, and make **decisions** about future campaigns based on these **trends**.

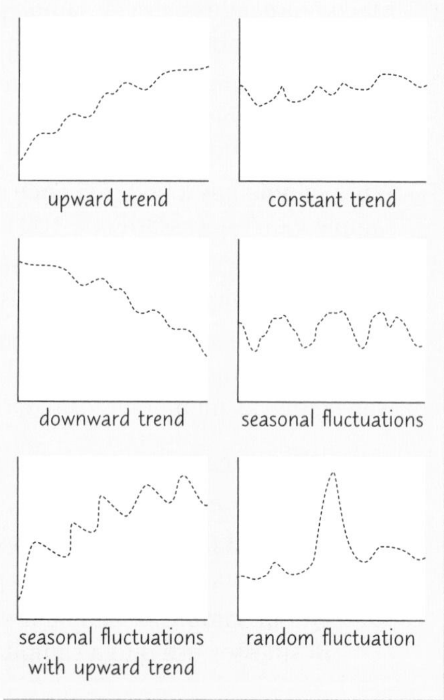

Extrapolation** can be used to **Predict Future Sales

1) **Trends** in sales data from previous years can be continued into the future (**extrapolated**) to **forecast future sales.** This allows managers to set **sales targets**. Sales **performance** can be measured against these targets.
2) For example, if sales have increased by **8% a year** for the past five years, extrapolation will predict that they'll **continue** to do so in future years.
3) In reality, increases or decreases **won't be the same** every year — marketing can use the **average** increase or decrease over a **few years** to extrapolate into the future:

- The revenue for this business increased by **£40 000** between 2010 and 2014 (**4 years**) — that's an **average** of **£10 000 a year** (40 000 ÷ 4). This average can be used in extrapolation.
- So in **2017** you might predict that the revenue will be **£310 000**. In order to achieve this target, marketing might set the objective of increasing sales by **3.5%** each year for the next **3 years**.
- However, this prediction **doesn't** take into account that the rate of growth was **slowing down** between 2010 and 2013 (the increase in growth between 2013 and 2014 could have been a **random fluctuation**). It also doesn't factor in other influences like **market share** or **market growth.**

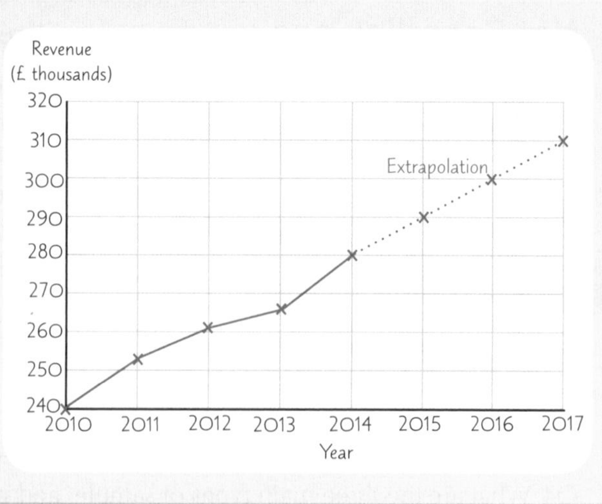

4) Extrapolation is most useful in fairly **stable** environments, e.g. where the **size** of the **market** or the number of **competitors** is **unlikely** to **change** much.
5) Extrapolation relies on **past trends** remaining **true**. Unfortunately, the **pace of change** in the market can be very fast, so extrapolations from the past don't always predict the future very accurately — it's best to use it for predicting just a **few months** ahead because customer desires and technology constantly change.
6) **Sudden unexpected events** are the biggest pitfall for extrapolation. Changes in the market due to things like **new technology** make extrapolation from past data completely useless.

Interpreting Marketing Data

Correlation** shows how **Closely** two **Variables** are **Related

1) **Correlation** is a measure of how **closely** two variables are **related** — for example, the age of customers and their income. Correlation may be **positive** or **negative**, **strong** or **weak**, or there may be no apparent correlation at all.
2) You can draw a **line of best fit** through a set of correlated points — the line should be as **close** as possible to **all** the **points** on the graph.

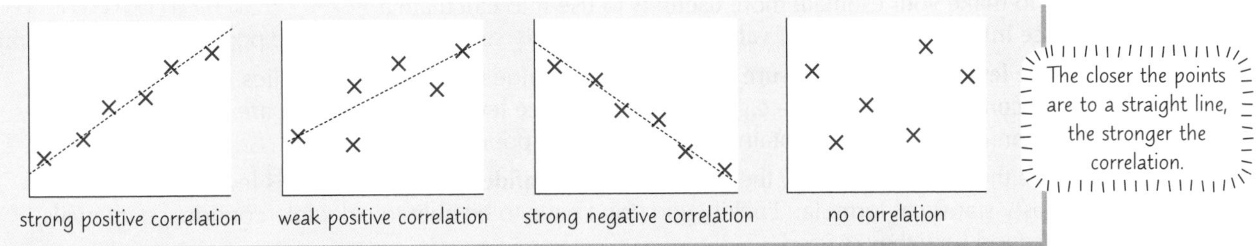

3) It's a **useful tool**, but correlation **doesn't** prove **cause and effect**. **Other variables** may be important — e.g. there might be a **strong positive correlation** between ice cream sales and sun cream sales, but one does not **cause** the other. They're both **affected** by an **external factor** — e.g. the weather.
4) **External factors** have to be taken into account when **reviewing correlation**. For example, if sales of sports equipment increased during a **marketing campaign** then you might say sales increased because of the marketing campaign. However, if the marketing campaign happened to **coincide** with the Olympic Games then it's not clear whether marketing or the event had a **bigger impact** on sales.
5) If there's a **correlation** between two variables, managers might assume that the trend will **carry on**. They can **extrapolate** the graph — draw a **line of best fit** and then keep the line going to **project** the trend **further** along the **horizontal axis**. For example, if the graph shows the **cost** of **car repairs** against the number of **miles driven**, the line can be **extrapolated** to **predict** the cost of repairs after **any** number of miles. However, they need to be cautious about extrapolating too far beyond the known data as the trend might not continue.

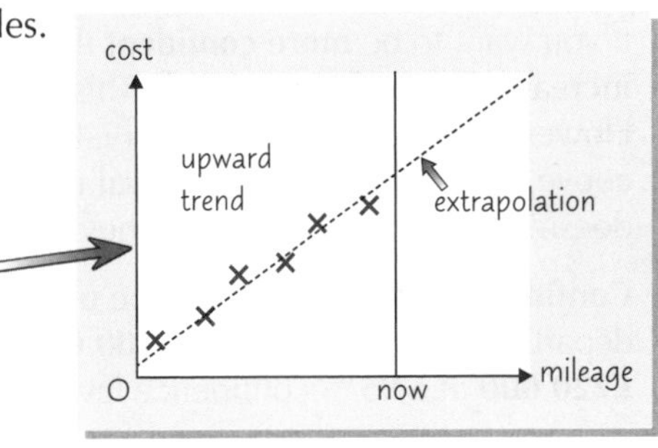

Sales Forecasts** can help **Other Departments

1) Sales forecasts allow the **finance** department to produce **cash flow** forecasts — they can use **predicted sales** to work out how much money is expected to **come in** and how much they have to **spend**. (See page 73 for more on cash flow forecasting.)
2) Sales forecasts also allow **production** and **human resources** departments to prepare for the expected level of sales. They can make sure that they have the right amount of machinery, stock and staff. (See page 88 for more on HR planning.)

Practice Questions

Q1 What is a trend?

Q2 What is extrapolation? How can a business use extrapolation?

Q3 What is correlation?

Exam Question

Answer on p.199.

Q1 The graph on the right shows the sales figures for a children's computer tablet.

Revenue (£ thousands): 100, 110, 120, 130, 140, 150, 160
Year: 2010, 2011, 2012, 2013, 2014, 2015

a) By drawing and extrapolating a line of best fit on the graph, estimate the revenue in 2015. [3 marks]

b) Do you think this estimate is likely to be accurate? Justify your answer. [16 marks]

A little less extrapolation, a little more action please...

Extrapolation is all about identifying a trend and then predicting what will happen next. It's important for businesses to look at past performance because it will give them an idea of how a product will sell in the future. But don't forget, it's not 100% reliable — sudden events can really throw a spanner in the works and mess up your marketing strategy.

Interpreting Marketing Data

A bit of statisticky stuff first and then some ways that technology is used to find out about you and your interests.

Confidence Intervals are a Margin of Error for sample results

1) No matter how carefully you select your sample there's a good chance that it **won't** represent the **whole population** accurately. Any result taken from the sample will just be an **estimate** of the equivalent value for the **population**.
2) One way to make your estimate more useful is to use it to calculate a **confidence interval** — a **range of values** that you're fairly sure the value for the population will lie within.

The population is the whole group that you want to find out about. E.g. all a business's customers.

3) **Confidence levels** indicate how **sure** you are that the value for the population lies **within** the **confidence interval** — e.g. a **95% confidence level** means that you are 95% certain that your confidence interval contains the value for the population.
4) You choose the **confidence level**, then **calculate** the **confidence interval** for this level using a nasty statistical formula. Luckily you don't have to be able to calculate confidence intervals, just understand how they're used.

Example: A cleaning company sets an objective of **80% customer satisfaction**. They ask a sample of their customers and find that **84%** of them are satisfied. Using this estimate and a **confidence level** of **95%**, they calculate a **confidence interval** of **82%** to **86%** customer satisfaction.

This means that they are **95% confident** that the percentage of satisfied customers lies between 82% and 86%. So they can be fairly sure that **more than 80%** are satisfied, which means that they've **met their objective**.

5) If you want to be **more confident** that your interval contains the **value** for the **population**, you can **increase** the **confidence level**. This will give you a **wider** confidence interval.
However, wide confidence intervals can be too **vague** to be helpful. E.g. for the cleaning company example above, a 99% confidence interval might be calculated as **78%** to **90%** customer satisfaction. This interval doesn't help them to decide if they've met their objective because it includes values **below** their target of 80%.
6) **Confidence intervals** can also be used to show uncertainty in **predicting** other figures — e.g. if the marketing department predicts sales of **£200 000**, they might say that the actual sales will be between **£180 000** and **£220 000** at a **95%** confidence level.

Technology can be used to gather Information about Customers

Many companies now use **technology** to gather **information** about the **lifestyles** of their **customers** and the **products** that they **buy**. This helps them to make sure that **promotions** are **targeting** the right people.

1) Lots of supermarkets offer **loyalty cards** which give customers money back according to how much they spend. The **benefit** for the supermarket is that it not only allows them to form a **database** of customer names and addresses, but also their **preferences** based on what they **buy**. E.g. they could target an offer on pet insurance at people who bought pet food. This would make the campaign **cheaper** and **more effective**.
2) **Social networking websites** are another way that businesses use technology to find out more about their customers.
   - Facebook® has tools that **analyse** which other pages a company's **followers** are **interested** in — this allows the company to build a **profile** of its customers for relatively **minimal cost**.
   - Facebook® can also be used to find out the **demographics** (see p.16) of people interested in existing products — so if a company wants to **market** a **new product** it can see what kinds of people like **similar products**.
   - Companies who **advertise** on social media sites can make their adverts visible only to the people who have shown an interest in **similar products** before — this is **cheaper** and more **effective** than targeting everyone who uses the website.
   - Businesses can also use **social media** to follow **what people are saying** about their products and also competitors' products. This is **cheaper** and **more immediate** than organising surveys.
3) **Search engines** like Google™ often use targeted advertising too — they show adverts that are **relevant** to the topic the user searched for.
4) Controversially, some stores use **Wi-Fi® signals** from customers' **phones** to track their movements — they can then use this data to help them plan the **best store layout**. For example, they can identify the areas of the store that **most customers** walk past and display their **best promotions** and **offers** there.

Interpreting Marketing Data

IT can be used to help Analyse Marketing Data

Most companies use **software** to do their marketing analysis. The **advantages** of this are:

1) Computers can process much **more data** than people can. Computer software can analyse huge amounts of data and produce sales forecasts more quickly than people can. Using computers can also **reduce** the risk of **errors**.
2) There are many types of market analysis software, so a business can find a program that fits its **needs** exactly. For example, marketing analysis software allows managers to investigate "**what if?**" scenarios. They can work out the impact of **potential changes** in expenditure or sales, which helps them to plan their marketing decisions.
3) IT can also be used to analyse data gathered at the **point-of-sale**. As soon as an item has been sold, it is recorded — so the effect of vouchers/coupons and marketing campaigns can be seen immediately.
4) '**Big data**' is a new term used to describe the **vast quantities** of data from all sources, e.g. data with a structure such as sales and customer information, and unstructured data such as that from social networking. The trouble is there is so much data and it streams in so fast that normal computers aren't sufficient to handle it. Large companies are investing in ways of **analysing big data** to draw **useful correlations**.
5) There are **downsides** to analysing marketing data using IT:

- Buying **software** can be **expensive**. If a new version of the software is released and the business decides to **upgrade**, it costs even more money.
- Staff need to be **trained** to use the software, which might be **expensive** and **time-consuming**. If the company **upgrades** their software at any point, further training might be needed.
- There's a risk that having software that can deal with loads of data will lead to the company valuing the **quantity** of information over its **quality**. A business might produce lots of pretty graphs, but if nobody's drawing **conclusions** about what the **trends** mean for the company they're not useful at all.
- Companies with lots of data might find that their **computer systems** aren't up to the job of **handling** it, e.g. if it takes too long to upload all the information. If this happens, they might have to **outsource** (see p.65) their marketing analysis to a **specialist company** or stick to analysing just a **proportion** of the available data.

Example

Problem: When Tesco launched its **loyalty card**, Clubcard, in 1995, it took **30 hours** every time they **transferred the data** they'd collected from their computers to the computers of the **data analysis** firm that interpreted it.

Solution: Tesco decided that it would be easier to **interpret** just **some of the data** and then apply their findings to the **rest of the data**. They agreed that the **data analysis** firm dunnhumby would look at 10% of the data once a week and **extrapolate** their findings to the other 90% of Clubcard holders. Dunnhumby have since introduced **new software** which allows them to analyse the behaviour of **all** Clubcard holders without relying on extrapolation.

Practice Questions

Q1 Why are confidence intervals used when reporting market research data?

Q2 Give three ways that technology can be used to gather information about customers.

Q3 Give two advantages and two disadvantages of using IT to analyse data.

Exam Question

Q1 Using sample data, a business estimates the average age of their customers and calculates a 99% confidence interval for this age. The interval extends from 44 to 60. Which of the following is most likely to be the true average age of their customers?

A 42   B 50   C 61   D 69   [1 mark]

Confidence interval — a short break for a little pep talk...

Increasing the confidence level means you're more sure of your results, but that the interval will be less precise and probably less useful. E.g. it's not very helpful to claim that, at the 99.9% confidence level, between 10% and 90% of the population would buy the new product.

Interpreting Elasticity of Demand

OK, so price isn't the only thing that affects demand, but it can certainly have a pretty major impact...

Price Elasticity of *Demand* shows how *Demand* changes with *Price*

1) The **price elasticity** of a product is how much the price change **affects** the demand. It is found using this **formula:**

$$\text{Price elasticity of demand} = \frac{\text{\% change in quantity demanded}}{\text{\% change in price}}$$

2) Price elasticity of demand is **always negative** (a positive change in price causes a negative change in demand, and a negative change in price causes a positive change in demand) so you can just **ignore** the **minus sign**.
3) If the price elasticity of demand is **greater than 1** (ignoring the minus sign), the product is **price elastic**. If the price elasticity of demand is **less than 1**, it's **price inelastic**. So, –1.5 is price elastic and –0.5 is price inelastic.

Example: A price **rise** of **10%** results in a **30% reduction** in demand.

Price elasticity of demand = $\frac{-30\%}{+10\%}$ = **–3** so this product is **price elastic**.

As price goes up, demand falls — and vice versa.

You won't have to work out elasticity coefficients in your exam — just use and interpret them.

Example: A price **reduction** of **20%** results in a **5% increase** in demand.

Price elasticity of demand = $\frac{+5\%}{-20\%}$ = **–0.25** so this product is **price inelastic**.

This is called the elasticity coefficient.

4) For **price elastic** products, the **% change in demand** is **greater than** the **% change in price**.
5) For **price <u>in</u>elastic** products, the **% change in demand** is **less than** the **% change in price**.

Price Elasticity affects *Revenue* and *Profit*

1) **Sales revenue = price of product × quantity sold** (see p.6). Price elasticity shows how price affects sales revenue.
2) If a product is **price elastic**, a **price increase** will make **sales revenue go down**. The money lost from the **% decrease in sales** will be **more than** the money gained from the **% increase in price**.

Example: **100 scarves a year** are sold for **£10 each** giving a revenue of **£1000**. Price elasticity coefficient = **–2.5**. If the company **increases** the price by **10%** to **£11**, demand will **decrease** by 10% × 2.5 = **25%**. So 75 scarves will be sold at the new price, which **decreases revenue** to 75 × £11 = **£825**.

3) For **price elastic products**, a firm can **increase revenue** by reducing price, as it increases the number of sales.
4) If a product is price **inelastic**, a rise in **price** will make **sales revenue go up**. The money lost from the **% decrease in sales** will be **less than** the money gained from the **% increase in price**.

Example: If the scarves' price elasticity coefficient is **–0.5** and price **increases** by **10%**, demand will **decrease** by 10% × 0.5 = **5%**. So 95 scarves will be sold at the new price, which **increases revenue** to 95 × £11 = **£1045**.

5) For **price inelastic products**, **decreasing** the **price** will make **sales increase** slightly, but sales **revenue goes down** because the price has fallen and only a few more units have been sold.

Price Elasticity of Demand *Depends* on *Ease* of *Switching*

1) **Necessary products** like milk are **price inelastic**. Changing the prices doesn't have much affect on demand. If consumers can **switch** to **similar** or **competitor** products, demand will be **price elastic**. E.g. if Princes tuna increases in price, people might buy John West tuna instead.
2) Businesses try to **differentiate** their products to create **brand loyalty**. **Loyal** customers won't switch even if the price goes up, so this makes the product **less** price elastic.

iPhones® are price inelastic due to the strength of the Apple® brand.

3) Price elasticity of demand increases over time as customers have chance to find alternative products. The **internet** makes it easy to find alternatives and so **increases price elasticity**.
4) **Product types** tend to be **price inelastic**, but individual **brands** tend to be **price elastic**.
5) Items costing a **greater proportion** of consumers' incomes will be more **price elastic**. Customers won't be too concerned about a 10% rise in the cost of a newspaper, but a 10% increase in the price of a car might cause them to look for **alternatives**.

Petrol sales are inelastic but sales of an individual company's petrol are elastic.

Interpreting Elasticity of Demand

Income Elasticity of Demand shows how Demand changes with Income

When people earn **more money**, there's **more demand** for some products, and **less demand** for other products.

$$\text{Income elasticity of demand} = \frac{\%\text{ change in quantity demanded}}{\%\text{ change in real income}}$$

Example: A **rise** in income of **10%** results in a **5% increase** in demand.

$$\text{Income elasticity of demand} = \frac{+5\%}{+10\%} = +0.5$$

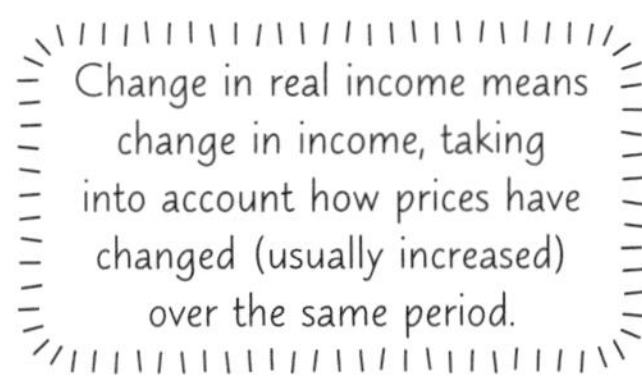

1) **Normal goods** (e.g. fresh fruit and vegetables) have a **positive income elasticity of demand** that's **less than 1**. This means that as **income rises**, the **demand rises** — but at a **slower rate** than the increase in income.
2) **Luxury goods** (e.g. designer clothes and fine wines) have a **positive income elasticity of demand** which is **more than 1**. This means that the **demand for luxury goods** grows **faster** than the increase in income.
3) In a business sense, "**inferior**" goods are cheaper 'value' products — e.g. a **cheaper supermarket value brand** of baked beans compared to **Heinz® Baked Beans**. Inferior goods have a **negative income elasticity of demand** — **demand falls** when **income rises** and **demand rises** when **income falls**.

If demand rises, revenue increases. If demand falls, revenue decreases.

Elasticity helps a business make Choices

1) **Price elasticity** helps a manufacturer **decide** whether to **raise** or **lower** the price of a product. They can see what might happen to the **sales**, and ultimately what will happen to **sales revenue**.
2) **Income elasticity** helps a manufacturer see what will happen to sales if the **economy** grows or shrinks.
3) Here are examples of the **marketing decisions** that might be made about two products:

Tin of value tomato soup — price elasticity of demand = –3.0, income elasticity of demand = –0.5

- **Reduce** the price to **increase demand** and **sales revenue**, but **only** if the profit margin is big enough.
- In times of **economic growth**, sales will **fall** so the **brand image** of the product may need to be changed to appeal to better-off customers. In times of **recession**, demand for the product will **increase**.

New designer kitchen — price elasticity of demand = –0.4, income elasticity of demand = +1.5

- **Increase** the price — demand will **fall slightly**, but revenue and profit will still **increase**.
- In times of **economic growth**, sales will **grow** so the aspirational **brand image** should be maintained. In times of **recession**, demand for the product will **fall**, so **incentives** such as discounts and interest-free repayments over a number of years could be introduced to **encourage sales**.

Practice Questions

Q1 If a product has an elasticity coefficient of –0.9, is it price elastic or inelastic?

Q2 Give three factors that affect price elasticity.

Q3 What kind of products become less popular when there's an increase in income?

Exam Questions

Answer on p.199.

Q1 A company sells 200 horses a year for £1500 each. If the elasticity coefficient is –0.7, calculate the impact on revenue that a 15% increase in prices will have. [7 marks]

Q2 The price elasticity of demand for a pack of sausages is estimated to be –0.2. Explain what this means and analyse the effect changes in price will have on revenue. [9 marks]

Rubber prices are usually the most elastic...

The clues are in the names — price elasticity shows how much price influences demand, and income elasticity shows how much income affects demand. Luckily, you won't be asked to calculate the elasticity coefficients in your exams.

Marketing Decisions — STP

Now it's time to divide and conquer the market. That's what STP is all about.

STP — Segment, Target, Position

STP aims to **focus** marketing efforts where they'll be **most effective**. It is a marketing process with **three stages**:

There are Different ways to Segment a market

1) Segmentation **divides** a market into **groups** of buyers. Each group will have different wants and needs, and require a **different marketing mix** (see p.40). E.g. they'll differ in how much they're prepared to spend, and where and when they shop. They'll also use different forms of **media** — e.g. TV, magazines, social media platforms.
2) Here are some of the methods or 'bases' used to segment a market:

Demographic

Age, e.g. Saga Holidays are aimed specifically at the over-50s.

Gender, e.g. yoghurts are mainly marketed towards women.

Socio-economic class, e.g. businesses can segment their market based on the kind of **jobs** people have — e.g. **modern one bedroom flats** might be marketed at **young professionals**.

Family size, e.g. large "**family packs**" of breakfast cereal, loo roll, etc. are aimed at large families.

Geographic

The market can be divided according to **neighbourhood**, **city**, **county**, **country**, or **world region**, e.g. Asia. It's a method mostly used by **multinational** companies as their customers have a range of cultures, lifestyles and climates and are likely to need **different marketing mixes**. An example closer to home is that the core market for **Irn-Bru** is **Scotland**.

Income

E.g. CHANEL makeup is aimed at customers with **high incomes**, and Tesco's own-brand makeup is aimed at lower-income customers. **Luxury products** are usually aimed at high income groups.

Behaviour

Amount of use, e.g. mobile phone suppliers market **differently** to heavy users and light users.

Lifestyle, e.g. busy **young workers** might tend to buy lots of microwaveable ready-meals, so a company making **ready-meals** might target this market segment.

3) Segmentation is useful for **identifying new customers**, **markets** and **products**. It can also help to identify the **best way** to market a product (e.g. advertising high-end cosmetics in Vogue magazine).
4) However, segmentation can cause companies to **ignore the needs** of **potential customers**. It can be difficult to **break** the market into **obvious segments** and even more difficult to find ways of marketing to **specific demographics**.

Target Big enough segments, with Potential Growth and Little Competition

Once you've segmented the market, you need to decide **which segments** to **target**. There are **three approaches**:

Concentrated marketing involves targeting **one or two segments**. It's a good approach for smaller businesses with **limited resources**. The segment must be **big enough** for a decent return, have **growth potential** (e.g. sports clothing for pensioners). It should also have a **need** that the business can meet (that **isn't** already met by lots of **competitors**).

Differentiated marketing is where **several segments** are targeted, and the product and marketing mix is **adapted** to appeal to **each** segment. This is only really feasible for **large companies** with large budgets. E.g. the same colouring book could be advertised to children as a fun activity, or to adults as a relaxation aid.

Undifferentiated marketing is where the segments are **ignored** and the company tries to reach the **entire market** with a single product and marketing mix. It makes sense for **widely used products**, e.g. toothpaste. It has the advantage of potentially **high sales volumes** and **relatively low marketing costs**.

Marketing Decisions — STP

Businesses can target **Niche** or **Mass Markets**

1) Concentrated marketing is also known as **niche marketing**.
2) Focusing on **niche markets** often means small businesses don't have to compete **directly** with larger businesses (who don't normally target niche markets). E.g. a small business selling microwave meals could **establish a niche** by **specialising** in, say, meals for people with nut allergies — this allows the business to make a profit even though there are lots of large ready-meal businesses.
3) A small manufacturer can **meet the demand** of a small niche more easily than it can meet the demand of a **mass market**. It can also be easier to market their product to a niche. E.g. a new type of fishing bait could be promoted in a fishing magazine.
4) Some products are aimed at a **mass market** (often with undifferentiated marketing) — they're designed to appeal to **lots of consumers**, e.g. Coca-Cola®.

Position a product in **Customers' Minds**

1) Once a company has decided which **segments** it's going to **target**, it needs to think about **positioning**.
2) Positioning is **creating an image** of your brand or product in the **mind** of your **target customer**. It's getting **them** to develop the opinion of your product that **you** want them to.
3) Customers have a **mental map** of the market and will **position** new products relative to the alternatives. So a business needs to look at where would be the most effective place to **position** its brand or product in relation to its **competitors**. E.g. if it can't **compete** with competitors on **price** or **quality** it might push the **convenience** or **ethical nature** of the product.
4) To position your product well, you need to convince the target customers that your product has **benefits** for them and to **differentiate** it from the competition in a way that is **relevant** to them.

Example: An **outdoor clothing** company targeting **young back-packers** might choose to position its range of outdoor clothing as more **ethical** than **rival products** because its market **research** has highlighted **ethical sourcing** as a feature that young back-packers **care about**.

Influences on positioning

- **State of the market** — if the economy is in **recession** then companies will be more likely to **position** their brand or product to make customers think it offers the **best value for money**. Whereas in a booming market they might emphasise that their product is **great quality** or **environmentally-friendly**.
- **Company's current products** — if the company's other products are seen as **reliable** and **cheap** they are likely to try and position any new products in a similar place.
- **Attributes of the company** — companies need to position products to match their **strengths** and **weaknesses**. E.g. if a business is really **innovative** then it will focus on how its products are **cutting-edge** and **unique**.

Practice Questions

Q1 Outline the STP process.

Q2 Give four bases for segmenting the market.

Q3 Give two things you should consider when picking a segment to target.

Exam Questions

Q1 A small manufacturer is launching a new brand of luxury suntan lotion. Analyse how the STP process could be used in marketing the lotion. [9 marks]

Q2 A new archery equipment store has opened. To what extent do you think that targeting specific markets is the best marketing strategy for the store? [25 marks]

Any customer can have a car painted any colour — so long as it is black...

That's what Henry Ford famously said in 1909 about one of the first mass marketed cars — the Model T. Mr Ford churned them out cheaply and advertised them in mass media. Then along came General Motors, who segmented the market by income and type of car wanted — their aim was to make a car for each segment. Which was a lot of cars.

Marketing Decisions — The Marketing Mix

The marketing mix used to just have 4Ps in it. But lucky for you, some marketing guru thought up an extra 3Ps.

The *Traditional Marketing Mix — Product, Price, Place, Promotion*

The marketing mix describes the **factors** that firms consider when **marketing** a product — they're the factors that'll make customers either buy a product or not buy it.

It used to be known as the **4Ps**. The **price** has to be right, the **product** has to be right, the product must be distributed through the right **places**, and it has to be **promoted** in the right way.

Cindy thought the 7Ps were Party, Party, Party, Party, Party, Party and Penguin.

The *Extra 3Ps — People, Physical Environment, Process*

Service industries supply **people** to **help** or **work** for customers — they have become the **biggest sector** of the UK **economy** and so **3 extra Ps** have been added to the **marketing mix**. These Ps are particularly **important** for services, but are part of the marketing mix for **physical goods** too.

People — People are the most important part of a service business. A customer is more likely to buy a service if the people providing it are **well-trained**, **knowledgeable**, **reliable**, **friendly** and **efficient**.

Physical Environment — The presentation of the **environment** where a service is delivered is important. E.g. customers expect a hair salon to be **clean** and **stylishly decorated**, with a comfy sofa on which to read magazines as you wait. Grubby seats and peeling wallpaper won't attract many customers.

Process — This includes things such as **waiting times**, the **ordering** and **payment systems** and any **after-sales service**. E.g. the option to pay with PayPal might influence whether a customer buys from a particular online company.

There's more on each of the 7Ps on pages 42-53.

In an **integrated marketing mix** the 7Ps need to **work together** and **complement** each other — if just one of the factors is **wrong**, it can **decrease** the **revenue** generated from the product.

Example: A company develops an innovative new **product**, but has an inefficient ordering and delivery **process**. This means customers have **trouble ordering** the product, and have to **wait** weeks for it to be delivered. The company will get a **bad reputation** among customers and will sell **fewer products.**

Different Factors influence the Integrated Marketing Mix

1) The integrated marketing mix shouldn't be based on guess work — the right **market research** helps companies develop the right mix of the 7Ps, and make the best **marketing decisions** based on these Ps.
2) **Competitors** in the market can influence the marketing mix — the **price** of a product will be directly influenced by the price of similar products. A high level of competition might mean the company spends more on **promotion** and more **people** are recruited and trained to offer better **customer service** than competitors.
3) The **target market segment** influences the marketing mix. E.g. wealthy consumers will be **less price sensitive** than low income consumers. Also, certain market segments will see different forms of **media promotion** — e.g. young working people, who could be the target market for a new trendy ready-meal brand, might not see adverts on daytime TV.
4) Where the company wants to **position** a **product** in the minds of customers will impact all areas of the marketing mix. For example, PANDORA bracelets highlight that their product is high quality by having **well-trained** and **knowledgeable staff** selling **expensive** products in **exclusive**, **stylish stores**.
5) The **location** of a business will determine what is realistic when it's putting together its marketing mix. E.g. a business that's based in Alaska might not be able to include next-day delivery to the rest of the world as part of its **process**.
6) The **type of product** you are marketing will affect the importance of each of the 7Ps in the marketing mix. E.g. **promotion** and **physical environment** aren't that important for **cheap** products (e.g. plastic cups) whereas they are very important for **expensive** products (e.g. high-end sports cars).
7) Whether you're selling **goods** or a **service** will affect the mix, as will whether you're selling to another **business** or to **consumers**.
8) Other factors to do with the product, such as the **product life cycle** and the business's **product mix** influence the marketing mix. These factors are covered on p.42-45.

Marketing Decisions — The Marketing Mix

*The **Resources** of a **Business** affect the **Marketing Mix***

The integrated marketing mix is influenced by factors within the business:

1) The **marketing** and **corporate objectives** of a business will affect the marketing mix — for example, if an airline wants to increase its **brand loyalty** it might offer frequent fliers an exclusive departure lounge, extra customer service and **promotions** on the **prices** of certain tickets.
2) Many businesses have to **compromise** on certain aspects of the marketing mix due to their **finances**. E.g. a small firm might not have enough **money** to promote a niche product through TV adverts, promotional pricing and point-of-sale displays, so they must choose the **most effective** method of promotion that they can afford.
3) Suppliers tend not to offer **credit** or **discounts** to small businesses so they are only able to produce **small quantities** of goods at a time. This will impact the **price** and **process** aspects of the marketing mix.
4) Businesses that don't have the right **software** to monitor customers' details will have to spend extra money on **promoting** products as they **can't** market directly to **repeat customers**.
5) A company with a well-respected, luxurious **brand image** will be able to charge more for their products than a budget brand. In fact, it'd probably be a **bad idea** for them to lower their prices as this might affect their image.
6) The **knowledge and skills of employees** might mean businesses can justify **increasing prices**. E.g. at Halfords, employees will help you find the correct bulb or wiper blade for your car and even fit it (for an extra payment). However, these services need to be **promoted** so people know about them.

Changing** the **Marketing Mix** can help to make a business **More Competitive

1) **Markets** are **dynamic** (constantly changing) — new competitors/products are constantly **entering** the market and failed ones are **leaving**. The integrated marketing mix needs to **adapt** to these changes.
2) In order to **remain profitable**, companies need to keep **reviewing** their **marketing mix** and **altering** their marketing decisions, taking into account the actions of **competitors** and **other changes** in the marketplace.
3) For a company to stay profitable, it needs to stay **competitive**. A business is competitive if it has something that **customers want** or **need** that **other** similar **businesses don't** have.

- A company can **improve** its **competitiveness** by **changing** any one of the seven elements in the **marketing mix**. They can improve the **quality** of the **product**, reassess their methods of **promotion**, use new **pricing strategies**, and reconsider **channels** of distribution. Businesses can increase the **skills of staff** (e.g. teach hairdressers head massage techniques), make their **processes** better for the customer (e.g. make appointments bookable online), or make their **physical environment** more inviting.
- **Technological advances** are another reason why companies might change the mix. Widespread **internet** access has meant that many firms have **changed** their **method of distribution**. Also, products need to change as technology advances. E.g. computer games are now available as **digital downloads**.
- **Social factors**, such as an increasing number of pensioners, might prompt a change in a **product**, or how it is **promoted**.
- **New laws** can affect the marketing mix, e.g. a new standard for crash helmets would mean adapting **products**, and laws about how and where junk food can be advertised would change the **promotion** factor.

Practice Questions

Q1 What is the marketing mix?

Q2 List the 7Ps.

Q3 Give four influences on the marketing mix.

Exam Question

Q1 Enid owns a snack van. Her revenue has fallen since a competitor entered the market.
Evaluate the changes she could make to her marketing mix to regain market share. [16 marks]

A handy tip to remember the 7Ps — they all begin with P...

The integrated marketing mix brings together the 7Ps — if a firm wants to change one of the Ps it needs to consider the impact it will have on the others. Kind of like fitting a carpet — you might try and adjust one corner to get it to fit but then a problem pops up in another corner. But enough of the carpet related analogies, you've got some work to do...

Marketing Mix — Product

There's a lot to think about before bringing a new product onto the market. Businesses need the right mix of new, growing and mature products to survive in the long-term. And the wrong product can be a pricey mistake.

There are Three Types of Consumer Products

1) **Convenience products** — these are **inexpensive**, everyday items bought **regularly** by **lots** of people. They're often bought out of **habit**, e.g. a coffee on the way to work. Consumers don't put too much thought into buying them and they don't bother shopping around for cheaper alternatives because they **wouldn't save much**.
2) **Shopping products** — these are things like clothes, computers and washing machines that are bought **less regularly** than convenience products. They're **more expensive** and are sold in **fewer places** than convenience products. People might pay more for a **particular brand**, e.g. a Bosch hob or a Jack Wills sweater.
3) **Speciality products** — these are things consumers believe are **unique** in some way, and they'll **travel** to find the exact brand — e.g. designer handbag, celebrity hair stylist or luxury car. Perceived **image** and **quality** are more important to consumers than price for speciality products, so **higher profits** can be made from them.

Businesses need a Variety of Products — a Mixed Product Portfolio

1) A **product line** consists of related products (including different sizes of the same product) with similar **characteristics**, **uses** or **target customers**.
2) The **product mix** is the **combination** of all the **product lines** that a business produces.
3) Businesses aim to have a **product mix** that contains a variety of different products, all at different stages of the **product life cycle** (see p.44). That way if one product fails, the business should still be able to depend on the others.

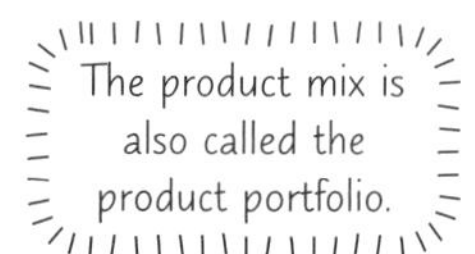

The Boston Matrix is a model of Portfolio Analysis

1) The Boston Matrix compares **market growth** with **market share**. Each **circle** in the matrix represents **one product**. The **size** of each circle represents the **sales revenue** of the product.

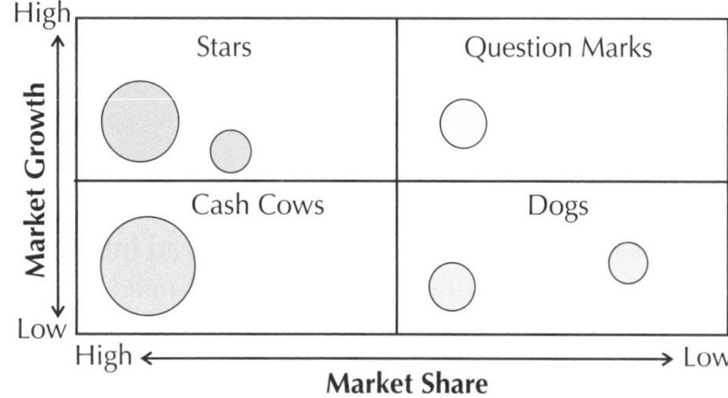

All **new products** are **question marks** (sometimes called **problem children**) and they have small market share and high market growth. These aren't profitable yet and could succeed or fail. They need **heavy marketing** to give them a chance. A business can do various things with question marks — **brand building**, **harvesting** (maximising sales or profit in the short term) or **divestment** (selling off the product).

Cash cows have high market share but low market growth. They're in their **maturity** phase. They've already been promoted and they're produced in high volumes, so costs are low. Cash cows bring in plenty of **money**.

Stars have high market growth and high market share. They're in their profitable **growth** phase and have the **most potential**. They're future **cash cows**. BUT... competitors are likely to try to take advantage of this **growth market** too, so a firm will need to **spend** a lot on **promoting** their product to keep their **market share**. Also, money might need to be spent to **increase capacity** (see page 56) to keep up with **demand**.

Dogs have low market share and low market growth. They're usually pretty much a lost cause. If they're still profitable, e.g. a chocolate bar that is still popular, but no longer growing, the business will **harvest profit** in the **short term**. If the product is no longer making a profit it can be **sold off**.

Jack had low growth — so he tried standing on two legs to make himself look taller.

2) The **Boston Matrix** is a **valuable** way of showing where a business's products are **positioned** in the market.
3) A business's marketing **decisions** will depend on the products' **positions** in the matrix. For example, a business can use money from its **cash cows** to **invest** in its **question marks** so they can become **stars**.
4) But the Boston Matrix **can't predict exactly** what will happen to a product. A product's **profit** may be **different** from what the matrix suggests (e.g. a dog can have strong cash flow and be profitable despite falling sales).

Marketing Mix — Product

New Products can be great for a business

There are three main reasons why it is worthwhile for companies to develop new products:

1) New products can bring in **new customers**.
2) They give a **competitive** advantage.
3) They allow companies to maintain a **balanced product portfolio**.

Competition and **Technology** can inspire **New Products**

Most new products come about for one of three reasons:

1) **Technological developments** mean that a company can now offer the customer something that it couldn't offer before, e.g. 3D TV. In the long term, the new product is likely to be a **replacement** for the old one.
2) A company might develop an **imitative** new product in response to one which has been launched by a **competitor**, e.g. lots of companies decided to develop bagless vacuum cleaners after the launch of the Dyson™.
3) Somebody within the company (usually the owner or a manager) identifies a **gap in the market** for an **innovative** product. Products such as The Sony WALKMAN® or 3M's Post-it® Notes originally fitted into this category. In order to create **innovative products**, companies have to spend lots on **research and development (R&D)**. It is a **high risk** strategy but also carries the **highest potential rewards**.

New Products need a **Unique Selling Point (USP)**

Every successful new product, whether it is innovative, imitative or a replacement for an existing product, needs to have something that **differentiates** it from the **competition**. This is known as a **Unique Selling Point** or a **Unique Selling Proposition (USP)**. USPs can be **tangible benefits** and **intangible benefits**.

1) **Tangible benefits** can be **measured**. Products with tangible benefits that could be used as USPs are things like low-calorie pizza, energy-efficient fridges and savings accounts with high rates of interest.
2) **Intangible benefits** are things that **can't be measured**. They're based on concepts such as reputation and product image. E.g. beauty products market themselves as making the consumer **feel good** and certain makes of car are perceived as being **reliable**.
3) A product's tangible and intangible benefits are important, but there are other things the consumer considers. These might be things like **customer service**, **money-back guarantees**, and availability of **spare parts**.
4) **Service** businesses need USPs too. E.g. Butlins, a chain of holiday camps, claim that so much is included in the price that you won't have to spend any extra money while you're there.

Jim had read the whole manual, but he still couldn't find his laptop's USP.

Practice Questions

Q1 What are the three types of consumer product?

Q2 Sketch and label the Boston Matrix.

Q3 Explain why the Boston Matrix is a valuable tool for portfolio analysis.

Q4 What is the benefit for a company of having a product with a unique selling point?

Exam Questions

Q1 Explain why a small company which is new to the market might prefer to launch an imitative, rather than innovative, product. [4 marks]

Q2 Discuss the usefulness of the Boston Matrix to a biscuit manufacturer. [9 marks]

Glitches in the Boston Matrix create Cash Dogs...

It's really important for a business to have a balanced product portfolio — lots of cash cows might seem like a good thing but the business will worry that the market is growing too slowly and that there are no extra sales to be made from those products. Having lots of stars isn't really a problem though, as long as you can maintain their market share...

Marketing Mix — Product

All products are born with no sales at all. If they're looked after, they grow into big strong products with lots of sales, then they get married and have lots of spin-offs ... er, maybe.

Products** have a **Life Cycle

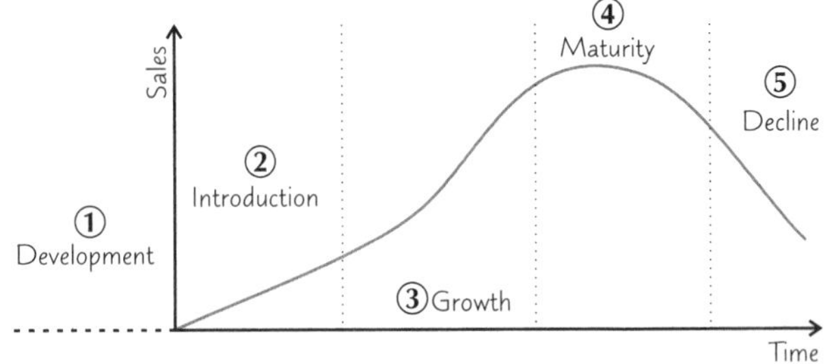

1) The product life cycle shows the **sales** of a product over **time**.
2) It's **valuable** for planning **marketing strategies** and changing the **marketing mix**.
3) **Marketing decisions** will be based on where a product is in its **life cycle** (see next page).

1 — Development

1) The **research and development** (R&D) department **develop** the product.
2) The **marketing** department does **market research**.
3) The **costs** are **high**, and there aren't any sales yet to cover the costs.
4) Development has a **high failure rate**. This is because there's often **not enough demand**, or because the business can't make the product **cheaply** enough to make a profit.

2 — Introduction

1) The product is **launched**, either in one market or in several markets. It's sometimes launched with **complementary** products — e.g. the PlayStation® was launched with games.
2) The business often **promotes** the product heavily to build sales — but businesses need to make sure they've got enough **resources** and **capacity** to **meet the demand** that promotions create.
3) The **initial price** of the product may be **high** to cover **promotional costs**. This is called **skimming**.
4) Alternatively, the price can start off **low** to encourage sales. This is **penetration pricing**.
5) Sales go up, but the sales revenue has to pay for the high **fixed cost** of development **before** the product can make a **profit**. The business usually ditches products with disappointing sales after this stage.
6) There aren't many **outlets** for the new product — businesses have to work hard to persuade retailers to sell it.
7) Competition may be **limited** (if it's an **innovative** product).

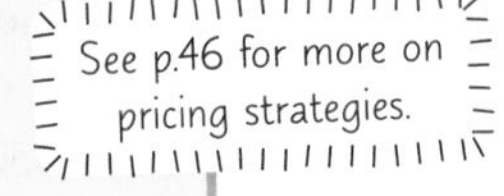
See p.46 for more on pricing strategies.

3 — Growth

1) Sales grow fast. There are **new customers** and **repeat** customers.
2) **Competitors** may be attracted to the market. Promotion shows **differences** from the competitors' products.
3) The product is often **improved** or **developed**, and it may be targeted at a different market segment.
4) Rising sales encourage **more outlets** to stock the product.

4 — Maturity

1) **Sales** reach a **peak** and profitability increases because **fixed costs** of **development** have been **paid for**.
2) At **saturation** (when the market is full and has reached maximum growth) sales may begin to drop, depending on the product. Sales are more likely to drop for long-lasting products that customers do not need to replace regularly. The price is often reduced to stimulate **demand**, which reduces profits.
3) There aren't many new customers. **Competition** within the industry becomes fierce so sales might **suffer**.

5 — Decline

1) The product doesn't **appeal** to customers any more. **Sales fall** rapidly and profits decrease.
2) On the other hand, the product may stay profitable if **promotional costs** are **reduced** enough.
3) If sales carry on falling, the product is **withdrawn** or **sold** to another business (**divestment**). Sometimes, sales might pick up again if competitors leave the market first.

Marketing Mix — Product

Extension Strategies keep a product Going Strong for Longer

Extension strategies try to prolong the life of the product by changing the **marketing mix**. They include:

1) **Product development** — businesses **improve**, reformulate or **redesign** a product. They can change the design of **packaging** to make it look more up to date, or make **special editions** of the product. This can also give a **new focus** to existing **marketing** campaigns.
2) **Market development** — businesses can find **new markets** or **new uses** for existing products. They can aim an existing product at a new market **segment** (e.g. Hunter® boots are now marketed as a fashion item as well as practical outdoor footwear).
3) A business can change the way the product's **distributed** — by selling through the **internet**, selling through **supermarkets** or convenience stores, etc. Alternatively, they could try marketing it in a **different country**.
4) A business can change the way the product's **priced**, or use special offers or competitions.
5) A business can change the way they **promote** the product — by running a new **ad campaign**, for example.

Decline isn't inevitable — it's usually caused by products becoming obsolete, changing consumer tastes or poor marketing. Quality products with excellent original design (e.g. Cadbury Dairy Milk) can carry on selling for **decades**.

The Product Life Cycle is Valuable when changing the Marketing Mix

1) Businesses need to know what stage of the **product life cycle** a product is at in order to **adapt** the **marketing mix** correctly. Their marketing **decisions** are partly based on the **product life cycle**.
2) When a product is in **development**, the focus should be on **product** and **price** — marketing can do research into what **product** people **want** and **how much** people are willing to **pay** for it. In the final stages of development, the marketing mix changes may start to focus on **how** they are going to **promote** it and **where** they are going to **sell it**.
3) As the product is first **introduced**, marketing usually focuses heavily on **place** and **promotion** to get the product out there and raise awareness of it. Marketing also need to think about training **people** to be more **knowledgeable** about the product. Depending on how well the product is received, the **price** might be adjusted.
4) As the product enters the **growth** stage, the marketing mix may be more focused on **people**, **physical environment** and **process**. People will need to be **well-trained** to deal with queries from new customers and the company can also be more picky about the **physical environment** (e.g. they might redesign their website). The **process** has to be improved to keep the additional customers happy with the service they are receiving.
5) During the **maturity** stage of the life cycle, the marketing mix may focus on **price** and **promotion** again. The **price** of the product can be reduced and the unique features of the product can be **promoted** in order to stay competitive. Marketing might look at **adapting the product** to keep their sales up for as long as possible.
6) When sales of the product begin to **decline**, marketing will decrease the amount of money they spend on each of the 7Ps. **Promotion** may stop altogether, **discounted prices** will be offered, the product may be **pulled out** of some stores and they will **stop training** people.

Practice Questions

Q1 What are the stages of the product life cycle?

Q2 Why does profitability increase in the maturity phase of the product's life cycle?

Q3 What are extension strategies?

Q4 How does the promotion of a product change during its life cycle?

Exam Question

Q1 A software developer is ready to launch a new computer game.
To what extent could the marketing mix be affected by the life cycle of the game? [25 marks]

No product can live for ever — except maybe the wheel...

There's a lot to learn on these pages, I'll give you that. If you take it step by step though, it's fairly straightforward — it really just goes through the different stages in the life cycle of a product. And if you know the product life cycle inside out, it won't be so hard to learn the other bits mentioned here about extension strategies, the 7Ps and so on.

Marketing Mix — Pricing

The basic rules of pricing are obvious — a firm needs to price its product so that it covers its costs but is still affordable for the consumer. Products often change price at different stages in their life cycle.

Several Factors affect Pricing Decisions

1) The **price** of a product is affected by all of the other Ps in the **marketing mix** — e.g. during heavy **promotion** of a product, its **price** may be **reduced**.
2) The price is often set to **cover the cost** of making the product (or buying it from a wholesaler) and **make a profit**. This is called **cost-plus pricing**. The percentage amount that's added on to the cost is called the **mark-up**.
3) The price must be **acceptable to customers** — it depends how **price sensitive** the target market is. Affluent consumers are less price sensitive than those at the other end of the scale.
4) The **price elasticity of demand** (see page 36) influences the pricing of a product. This depends on the **availability of substitutes**, the **type** of product, the **age** of the product, whether it's an **expensive purchase**, and **loyalty** to the brand.
5) The stage of the **product's life cycle** (see page 44) will also affect pricing decisions — for example, if sales are declining then price may be **reduced**.
6) The price has to be in line with the company's **objectives**. E.g. they might be aiming to increase their **market share**, make the **maximum profit**, or keep their **brand image** up-market.
7) The price of **competitor products** influences pricing decisions. If the price is set **above** that of competitor products without it being **differentiated** in some way then no one will buy it and it may bring the company **bad publicity**. However, if the price is too far **below** that of others, particularly the major players', then customers will question its **quality**.

No one was sure which was falling faster — Jim, or demand for tiny swimming trunks.

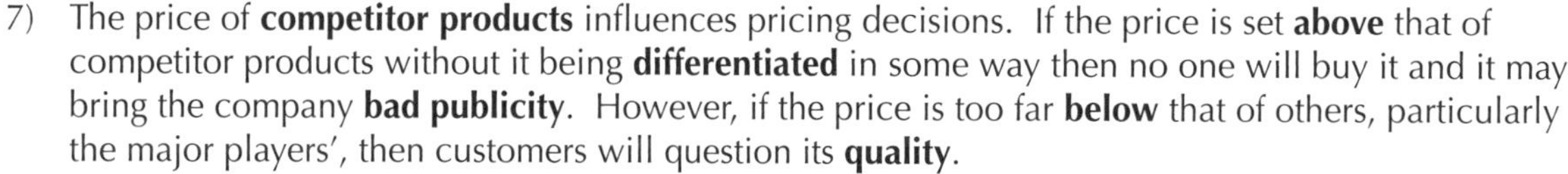

Companies use Promotional Pricing Strategies for New Products

Price Skimming

1) **Price skimming** is when **new** and **innovative products** are sold at **high prices** when they first reach the market. Consumers will pay more because the product has **scarcity value**, and the high price boosts the **product's image** and increases its appeal. **Technological products**, e.g. computers, tend to be priced using this method.
2) Prices are usually then **dropped considerably** when the product has been on the market for a year or so — by this point everyone prepared to pay extra for being one of the first to own the product has got one. Also, competitors will have entered the market with **imitative products** at **lower prices** — unless a company can prevent this by using **patents** or **trademarks**.
3) Some companies use price skimming as a **long term strategy** to keep their brands **more exclusive**, e.g. Apple® and Ray-Ban® sunglasses.
4) However, **potential customers** can be put off by the initial high price and customers who bought the product at its initial price may be **annoyed** and **frustrated** when it suddenly drops in price after launch.

Penetration Pricing

1) **Penetration pricing** is the opposite of skimming. It means launching a product at a **low price** in order to **attract customers** and gain **market share**. It is especially effective in markets which are **price-sensitive**, e.g. a new washing powder or food product.
2) Penetration pricing works best for companies that can benefit from **lower costs** when manufacturing **large quantities** of a product.
3) A **problem** with penetration pricing is that customers expect the low price to **continue**, so it's difficult to raise it without losing customers. It can also damage how the **brand image** is perceived.
4) Price penetration isn't just for new products — it can be used as an **extension strategy** to prolong a product's life (see page 45).
5) Penetration can also be used to target a more **budget-conscious** market segment. E.g. an airline might set up a **no-frills, low-cost service** in addition to its regular service. That way they can keep their **existing customer base** who are prepared to pay more, as well as maintaining their premium brand image.

Marketing Mix — Pricing

There are lots of other **Pricing Strategies**

1) **Predatory pricing** is when a business **deliberately lowers prices** to force another business **out of the market** (which is illegal under EU and US laws) — e.g. a large nationwide company might target a successful but small local competitor by lowering their prices in that specific area until the small competitor **goes out of business**. Once the competitor has gone they will **raise** their prices again.
2) **Competitive pricing** is when companies **monitor** their **competitors' prices** to make sure that their own prices are set at an equal or lower level. **Supermarkets** and **department stores** often use this method. Some stores will **refund the difference** in price if the product is cheaper somewhere else.
3) **Psychological pricing** bases the price on customers' **expectations**. A **high price** may make people think the product is really **high quality**. An **insignificant** price change can have a big **psychological impact** on the customer, e.g. £99.99 seems a lot better than £100 even though it's only 1p difference.
4) **Loss leaders** are products sold at or below cost price. These products may well **lose money**, but the idea is that they'll **make a profit** for the business **indirectly** anyway, e.g. by enticing customers into the shop where they'll probably buy full-priced items too. The loss leaders can be widely **advertised** to encourage this. This tactic can work well in **supermarkets**, where customers will usually buy lots of **other items** as well as the loss leader.
5) **Price discrimination** is when a company sells its product at different prices to **different groups of consumers**. E.g. zoo ticket prices often vary according to the **age** of the customer.

Dynamic Pricing responds to **Changes In Demand**

1) Dynamic pricing aims to increase revenue by changing prices depending on **competitor prices** and **demand**.
2) Hotel rooms, air travel and rail tickets are often dynamically priced. Prices change as the **travel date** gets **nearer**. They can also change according to the **day** or **time** that a customer wants to travel.
3) If demand is **high** at a particular time, prices **rise**, and if demand is **low**, prices go **down**. It also allows firms to make **increased profit** at busy times and offset some of the costs of having **excess capacity** during quiet periods (as well as creating **extra demand** at these times).

Industrial Marketing has Different **Pricing Influences**

1) Many businesses sell to **other businesses** rather than directly to consumers. E.g. photocopier companies market their products to businesses, brake suppliers market their products to bike manufacturers.
2) When businesses are selling to other businesses they try to build a **good ongoing relationship** with the customer, which may be worth **sacrificing** some immediate **profit** for. They want the customer to make **repeat purchases** and they might be able to make **extra profit** by providing spare parts and servicing.
3) Like with consumer marketing, **price** depends on the **competitiveness** of the market.
4) Other parts of the **marketing mix** differ in industrial marketing too. E.g. **promotions** tend to be less persuasive and more **informative** as business buyers will be more **knowledgeable** and **objective**.
5) **Place** will also differ, e.g. **trade shows** are important for industrial marketing.

Practice Questions

Q1 What are price skimming and price penetration?

Q2 Give an example of dynamic pricing.

Q3 What influences pricing in industrial marketing?

Exam Questions

Q1 Explain why a hotel might use dynamic pricing for its rooms. [4 marks]

Q2 A small company is launching a new brand of fruit juice. Suggest a pricing strategy it should consider, and analyse the advantages and disadvantages of this strategy. [12 marks]

Price skimming — a way of milking profits...

When it comes to pricing, most companies use a cost-based method and throw in the occasional bit of promotional pricing to keep consumers interested. But remember — price isn't the only thing that bothers customers...

Marketing Mix — Promotion

Promotion — basically it means using advertising, branding, sales promotion and PR to sell more products.

Promotion is part of the **Marketing Mix**

1) Promotion is designed to **inform** customers about a product or service, or **persuade** them to buy it. **Industrial promotion** tends to be **informative**, whereas **consumer promotion** tends to be **persuasive**.
2) **Promotional objectives** include increasing **sales** and **profits**, and increasing **awareness** of the product.
3) All promotion has to get the customer's **attention** so that they can be informed or persuaded about the product.

Many companies choose to **Advertise** through the **Media**

1) Adverts are used to **promote goods** and **services** — and also to promote a firm's **public image**. Advertising uses various **media** including print, film, TV, radio, billboards (also called hoardings) and the Internet.
2) The choice of media depends on the **number of target customers** and how many of them **see** the ad. TV adverts at prime times are very expensive. Ads shown when fewer people are watching are cheaper, but don't reach as many people. The cost must be **worth it** in terms of the **extra sales** or **awareness** created.
3) **Digital advertising** is **cheaper** than traditional forms:

- Businesses can **target** online adverts to customers who've shown an **interest** in that type of product by browsing for it online.
- **Advertising** on **mobile phones** is becoming increasingly important, e.g. banners in apps — sometimes the advertiser is only charged when their advert is **clicked on**, so no money is wasted on unseen ads.
- **Viral marketing** is when companies get users to **pass on adverts** to their friends through social networking platforms or email, etc. The adverts have to be considered **interesting enough** for people to pass along, e.g. a hilarious video, or something that offers something for **free**.

The TV remote — scourge of TV advertisers everywhere.

4) The **impact** of an ad is very important. An advert that covers a two-page spread in a magazine has much more impact than a single page, or a small ad stuck in the classified section at the back.
5) **Specialist media** are used to advertise specialist products to **niche markets**. For example, a manufacturer of fish hooks would do better to advertise in a monthly fishing magazine than in the Daily Telegraph newspaper.
6) Companies need to follow **legal constraints** on advertising some products. E.g. cigarette advertising is banned.

Advertising changes during a **Product Life Cycle**

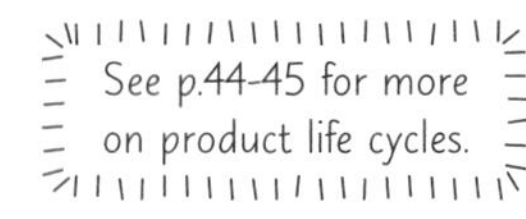
See p.44-45 for more on product life cycles.

1) Products are often heavily advertised at **launch**. If a product is completely **new** to the market, the adverts are **informative**. They tell customers about the product.
2) During the **growth** phase, advertising **differentiates** between brands, persuading consumers that the product is better than competitor products. The objective during this phase is to **maintain** or **increase market share**.
3) When a product is at the **mature**, **saturation** phase, consumers need to be **reminded** of it. If the manufacturer has an **extension** strategy, they can use advertising to inform consumers about, say, any **improvements** to the product.

Branding is a key aspect of **Product Image**

Branding differentiates a product from the competition. Customers recognise it through its name, logo or slogan. Brands can be **individual** products, e.g. Sprite®, or "**family brands**" covering a **range** of products, e.g. Heinz®.

1) If a business convinces customers that their brand is **superior** to others, they can charge a **premium price**.
2) Customers often remain **loyal** to a brand as they have **confidence** in its quality. New products launched under the same brand will often be **accepted more readily**, without much being spent on promotion.
3) Packaging is important to **distinguish** the product, e.g. the Coca-Cola® bottle. This is more true for some products than others, e.g. **fancy chocolates** need attractive packaging, but bulk orders of **printer toner** don't.
4) Popular brands often **eliminate competition** and **deter new competitors**. If there are no alternative products, then the price will become **inelastic** and can be **increased** without reducing demand much.
5) Some brand names have an **ethical** or **environmentally-friendly** image. The companies behind them aim to appeal to consumers concerned about these issues.

Marketing Mix — Promotion

Not All *promotion involves* ***Advertising***

1) Companies often offer **sales promotions**. These are things like **special offers**, e.g. "buy one get one free" (**BOGOF**), competitions and free gifts. Sales promotions can aim to **raise awareness** or **increase sales** of a product. Manufacturers also aim sales promotions at the **retailer** to encourage them to **stock** more of their products.
2) **Merchandising** means ensuring that retailers are displaying a company's products as effectively as possible. Some merchandisers offer retailers **point of sale displays** (e.g. special colourful racks with the company logo).
3) **Direct mail** means **mailshots** sent out to customers. The customer usually hasn't **asked** to receive them. Businesses that keep information about their customers on a database can **target** their direct mail to particular consumer groups either through post or email. Direct mail that is untargeted ("**junk mail**") can sometimes be a **waste of money**, because it often just gets thrown away.
4) **Personal selling** or **direct selling** is personal communication between a **salesperson** and a customer. Personal selling can involve sales assistants in shops as well as travelling salespeople and phone salespeople.
5) **Relationship marketing** involves forming **long-term relationships** with customers. This costs **less** in marketing than continually attracting new customers. For example, a business could offer existing customers **special offers** or **loyalty cards**. **Social media** is very useful for **relationship-building** with customers.
6) **Event sponsorship** makes consumers **aware** of a firm and its product. It also gives the firm a **good image**.
7) **Direct Response TV Marketing** encourages consumers to contact the advertiser directly to purchase a product they have seen advertised on television. **Shopping channels** are an example of this kind of promotion.

PR *gets businesses or products* ***Good Publicity*** *in the* ***Media***

1) **Public relations** (**PR**) involves **liaising** with the **media**, writing **press releases**, and answering **press enquiries**.
2) PR departments write **brochures**, **newsletters** and **leaflets** giving information about the company.
3) Public relations deals with things like **product launches**, **conferences** and other **special events**.

The ***Promotional Mix*** *reflects* ***Product***, ***Budget*** *and* ***Competitor Activity***

1) Businesses use a **mixture** of methods to promote products. This is called the **promotional mix**.
2) The promotional mix depends on: the **product** itself, the **market**, **competitor activity**, the **product life cycle** and the **budget** available.
3) In general, **convenience** products purchased by the **consumer** are promoted by **advertising**.
4) **Expensive** and **complex** products are more likely to be promoted by **personal selling**. So are products or services sold in the **industrial market**.
5) **Shopping products**, e.g. perfumes and bikes, and **speciality products**, e.g. luxury cars, are often sold by a combination of **advertising** and **personal selling**. TV, print and billboard adverts **attract the buyer** into the showroom, where the salesperson takes over.
6) Manufacturers use different methods to sell their product to a **retailer** than to sell it to the **final customer**. Businesses often use **salespeople** to get **shops** to stock their product, and **advertising** to persuade **customers** to buy the product in the shops.
7) The promotional mix reflects the **economy**. E.g. in a **recession**, McDonald's may promote their 'Saver Menu'.

See p.42 for more on convenience, shopping and speciality products.

Practice Questions

Q1 What is promotion designed to do?

Q2 In which phase of the product life cycle does advertising stress differences with competitor products?

Q3 Give three ways that branding helps a company maximise its sales.

Exam Question

Q1 Analyse how, in addition to advertising, a manufacturer of breakfast cereal could promote its product. [9 marks]

We want people to buy our product — that's why we tell them to BOGOF...

When it comes to promotion, it's all in the mix. You'll need to suggest which combination of methods would best suit a firm, and why. The optimum mix for a product will change depending on where it is in its life cycle.

Marketing Mix — Place

Distribution is important. This is the "place" part of the marketing mix. If a product can't get to the marketplace, no one can buy it. Needs go unfulfilled, companies don't make profits, anarchy reigns...

It's ***Vital*** *to get the* ***Product*** *to the* ***Consumer***

A **channel** of **distribution** is the route a product takes from the producer to the consumer. A product usually passes through **intermediaries** on the way from producer to consumer — e.g. **retailers**, **wholesalers** and **agents**.

1) **Retailers** are **shops** who sell to consumers. They're usually the **final stage** in the distribution channel. Tesco, Argos and amazon® are **retailers**. Retailers can be physical shops or online "e-tailers".
2) **Wholesalers** buy products cheaply in **bulk** (particularly convenience items) and **sell them on** to **retailers**. Wholesalers make life **easier** for retailers and manufacturers:

- Wholesalers **buy** goods from manufacturers in bulk and **sell** them in **smaller quantities** to **retailers**. This is called "**breaking bulk**" — a wholesaler takes the goods off the manufacturer's hands and **pays** for the whole lot. Manufacturers don't have to **wait** for customers to buy the goods before they see any cash.
- Wholesalers make distribution **simpler**. Without a wholesaler, the manufacturer would have to make **separate deliveries** to lots of retailers, and send each and every retailer an **invoice**. Selling to one wholesaler cuts down the paperwork and the number of journeys.
- Wholesalers can **store more goods** than a retailer can — they act as the retailer's storage cupboard.

There are ***Different Channels*** *of* ***Distribution***

Direct Selling (0-level channel): Manufacturer ⇒ Consumer

The **Internet** has made it **easier** for producers of **shopping** and **speciality** goods to sell **direct** to the consumer. Buying and selling on the Internet is called **e-commerce**. This allows access to a **worldwide market**. For small firms, a low-cost option is to sell goods using **electronic marketplaces** (e.g. eBay®).
Direct selling is done through door-to-door sales, TV shopping channels, telephone sales and websites.
Accountants, electricians and hairdressers sell their **services** direct to the consumer.

Indirect Selling (1-level channel): Manufacturer ⇒ Retailer ⇒ Consumer

Large supermarkets buy **convenience** and **shopping** goods in bulk direct from the manufacturer and have them delivered straight from the manufacturer or via their own warehouses. This is a faster method for **perishables**.

Direct Selling through an agent (1-level channel): Manufacturer ⇒ Agent ⇒ Consumer

An **agent** is like a **sales representative**, except they are **not employed** by the company whose goods they sell. They get **commission** (a percentage of the value of the goods they sell) instead of being paid a **salary**.
E.g. Avon products are sold by **agents** who sell Avon products in their own name rather than as an Avon employee.

Indirect Selling (2-level channel): Manufacturer ⇒ Wholesaler ⇒ Retailer ⇒ Consumer

This is the **traditional** distribution channel used for **convenience goods**, e.g. by fast-food chains.

Retailers *often use* ***Multi-Channel Distribution***

Multi-channel distribution is when businesses sell through more than one method, e.g. online and in store. It gives **flexibility** for customers and a **wide market coverage** for manufacturers.

1) Supermarkets and fashion retailers which have **high street stores** as well as an **internet store** are using a **multi-channel strategy**. This may lead to added costs, but it allows them to target a wider market.
2) Stores which **only** sell **online** may have **cheaper costs**, because they use a **single** channel of distribution. However, they can have **problems** establishing **brand loyalty**. Also, customers often like to see and feel goods before they buy them, which is a **limitation of e-commerce**.

Example: Apple® uses multi-channel distribution. You can buy an iPad® **directly** from an **Apple® Store**, either **online** or in a **physical shop.** Alternatively, you can buy it from an **online retailer** such as amazon®, or from a retailer such as ASDA or PC World, either **online** or from a **retail outlet**...

Marketing Mix — Place

Businesses choose a **Channel** of **Distribution** to **Suit Their Needs**

The choice of distribution channel is a compromise between **cost**, **ease** and **control**.

1) It's **more profitable** to **sell direct** to the customer. Each intermediary (party) in the distribution chain takes a **slice of profit** from the manufacturer — wholesalers and retailers have to make money too. Businesses that **sell direct** can offer their product at a **lower price** than **retailers** at the end of a long distribution chain.
2) On the other hand, it's **easier** to use **intermediaries**, especially for convenience goods. It'd be a hassle to distribute a small amount of product to lots of little shops. It's easier to sell to a **wholesaler** who can deliver products from several manufacturers in a single delivery. Using wholesalers often means more **market coverage**.
3) The **fewer intermediaries** in the distribution chain, the more **control** a manufacturer has over how its products are sold. It has more say in the **final selling price** and how the product is **promoted**. For example, some companies aim to **protect** their brand's up-market image by not allowing it to be sold in supermarkets.
4) UK **retail trends** have **changed** in recent years, as retailers have found **cheaper** or **more effective** ways of distributing their products. **Out-of-town retail parks**, **concessions** (shops within shops), and **mail-order catalogues** have **cheaper overheads** than high street stores and often offer customers other **benefits**, such as **free parking**. **Factory outlets** allow firms to make a return on **imperfect goods** (seconds) or **last season's stock**.

Short Distribution Channels	Long Distribution Channels
• Industrial products	• Consumer products
• Few customers	• Many customers
• Expensive, complex goods	• Inexpensive, simple goods
• Infrequent sales	• Frequent sales
• Bespoke (custom-made) products	• Standard products
• Bulky products	• Small products
• Services	• Goods

There are no real hard and fast rules about which distribution channel a business might choose, but there are a few trends.

The **choices** of distribution channels for **new** and **small business** can be **limited** as they struggle to place their products **directly** into major chains. They might have to sell through established **agents** or **wholesalers**, which will directly impact on their profits.

A product's place **Within an Outlet** is important too

1) Manufacturers try to influence retailers to give their products more **prominence**.
E.g. a drinks manufacturer might supply a fridge with their **branding** all over it. Leading brands such as Kelloggs® and Coca-Cola® create lots of **product varieties** to get more **shelf space** and squeeze out the competition.
2) Supermarkets use tactics to get you to buy more — e.g. they put **everyday essentials** such as bread and milk at the back so you have to walk through the **whole shop** and are tempted to buy **other products** on the way.
3) In e-commerce, businesses try to get their product to appear at the **top** of the lists on e.g. amazon® or Google™. They do this by including **keywords** in their description and getting lots of **positive customer ratings**.

Practice Questions

Q1 What is the role of a wholesaler?

Q2 Describe two distribution channels.

Q3 Why do businesses often use multi-channel distribution?

Exam Questions

Q1 Analyse the possible influences on the choice of distribution channel for a firm selling clothes aimed at young people. [9 marks]

Q2 Evaluate e-commerce as a means of distributing luxury consumer goods. [12 marks]

I'm a new product — get me out of here...

Distribution can seem like a mundane, boring thing. Yes, it is all about warehouses full of cardboard boxes, fleets of trucks going from A to B and people popping catalogues through your letterbox. But on the other hand it's a vital part of the wondrous marketing mix. Where you can buy something is a big factor in deciding whether to buy it.

People, Process and Physical Environment

You are probably a bit P'd out, but there's still the final three Ps to go. As the service sector now dominates the UK's economic activity, these final Ps have been added as they're super-relevant to service businesses.

People are a Vital Part of providing Goods and Services

1) With **services** such as banking, hairdressing and dining out, the customer's experience is highly dependent on the **people** dealing with them. E.g. an attentive waiter with a good knowledge of the menu will make a customer's experience far more enjoyable. Sometimes the person is the **only aspect** of a service a customer sees — e.g. they might not be able to see the work done on their central heating pipes, but most customers would prefer to use a pleasant plumber who explains things well.
2) If employees are **friendly, polite and knowledgeable**, people are **more likely** to buy the goods or service from them, **promote** them by word-of-mouth and **return** again and again — so it makes sense for businesses to focus on providing excellent **customer service**. The **Internet** makes this aspect really important as customers will often put a **review** of their experience online.
3) When you buy things in a shop, you'll usually be served by a **person**, but some **goods** have more of a service element — e.g. someone buying a child car seat might go into a **specialist shop** and seek **advice** on the best seat for their needs and be shown how to fit it correctly. If you buy a computer, you might need **after-sales personnel** to help you set it up. People are an **important** part of the customer's experience.
4) In **e-commerce**, customers can usually enquire about a product either through **e-mail** or by **phone**. Getting a **prompt, knowledgeable** reply to an e-mail will encourage a customer to **buy** the product and **review** the company favourably.
5) For **business customers**, access to someone who can explain **technical aspects** of the product is important. Also, business-to-business **sales people** need to have the **interpersonal skills** to form **good ongoing relationships** with business customers.

The Process is the System of providing Goods and Services to customers

The **process** is how easy it is for customers to get **what they want, when they want it**. It's the customers' **experience** of the business. Some **process** elements that concern customers are:

- How easy is it to get an **appointment** at a time that suits them?
- How long do they have to wait? E.g. for their food in a restaurant.
- Are the advertised products **in stock**?
- What **payment methods** are available?
- How **user-friendly** is the **website**?
- What **after-sales service** is offered — e.g. is the builder's work **guaranteed**?
- Will a **phone enquiry** be answered by a person or a machine?
- How **quickly** will a business respond to complaints?

Kevin the koala won the cuteness selection process.

1) Businesses have to **decide** how to **balance** maximising profits while keeping customers happy with their processes. E.g. in a call centre it is convenient for operators to put customers **on hold** during periods of **high demand** — however, **customers** can get **annoyed** if they are waiting for too long.
2) Different businesses place **different degrees of importance** on processes. E.g. ASDA has invested in hybrid tills which can be operated by a member of staff or as a self-service till so all the checkouts are always open and queues are kept short. Whereas Aldi places more emphasis on low prices than on short queues.
3) Process aspects can be used in **promotion**. E.g. an online retailer might advertise 'next day delivery as standard'.
4) **Technology** can be used to improve processes. For example:

   Queue management technology is used by **airports** to direct customers to **shorter queues** and inform them how long their waiting time will be — known waits seem shorter than unknown waits.

   Lots of e-tailers offer the option to **pay through PayPal**, meaning customers can use their **address** and **payment details** already linked to their PayPal account.

5) In **e-commerce**, good processes are important. Customers will leave **feedback** about how promptly their product arrived, and how well any **complaints** were dealt with. Also, the **ranking** (how close to the top the product features) on sites such as amazon®, is affected by things like how **quickly** goods are shipped, how often the product is **out of stock** and how often the product is **returned**.

People, Process and Physical Environment

Physical Environment is the customer's Surroundings

1) **Physical environment** includes things like:
   - **Decor and cleanliness** — the decor should fit in with the **nature** of the business. Cleanliness is important in **all** businesses, especially **restaurants** and **hotels**.
   - **Appearance of the website** — a good website should reflect the business's **nature** and **ethics**. A professional-looking website will create a good impression of the business.
   - **Appearance of staff** — businesses can give customers an **impression** of the business through the appearance of their staff, e.g. they could be dressed **casually**, **smartly**, in **uniform**, etc.
   - **Layout** — how easy it is to **find your way around** a physical location or a website. Customers can get **annoyed** if they can't find the item they want, so they might use **another store** or **website** instead.
   - **Practicality and safety** — customers need to have **access** to the products and be able to **purchase** them **safely** — for example, heavy goods shouldn't be on the top shelf in a supermarket.
2) The physical environment can **influence** whether a customer buys goods or services from the business. For example, a travel agent might have a **modern**, **clean** and **stylish** office to give customers the impression that their holidays will be up to the same standards.
3) The physical environment can also give an **impression** of the **nature** of the business. For example, banks often have **neutral decor** and look very **clean** to reflect the **seriousness** of the business — staff wear **uniforms** or **suits** so that the bank comes across as **professional**.

Businesses make Decisions about these 3Ps

As part of an **integrated** marketing mix, **decisions** about people, process and physical environment **depend** on the **type** of product and the **other elements** of the mix.

Decisions about the 3Ps at a luxury hotel and a budget hotel

A **luxury hotel** needs to provide a **high quality experience** that customers are willing to pay a **high price** for, whereas a **budget hotel** will aim to **minimise** their **costs** to allow them to offer **cheaper prices**.

- **People** — a luxury hotel will want to hire the **best staff** possible, and **train** them to an even higher standard. For example, they will want experienced, quality chefs. A budget hotel will hire staff who are less experienced or less qualified — this usually means that they will be paid a **lower wage**.
- **Process** — a luxury hotel will offer a **high level of care** throughout your visit. For example, staff will carry your bags to your room, clean and tidy daily, provide room service, etc. A budget hotel might offer more of a **no-frills service** to keep their costs down.
- **Physical environment** — a luxury hotel will consider their **physical location** and **decor** very carefully to make sure it **appeals** to their **target market**. For example, they might choose a large country estate, or **prime location** in a city, and will have **expensive** decoration, whereas a budget hotel might be in a slightly **less convenient location** and might concentrate more on a clean, neutral look.

Practice Questions

Q1 Explain why it is worthwhile for a business to recruit suitable people.

Q2 Give three examples of process elements that matter to customers.

Q3 How can businesses use technology to improve processes?

Q4 Give five aspects of the physical environment that businesses need to think about.

Exam Questions

Q1 How important do you think the physical environment is likely to be to a café? Justify your answer. [16 marks]

Q2 Evaluate the effect of people, process and physical environment on the other elements of the integrated marketing mix for a national hairdressing chain. [16 marks]

Business, GSOH, seeks customers for long-term relationship...

It's hard to split things up into 'purely goods' and 'purely services'. Most 'goods' businesses have an element of 'service', and many 'service' businesses sell something too — e.g. hairdressers sell shampoo, etc. Anyway, it's the service elements these P's are most important for. Just don't forget them when you're talking about the marketing mix.

Operational Objectives

This section might sound complicated, but actually, it's not. 'Operations' is just a fancy word for the real reason businesses exist in the first place — to make stuff.

Operational Objectives are Targets set for Production

Setting operational objectives can help a company achieve its **overall objectives** (see p.3-5) — operational **decisions** will become **focused** on meeting these objectives. The **performance** of the production department can be **reviewed** and **assessed** on its ability to meet these operational objectives:

QUALITY — This type of objective is likely to involve either **maintaining** or **improving** levels of quality. For example, a company might aim to ensure that **95%** of their products last **five years** or longer, or they might aim to **reduce** the number of **customer complaints** that they get in a month.

COSTS — Many firms aim to **cut costs**, especially if they compete on **price**. Depending on the type of business, there are different ways of doing this. The firm can cut its **fixed costs** or **variable costs** (see p.6) — e.g. the firm might **restructure** to remove a layer of management, or the costs of an individual **product** can be reduced (e.g. an airline might stop offering meals on a particular route).

FLEXIBILITY — Businesses need to be able to **react** to what customers want. For example, they need to be able to vary the **amount** of goods or services that they are producing so that **volume** doesn't **exceed demand** or vice-versa. E.g. if a business knows people buy fewer healthy choice ready-meals at Christmas, it might reduce production in December. Some companies ensure their workforce is flexible by employing people on **zero-hours contracts**.

Zero-hours contracts are when a worker is employed without a guaranteed minimum number of hours per week.

EFFICIENCY — Efficiency objectives aim to make **better use of resources** in order to reduce costs and increase profit. This might mean increasing **capacity utilisation** (increasing output so it's closer to the maximum amount of goods the firm could produce with current levels of staff and machinery) or taking steps to improve **labour** and **capital productivity** (how much output a particular worker or piece of machinery generates in a set time period).

See p.56-57 for more on capacity utilisation.

INNOVATION — Businesses can set their **Research & Development** (R&D) department innovation targets, e.g. a car manufacturer might set an objective to produce a zero-emissions car by 2018. These objectives can be **hard** to **achieve**, as unexpected problems often occur.

ENVIRONMENT — **Pressure** from **customers** and the **Government** often leads to firms setting environmental objectives, such as cutting **carbon emissions** or using a greater number of **recycled** raw materials.

SPEED OF RESPONSE — The **speed** at which a business can operate is important. This might mean decreasing the **production time** of a product, decreasing the **waiting time** for customers or getting new products to market **more quickly**. These objectives are often closely related to the company's **efficiency** objectives.

DEPENDABILITY — Customers need to be able to depend on a **business** and businesses need to be able to depend on their **suppliers**. E.g. if a store always has items in stock then customers are more likely to shop there, even if the products are more expensive. A **reliable** business can often **charge more** for its goods and services.

Added Value is a key Operational Objective for any Business

Businesses transform **raw materials** into **finished products** to sell. **Adding value** means increasing the **difference** between the **cost** of the raw materials and the **price** that the customer pays. Adding **value** will usually increase **profits**.

ADDED VALUE = SALES REVENUE – COST OF BOUGHT-IN GOODS AND SERVICES

Added value can be achieved by either **increasing** the **selling price** of the product or by **reducing** the **costs** of the raw materials. Customers will pay more for a **better quality** product, but there are other ways to increase the **value** of a product — e.g. if a business is **environmentally friendly**, offers a **quick speed of response** and is **dependable** then it can justify charging a higher selling price than its competitors.

Operational Objectives

Operational Objectives are influenced by **Internal** and **External** Factors

INTERNAL

- **Nature of the Product**: a computer technology firm is likely to have very different targets to a family-run bed and breakfast. The **computer technology company** is likely to focus on **innovation** whereas the **B&B** may be trying to increase its **capacity utilisation** by having lots of rooms full.
- **Availability of Resources**: many businesses would like to **increase output** but are limited by whether they have enough **resources**. For example, it won't be possible to produce 500 hand-painted dolls' houses in 3 days if the company only employs five carpenters.
- **Other departments**: objectives and decisions made in the **finance**, **marketing** and **HR** departments will affect what the production department can actually achieve, and vice-versa.
- **Overall objectives**: for example, if a business is concerned about its **environmental impact**, the production process will have to be more environmentally friendly.

EXTERNAL

- **Competitors' Performance**: many firms set targets in **reaction** to their **rivals' actions**. For example, if a rival gains market share, you would also probably try to increase your share of the market to make sure they don't overtake you (or leave you even further behind). **Competition** from **abroad**, e.g. China, is forcing companies to set stricter **cost** and **efficiency** objectives.
- **Market conditions**: e.g. if customers are spending less money in a **particular market**, or if there are **more competitors** in a market, this can affect any operational objectives.
- **Demand for Product**: businesses should try to make sure that **output** is not higher than **demand,** so they might set an objective to increase **flexibility** of production (see p.54).
- **Changing Customer Needs**: e.g. if customers indicate that they'd like a firm to behave more **ethically** this can affect **costs** and **environmental** objectives.
- **New technology**: the production process often needs to **adapt** to make the most of new technology.

Operational Objectives can affect the **Method of Production**

There are **five common methods** of production:

Job production	Production of **one-off items** by **skilled workers.**
Flow production	Mass production on a **continuous production line** with **division of labour.**
Batch production	Production of **small batches** of **identical items.**
Cell production	Production divided into **sets of tasks**, each set completed by a **work group.**
Lean production	Streamlined production with **waste at a minimum.**

1) A business that is trying to improve the **quality** of its goods might use **job** or **cell** production.
2) **Batch** or **flow** production methods could be used by a business trying to achieve **efficiency**, **dependability** and **speed of response** objectives.
3) **Lean production** could help to meet **environmental** and **efficiency** objectives whilst ensuring high **quality**.

Practice Questions

Q1 Identify eight types of operational objective.

Q2 How could a company increase the added value of one of its products?

Q3 Name two different internal factors that could influence operational objectives.

Exam Questions

Q1 Explain how external factors influence the operational objectives of a business. [6 marks]

Q2 Analyse the effects on the operational objectives of a global coffee shop chain if the price of coffee beans increases rapidly. [9 marks]

Increase the flexibility of your workforce through daily yoga sessions...

What do you mean it's not that kind of flexibility? Anyway, make sure you learn the different operational objectives and the internal and external factors that can influence them. Don't forget those production methods either...

Capacity Utilisation

Businesses need to analyse capacity utilisation data before making important operational decisions...

Capacity is Maximum Output with the Resources Currently Available

1) The **capacity** of an organisation is the **maximum** output that it can produce in a given period without buying any more fixed assets — machinery, factory space, etc.
2) Capacity depends on the **number of employees** and how skilled they are.
3) It also depends on the **technology** the business has — what **machinery** it has, what state it's in, what kind of computer system it has, etc.
4) The kind of **production process** the business uses will also affect its capacity.
5) The amount of **investment** in the business is also a factor.

Check out the capacity on that...

Capacity utilisation is how much **capacity** a business is **using**. The following formula can be used to calculate it:

$$\text{Capacity Utilisation (\%)} = \frac{\text{Output}}{\text{Capacity}} \times 100$$

Examples: a hotel with half its rooms booked out has a **capacity utilisation** of **50%**.
A clothing factory with an output of 70 000 shirts per month and a capacity of 100 000 shirts per month is running at **70% capacity utilisation.**

90% Capacity Utilisation is better than 100% Capacity Utilisation

High capacity utilisation is better than low capacity utilisation. However, **100% capacity utilisation** has drawbacks:

1) Businesses have to consider all their **operational objectives** when they plan their capacity usage. **Cost** isn't the only thing to think about — it might not be possible to operate at 100% capacity and keep **quality** levels high.
2) The business may have to **turn away** potential **customers** because it can't increase output any more.
3) There's no **downtime** — machines are on **all the time**. If a machine **breaks down**, it'll cause **delays** as work piles up **waiting** for it to be fixed. There's no time for equipment **maintenance**, which can reduce the life of machinery.
4) There's no **margin of error**. Everything has to be perfect first time, which causes **stress** to managers. **Mistakes** are more likely when everyone's working flat out.
5) The business can't **temporarily increase output** for seasonal demand or one-off orders.
6) If output is greater than demand, there'll be **surplus stock** hanging about waiting to be sold. It's not good to have valuable **working capital** (see p.72) tied up in stock.

Businesses should plan production levels to achieve almost full capacity utilisation.

Firms with High Capacity Utilisation can Increase their Capacity

Firms that are operating at close to 100% capacity utilisation don't just stop accepting new orders. They have ways of **increasing** their **capacity** so that they can **match** their **output** to **demand**. The best way to do this depends on whether the rise in demand is expected to be **temporary** or **long-term**.

1) Businesses can **increase capacity** by using their facilities for **more** of the **working week**. They can have staff working in two or three **shifts** in a day, and on weekends and bank holidays.
2) Businesses can buy **more machines**, if they can afford them (and the staff needed to operate them).
3) Businesses can **increase** their **staff levels** in the long run by recruiting new permanent staff. In the short run they can employ **temporary staff**, **part-time staff**, or get their staff to work **overtime**.
4) Businesses can also increase their capacity by increasing **productivity**. They can reorganise production by reallocating staff to the busiest areas, and they can increase employee **motivation**.
5) If the rise in demand is **temporary** then businesses might choose to **subcontract** work:

- **Subcontracting** (or **outsourcing**) is when a business uses another firm to do some work on its behalf. E.g. a manufacturer of detergent might make detergent for a **supermarket** and package it with the supermarket's own label.
- Companies can **subcontract** work to other businesses in **busy periods**. This means they can meet **unexpected increases in demand** without increasing their own capacity and having the costs of extra staff and facilities all year round.

Capacity Utilisation

Under-Utilisation is *Inefficient* and increases *Unit Costs*

Low capacity utilisation is called **under-utilisation**. It's **inefficient** because it means a business is **not** getting **use** out of **machines** and **facilities** that have been paid for.

1) Under-utilisation increases costs because it causes **fixed costs** to be spread over **fewer units of output**, so **unit costs increase**.
2) Higher capacity utilisation means an increase in the number of units output **without** increasing the **fixed costs**. So the **total costs** are spread over **more units**.

For more on unit costs, see p.7. Remember, total costs = fixed costs + variable costs.

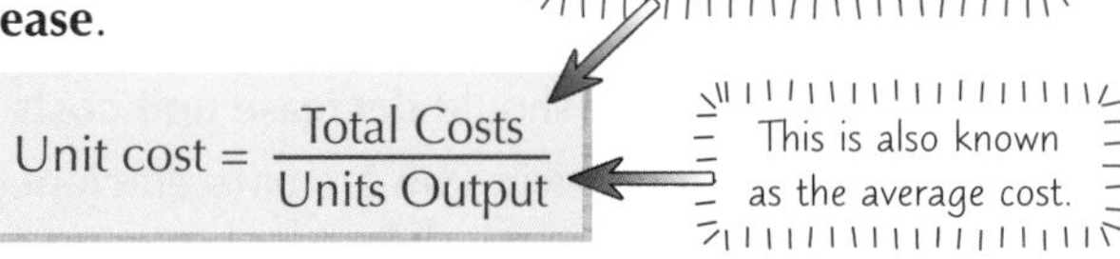

Example: A chocolate factory's total costs are **£7200** a month. In November, the factory output **18 000** chocolate bars, giving a unit cost of **£0.40**. In December, staff holidays caused output to fall to **16 000 bars**, meaning that the unit cost rose to **£0.45**.

Firms deal with Under-Utilisation in Two ways

Sometimes firms have **too much capacity** and **not enough demand** for their product, which leads to **under-utilisation.** When this happens, they'll **first** try to **increase demand**, but if that doesn't work, they need to **reduce capacity**.

1) Businesses stimulate demand by changing the **marketing mix** (see p.40-41). E.g. they can change the **promotion** of a product, or change its **price** or its **distribution**.
2) Businesses can also fill spare capacity by **subcontracting** work for other firms. It's often better to make goods for a **competitor** and make a bit of money than it is to leave **machinery** sitting around doing **nothing**.
3) If a business can't increase demand for their product, they need to **reduce their capacity** by closing part of their production facilities. This is called **rationalisation** (or **downsizing**).
4) Businesses can reduce capacity in the **short term** by stopping **overtime** or reducing the length of the working week, allocating staff to **other work** in the business, and by not renewing **temporary contracts**.
5) Businesses can reduce capacity in the **long term** by not **replacing** staff as they retire (natural wastage), making staff **redundant**, and by **selling off** factories or equipment.

Firms have to consider how their Capacity Needs will Change over Time

1) Demand **changes** over time, so firms must think about demand in the **future** as well as the current demand.
2) The key to **long-term** success is planning **capacity** changes to match long-term changes in demand. You can use **market research** to help **predict** future demand, but it's not 100% certain. There's always an element of **risk**.
3) **Short-term** changes in **capacity utilisation** provide **flexibility**. Firms should be flexible and **temporarily** increase existing capacity utilisation if an increase in demand isn't expected to continue **long-term** — e.g with seasonal goods like Christmas crackers, goods heading towards decline in their life cycle, and one-off special orders.
4) **Long-term** solutions end up giving **lower unit costs** — as long as **predictions** of demand turn out to be **true**.

Practice Questions

Q1 Calculate capacity utilisation for a restaurant that has 64 seats but only 44 people dining each night.

Q2 Give five ways in which a firm can increase its capacity.

Q3 Calculate the unit cost of one shirt, if a factory makes 450 shirts a month and has total monthly costs of £1719.

Answers on p.200.

Exam Question

Q1 A cinema is open 7 days a week. It only has one screen, with 300 seats, and shows 3 films a day. The cinema gets 2205 customers per week.

a) Calculate the cinema's capacity utilisation. [3 marks]

b) Use your calculation to advise the cinema on its plans for the future. [6 marks]

She cannae take any more, Jim...

Businesses need to keep an eye on capacity utilisation. Under-utilisation is a consequence of low demand. When a business launches a product, capacity utilisation often starts out low and then builds up as demand for the new product increases. It really is worth your while knowing how businesses should deal with high and low capacity utilisation.

Increasing Efficiency and Productivity

The more efficient you are at revision, the quicker this page will all be over.

Productivity and Efficiency are Not the Same Thing

Dave's productivity currently stood at 900 rabbits per hour.

1) **Productivity** is measured as the **output per worker** in a given time period.
2) **Efficiency** is all about getting **more output** from a given amount of inputs. Being efficient just means **reducing the waste** of all the inputs, e.g. time and materials. Greater efficiency should **decrease unit costs** and **increase profits**.
3) Increasing productivity can increase efficiency, but this **isn't** necessarily the case. E.g. a farmer shearing 8 sheep per hour and getting all the wool is **less productive** but **more efficient** than a farmer shearing 20 sheep per hour but wasting half the wool.

Labour Productivity measures How Much each Employee Produces

Companies need to know how productive their workforce is, because changes in labour productivity can have a massive impact on the business. This is especially true in **labour-intensive** firms, where labour costs are a high proportion of total costs.

$$\text{Labour Productivity} = \frac{\text{Output per period}}{\text{Number of employees}}$$

Example: A factory employs 90 workers to produce 9000 DVD players per week.
Labour Productivity = 9000 ÷ 90 workers = **100** DVD players per worker per week.

1) The **higher** the labour productivity, the **better** the workforce is performing. As labour productivity **increases**, labour costs per unit **fall** (see p.84).
2) If labour productivity is **low**, managers will try to increase it (see below).

Increasing Labour Productivity influences Efficiency

Increasing productivity can **improve** the efficiency of a business. If the **same number of workers** are producing **more units of output** in the **same amount of time** then unit costs will be lower.

Ways to increase labour productivity

- Labour productivity can be improved by **improving worker motivation** (see p.90-91).
- **Training** can make workers more productive.
- **New technology** can increase the speed at which workers can do their job.

However, **increasing productivity** is not always a good thing for the business or for the workers.

1) Encouraging workers to produce more by offering **bonuses** and **incentives** for increased output could mean that the **quality suffers** or that **more waste** is produced.
2) If the business is not planning to **increase its capacity**, then training workers to be more productive could result in **redundancies** and **job losses** — this will **lower morale** amongst staff.
3) New technology can be very **expensive** and businesses need to decide whether it's worth **investing** in new machines and software.

- Businesses will base their **decisions** about labour productivity on the **value added** and **efficiency**.
- If labour costs only make up a **small percentage** of the **production costs** then it may not be worth investing lots of time and effort into increasing labour productivity.
- Increasing productivity could lead to **more waste** of raw materials which could reduce value added and will have a negative impact on the environment.

Lean Production Methods aim to Increase Efficiency

Lean production isn't a good thing for everyone — it can mean that jobs are lost as efficiency increases.

1) **Lean production** is an **efficient** form of production that keeps **waste** (of time and resources) to a **minimum**.
2) **Inefficient** production methods increase **costs**, so **lean** production can **save** businesses a lot of money.
3) Businesses can use lean production to help them meet some of their **operational objectives** (see p.54). E.g. reducing waste will have a **positive impact** on **costs**, **value added** and the **environment**.
4) **Lean** production methods include **just-in-time**, **time-based management** (see next page) and **kaizen** (see p.63).

Increasing Efficiency and Productivity

Just-In-Time (JIT) Production keeps stock levels Very Low

1) **Just-in-time** production aims to **reduce** waste of materials and products by having as **little stock** as possible. Ideally, all raw materials come in one door, are made into products and go straight out another door — all **just in time** for delivery to customers.
2) JIT is based on very efficient **stock control** (see p.64). **Kanban** is the JIT system of triggering **repeat orders**. When staff reach coloured kanban cards towards the end of a batch of components, they order more straight away. The **supply** of components is **linked directly** to the **demand** for components, and there's no need for lots of stock.
3) JIT has **advantages** — **storage costs** are reduced and **cash flow** is improved as money isn't tied up in stock. There's **less waste** because there's less out-of-date or damaged stock lying around. The business is more **flexible** so it can cope with changes in **demand** and easily **adapt its products** to suit changing customer requirements.
4) There are **disadvantages** — no stock means customers can't be supplied during **production strikes**. Suppliers have to be **reliable** because there isn't much stock of raw materials to keep production going.

Time-Based Management means companies have to be Flexible

1) The time-based management approach aims to **reduce wasted time** in the production process.
2) Time-based management means that as well as competing on price and quality, companies can also **compete** on **time** by trying to be the **fastest** to get their product on the market. It's often used to produce **technological** items and **high fashion** clothes — areas where consumer needs change fast.
3) Time-based management depends on **flexible production facilities**, e.g. a fashion retailer might need a machine that can sew buttons onto coats one week and attach zips the next.
4) **Effective communication** between managers and production staff is essential, so the business needs to have a culture of **trust**. Staff also need to be **multi-skilled** — so **training** is important.

Advantages of Time-Based Management

- It **reduces lead times** — the time between a customer placing an order and taking delivery. So the cost of holding stock falls (see p.64).
- Reduced lead times also mean that **customer needs** can be satisfied **quicker**, giving the company a **competitive advantage**.
- **Machinery** with more than one function makes it possible to offer a more **varied** product range.
- It can help to **drive innovation** by decreasing research and development time.

5) However, some people have **criticised** time-based management for placing speed above **quality** — customers get a product sooner, but it might be faulty or not last as long.

Practice Questions

Q1 A council employs 4 workers to cut grass. They each work 35 hours per week. In total they cut 168 000 m^2 of grass each week. What is the labour productivity of the workers?

A 42 000 m^2 per worker per hour B 4800 m^2 per worker per hour
C 1200 m^2 per worker per hour D 6000 m^2 per worker per hour

Q2 Give three ways a company can increase its labour productivity.

Q3 What is lean production?

Q4 Give two advantages of just-in-time production.

Exam Questions

Q1 A guitar manufacturer wants to lower the price of its guitars but wants to ensure that the value added remains the same. Analyse how efficiency and productivity could be improved to meet these goals. [12 marks]

Q2 To what extent do you agree that all firms should use lean production methods? [12 marks]

Just-in-time production is a good idea — just-in-time revision isn't...

Hopefully you're reading this a good few weeks before the exam and you've got time to read and scribble until it's properly embedded in your memory. If you are tight for time though, don't panic. Just do as much as you can.

Increasing Efficiency and Productivity

Most modern businesses rely heavily on technology, from automated production lines to computer systems. Technology can make a firm more cost-effective and efficient, but it needs constant updating and maintenance.

*Businesses use **Two** main types of **Technology***

The main technologies that companies use in day-to-day operations are:

1) **Robotic Engineering** — using robots as part of the manufacturing process.
2) **Computer Technology** — computers are used by businesses in lots of different ways. Product development, business communications and finance departments all depend heavily on IT systems.

*Using **Robots** can **Reduce Staffing Costs***

1) **Robots** are mostly used to replace human staff for **tasks** which are **dangerous**, **repetitive** or **boring**.
2) **Factories** and **production plants** often use **automated pickers** to take goods from the production line and pack them into boxes. It's usually **cheaper** and **faster** for robots to do this job instead of humans.
3) Companies that are planning to replace human workers with robots need to weigh up the **advantages** of using robots against the **demotivating effect** that it is likely to have on staff.

Developments in IT** can make **Companies** more **Efficient

1) **Computer-aided design** (CAD) uses computers to design new products, or make alterations to existing products. CAD produces 3D mock-ups on screen — this can also be useful for marketing things like new kitchens.
2) **Computer-aided manufacturing** (CAM) uses computers to produce a product, usually involving **robots** or 'computer-numerically controlled' (CNC) machines. CAM is often combined with the CAD process — products are digitally designed, and the design data fed straight into the production machine. This is called **CAD/CAM**.
3) **3D printing** can be used to produce a **prototype** from a CAD. This is a lot **cheaper** than the CAD/CAM process as you don't need to build robots to make a single item.
4) Computers make **stock control** easier. Holding stock information in a database makes it much easier to monitor when you need to order new stock. In retail, **Electronic Point of Sale (EPOS)** systems rely on barcodes to record which products are being purchased, which means stock can be re-ordered automatically. **Electronic data interchange** can be used to automatically share sales information with a supplier — having a good stock control system makes it easier for companies to move to a **just-in-time** supply system (see p.59).
5) **Spreadsheets** are very useful in marketing and finance departments. E.g. in marketing they can calculate the impact of **potential changes** in expenditure or sales, which makes **decision-making** easier.
6) **Email** is a fast and efficient method of **communicating**, both internally and externally. E.g. companies can advertise cheaply to a **target audience** of their previous customers through email.
7) The **internet** allows businesses to reach a **huge customer base**, and do business **24 hours a day**, all over the world. Customers can order products using a business's **website** rather than phoning or posting an order.

*Firms need to consider the **Advantages** and **Disadvantages** of **Technology***

Most companies invest a lot of money in technology. Technology is beneficial if it leads to:

1) **Increased productivity** and **quality** — machines are often quicker and more accurate than humans.
2) **Reduced waste** through more effective production methods.
3) More **effective** and **efficient delivery** of goods and services to the customer.
4) More **effective marketing** campaigns that target the right customers.
5) **Reduced** administrative and financial **costs**.
6) **Better communications** both internally and externally.

However, introducing new technology or updating older systems can create problems:

1) **Initial costs** of technology may be **high**.
2) Technology requires **maintenance** and **constant updating** in order to stay current, which can also be **expensive**.
3) New IT systems may create an **increased** need for **staff training**.
4) Some technologies might replace manual work, leading to **staff redundancies**.

Increasing Efficiency and Productivity

A **Capital-Intensive** firm has **Lots** of **Machinery**

1) A **capital-intensive** business uses more **machinery** and relatively few **workers**.
2) **Larger** firms tend to be more **capital-intensive** than smaller companies. E.g. the Morgan Motor Company makes a small number of hand-built sports cars using lots of **labour**, whereas BMW uses more **robots** and machinery.
3) A rise in the **cost** of **labour** can also cause companies to **switch** to a **capital-intensive** method of production.

Advantages of Capital-Intensive Production	Disadvantages of Capital-Intensive Production
• **Cheaper** than manual labour in the **long term**. • Machinery is often **more precise** than human workers, which might lead to more **consistent quality** levels. • Machinery is able to work **24/7**. • Machines are **easier** to **manage** than people.	• High **set-up** costs. • Machines are usually only suited to one task, which makes them **inflexible**. • If machinery **breaks down**, it can lead to long **delays**. • The fear of being replaced by a machine can cause workers' **motivation** to **decrease**.

A **Labour-Intensive** firm is very **People-Heavy**

1) A **labour-intensive** firm uses more **workers** and less **machinery**. For example, the **NHS** is very labour-intensive.
2) In countries where labour is relatively **cheap** (e.g. China), **labour-intensive** methods of production are common.

Advantages of Labour-Intensive Production	Disadvantages of Labour-Intensive Production
• People are **flexible** and can be **retrained**. • **Cheaper** for **small-scale** production. • Labour-intensive methods are also **cheaper** where **low-cost labour** is available, e.g. China and India. • Workers can **solve** any **problems** that arise during production and suggest ways to **improve quality**.	• It's **harder** to **manage** people than machines. • People can be **unreliable** — they can get sick. • People can't work without **breaks** or **holidays**. • **Wage increases** mean that the cost of labour can increase over time. • Labour costs as a % of turnover (p.84) are **high**.

Businesses need to have the **Right Mix** of **People**, **Machines** and **Materials**

1) Businesses should try to **optimise resources** (**materials**, **machinery** and **people**) in order to meet objectives. How hard it is to get this right depends on the **complexity** of the product and the number of **production stages**. A business needs to strike the right **balance** between **labour-** and **capital-intensity** at each stage of production.
2) The **design** of the product affects the mix — e.g. freshly squeezed orange juice has just one component (oranges), but a car has hundreds. The **higher** the number of **components**, the more **complicated** the product is to produce, so the **harder** it is to get the correct mix of people, machines and materials.
3) Businesses can have problems getting the right mix if there's a **shortage** of suitably skilled **labour**. E.g. at the moment there's a very limited supply of **nurses**, **geologists** and **civil engineers** in the UK.
4) Businesses are also limited by their **finances**. Most companies would have the **latest technology** if they could **afford** it, but in reality **smaller firms** can rarely afford to keep updating their machinery.

Practice Questions

Q1 What is meant by CAD? How can a business use it?

Q2 Give three advantages and three disadvantages of using technology in business.

Q3 Give three benefits of capital-intensive production and three drawbacks of labour-intensive production.

Exam Questions

Q1 Plastoise is a plaster ornament manufacturer that specialises in making plaster animals.
Analyse how they could use technology to develop, design and make new products. [9 marks]

Q2 A plumbing supplies manufacturer is changing its production system to be more capital-intensive.
To what extent will this affect the business, the employees and the customers? [25 marks]

If these pages are repetitive and boring — they're the work of a robot...

Reading through this lot is enough to make you wonder how big businesses ever coped before technology came along. Robots might be cheaper than humans, but they tell lousy jokes, don't flirt, and are no good at making tea...

Improving Quality

Increased competition means that firms now compete through quality as well as price.
High quality can increase revenue and reduce costs.

*A **High Quality Product** can **Increase Profits** but may have **Drawbacks***

1) It's **important** that companies produce **quality** goods — poor quality leads to **customer dissatisfaction** and a **bad reputation** for the business.
2) Most **customers** realise that **lower priced** goods won't be as **high** quality as more **expensive** ones, but they do expect a product to be **fit for purpose** (to do the job it's intended for).
3) Producing high quality products allows for **premium pricing** and gives workers pride in their work, which can increase **morale** and **motivation**.
4) It also allows the business to **reduce its costs** and **increase its revenue**:

- Less **raw materials** and less **worker** and **machinery** time get used up by **mistakes**.
- You don't need as much **advertising** and **promotional** material to persuade **shops** to stock high quality goods.
- There are **fewer complaints** and **refunds** so employees can spend their time on other things.
- You don't need to **discount** prices to sell **damaged stock**.
- Quality can function as a **unique selling point (USP)** for your product.
- High quality products improve the **image** and **reputation** of the business.
- Quality goods and services make it easy to keep **existing customers** and **attract new customers**.

5) However, it can be **difficult** for companies to improve the quality of their products **efficiently**.
6) There is a **limit** to how much quality can be improved — workers have to know when the quality is **good enough**. Trying to make every single product 100% perfect could prove **costly** to the business.
7) If a company **outsources** some of its work it can be difficult to make sure the outsourced work is of the **same quality** that is expected within the business.

Quality Control** and **Quality Assurance** are **Different Things

There are **two main** ways for a company to **check** it's producing goods of a suitable quality:

1) **Quality control** means **checking goods** as you make them or when they arrive from suppliers to see if anything is wrong with them. It's often done by specially trained **quality inspectors**.
2) **Quality assurance** means introducing measures into the **production process** to try to ensure things don't go **wrong** in the first place. It assumes you can **prevent errors** from being made in the first place, rather than **eliminating faulty goods** once they've been made.

Quality Control (QC)	Quality Assurance (QA)
• Assumes that errors are **unavoidable**. • **Detects** errors and puts them **right**. • Quality control **inspectors** check other people's work, and are **responsible** for quality.	• Assumes that errors are **avoidable**. • **Prevents** errors and aims to get it right **first time**. • Employees **check** their own work. Workers are responsible for passing on **good quality** work to the next stage of the production process.

Quality Assurance** can be more **Motivating** than **Quality Control

1) **Quality assurance** is a more modern approach to quality control.
2) Under a self-checking system, it's **everyone's responsibility** to produce good work. Everyone should try to get it **right first time**. Workers can **reject** components or work in progress if they're not up to standard. They don't pass the poor quality off as **someone else's problem**.
3) **Empowering** employees to **self-check** the quality of their work can be highly **motivating**.
4) **Training** is important for quality assurance. Workers have to be trained to produce good quality products and services. New recruits get this as part of their **induction**. Experienced workers might need to be **retrained**.
5) Workers must be **motivated** and **committed** to quality for quality assurance schemes to work.
6) The ultimate aim of quality assurance is to create a culture of **zero defects**.
7) Both methods have their **drawbacks** — unless **all products** are tested during quality control, some **faulty** products will slip through. Quality assurance can result in products only being '**acceptable**', not of a **high standard**.

Improving Quality

Total Quality Management assures Commitment To Quality

1) **Total Quality Management** (TQM) means the **whole workforce** is committed to quality improvements. The idea is that **every department** focuses on quality in order to improve the **overall quality** of the products and services.
2) With TQM, every employee has to try to **satisfy customers** and **co-workers** — customers need to be happy with products or services they are being sold, and co-workers need to be happy with work you are passing on to them.

Advantages of TQM	Disadvantages of TQM
• Because all employees are involved with improving quality, TQM can help them to bond as a **team**. • TQM boosts a company's **reputation** for providing quality services or products. • TQM usually leads to fewer **faulty** products being made — so the business creates less **waste**.	• It can take a **long time** to introduce TQM. Companies might not see immediate improvements in quality. • TQM can **demotivate staff** — it can seem like a lot of effort to think about quality in all parts of the business. • TQM is usually **expensive** to introduce — it often means investing in **training** for all employees.

Businesses may use Other Methods to Improve Quality

Quality Circles

1) **Quality circles** meet at regular intervals to discuss quality control issues.
2) They use the knowledge of employees from **various departments** and **all levels** of the organisation.
3) Quality circles aim to **identify** and **solve** specific quality problems that arise.
4) They are a great way to get staff **involved** and can lead to increased **motivation** and **productivity**.
5) However, suggestions can often be **unrealistic** and management may **not listen** to the floor staff.

Kaizen

1) The **kaizen** approach is a **lean production method** (see p.58-59) that means that employees should be **improving** their work slightly **all the time**, instead of just making one-off improvements.
2) Employees are **encouraged** to question **why** a problem has occurred.
3) Employees at the bottom of the hierarchy have to be given some control over **decision-making**.
4) **Kaizen** helps workers feel involved in **quality assurance**. It's also **cheap** to introduce.
5) The downside of **kaizen** is that, because it makes **small changes** over time, it's not great for businesses that **urgently** need to improve quality. It needs the firm to be willing to commit to the method in the **long term**.

Practice Questions

Q1 Give two reasons why high quality reduces costs.

Q2 What's the difference between quality control and quality assurance?

Q3 Describe two advantages and two disadvantages of TQM.

Q4 What are 'quality circles'?

Staff adopted a new quality assurance method — if they didn't turn up to work, nothing could go wrong...

Exam Questions

Q1 Lightoptic manufactures table lamps. Recently a large number of customers have been complaining about the quality of the lamps. To what extent do you think that introducing further quality control will help the matter? [16 marks]

Examiners — the ultimate quality control inspectors...

Poor quality products can have huge impacts on a business. They can lead to decreased sales, a poor reputation, waste or discounted goods, complaints, and additional costs in bringing them up to scratch. Companies like to get it right first time — just like in your exam really, get it spot on first time and bathe in the glory of your achievements.

Managing Inventory

Managing inventory is a fancy name for keeping track of stock levels.

It's **Costly** to hold lots of **Stock**

1) A business's **stock** includes the **raw materials** needed for making a product, the materials that are currently being used for **products-in-progress** and the store of **finished goods** that a firm holds to supply to customers. These days, firms don't tend to hold much stock — because of the **costs** involved.
2) **Storage costs** are the most **obvious cost** of holding stock. Storage costs include **rent** for the warehouse and also the non-obvious costs of **heating**, **lighting**, **refrigeration**, **security** etc.
3) **Wastage costs** are the costs of **throwing away** useless stock. The longer a business holds stock, the more likely it is to create waste. Stock gets **physically damaged** as time goes on, and can also go **out of fashion**.
4) The **opportunity cost** (see p.21) is the cost of **investing** money in stock instead of **something else**. Capital tied up in stock is **unproductive** and could be used more productively elsewhere.

Stock Control aims to keep levels of stock **Just Right**

1) Most businesses try to **minimise** the level of stock they're holding. The **maximum** level of stock a business wants to hold depends on the size of their warehouses, their production method (see p.55) and on **opportunity cost**.
2) Businesses that use **flow production** need a **large stock** of **raw materials**, whereas **batch production** leads to large stocks of **work-in-progress**. **Job production** often means there is **no stock** of **finished goods** to be stored and **cell production** usually relies on **just-in-time** stock control (see p.59).
3) A business needs a **minimum** level of stock so that it **won't run out** of raw materials or finished goods. This minimum stock level is called **buffer stock**.
4) The **amount** of **buffer stock** needed depends on the storage **space** available, the kind of product (**perishable**, or something that keeps), the **rate** at which stocks are used up, and the **lead time**.
5) The **lead time** is the time it takes for goods to **arrive** after ordering them from the supplier. The **longer** the lead time, the **more buffer stocks** you need to hold — if customer demand suddenly went up, you wouldn't want to wait a long time for stocks to arrive from the supplier.
6) The **re-order quantity** is the amount the company orders from its supplier. The stock level at which this re-order is placed is called the **re-order level** and is calculated using:

Re-order level = lead time (in days) × average daily usage + buffer stock level

If lead time is in weeks, use the average weekly usage.

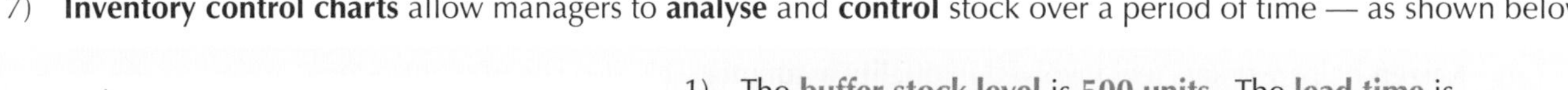

7) **Inventory control charts** allow managers to **analyse** and **control** stock over a period of time — as shown below.

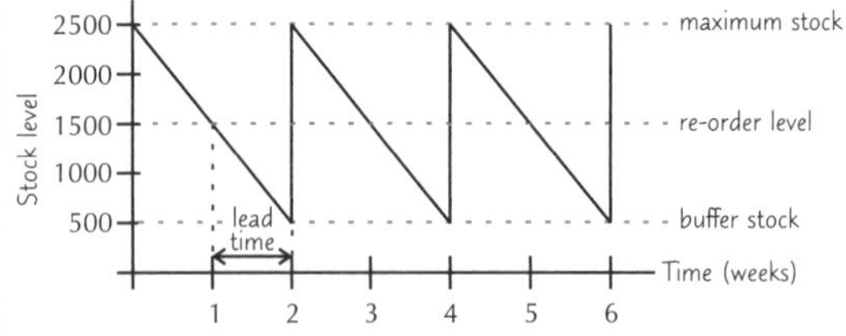

1) The **buffer stock level** is **500 units**. The **lead time** is **1 week**, and the business uses **1000 units** a week. That means they have to **re-order** stock when they have: 1 × 1000 + 500 = **1500** units left (so they don't go below their buffer stock level). 1500 units is the **re-order level**.
2) The **re-order quantity** is **2000 units**. This takes them back to their **maximum stock level** of 2500 units.

Practice Questions

Q1 Name three costs involved in holding stock.

Q2 In inventory control, what is the lead time?

Q3 Find the re-order level if lead time is 5 days, daily usage is 9 units and 7 units of buffer stock are required.

Exam Question

Q1 A bakery monitors its stock levels of flour over a 10 day period. They started with 70 bags of flour, they use 20 bags per day and keep a stock buffer of 10 bags. Each time they place an order it takes 2 days to arrive and they order 60 bags each time. Draw a stock control chart to show the bakery's stock of flour. [4 marks]

Answers on p.200.

It's time to sit back and take stock of what you've learnt...

Make sure you know and can read off all the different parts of an inventory control chart. You'll also need to know all the definitions on this page and how to calculate re-order level. This revision lark is a piece of cake, isn't it?

Managing Supply Chains

Every business in the supply chain needs to pull their weight, or production just doesn't happen...

Businesses need to have **Flexible** and **Dependable Supply Chains**

1) A **supply chain** consists of the **group** of firms that are involved in **all** the various **processes** required to make a **finished product** or **service** available to the customer.
2) The chain **begins** with the provider of **raw materials** and **ends** with the firm that sells the **finished product**.
3) The members of a supply chain will **vary** depending on the type of product or service, but will typically include **suppliers**, **manufacturers**, **distributors** and **retailers**.
4) **All** the **members** of the supply chain need to be **dependable**. If any of them are **unreliable**, the product won't be on the shelves when it needs to be, or the **quality** will be **poor**, which reflects **badly** on the company selling it.
5) Businesses need to be **flexible** on the **time taken** to supply goods and the **volume** of goods they supply. They can utilise a **flexible workforce** or use **outsourcing** (see below) to help manage sudden **changes in demand**.
6) A supplier that can offer **faster response** times than its competitors is more likely to gain the contract. This might be achieved through maintaining a **range of delivery** contracts to suit a business's needs.

"We should be able to get those components to you by 1952."

Businesses need to match **Supply** to **Demand**

Peripheral workers can help deal with changes in demand

1) **Core workers** are employees who are **essential** to a business, like senior managers and skilled workers. They are employed on **full-time**, **permanent** contracts. They are the workers that the company couldn't function effectively without, even if demand is low.
2) **Peripheral workers** are employees who **aren't essential** to a business, but that the business employs when they need **more staff**. Businesses keep their **fixed costs down** by employing peripheral workers on **temporary**, **part-time** or **zero-hours** contracts.
3) Peripheral workers can help a business deal with unforeseen or foreseen **increases in demand**. E.g. a supermarket might employ seasonal workers in order to deal with greater demand at Christmas time.

Outsourcing can help a business to meet demand

1) **Outsourcing** (or **subcontracting**) is when businesses **contract out** some activities to other businesses rather than doing them **in-house**.
2) Businesses can outsource some or all of the **product manufacturing** to deal with **increased demand**. They might also outsource things like **finance**, **recruitment**, **advertising** and **IT** — things that the business doesn't **specialise** in but sometimes needs.
3) Outsourcing can **benefit** businesses because they might be able to **accept contracts** which they would otherwise have turned down. They can also benefit from the **specialised knowledge** of the businesses they outsource to. Outsourcing also means that the business doesn't have to pay for permanent staff when they're only needed occasionally, so it **reduces costs**.
4) The main **disadvantage** of outsourcing is that the business doesn't have **control** over the **quality** of the outsourced work — if the work is bad, it can have a **negative effect** on the business's reputation.

Mass customisation allows businesses to supply tailor-made products

1) **Mass customisation** is a method of **producing to order** (products are made **after** the order is placed). It combines the **flexibility** of a custom-made product with the low cost of **mass production**.
2) A business that develops its capacity for mass customisation must have a **flexible** and **efficient production process** and **supply chain**.
3) It allows for an **increase in customer choice** without a corresponding increase in costs and it can lead to a **competitive advantage**.
4) However, it can be **very difficult** for a business to make mass customisation **efficient** and **profitable**. Customised products can be **expensive** and it can take a **long time** for them to be delivered to customers — this is acceptable for **luxury items** but not for everyday things.

Managing Supply Chains

Companies need to Choose their Suppliers Carefully

The most **effective suppliers** are those who offer products or services that **match** (or **exceed**) the **needs** of your business. So when you are looking for **suppliers**, it's best to be **sure** of your **business needs** and what you want to achieve. The most important factors to consider are:

Price — The **total cost** of acquiring the product. Firms have to decide **how much** they are willing to pay and whether **cost** is their **first priority**. If they want to cut down the time it takes to serve customers, suppliers that offer faster delivery will rate higher than those that compete on price alone. The **cheaper** a supplier is, the more **value added** to the final product. However, the **cheapest** supplier isn't always the **best** as they will often supply **lower quality** products.

Payment Terms — Companies need to know **how much** they need to pay, **how** it has to be paid and **when** it should be paid by. **New companies** will often have to pay for all the goods **up front**, whereas companies with a **well-established relationship** with their supplier will be given **credit**, which **delays** the payment for a certain amount of **time** (often 30 days).

Quality — The **quality** of supplies needs to be **consistent**. In recent years, customers have become much **more selective** about the quality of the product. Customers will associate **poor quality** with the business they buy from, not their suppliers.

Capacity — Businesses need to select **suppliers** who are able to **meet** any **peaks** in **demand** for particular products / services.
Big businesses usually opt to buy in bulk in hope of getting a **discount**.

Reliability — If **a supplier** lets a **firm** down, that firm may not be able to supply its **own** customers. Suppliers need to **deliver high-quality products on time**, or give plenty of **warning** if they can't.

Flexibility — **Suppliers** need to be able to **respond easily** to **changes** in a company's **requirements**. Efficient production relies on suppliers who can provide extra (or fewer) supplies at **short notice**. Flexible suppliers will also be willing to adapt to meet the company's other requirements — such as becoming more **environmentally-friendly**.

*Companies build **Relationships** with their **Suppliers***

Mr MacDonald and Mr Paulin had spent three days choosing a supplier for a new stapler.

A **strategic working relationship** is one where both companies in the relationship can get **long-term benefits** from **working together**. There are several ways for companies to build strategic working relationships with their suppliers:

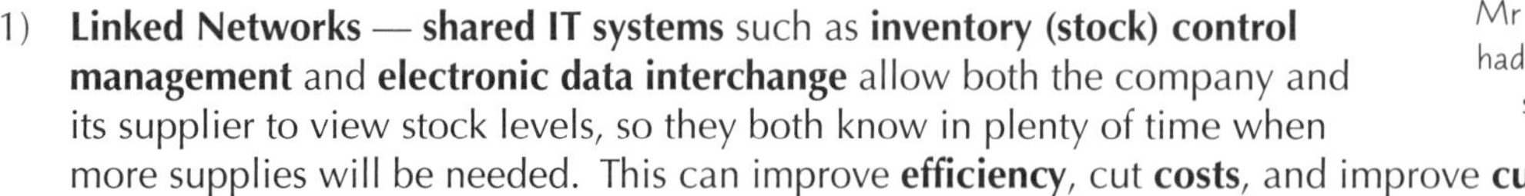

1) **Linked Networks** — **shared IT systems** such as **inventory (stock) control management** and **electronic data interchange** allow both the company and its supplier to view stock levels, so they both know in plenty of time when more supplies will be needed. This can improve **efficiency**, cut **costs**, and improve **customer value**.
2) **JIT (Just-in-Time) Systems** (see p.59) — these are becoming a popular way of managing operations. The goal of JIT systems is to have only the **right amounts** of **materials** arrive at precisely the **times** they are **needed**. Because supplies arrive just as they are needed, you don't need a big warehouse, and there's **less waste**.
3) **Shared Costs** — if a business and its supplier are producing similar goods, there's a good chance they'll be able to save money by sharing **specialist equipment** and storing their goods in the same **warehouse**.
4) **Innovation** — companies who work **closely** with their suppliers are able to **share new ideas** and ultimately make or save **more money** through innovation. They could work together to improve the **manufacturing process**, develop a **new product** or even alter the **supply network** — all these things can help both the company and the supplier to save money.

Managing Supply Chains

A Well-Managed Supply Chain can Improve Operational Performance...

1) If a business works **closely** with the **right suppliers**, operational **performance** will improve.
2) **Productivity** will **increase**, which causes **costs** to fall (see p.58), so **profits** will increase.
3) A business with an **efficient supply chain** is in a much better position to meet its customers' **expectations**.
4) Businesses should constantly be looking to improve their **supply chain**, and they can do this in several ways:

   1) A company's buyers need to make sure that they **only buy** the **supplies** that the **company** really **needs**.

   2) They also need to understand the difference between a **strategic supplier**, who provides goods or services that are essential to the business — such as high-value raw materials, and a **non-strategic supplier** who provides low-value supplies such as office stationery. It's important to spend **more time** selecting and managing **strategic suppliers** than non-strategic suppliers.

   3) It's often easier, and generally more **cost-effective**, for businesses to **limit** the number of **sources** they buy from. However, it's **dangerous** to have just **one supplier** because if there are ever problems with that supplier, the business has nowhere to turn.

   4) It's always worth having an **alternative supply source** ready to help in difficult times. This is really important for suppliers who are essential to the success of the business.

...and efficiently Match Supply to Demand

When demand for a product **increases** the whole supply chain needs to adapt. For example:

See p.65 for more on peripheral workers and outsourcing.

- The **retailer** might hire more **peripheral workers** on **short-term** contracts to keep the shelves full and to deal with customers.
- The **distributor** could increase the number of deliveries by **outsourcing** some work to another distributor.
- The **manufacturer** could temporarily increase its **capacity utilisation** (see p.56) to 100% and get more raw materials from its **alternative supply sources**.
- The **supply sources** may have to be able to supply more **raw materials**.

Practice Questions

Q1 Give three types of company that you would expect to find as part of a supply chain.

Q2 What is mass customisation?

Q3 Give six qualities that a business would look for in a supplier.

Q4 What is the difference between a strategic supplier and a non-strategic supplier?

Q5 Why is it risky for a business to rely on a single supplier?

Exam Questions

Q1 Alpha Beefs Ltd is looking for a supplier of beef to use in its new range of beef pies.
Discuss the factors it should consider before deciding which one to choose. [8 marks]

Q2 Mr Brown, director of Brown's Brushes Ltd, wants to improve his relationship with his wood supplier.
Discuss the ways in which he could achieve this. [8 marks]

Q3 Gordon's Cycles is a custom-made bike manufacturer. In July, demand for their bikes increased by 50%.
Analyse the short-term and long-term impacts on different parts of the supply chain. [12 marks]

Supply me to the moon, let me sing among the stock...

If you're a business, the relationship with your supplier might be the best one you'll ever have. Or the worst. If your suppliers do what they're supposed to when they're supposed to, there's a good chance that the production process will all run to plan. If they're late, or just don't deliver, production stops — which isn't an ideal situation...

Financial Objectives

Here's where the real fun starts — it's finance time.

Financial Objectives are what the business wants to Achieve Financially

1) **Financial objectives** are **financial goals** that a business wants to achieve. Businesses usually have **specific targets** in mind, and a **specific period of time** to achieve them in. E.g. a business might have an objective to increase its profits by 10% within three years.
2) The financial objectives will be set by **financial managers** and will help the business achieve its corporate objectives. They must also be **consistent** with the **functional objectives** of the other departments.
3) Financial objectives can improve **coordination** between teams, act as a **focus** for **decision-making** and allow shareholders to judge whether a business would be a worthwhile **investment**.
4) Businesses look at their **financial data** (e.g. cash flow figures and profit margins) to assess their **financial position**. They can then **set objectives** based on what they need to improve.

Companies set Revenue, Costs and Profit Objectives

For more on revenue, costs and profit, see p.6

1) **Revenue objectives** are often set to **increase** the **value** or **volume** of **sales**. Examples might be 'increase sales revenue by 5% in the next year' or 'beat a competitor's monthly sales'.
2) **Costs objectives** are usually set to **minimise costs**. Examples of costs objectives for the next year could be 'reduce costs of raw materials by 10%', or 'reduce fixed costs by 15%'. If costs are reduced and the business still sells the same number of products at the same price, this will **increase** its overall **profits**. Businesses have to be careful that cutting costs doesn't reduce the **quality** of their products or services, or raise **ethical questions** about how they operate — otherwise sales might drop and they'd end up with **lower profits** instead of higher profits.
3) **Profit objectives** might set a target figure for profit or for a percentage increase from the previous year. Since revenue, costs and profit are closely linked, achieving revenue and costs objectives can help achieve profit objectives.

Cash Flow Objectives aim to Improve Cash Flow

1) **Cash flow** is all the money flowing **into** and **out of** the business over a period of time, calculated at the exact time it **enters** or **leaves** the bank account or till. On the other hand, **profit** includes all transactions that will lead to cash in or out, now, or in the **future**.
2) Cash flow calculations are pretty much the most important thing to a business in the **short term**. Businesses need cash to survive. Looking at the **long term**, making a profit is the **main objective**.
3) If a business allows payments to be made on **credit** (see p.72), this may **damage** their cash flow. Similarly, if a business needs to spend a lot of money on a new computer system or machinery, the outflow of cash could lead the business to a potential **crisis**. If a business **produces too much**, they'll have to **pay** suppliers and staff **so much** that they'll become **insolvent** before they have the chance to **get paid** by their customers. This is called **overtrading**.
4) **Cash flow objectives** are put in place to help **prevent** cash flow problems. Businesses may set objectives to spread revenue or costs more **evenly** throughout the year, acquire a specified amount of **liquid** assets (an asset that can be turned into cash quickly) or target a **minimum cash balance**.

<u>Insolvency</u> means that a business is unable to pay its debts. If a sole trader or partnership business is insolvent, the owner may have to declare <u>bankruptcy</u>.

Return on Investment Objectives help a business stay Profitable

1) Businesses might set objectives for **return on investment** (**ROI**), calculated using this formula:

$$\text{Return on investment (\%)} = \frac{\text{Return on investment (£)}}{\text{Cost of investment (£)}} \times 100$$

Return on investment (£) = Financial gain from investment – costs of investment

2) Return on investment measures how **efficient** an investment is — it compares the return from a project to the amount of money that's been invested in it. The **higher** the ROI, the **better**. Companies might set a target value for the ROI of an investment or use it to compare the profitability of two potential investments.

Financial Objectives

Businesses *set* ***Objectives*** *for* ***Long-Term Investments*** *and* ***Funding***

1) **Capital** is simply wealth in the form of money or other assets owned by a business.
2) **Capital expenditure** (or investment) is the money spent to buy fixed assets. These are things that are used over and over again to produce goods or services, like **factories** or **vehicles**.
3) Businesses may set an **investment objective** to help achieve a set amount of capital expenditure during a year. E.g. 'Capital expenditure of £150 000 to fund purchase of new equipment'. Alternatively a business may wish to reduce capital expenditure.
4) **Capital structure** refers to the way a business raises capital to purchase **assets**. A business's capital structure is a combination of its **debt capital** (borrowed funds) and its **equity capital**. Equity capital is the capital raised by **selling shares**, and is sometimes known as share capital.
5) A common **capital structure objective** is to set a **debt to equity ratio**, e.g. 1.5 : 1 after 4 years. Sometimes businesses set targets to reduce the proportion of **debt** in their **long-term funding**.

Internal *and* ***External*** *factors influence* ***Financial Objectives***

There are many factors that influence a company's **ability** to **achieve** its objectives, and managers need to take these factors into account when they set financial objectives.

<u>Internal factors influencing financial objectives</u>

1) **The overall objectives of the business** — Financial objectives need to be consistent with the corporate objectives of the business. E.g. a company with a strong **environmental** standpoint might be more interested in minimising its carbon footprint than in maximising its profits.
2) **The status of the business** — New businesses might set **ambitious** targets for revenue because they're trying to grow quickly and establish themselves in the marketplace. **Established** companies might be satisfied with **smaller** increases in revenue if they're not actively trying to grow.
3) **Other areas of the business** — Financial objectives might be limited by what's happening in other departments of the business. E.g. if a business has a **high turnover of sales staff**, an objective to increase revenue might be **unrealistic** because experienced staff are needed to encourage customers to spend more.

<u>External factors influencing financial objectives</u>

1) **The availability of finance** — **Cash flow** targets might depend on how easy it is for the business to get **credit**.
2) **Competitors** — If **new competitors** enter the market, or **demand** for competitors' products **increases** (due to a special offer or price reduction, etc), a business might set an objective to **cut costs** to be more competitive.
3) **The economy** — In a period of economic **boom**, businesses can set **ambitious** profit targets. In a **downturn**, they have to set more **restrained** targets, and they might also set targets to **minimise costs**.
4) **Shareholders** — Shareholders usually want the best possible **return** on their investment — this might put pressure on businesses to set objectives to increase **profits** or **dividends**.
5) **Environmental/Ethical influences** — E.g. sourcing fair trade supplies may affect costs objectives.

Practice Questions

Q1 Give an example of a revenue, a profit and a costs objective.

Q2 Why would a business set a cash flow objective?

Q3 Give two external factors that influence a company's financial objectives.

Exam Question

Q1 Greenwood Desks is a new business aiming to create bespoke desks 'to-order' for both businesses and individuals. Greenwood Desks promise to use only sustainable resources in the production process, and also offer customers a credit period of 6 months. To what extent are cash flow objectives the most important objectives for Greenwood Desks? Justify your answer. [12 marks]

We're choosing another location for the wedding — we're re-venueing...

Make sure everything here is clear before moving on — this stuff is pretty important for the rest of the section. Learn all of the different types of objectives and why they're important, and walk yourself through the internal and external factors that influence financial objectives — you never know where they'll pop up in the exams. Eesh.

Measuring and Increasing Profit

Revenue and profit are different animals — revenue is the money received from sales, whereas profit is found by deducting costs from the revenue. There are different types of profit though, so cast your eyes over this spread.

Businesses *want to* **Maximise** *their* **Profits**

1) Most businesses exist to make a **profit** — if a business makes large profits then it is **successful**. Even successful businesses want to **increase profits** and become **more successful**.
2) Businesses **measure** their profits on a regular basis. They **compare** their profits from the current period (usually a year) to the profits from previous periods to measure their **progress**.
3) If profits go **down**, this is **bad news**, even if the business is still making large profits. For example, if a business makes a profit of £100 million in a year, this might sound like good news, but if the previous year's profit was £125 million then it's a **bad sign**.
4) This is why businesses work out the **percentage increase** or **decrease** in their profits from year to year — it makes it easy to see how well they're performing in comparison with other years.
5) If profits are decreasing, the business needs to investigate **why** this is happening and **take action** to fix it.

The formula for measuring the **percentage change in profit** is:

$$\text{Percentage Change in Profit} = \frac{\text{Current Year's Profit} - \text{Previous Year's Profit}}{\text{Previous Year's Profit}} \times 100$$

Businesses *use different* **Methods** *to* **Increase Profits**

1) Businesses can **improve** their **profits** by increasing their **prices** (if the demand for their products is price inelastic — see p.36-37) or **reducing** their prices to increase **demand** (if demand is price elastic). The **downside** is that increased prices could mean **reduced sales**, and reduced prices may not increase sales.
2) They could also try to **reduce** their **costs of production**. However, reducing production costs may lead to a **lower quality product**, which could damage the number of sales.
3) Businesses may use **advertising** to increase **demand** for a product, which could increase sales and profit. Unfortunately, advertising can be expensive and there is no guarantee that profits will increase.
4) **Improving** the **quality** of a product can reduce costs from returns or from items that are **not** of an acceptable quality for **sale**. This should lead to an increase in profits, as long as the costs of improving the quality don't outweigh the savings.

There are **Different Ways** *of* **Reporting Profit**

The general profit formula given on p.6 is Profit = Total Revenue – Total Costs.

Businesses are interested in **different measures** of profit:

1) **Gross profit** is the amount left over when the **cost of sales** is **subtracted** from **sales revenue**. Cost of sales includes the costs **directly related** to making the product, e.g. the cost of materials.

   Gross Profit = Sales Revenue – Cost of Sales

2) **Operating profit** takes into account all revenues and costs from **regular trading**, but not any revenues or costs from **one-off** events such as the sale or purchase of another business. Operating profit considers both the cost of sales and **operating expenses**, such as administrative expenses. If a company's **gross profit** is **increasing** but its **operating profit** is **decreasing**, it usually means the company is **not controlling** its **costs**.

   Operating profit = Sales Revenue – Cost of Sales – Operating Expenses

3) **Profit for the year** also takes into consideration profit or loss from **one-off events** and **financial costs**, e.g. interest payments and tax. It's the measure of profit that dividend payments are based on.

   Profit for the Year = Operating Profit + Other Profit – Net Finance Costs – Tax

Example

Hannah's Hammers is a small company selling hammers with a floral design. The cost of producing each hammer is **£2**, and they are sold for **£5** each. Hannah also has operating expenses of **£9000** a year.
If Hannah sells **10 000** hammers in a year, her **sales revenue** is 10 000 × £5 = **£50 000**.
Hannah's **gross profit** is £50 000 – (£2 × 10 000) = **£30 000**.
Her **operating profit** is £50 000 – £20 000 – £9000 = **£21 000**.

Measuring and Increasing Profit

Profit Margins *show how* ***Profitable*** *a business or product is*

Return on investment (see p.68) is also used to measure profitability.

1) As well as measuring profits, businesses are interested in measuring **profitability** — the amount of profit **relative** to **revenue** or **investment**.
2) Profit margins measure the relationship between the **profit made** and the **sales revenue**. They tell you what **percentage** of the selling price of a product is actually **profit**.
3) Profit margins can be used to make **comparisons** over a period of time, or compare the profitability of different companies. Other ways of analysing profitability are given on pages 108-110.

Gross Profit Margin

1) The **gross profit margin** measures gross profit as a percentage of sales revenue:

$$\text{Gross Profit Margin (\%)} = \frac{\text{Gross Profit}}{\text{Sales Revenue}} \times 100$$

2) What counts as a good gross profit margin depends on the **type of business**, but the **higher** the percentage the better. A business with a high sales volume (e.g. a bakery) can afford to have a low gross profit margin.
3) The margin can be **improved** by **increasing prices** or **reducing** the direct **cost of sales**.

Operating Profit Margin

1) The **operating profit margin** takes into account all the costs of regular trading. Again, it's a percentage:

$$\text{Operating Profit Margin (\%)} = \frac{\text{Operating Profit}}{\text{Sales Revenue}} \times 100$$

2) It's best to have a **high** operating profit margin, although it does depend on the type of business. Operating profits can be **improved** by **increasing prices** or **reducing the cost** of sales or operating expenses.
3) It's useful to **compare** operating profit margin with gross profit margin over a **period of time**. A business with a **decreasing operating profit margin** compared to gross profit margin is struggling with operating expenses.

Profit for the Year Margin

1) The **profit for the year margin** measures the profit for the year as a percentage of sales revenue:

$$\text{Profit for the Year Margin (\%)} = \frac{\text{Profit for the Year}}{\text{Sales Revenue}} \times 100$$

2) A high profit for the year margin is attractive to **shareholders**, because it can indicate that they may receive high dividends. Similarly this can attract potential shareholders.

Practice Questions

Q1 If a business makes a profit of £50 000 in 2018 and £52 000 in 2019, what is the percentage change in profit?

Q2 Calculate the profit for the year for Hannah's Hammers (see previous page), given that the business paid tax of £6000, made £3000 profit from sales of assets and had net finance costs of £2000.

Q3 Give two ways in which the gross profit margin can be improved.

Answers on p.200.

Exam Questions

Q1 Dogs4eva had a gross profit margin of 18% in 2013 and 11% in 2014.
Analyse how the company's revenue and costs may have changed from 2013 to 2014. [6 marks]

Q2 A business has sales revenue of £2 million. Its gross profit is £750 000, and its operating expenses are £250 000.
a) Calculate the operating profit margin. [4 marks]
b) Analyse what the business could do to improve the operating profit margin. [9 marks]

I'm just about 100% fed up with all these percentage calculations...

OK, I admit this hasn't been the world's most interesting page but this is all really important stuff, so make sure you get your head around it before moving on. You need to be able to calculate the profits and their margins, so learn the formulas. You also need to understand what they mean for a business and how firms can improve their profitability.

Cash Flow Forecasting

Remember cash flow (p.68)? Well, cash flow forecasts are dead important for businesses. They're used to predict when money will come in and out of the business over a period of time, and can help prevent nasty monetary surprises.

The Cash Flow Cycle is the Gap between Money Going Out and Coming In

1) Cash **inflows** are sums of money **received** by a business, e.g. from product sales or loans. Cash **outflows** are sums of money **paid out** by a business, e.g. to buy raw materials, or pay wages.

2) Businesses need to **pay out money** for the costs of producing an order, or for assets like machinery, **before** they **get paid** for that order. This **delay** between money going out and money coming in is called the **cash flow cycle**.

3) It's important to make sure there's always **enough money** available to make payments. Not paying suppliers and employees can be something of a **disaster**. For **new businesses** the cash flow cycle can be a **big problem** because they need money for **start-up costs** before they've made any sales at all. The money available to a business for its day-to-day running costs is called **working capital**.

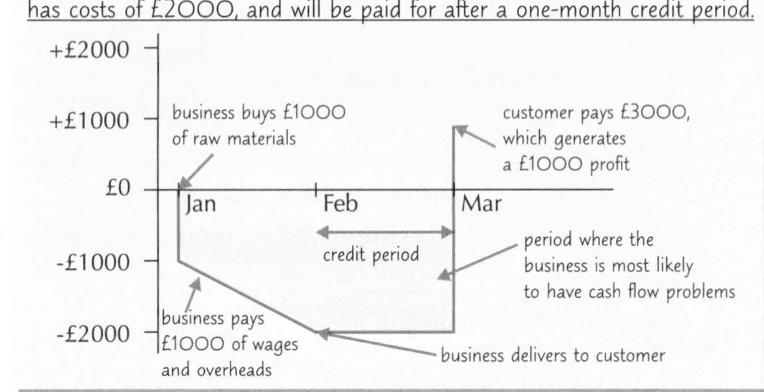

4) The **length** of the **cash flow cycle** depends on:

- <u>**The type of product**</u> — this determines the **length of time** it takes to produce and **how long** it's held in stock. E.g. a butcher wouldn't hold stock for long, so there would only be a short delay between paying suppliers and selling to customers.
- <u>**Credit payments**</u> — Buying **on credit** means that the goods are received, but the buyer has an agreed period of time (credit period) before payment is due. E.g. a sofa company may allow customers three months from the purchase date to pay for their sofa. Businesses also buy **on credit** from their **suppliers**.

5) People who are **owed** money by the business are known as **creditors**. Money that the business owes is known as **payable**. People who **owe** the business money are called **debtors**. Money that is owed to the business is known as **receivable**.

6) The **ideal cash flow situation** is where there's a short period of time from the start of production to the sale of goods, and where the business is given a longer credit period by its creditors (e.g. suppliers) than it gives its debtors (e.g. customers).

Businesses have Various Canny Tricks to Improve Cash Flow

Businesses have various methods to **improve cash flow**, but they can have **drawbacks**.

1) **Overdrafts** can be arranged with banks to allow a business to borrow money according to its needs, up to a preset amount. These can be useful in times of need, but in the long term overdrafts can be very **expensive**, as the business will need to pay **interest** on the borrowed money.
2) Businesses can try to hold less **stock**, so less **cash** is tied up in stock. But this could cause problems if there is a sudden increase in demand for a product, as they may run out.
3) Businesses try to **reduce the time** between **paying** suppliers and **getting money** from customers. They try to get their **suppliers** to give them a **longer** credit period — and give their **customers** a **shorter** credit period. However it's important to **balance** the need to manage cash flow with the need to keep suppliers and customers **happy** — you don't want customers to go elsewhere.
4) **Credit controllers** keep **debtors** in control. They set credit limits and remind debtors to pay up.
5) **Debt factoring** gives instant cash to businesses whose customers haven't paid their invoices. Banks and other financial institutions act as **debt factoring agents**. The agent pays the business about **80%** of the value of the invoice as an **instant cash advance**. The agent gets the customer to pay up, and then **keeps** about **5%** of the value of the invoice — debt factoring costs money and the agent needs to make a living.
6) **Sale and leaseback** is when businesses **sell** equipment to **raise capital**, and then **lease** (rent) the equipment back. That way, they get a big **lump sum** from the sale, and pay a **little** bit of money each month for the lease of the equipment. Of course, they don't get to own the equipment again unless they get enough cash to buy it back — and they have to pay the lease in the meantime.

Cash Flow Forecasting

Businesses make **Cash Flow Forecasts** to help them make **Decisions**

1) **Cash flow forecasts** (also called cash budgets) show the amount of money that managers **expect** to **flow into** the business and **flow out** of the business over a period of time in the **future**.
2) Managers can use cash flow forecasts to **make sure** they always have **enough** cash around to pay **suppliers** and **employees**. They can **predict** when they'll be **short of cash**, and arrange a **loan** or **overdraft** in time.
3) Businesses show cash flow forecasts to **banks** and venture capitalists when trying to get **loans** and other finance. Cash flow forecasts prove that a business has an idea of where it's going to be in the future.
4) They can be used to check that a firm isn't holding **too much cash**, i.e. cash that could be invested in the business instead.
5) **Established** firms base forecasts on **past experience**. **New** firms have no past data, so their forecast should consider the business's **capacity**, experiences of **similar firms** and customer trends shown by **market research**.

Example: A new firm starts up with a loan of £18 000 and £5000 of capital. It expects to sell £5000 of goods in January, £35 000 in February, £35 000 in March and £40 000 in April. All customers will get a **one month credit period**. Wages and rent will cost £15 000 in total each month, and other costs are expected to be £5000 in January, £8000 in February, £2000 in March and £2000 in April.

	Item	Jan	Feb	Mar	Apr
Cash in	Sales revenue		£5000	£35000	£35000
	Other cash in	£18000			
	Total cash inflows	**£18000**	**£5000**	**£35000**	**£35000**
Cash out	Wages and rent	£15000	£15000	£15000	£15000
	Other costs	£5000	£8000	£2000	£2000
	Total cash outflows	**£20000**	**£23000**	**£17000**	**£17000**
Net monthly cash flow	**Net cash flow**	**(£2000)**	**(£18000)**	**£18000**	**£18000**
	Opening balance	£5000	£3000	(£15000)	£3000
	Closing balance	**£3000**	**(£15000)**	**£3000**	**£21000**

This shows cash coming in from sales and from the initial start-up loan.

This shows cash going out to pay for the firm's costs.

Net cash flow = cash inflows – cash outflows

The opening balance is money in the bank at the start — for January it's £5000.

Closing balance = opening balance + net cash flow

The closing balance for last month is this month's opening balance.

There's a one month credit period, so each month's sales revenue isn't received until the following month.

Figures in brackets are negative.

According to this, the business will have £21 000 in the bank by the end of April. But it'll still owe £18 000 from the start-up loan...

Cash Flow Forecasting isn't always accurate

1) Cash flow forecasts can be based on **false assumptions** about what's going to happen.
2) Circumstances can **change suddenly** after the forecast's been made. **Costs** can **go up**. Machinery can **break down** and need mending. **Competitors** can put their prices up or down, which **affects sales**.
3) Good cash flow forecasting needs lots of **experience** and lots of **research** into the market.
4) A **false forecast** can have **disastrous** results. A business that runs out of cash could end up **insolvent**.

Practice Questions

Answers on p.200.

Q1 Give two methods a business may use to improve cash flow.

Q2 Give two reasons why a cash flow forecast is useful to someone setting up their own small business.

Q3 If a company has a total cash in of £8000 and a total cash out of £9500, what is its net cash flow?

Q4 If a company has an opening balance of £20 000 and its net cash flow is (£7000), what is the closing balance?

Q5 How can you work out a company's opening balance in any given month?

Exam Questions

Q1 Analyse the ways in which a car sales company could improve its cash flow. [12 marks]

Q2 To what extent can a business successfully and accurately predict future cash flow? Explain your answer. [12 marks]

Dunno 'bout you, but cash flows through my wallet like water...

Cash flow is important — without it, businesses can end up insolvent and individuals could go bankrupt. Make sure you know how to calculate the figures in the forecast on this page. It can be tricky to start with, so go over it a few times if you need to. Don't forget to learn the ways that businesses can improve cash flow. It'll be worth it in the exams.

Setting Budgets

Businesses make financial plans. They set targets for how much money they're going to make, and how much they're going to spend. Then they check to see how they've done. It sounds simple enough...

A **Budget** is a **Financial Plan** for the future

A **budget** forecasts **future earnings** and **future spending**, usually over a 12 month period. Businesses use different budgets to estimate different things. There are three types of budget:

Marketing data is used in financial planning.

1) **Income budgets** forecast the amount of money that will come into the company as revenue. In order to do this, the company needs to predict **how much** it will sell, and at what **price**. Managers estimate this using their **sales figures** from previous years, as well as **market research.**
2) **Expenditure budgets** predict what the business's **total costs** will be for the year, taking into account both fixed and variable costs. Variable costs increase with output, so managers must predict output based on sales estimates.
3) The **profit budget** uses the **income budget** minus the **expenditure budget** to calculate what the expected **profit** (or **loss**) will be for that year.

Budgets affect **All Areas** of the business

1) The expenditure budget forecasts **total** expenditure. This is broken down into **department** expenditure budgets — each department is allotted a certain amount of money to spend.
2) **Budget holders** are people **responsible** for spending or generating the money for each budget. For example, the budget holder of the expenditure budget for marketing could be the head of the marketing department.
3) Department expenditure budgets are broken down into budgets for **specific activities** within the department. These help local managers control and coordinate their work.

Item of Expenditure	Expenditure (£)
Wages	150 000
Marketing	50 000
Raw Materials	100 000
Research and Development	25 000
Total Expenditure	**325 000**

The **Budget Setting** process involves **Research** and **Negotiation**

1) To set the **income budget**, businesses **research** and **predict** how sales are going to go up and down through the year, so that they can make a good prediction of **sales revenue**.
2) To set the **expenditure budget** for **production**, businesses research how labour costs, raw materials costs, taxes and inflation are going to go up over the year. They can then figure out the **costs** of producing the volume of product that they think they're going to sell.
3) **Budgets** are **influenced** by a company's **objectives** — e.g. if they aim to increase sales, this will affect their predicted sales revenue and cost of sales, and they might allocate more of the expenditure budget to marketing.
4) Annual budgets are usually agreed by **negotiation** — when budget holders have a say in setting their budgets, they're **motivated** to achieve them.
5) Budgets should **stretch** the abilities of the business, but they must be **achievable**. **Unrealistically** high income budgets or low expenditure budgets will **demotivate** staff. No one likes being asked to do the **impossible**.
6) Once they've agreed the budget, budget holders **keep checking** performance against the budget. This is called **variance analysis**. There's more about variance and variance analysis on p.76-77.

Budgets have **Advantages** and **Disadvantages**

Benefits of budgeting

- Budgets help to **achieve targets**, like keeping costs low or revenue high.
- Budgets help **control** income and expenditure. They show where the money goes.
- Budgeting helps managers to **review** their activities and make decisions.
- Budgeting helps focus on the **priorities**.
- Budgets let heads of department **delegate** authority to budget holders. Getting authority is **motivating**.
- Budgets allow departments to **coordinate** spending.
- Budgets help persuade **investors** that the business will be successful.

Drawbacks of budgeting

- Budgeting can cause **resentment** and rivalry if departments have to compete for money.
- Budgets can be **restrictive**. Fixed budgets stop firms responding to changing market conditions.
- Budgeting is **time-consuming**. Managers can get too preoccupied with setting and reviewing budgets, and forget to focus on the real issues of **winning business** and **understanding** the **customer**.
- **Inflation** is difficult to predict — some prices can change by levels much **greater** than average.
- Start-up businesses may struggle to gather data from other firms, so the budget may be **inaccurate**.

Setting Budgets

Budgets can be Updated Every Year or developed from Scratch

1) **Start-up businesses** have to develop their budgets **from scratch** (known as **zero-based budgeting**). This is difficult to do because they don't have much information to base their decisions on — they can't take into account the previous year's sales or expenditure. This means that their budgets are likely to be **inaccurate**.
2) After the first year, a business must decide whether to follow the **historical budgeting** method, or to continue using the **zero-based budgeting** method.

Historical budgets are updated each year

1) This year's budget is based on a percentage increase or decrease from last year's budget. For example, a business expecting 10% revenue growth might add 10% to the advertising, wages and raw materials purchasing budgets.
2) Historical budgeting is **quick** and **simple**, but it assumes that business conditions stay **unchanged** each year. This isn't always the case — for instance, a product at the introduction stage of its **life cycle** (see p.44) needs more money spent on advertising than one in the growth or maturity stages.

Zero-based budgeting means starting from scratch each year

1) Budget holders **start** with a budget of **£0**, and have to **get approval** to spend money on activities.
2) They have to **plan** all the year's activities, ask for money to spend on them, and be prepared to **justify** their requests to the finance director. Budget holders need good **negotiating** skills for this.
3) Zero-based budgeting takes much **longer** to complete than historical budgets.
4) If zero-based budgeting is done properly it's **more accurate** than historical budgeting.

Budgets affect how Flexible a business can be

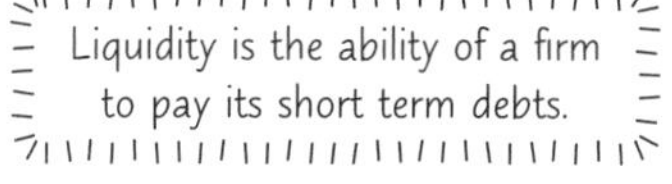

1) **Fixed budgets** provide **discipline** and **certainty**. This is especially important for a business with **liquidity** problems — fixed budgets help control **cash flow**.
2) **Fixed budgeting** means budget holders have to stick to their budget plans throughout the year — even if market conditions change. This can **prevent** a firm reacting to **new opportunities** or **threats** that they didn't know about when they set the budget.
3) **Flexible budgeting** allows budgets to be altered in response to significant changes in the market or economy.
4) **Zero-based budgeting** gives a business more **flexibility** than **historical budgeting**.

Mary had no problems with flexibility

Practice Questions

Q1 Name the three main types of budget that a business will set, stating what each tells you.

Q2 If a business has an income budget of £125 000 and a profit budget of £30 000, what is its expenditure budget?

Q3 State three benefits and three drawbacks of using budgets.

Q4 What is historical budgeting?

Q5 Explain the difference between fixed and flexible budgets.

Answer on p.200.

Exam Questions

Q1 To what extent might fixed budgets help a manufacturer in the fast-changing computer software sector? [16 marks]

Q2 a) Explain the benefits that setting a budget will have for a new business. [6 marks]
b) Analyse the problems that a new business might have in setting budgets for the first time. [9 marks]

I set myself a word budget today and I'm just about to run out...

Budgets are multi-purpose — they help businesses forecast their future spending and they can help to motivate people. Make sure you know how they're constructed and how to explain their benefits and drawbacks.

Analysing Budgets

Budgets are often reviewed using variance analysis. Variance is the difference between actual and budgeted spend. Understanding variances helps managers make decisions and fix problems, and it'll help you sail through your exams.

Variance is the Difference between Actual figures and Budgeted figures

1) A variance means the business is performing either **worse** or **better** than expected.
2) A **favourable variance** leads to **increased profit**. If revenue's more than the budget says it's going to be, that's a favourable variance. If costs are below the cost predictions in the budget, that's a favourable variance.
3) An **adverse variance** is a difference that **reduces profits**. **Selling fewer items** than the income budget predicts or **spending more** on an advert than the expenditure budget for marketing allows is an adverse variance.
4) If £10 000 is spent on raw materials in a month when the budget was only £6000, the variance is £6000 – £10 000 = –£4000, so there is a £4000 **adverse variance**.
5) Variances **add up**. For example, if actual sales exceed budgeted sales by £3000 and expenditure on raw materials is £2000 below budget, the variance is £3000 + £2000 = £5000, so there's a combined **favourable variance** of £5000. This is called **cumulative variance**.
6) Variances can be calculated for each budget each month, for each budget as a running total, and for groups of budgets as a monthly or running total variance:

(A) means an adverse variance.
(F) means a favourable variance.

	Jan Budget	Jan Actual	Jan Variance	Feb Budget	Feb Actual	Feb Variance	Cumulative Variance
Revenue	£100k	£90k	£10k (A)	£110k	£110k	£0	£10k (A)
Wages	£40k	£30k	£10k (F)	£40k	£41k	£1k (A)	£9k (F)
Rent	£10k	£10k	£0	£10k	£11k	£1k (A)	£1k (A)
Other costs	£5k	£6k	£1k (A)	£5k	£6k	£1k (A)	£2k (A)
Total costs	£55k	£46k	£9k (F)	£55k	£58k	£3k (A)	£6k (F)

Variances can be Bad — even if they say you're doing Better than Expected

1) When variances occur, it means that what has happened is **not** what the business was expecting. Businesses need to **know** about variances so that they can find out **why** they have occurred.
2) It's extremely important to spot **adverse** variances as **soon** as possible. It's important to find out which budget holder is responsible — and to take action to fix the problem.
3) It's **also** important to **investigate favourable variances**. Favourable variances may mean that the budget targets weren't **stretching** enough — so the business needs to set more **difficult targets**. The business also needs to understand **why** the performance is better than expected — if one department is **doing something right**, the business can **spread** this throughout the organisation.

Variances are caused by several factors, both Internal and External

External Factors Cause Variance

1) **Competitor behaviour** and changing **fashions** may increase or reduce **demand** for products.
2) Changes in the **economy** can change how much workers' wages cost the business.
3) The cost of **raw materials** can go up — e.g. if a harvest fails.

Internal Factors Cause Variance

1) Improving **efficiency** (e.g. by introducing automated production equipment) causes **favourable** variances.
2) A business might **overestimate** the amount of money it can save by streamlining its production methods.
3) A business might **underestimate** the **cost** of making a change to its organisation.
4) Changing the **selling price** changes sales revenue — this creates variance if it happens after the budget's set.
5) Internal causes of variance are a **big concern**. They suggest that internal **communication** needs improving.

Analysing Budgets

Variance Analysis means Identifying and Explaining variances

1) Variance analysis means **spotting** variances and figuring out **why** they've happened, so that action can be taken to fix them.
2) **Small** variances aren't a big problem. They can actually help to **motivate** employees. Staff try to **catch up** and sort out small **adverse** variances themselves. Small **favourable** variances can motivate staff to **keep on** doing whatever they were doing to create a favourable variance.
3) **Large** variances can **demotivate**. Staff don't work hard if there are large favourable variances — they **don't see the need**. Staff can get demotivated by a large **adverse** variance — they may feel that the task is **impossible**, or that they've **already failed**.

Businesses have to React to variances

When variances occur, businesses need to act on them. They can either change what the **business** is doing to make it fit the budget, or change the **budget** to make it fit what the **business** is doing. There are three factors that they need to take into account to make this decision:

1) Businesses need to **beware** of chopping and changing the budget **too much**.
2) Changing the budget **removes certainty** — which removes one of the big benefits of budgets.
3) Altering budgets can also make them **less motivating** — when staff start to expect that management will change targets instead of doing something to change performance, they don't see the point in trying any more.

Decisions based on Adverse Variances

1) They can change the **marketing mix**. **Cutting prices** will increase sales — but only if the demand is price elastic (see p.36). **Updating** the product might make it more attractive to customers. Businesses can also look for a **new market** for the product, or change the **promotional strategy** — e.g. by advertising the product more or doing point of sales promotion.
2) **Streamlining production** makes the business more **efficient**, so this reduces costs.
3) They can try to motivate **employees** to **work harder**.
4) Businesses can try to cut costs by asking their **suppliers** for a **better deal**.
5) Businesses may need to do additional **market research** to improve their forecasts in the future.

Decisions based on Favourable Variances

1) If the favourable variance is caused by a **pessimistic** budget, they can set more **ambitious targets** next time.
2) If the variance is because of **increased productivity** in one part of the business, they can try to get everyone else doing whatever was **responsible** for the improvement, and set higher targets in the next budget.
3) A favourable variance could indicate more **sales** than predicted, so a business may need to increase the **production** of a product or take on additional staff to meet demand.

Practice Questions

Q1 Define variance.

Q2 If a business sets an expenditure budget of £15 000 for marketing and the actual expenditure for marketing is £18 000, how much is the variance and what type of variance is it?

Q3 Why are variances a concern for businesses?

Q4 How do businesses deal with variances?

Answers on p.200.

Exam Question

Q1 a) Using the figures in the table on p.76, calculate monthly and cumulative variances for March. Assume all budgets remain the same as February, and that actual sales are £120k, wages are £39k, rent is £11k and other costs are £5k. [10 marks]

b) Explain what your answer to a) suggests about the budget planning process for this company. [6 marks]

Variance is one of those words that looks odd if you stare at it enough...

Variance variance variance... ahem... anyway. As well as knowing what businesses do when they set a budget, you need to know what they do when the real-life results don't quite match up to what the budget says. They don't panic and run about shouting "beeble beeble" in the car park. They just sort it out so it doesn't happen next time.

Break-Even Analysis

Break-even analysis is a great way of working out how much you need to sell to make a profit.

Breaking Even means Covering your Costs

1) The **break-even output** is the level of sales a business needs to **cover its costs**. At the break-even point, costs = revenue.
2) When sales are **below** the break-even output, costs are more than revenue — the business makes a **loss**. When sales are **above** the break-even output, revenue exceeds costs — the business makes a **profit**.
3) **New businesses** should always do a **break-even analysis** to **find** the break-even output. It tells them how much they will need to sell to break even. Banks and venture capitalists thinking of **loaning** money to the business will need to **see** a break-even analysis as part of the **business plan**. This helps them to decide whether to lend money to the business.
4) **Established businesses** preparing to launch **new products** use break-even analysis to work out how much **profit** they are likely to make, and also to predict the impact of the new activity on **cash flow** (see p.72-73).

Contribution is used to work out the Break-Even Output

1) **Contribution** is the difference between the **selling price** of a product and the **variable costs** it takes to produce it.

Contribution per unit = selling price per unit – variable costs per unit

See p.6 for more on fixed and variable costs.

2) The **total contribution** is worked out using one of the two formulas below:

Total contribution = total revenue – total variable costs OR **contribution per unit × number of units sold**

3) Contribution is used to **pay fixed costs**. The amount left over is profit.
4) **The break-even output** is where **contribution = fixed costs**. You calculate it using this formula:

$$\text{Break-even output} = \frac{\text{fixed costs}}{\text{contribution per unit}}$$

Example: Harry sets up a business to print T-shirts. The **fixed costs** of premises and the T-shirt printers are **£3000**. The **variable costs** per T-shirt (the T-shirt, ink, wages) are **£5**. Each printed T-shirt sells for **£25**.

Contribution per unit = £25 – £5 = **£20**

Break-even output = £3000 ÷ £20 = **150**

So, Harry has to sell **150** T-shirts to **break even**.

Draw a Break-Even Chart to show the Break-Even Output

1) Break-even charts show **costs** and **revenue** plotted against **output**. Businesses use break-even charts to see how costs and revenue **vary** with different levels of output.
2) **Output** goes on the **horizontal axis**. The scale needs to let you plot output from 0 to the maximum possible.
3) **Costs and revenue** both go on the vertical axis. Use a scale that lets you plot from 0 to the maximum revenue.
4) Plot **fixed** costs. (On the diagram on the right, fixed costs are the blue horizontal line.) **Add** variable costs to fixed costs to get the **total costs**, and plot them on the graph. (The total costs are shown by the purple line, starting at the same point as the fixed costs line.)
5) Next, plot **revenue** (selling price × number of units) on the graph. (It's the green line on the diagram.)
6) The **break-even output** is where the **revenue** line crosses the **total costs** line. On the diagram it's 150 units.

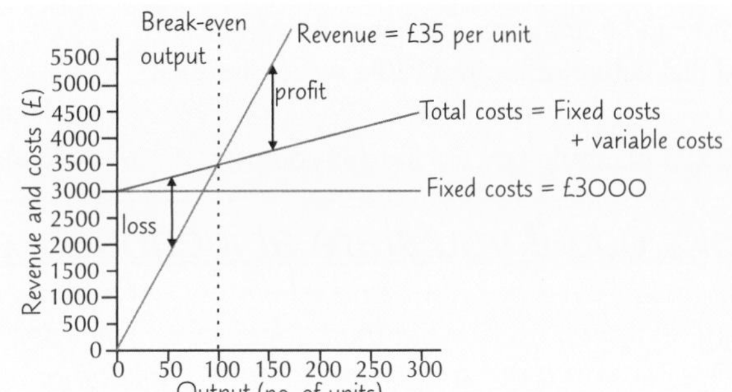

Changing either the variable costs or the price of the products will affect the break-even output.

This graph shows that if Harry increased the price of the T-shirts to £35 each, his break-even output would be lowered to 100 units.

When prices increase, the revenue line gets steeper, so the break-even output is lowered — if you charge more, you don't need to sell as many to break even.

Break-Even Analysis

The **Margin of Safety** is the amount between **Actual Output** and **Break Even**

Margin of safety = actual output – break-even output

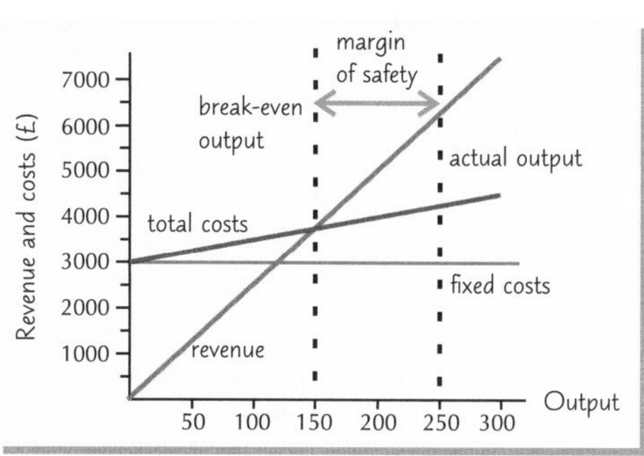

1) The diagram on the right shows the margin of safety for Harry's T-shirt business when his output is 250 T-shirts. If Harry sells **250** T-shirts, the **margin of safety** is 250 – 150 = **100**. He could sell up to 100 fewer T-shirts before he started losing money.
2) If his output changed to **300** T-shirts, the margin of safety would go up to 300 – 150 = **150**.
3) Knowing the break-even output and margin of safety allows businesses to make **important decisions** — if Harry's calculations show that his T-shirt business has a low margin of safety, he can take action to increase it by either **lowering his costs** or **increasing his revenue**.
4) This would **lower** his break-even output, so he'd have a **greater** margin of safety. A big margin of safety is useful for a business because it means less risk.

Break-Even Analysis has **Advantages** and **Disadvantages**

Advantages of break-even analysis	Disadvantages of break-even analysis
It's **easy** to do. If you can plot figures on a graph accurately, you can do break-even analysis.	Break-even analysis assumes that **variable costs** always rise steadily. This isn't always the case — a business can get **discounts** for buying in bulk so costs don't go up in **direct proportion** to output.
It's **quick** — managers can see the **break-even output** and **margin of safety** immediately so they can take **quick action** to cut costs or increase sales if they need to **increase** their margin of safety.	Break-even analysis is simple for a **single product** — but most businesses sell lots of different products, so looking at the business as a whole can get a lot more complicated.
Break-even charts let businesses **forecast** how variations in sales will affect **costs**, **revenue** and **profits** and, most importantly, how variations in **price** and **costs** will affect how **much** they **need** to **sell**.	If the **data** is wrong, then the **results** will be wrong.
Businesses can use break-even analysis to help **persuade** the bank to give them a **loan**.	Break-even analysis assumes the business sells **all the products**, without any wastage. But, for example, a restaurant business will end up throwing away food if fewer customers turn up than they're expecting.
Break-even analysis influences decisions on whether **new products** are launched or not — if the business would need to sell an unrealistic volume of products to break even, they would probably decide **not** to launch the product.	Break-even analysis only tells you how many units you **need** to sell to break even. It doesn't tell you how many you're **actually going to sell**.

Practice Questions

Q1 Write down the formulas for contribution per unit, total contribution and break-even output.

Q2 Write down two advantages and two disadvantages of break-even analysis.

Exam Questions

Q1 Bob is deciding whether to set up a business selling fishing equipment. Evaluate the value of break-even analysis in helping Bob decide whether or not to go ahead with the business. [12 marks]

Q2 Muneer Khan has a small restaurant. The average price per customer per meal is £13. The variable costs of materials and labour per meal are £5. The fixed costs of the restaurant are £1000 per month. Calculate the break-even number of customers per month. [4 marks]

Answer on p.201.

Ah, give us a break...

You might be asked to calculate the break-even output or draw it on a graph, so make sure you can do both. Make sure you can give examples of how break-even analysis is used by businesses to make decisions and plans, and learn some advantages and disadvantages of break-even analysis. Then give yourself a pat on the back. Yippee...

Choosing Sources of Finance

There are loads of different sources of finance for businesses, each with advantages and disadvantages. A business must choose carefully depending on what they need the money for and what's available to them.

All Businesses Need a **Source** of **Finance**

1) Businesses need finance to buy **fixed assets**, like factories, offices and machinery. Finance is also needed to pay **day-to-day costs**, like wages and bills, so that the business can survive.
2) Sources of finance can be **internal** or **external**. Internal finance is money from **within** the business, e.g. profit. External finance comes from sources **outside** the business, like bank loans or shareholder investments.
3) A business may require **short-term** finance to pay its suppliers or cover **temporary** shortages of cash. Short-term finance is usually repaid within **1 year**.
4) **Long-term** finance is needed for long-term investment. It can take a while for a business to benefit financially from investments like new machinery, so repayments of long-term finance are due over a **longer period**, usually 3 years or more.
5) When **choosing** a source of finance, a business must consider various things, including:

- **The legal structure of the business** — limited companies can sell shares, but this isn't an option for sole traders.
- **The amount of money required** — the larger the amount, the less likely it is that internal finance can be raised.
- **The level of risk involved** — a risky business is less likely to find a loan, although venture capital is an option.
- **If short-term or long-term finance is needed** — it depends on how long it will take the business to repay it.

Internal Finance comes from *Within* the business

Internal finance can be raised by putting **profits** back into the business, or **selling assets**.

Retained profit

1) **Profit** can be retained and built up over the years for **later investment**. This can work in the **short and long term**.
2) The main **benefit** of using profit for investment is that the business doesn't have to pay **interest** on the money. **Not all businesses** can use this method though — they might not be making enough **profit**.
3) **Shareholders** may object to this method as they may wish to receive the profits as **dividends**. Also, retaining profits may cause the business to **miss out** on investment opportunities.

Rationalisation

1) **Rationalisation** is when managers **reorganise** the business to make it more efficient. They can do this by **selling** some of their **assets** (e.g. factories, machinery, etc) to generate capital, then leasing them back when required.
2) Businesses don't need to pay **interest** on finance they raise by selling their assets.
3) The main **drawback** to selling assets is that the business **no longer owns** the asset. And leasing the asset back introduces another cost to the business. Also, assets like cars and computers **lose value** over time, so the business won't get back as much as it paid for them.

Some *External Sources* are suitable as *Short-Term Finance*

Overdrafts

1) **Overdrafts** are where a bank lets a business have a **negative** amount of money in its bank account.
2) Overdrafts are **easy to arrange** and **flexible** — businesses can borrow as **little** or as **much** as they need (up to the overdraft limit) and they only pay **interest** on the amount of the overdraft they actually use.
3) The main **disadvantage** of overdrafts is that banks charge **high rates** of **interest** on them. There may also be a **fixed charge** for using an overdraft. So they're **unsuitable** for using in the **long term**.

Debt factoring

1) **Debt factoring** is when banks and other financial institutions take **unpaid invoices** off the hands of the business, and give them an instant **cash** payment (of less than 100% of the value of the invoice).
2) The **advantage** of this for businesses is that they can **instantly** get money they are owed.
3) The **disadvantage** of debt factoring is that the debt factoring company **keeps** some of the money owed as a **fee**.

Choosing Sources of Finance

*Businesses can take out **Loans** to finance their projects in the **Long-Term***

1) Bank loans are an **external** source of finance. Businesses can borrow a fixed amount of **money** and pay it back over a fixed period of **time** with **interest** — the amount they have to pay back depends on the interest rate and the length of time the loan is for.
2) Banks need **security** for a loan, usually in the form of property.
3) Loans are a good **long-term** source of finance for a **start-up** business and for paying for **assets** like machinery and computers. They are **not** a good way to cover the **day-to-day** running costs of the business.

Advantages of bank loans

1) You're **guaranteed** the money for the duration of the loan (the bank can't suddenly demand it back).
2) You only have to pay back the **loan** and **interest** — the bank won't **own** any of your business and you don't have to give them a share of the **profits**.
3) The interest charges for a loan are usually **lower** than for an overdraft.

Disadvantages of bank loans

1) They can be **difficult** to arrange because a bank will only lend a business money if they think they are going to get it back. If the business doesn't own any property or other assets that can be used for security, they might not be able to get a loan.
2) Keeping up with the **repayments** can be difficult if cash isn't coming into the business quickly enough. The business might **lose** whatever the loan is secured on (e.g. their home) — the bank can sell it to get their money back.
3) The business might have to pay a **charge** if they decide to pay the loan back **early**.

Share Capital** is an **External Source of Finance** for **Limited Companies

1) **Private and public limited companies** can be financed in the **long-term** using **ordinary share capital** — money raised by selling **shares** in the business (see p.10).
2) Using share capital to finance a business has its **advantages**. E.g. the money **doesn't** need to be **repaid** (unlike a loan) and new shareholders can bring additional expertise into a business.
3) The **drawback** of selling shares is that the original owner(s) no longer **owns** all of the business — they may have to pay the shareholders a **dividend** (depending on profit) and also give them a **say** in how the business is run.

Venture Capital** and **Crowdfunding** are Other Sources of **External Finance

1) **Venture capital** is funding in the form of share or loan capital that is invested in a business that is thought to be high risk. **Venture capitalists** are professional investors who invest in businesses they think have the potential to be successful. They may also provide **business advice**, but applying for funding is a **long** process.
2) **Crowdfunding** is a method of financing a business or project using contributions made by a **large number of people**, usually done via the **internet** through organisations such as Kickstarter and Crowdcube. Contributors can give donations, loans or buy shares, depending on the business.
3) **Rewards** are sometimes offered for donations, such as early access to a product, or the product at a discounted price upon release. These can **reduce profits** if not controlled carefully. The crowdfunding organisations often take a small portion of the finance raised too, meaning not all of it reaches the crowdfunded business.

The Caterham Formula 1 team used crowdfunding in November 2014 to raise money to enter the team in the Abu Dhabi Grand Prix after going into administration.

Practice Questions

Q1 What is internal finance?

Q2 What is the difference between an overdraft and a loan?

Q3 What is meant by the term venture capital?

Exam Questions

Q1 To what extent is the choice of the source of finance important to the success of a business? [25 marks]

Q2 Discuss the advantages and disadvantages of financing a new business using a bank loan. [9 marks]

"Doctor, I've swallowed my wallet" — a classic example of internal finance...

Sources of finance might not be the most exciting topic in the world, but it's really important for businesses. Nearly all businesses set out to make a profit, and if they can't get enough money to pay for day-to-day survival, they won't last very long at all. Make sure you're clear on all the different ways that businesses can raise internal and external finance.

Human Resource Objectives

These pages are all about managing "human resources" — otherwise known as people.

Human Resource Management is about **Managing People**

1) The purpose of Human Resource Management (HRM) is to ensure that a business achieves the **maximum benefit** from its employees at the **minimum cost**. The human resources (HR) department needs to make sure that the business has the right **number of employees** with the right **skills**, **qualifications** and **qualities**.
2) Human Resource (HR) objectives are influenced by the objectives of the business **as a whole**. E.g. if the business is going to expand into a new market, the HR department might need to **recruit new staff** to suit the business needs.
3) They also work closely with **other departments**. These departments help HR to anticipate **workforce needs** and react to them — by **recruiting** new staff or **providing training**. HR needs to work with the finance department to determine a **suitable budget** for the department.
4) HR also decides how to treat staff — how to **use their skills**, how to **keep** them working for the company, how to **train** and **reward** them, and eventually how to **terminate** their employment.

Objectives help **HR** to **Manage People Effectively**

HR objectives help HR to manage staff successfully. Objectives for the HR department might include:

1 — Matching the Workforce to Business Needs

- HR needs to anticipate the **future size** of the workforce — if the organisation is **expanding** they'll need more workers, if it's **contracting** they won't need as many.
- They decide what **skill-level** the workforce **needs**, and whether staff should be employed **full-** or **part-time**. If the requirements of the business change, HR can decide whether to **train** current staff or **recruit** new workers from **outside** the business.
- They also work with other managers to decide **where** employees are needed if a business has several sites or branches, and **which departments** within a business require specific staff.
- HR also needs to think about **diversity** in all positions of the business, from **floor staff** to **directors**. A workforce that is diverse in **age**, **gender** and **race** will have a wide variety of skills, ideas and experiences.
- HR has a **budget** like all other departments. They have to make sure that staff wages are **appropriate** to the job and employee. They focus on getting the **right balance** between staying within the budget and having the **correct number** of staff, the right amount of **training** and **rewarding** more skilled/senior positions.

2 — Helping Employees Reach their Full Potential

- HR invests in **training** so workers can improve their **productivity**. They also make sure that employees have the right **equipment** to do their job properly.
- HR makes sure there are opportunities for **career progression**. Employees work better and are more **engaged** if they have **something to aim for**, like a **promotion** or taking on extra responsibility at work.
- In certain businesses, HR needs to make sure they focus on the **most talented** employees reaching their **full potential**. This can be achieved through extra **training** and '**fast-tracking**' schemes.
- They need to match **workforce skill-levels** to jobs. If a job is too **challenging** for an employee, this can lead to **demotivation** and **low self-esteem**. If the work is too easy, employees become **bored**.
- Effective **management**, good staff **organisation** and a pleasant **working environment** help to improve **morale** — happy employees are more likely to work to their full potential.

3 — Supporting Employee/Employer Relations

- Employee/employer relations are based upon **good communication**. HR **listens** and **reacts** to employee concerns. They can **advise** managers how to deal with problems in their departments.
- Employees who are given **responsibility** and are **involved** in decision-making feel **valued** and **trusted**.
- Improving the **relationship** between **employees** and **management** can reduce **absenteeism** and **labour turnover**. If employees feel **engaged**, they're more likely to be **loyal** to the business.
- **Breakdown in relations** can lead to **decreased productivity**, **low morale** and even **strike** action.
- Employee/employer relationships work best when the **values** of the employee **align** with the values of the employer. The employee should always bear in mind the values of the employer when making **decisions**.

Human Resource Objectives

Internal and *External Factors* influence *HR Objectives*

Internal factors

1) The **culture** within the business influences **HR objectives**. E.g. some businesses, like fast food restaurants, might not be worried about having a high labour turnover, so they wouldn't want HR to spend time and money trying to reduce it.
2) Other **departments** within the business influence HR. They give HR the information that they need to **predict** workforce needs.
3) The amount of **funding** available within the business.

External factors

1) The general state of the **economy** (boom or recession) will affect HR activities such as **recruitment** and **training**.
2) All UK businesses are subject to **UK** and **EU employment laws**. HR might have to change their objectives to fit in with **new legislation**.
3) Current **ethical** and **environmental** issues can influence HR objectives, e.g. the condemning of **zero-hours contracts**.
4) Improvements in **technology** might mean HR **recruit** people who can use a certain type of software or machine.

HRM Approaches can be *Hard* or *Soft*

There are **two schools of thought** in human resource management — **hard HRM** and **soft HRM**.

Hard HRM

1) Employees are seen as a **resource** like any other.
2) Employees are hired on a **short-term basis**.
3) Managers believe that employees are mainly motivated by **money** and think they will do as **little** work as possible.
4) Appraisals are **judgemental**.
5) Training is only done to meet **production** needs.

Soft HRM

1) Employees are the **most important** resource.
2) Employees are managed on a **long-term basis**.
3) Managers motivate employees through **empowerment** and **development** and think that working is **natural** for employees.
4) Appraisals are **developmental**.
5) Training is done to meet **development** needs.

1) **Hard HRM** can **benefit** a businesses because managers keep **control** of the workforce, so people are less likely to make **mistakes**. Since employees are seen as just another resource, it's easy for the business to **replace** them.
2) Businesses adopting hard HRM **don't** use employees to their **full potential**, so could be **missing out** on chances to increase **profits**. Hard HRM can also be **demotivational** for the workforce. Boring, repetitive jobs can make employees feel **undervalued**. They're unlikely to be loyal to their organisation, leading to **high staff turnover**.
3) **Soft HRM** is likely to increase **staff morale** because employees will feel **valued**. This will make it easier to **retain** staff, and the business will also benefit from the **skills** and **experience** of its staff. It encourages **commitment** and **good performance** from its workers, because they feel loyalty towards the organisation.
4) Soft HRM **isn't** always **appropriate** though — employees might not be interested in **development** or **empowerment**, and soft HRM usually involves more **costs** for businesses because it encourages **investment** in employees. The extra training is also **time-consuming**. There's also a risk that employees who have completed all the training might want to **leave** for a better job.

Practice Questions

Q1 Why is it important to have a diverse workforce?

Q2 How can the HR department help employees reach their full potential?

Q3 What are the external factors that influence HR objectives?

Q4 Why is it important for HR and other departments to work together?

Exam Question

Q1 Explain the difference between hard and soft HRM and analyse the costs and benefits of each. [12 marks]

Soft HRM is always practised in pillow factories...

HRM sounds quite tricky — you've got to make sure you've got the right number of staff who have the right skills and qualifications, then try to stop too many of them from leaving, and try to get them to turn up for work and leave at the end of the day in one piece. Phew. It's definitely a bit easier to learn about it than it is to actually do it...

Interpreting Human Resource Data

A business needs to measure the effectiveness of every resource used, and that includes its employees. People don't always like the idea of having their performance measured, but it's good for the business.

Human Resource Data** is **Analysed** before making **Decisions

1) There are many **figures** that HR consider when making decisions — these include **labour productivity**, **labour turnover**, **absenteeism**, **labour retention**, etc.
2) These figures are often calculated using a **performance management system** and are used to check that the business's human resources are always being used to **maximum efficiency**.
3) HR use this data to **make plans** for the human resource flow in the future (see p.88).
4) They will also compare these figures to their **competitors'** to see who is utilising their **human resources** better and if they need to **improve** in certain areas. E.g. if **labour retention** rates are **higher** in a competitor's business, HR need to look at why employees **don't want to stay** at their company.

***Labour Productivity** affects HR decisions*

HR needs to look at **trends** in **labour productivity** figures before making decisions on **training**, **recruitment** and **pay**.

$$\text{Labour Productivity} = \frac{\text{Output per period}}{\text{Number of employees}}$$

See p.58 for more on labour productivity.

1) HR can have a **positive impact** on labour productivity by employing a **diverse** workforce and making sure that all employees feel **engaged** and **motivated**. They can also make sure the right people are in the **right roles**. Doing these things will also **reduce levels of absenteeism** which will **increase productivity** even more.
2) If labour productivity is **increasing**, HR might choose to reward employees with **bonuses** and **increased salaries**. This will keep levels of **motivation** high and workers know their hard work is **valued**.
3) If labour productivity is **decreasing** then HR might choose to **retrain** staff, offer bigger **incentives** or, in extreme cases, offer **redundancies** and **replace** employees with more skilled labour.
4) HR will **compare** their labour productivity data to their **competitors'** and see if they need to **improve**, or if they are already ahead of the game. If productivity is **low** compared to competitors, they might need to look at how competitors are **managing** their **human resources** — this information is often **tricky** to get hold of.

HR Decisions** are affected by lots of **Different Performance Statistics

1) Two other important statistics that will affect HR decisions are **labour cost per unit** and **employee costs as a percentage of turnover**. They can be calculated using the following formulas:

$$\text{Labour cost per unit} = \frac{\text{Labour costs}}{\text{Units of output}}$$

$$\text{Employee costs as a \% of turnover} = \frac{\text{Employee costs}}{\text{Sales turnover}} \times 100$$

Unless you're told otherwise, assume labour costs are equal to employee costs.

Example: A bread manufacturer has labour costs of £500 000 per year.
They produce 2 000 000 loaves each year and have a turnover of £1 600 000.
Labour cost per unit = £500 000 ÷ 2 000 000 = £0.25 = **25p**
Employee costs as a percentage of turnover = £500 000 ÷ £1 600 000 × 100 = **31.25%**

2) Labour cost per unit shows **how much money** the business has to **pay employees** to make **one unit of output**.
3) Labour cost per unit can be reduced in two ways — by **reducing labour costs** or **increasing labour productivity**.
4) Employee costs as a percentage of turnover show what **percentage** of the money made is spent on **employees** — this is particularly useful when comparing **different-sized** businesses that make **similar** products.
5) **Controlling** employee costs is a main objective of the HR department — this could mean **increasing** or **decreasing** them. E.g. if they **recruit** more employees, employee costs will **increase** but they will look at labour cost per unit or employee costs as a % of turnover to see the **impact** the recruitment had on the business.
6) Employee costs can be decreased by **reducing wages** and **benefits** — HR will try to avoid this if possible as it could result in a **demotivated workforce** which could actually make the problem **worse**.
7) HR also needs to think about the **ethics** of the business when making decisions — it might be more important that staff are **treated well** and feel **valued** even though it will cost a bit more.

Interpreting Human Resource Data

Labour Turnover measures the Proportion of Staff who Leave each year

$$\text{Labour Turnover (\%)} = \frac{\text{Number of staff leaving}}{\text{Average number of staff employed}} \times 100$$

Average number of staff employed = (staff at the beginning of the time period + staff at the end of the time period) ÷ 2.

1) The **higher** the figure, the **larger** the proportion of workers **leaving** the firm each year.
2) **External causes** of high labour turnover include changes in regional **unemployment** levels, and the growth of other local firms using staff with **similar skills**.
3) **Internal causes** of high labour turnover include **poor motivation** of staff, **low wages**, and a lack of opportunities for **promotion**. Staff will **join other firms** to increase their pay and job responsibilities.
4) A **poor recruitment** process which selects incompetent candidates will also increase labour turnover.
5) Increased **delegation**, **job enrichment**, higher **wages** and better **training** can reduce employee turnover.
6) Businesses need **some** labour turnover to bring new ideas in. Labour turnover of 0% means no one **ever** leaves.

Benefits of high staff turnover	Disadvantages of high staff turnover
Constant stream of **new ideas** through new staff.	Lack of **loyal** and **experienced** staff who know the business.
Firm can recruit staff who've **already been trained** by competitors — saves money.	Firm **loses** staff it has **trained**, often to direct competitors.
If sales fall, firm can reduce workforce through **natural wastage** rather than costly redundancy.	**Training costs money** and **productivity drops** while new staff get trained.
Enthusiasm of new staff influences other workers.	**Recruitment** costs are high.

Labour Retention measures a Company's Ability to keep its Employees

$$\text{Labour Retention (\%)} = \frac{\text{Number of staff employed at end of period} - \text{Number of leavers}}{\text{Number of staff employed at end of period}} \times 100$$

1) **Labour retention** is closely related to **labour turnover**. The **higher** the turnover, the **lower** the retention rate.
2) A **low retention rate** means that the company only keeps a **small proportion** of its employees.
3) HR could deal with a **low retention rate** by improving the **induction** process. They could highlight the **opportunities** available to all employees and reinforce the **values** and **goals** of the business so that employees feel **included** and **valued**.

Practice Questions

Q1 Give three ways in which the HR department can help to increase labour productivity.

Q2 A firm produces 50 units per day and its labour cost per unit is £100. What are the firm's daily labour costs?

Q3 State two benefits and two drawbacks of a high labour turnover.

Q4 In 2014, 18 people left a firm which employs an average of 600 staff. Calculate the firm's labour turnover.

Answers on p.201.

Exam Questions

Q1 In 2005 the employee costs as a percentage of turnover of a business was 10%. By 2015 it had risen to 20%. Analyse why this could have happened and suggest ways the HR department could help to decrease it. [9 marks]

Q2 Last year a publishing company had a labour retention rate of 70%. Analyse how the human resource department could help to increase its labour retention. [9 marks]

Hopefully your information retention is at 100%...

All these formulas are quite easy really. Problem is, the numbers alone don't really tell you anything. You need to be able to interpret the figures and apply them to different businesses. E.g. high labour turnover isn't ideal at an aeroplane manufacturer but is totally acceptable at a fast-food restaurant. Now, do you want to go large for an extra £1?

Improving Organisational Design

Hurray, two pages on improving organisational design. It must be your lucky day.

Organisational Design shows Structure and Hierarchy

1) The traditional business structure is a series of levels, where each level has responsibility for, and **authority** over, the levels below. This is called a **hierarchy**, and can be shown on an organisational chart.
2) An **organisational chart** sets out who has **authority** and **responsibility** to make decisions.
3) It shows who individual employees are **accountable** to (who is directly **above** them in the hierarchy) and who employees are **responsible** for (who is directly **below** them in the hierarchy).
4) The chart also shows how the organisation is divided up, e.g. by **department**, by **product** or by **location**.

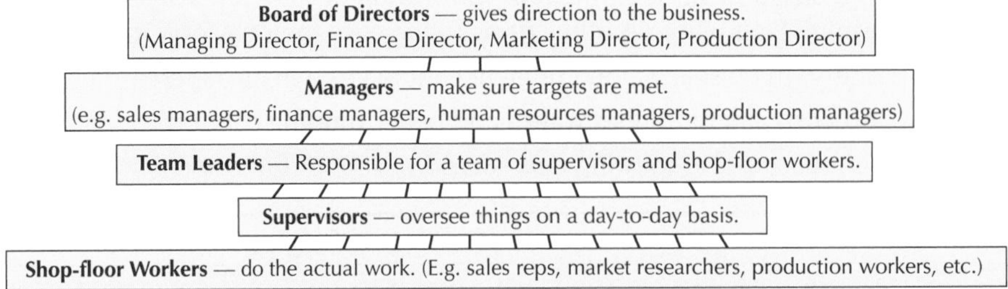

Structures can be Tall or Flat and have wide or narrow Spans of Control

1) Organisations with **lots of levels** in their hierarchy are called "**tall**". Tall structures have long **chains of command**. The chain of command is the path of **communication** and **authority** up and down the hierarchy.
2) Tall structures can affect **communication**. Messages take a **long time** to get from the top to the bottom, or vice-versa. **Decisions** take a long time to make, and there's a lot of **paperwork** to deal with.
3) "**Flat**" organisations only have a few levels in their hierarchy. People are given more **responsibility** and **freedom**.
4) Flat structures can lead to managers getting **overwhelmed** by too many people reporting to them. The **span of control** is the **number of people** who report directly to a manager. Managers in **flat** structures have **wide** spans of control. This means they have a lot of workers answering to them.
5) If the span of control is **too wide**, managers find it hard to manage **effectively**.
6) Managers in tall structures have **narrow** spans of control — they aren't responsible for many people. This allows them to **monitor** the people below them **more closely**.
7) If the span of control is **too narrow**, workers can become **demotivated** — they may feel that they're being **micromanaged** by interfering bosses.
8) It can be hard for a manager to keep a close eye on workers if the span of control is bigger than about 6 people. But if the workers are all doing the **same routine task**, they don't need as much supervision — so a span of control of 10-12 people (or more) is fine.

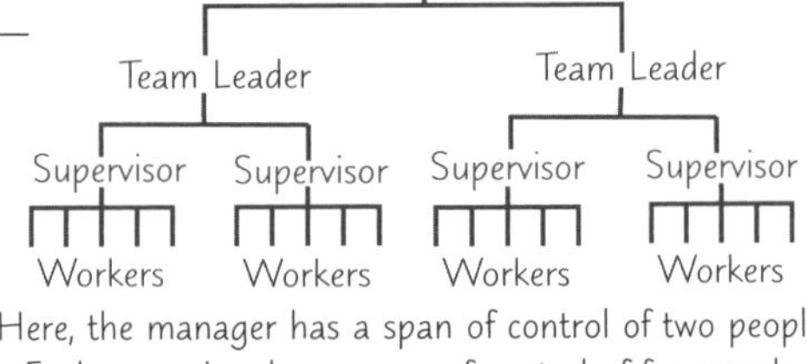

Here, the manager has a span of control of two people. Each supervisor has a span of control of five people.

Organisational design can be improved through delayering

- Delayering means **removing** parts of the hierarchy — it creates a **flatter** structure with **wider** spans of control.
- Delayering can help to **lower costs**. Cutting management jobs can save a lot of money in salaries. It gives junior employees **enhanced roles** with more responsibility and can improve **communication**.
- It can **cost businesses money** in the short term as the remaining staff need to be **retrained** in their new roles. If you **overdo** it, managers can end up **stressed** and overworked with **huge** spans of control.

For more details on delayering, see p.170.

Delegation relies on Trust Between the Two Parties

1) Giving responsibility for decision-making to people below you is called **delegation**.
2) The manager needs to **trust** the people they are **delegating** responsibility to. The best managers know the **strengths** and **weaknesses** of the people below them and delegate the right work to the right people.
3) The person being delegated to needs to **trust** that their manager isn't just passing on the work they don't like doing themselves. They should be given **challenging tasks** (to help them develop) as well as **routine tasks**.
4) The amount of delegation is heavily influenced by the **nature** and **culture** of the business — e.g. if the business wants its employees to be loyal and feel valued, it will delegate lots of responsibilities. A business that **delegates** a lot of responsibilities will need to have **many** levels of authority.

Improving Organisational Design

Centralised Structures keep Authority for decisions at the Top

In **centralised** organisations, all decisions are made by **senior managers** at the **top** of the business.

Advantages of centralisation

1) Business leaders have lots of **experience** of making business decisions.
2) Managers get an **overview** of the whole business, so decisions are **consistent** throughout the business.
3) Senior managers **aren't biased** towards one department so they can make the best decisions for the business as a whole.
4) Senior managers can make big decisions **quickly** because they don't have to **consult** anybody else.

Disadvantages of centralisation

1) Not many people are **expert** enough to make decisions about all aspects of the business.
2) **Excluding employees** from decision-making can be **demotivating**.
3) The organisation **reacts slowly** to change, allowing its **competitors** to get ahead. This is because the senior managers who make the decisions don't spend time on the shop floor, so they're slow to notice **consumer trends**.

Decentralised Structures share out the Authority to make decisions

1) Decentralisation **shares out authority** to more **junior** employees.
2) **National** and **multinational** firms **decentralise** decision-making, and **delegate** power to **regional** managers.
3) Managers have to make sure that the **work** of **all** a company's **employees** is **contributing** to the **goals** of the **business**. This can be **difficult** to achieve when a lot of **power** has been **delegated**.

Advantages of decentralisation

1) Involvement in decision-making **motivates employees.**
2) Employees can use **expert knowledge** of their sector.
3) Day-to-day decisions can be made **quickly** without having to ask senior managers.

Disadvantages of decentralisation

1) Junior employees may not have enough **experience** to make decisions.
2) **Inconsistencies** may develop between **divisions** in a business.
3) Junior employees may not be able to see the **overall situation** and needs of an organisation.

The **size**, **nature**, **objectives** and **culture** of a business will all affect whether a centralised or decentralised approach is used — this will then have an impact on the **structure** of the business.

- Businesses might centralise in order to save money in a more competitive market. A **centralised** approach can result in a flat and wide structure as levels of middle management are no longer needed.
- Businesses might **decentralise** as they are **expanding** and operating from a number of different locations. A **decentralised** approach will create more levels of authority and increase the amount of **delegation.**

Practice Questions

Q1 What are the disadvantages of a tall organisational structure?

Q2 Why might a flat structure be popular with junior employees in a business?

Q3 What is meant by "span of control"?

Q4 What's the difference between centralised and decentralised structures?

Exam Questions

Q1 A management consultant has advised Doug McLeod to alter the structure of his business by delayering.

a) Complete this sentence. Delayering will make the structure of Doug McLeod's business...

A Taller and wider B Flatter and narrower C Taller and narrower D Flatter and wider [1 mark]

b) Discuss the factors that Doug should think about before starting to delayer. [9 marks]

Q2 Evaluate the effectiveness of delegation in centralised and decentralised structures. [12 marks]

Delayering — isn't that taking off your cardigan when it's warm...

It's a shame you can't delegate the learning of your Business course to someone else. But then I guess you'd miss out on the joy of knowing the difference between centralised and decentralised structures and that would be sad...

Managing the Human Resource Flow

The human resource flow is how people move into, out of and within the business.

HR Planning starts with anticipating Future Staffing Needs

The **purpose** of human resource planning is to make sure that the business always has the **right number** of staff with the **right skills** to meet its needs. This is done by **predicting** the demand and supply of staff.

1) HR predict **how many** and **what kind** of workers will be **needed** (e.g. **skilled/unskilled**, **full/part time**).

- HR departments ask other **experienced managers** for their **opinions** and **advice**.
- **Past statistics** are used to see if employee numbers have **risen** or **fallen**.
- An increase or decrease in **demand** for a **product** means an increase or decrease in **need** for **workers**, so the HR department uses the company's sales forecasts to see whether demand for the company's products will rise, fall or stay the same.
- They'll need to decide whether they need **short-term staff** (e.g. if they're recruiting for a seasonal demand) or **long-term staff** (e.g. if they're anticipating growth or a change in production techniques).
- The introduction of **new technology** and **techniques** will alter the number of workers needed.
- HR analyse the **current staff details** to see how many are likely to **leave** or **retire** in the near future. They do an **internal staff stocktake** by looking at the number of employees and their **qualities** and **skills**.

The workforce should be flexible and adaptable enough to react to a changing environment.

2) HR also needs to assess the potential **supply** of **new workers**:

- They check the **level of unemployment** in the area to find out how many people are looking for work. HR departments see how many **school** and **college leavers** are seeking employment locally.
- **Local infrastructure** is important — good housing, transport and schools can **attract** people to the area. They see if **competitors** are recruiting a similar workforce — if so there'll be **competition** for workers.

Recruitment can be done Internally or Externally

1) When they've decided what new staff the business needs, HR draw up a **job description**, including the job title, the main **roles** and **responsibilities** of the job, salary, etc. They also write a **person specification**, detailing the **qualities** and **qualifications** required. HR also decide if they want to **advertise** the job **internally** or **externally**.

	Internal recruitment	External recruitment
Advantages	• Candidates already **know** the business, and the business knows the candidates. • **Short** and **cheap** process. • **Motivates** workers to go for a promotion.	• Brings in fresh **new ideas**. • Brings in **experience** from other organisations. • **Larger** number of applicants.
Disadvantages	• Leaves a **vacancy** in another department. • Can cause **resentment** among colleagues who aren't selected.	• **Long** and **expensive** process. • Candidates will need a **longer** induction process. • Have only seen a candidate at recruitment — might **not** be **representative** of what they're like at work.

2) Sometimes external recruitment will be done using professional **social media** sites such as LinkedIn — this allows businesses to reach a **large** number of people with very **specific** skills.

3) HR also take charge of the **selection procedure** for new staff:

- **Interviews** are the most common way of choosing candidates. Candidates can be interviewed **one-to-one** or by a **panel** of interviewers. Phone interviews are thought to be less effective than **face-to-face** interviews.
- Some organisations use **assessment centres** to help them **test** candidates. Tests include **psychometric** testing which assesses personality fit, **aptitude** tests which find out how good the candidate is at job tasks, and **group exercises** which show how candidates interact with other people in various situations.

4) A good **recruitment process** can help the HR department achieve its **diversity** objectives. They should make sure that they are recruiting workers with a variety of **skills** and from various different **backgrounds**.

5) Internal recruitment also helps to improve **employer/employee relations** as employees feel **motivated** by opportunities to progress in their career.

Managing the Human Resource Flow

HR Plan Employee's **Training** and **Development**

1) HR organises the **induction** and **training** programs of **new** staff. They also plan **retraining** and **development** of their current staff.
2) Training and development can be done **off-the-job** (e.g. studying part-time at a local **college**) or **on-the-job** (e.g. where the new worker is trained by an experienced worker).

	On-the-job training	Off-the-job training
Advantages	• Easy to **organise**. • **Lower cost** of training. • Training is **job specific**.	• Trainers are **specialists**. • **New ideas** are brought to the business. • **No job distractions** during training.
Disadvantages	• Trainer and trainee are **not productive** during training. • **Bad practices** are passed on. • No **new ideas** are brought to the business.	• Can be **expensive**. • **No benefit** to the business while training. • Training might **not be specific** to their day-to-day job.

3) Managing training correctly can help HR to make employees feel **engaged and involved** — it can make workers feel as if the business is **investing** in them and really **values** them. If workers feel valued by the business they are also **less likely** to be absent or to leave the company.
4) HR can also develop **specific** training programs to '**fast track**' its more talented workers.

HR Flow needs to be **Managed** during the **Tough Times**

1) Some departments might have **too much** labour if there has been a recent **drop in demand** or **new technology** has increased efficiency.
2) HR will first see if the surplus staff can be **redeployed** to other areas of the business. This allows the business to keep staff **morale** and **motivation** high while also filling other vacancies with staff that they **know** and **trust**.
3) If there is **no way** to redeploy staff then the business will have to make the surplus employees **redundant**.
4) Managing the HR flow in this way can make sure that the business has the **right number** of employees and they are being put where the business **needs** them the most.

HR Plans are influenced by **Internal** and **External Factors**

Internal Factors that Influence HR Plans	External Factors that Influence HR Plans
• **Corporate**, **marketing** and **production** plans. E.g. if production is expanding they will need to recruit more staff and offer more training. • Changes in **production style** may lead to retraining, recruitment or redeployment of staff.	• **Employment legislation** protects employees' rights and **restricts** companies' ability to dismiss or transfer workers. • **New technology** might change the **number** of staff and the **skills** needed — businesses might have to **retrain** their staff. • **Labour market trends** like **migration** and the **ageing population** have an effect on the **supply** of workers.

Practice Questions

Q1 What factors do HR consider when trying to predict a firm's future staffing needs?

Q2 Give two advantages of on-the-job training and off-the-job training.

Q3 Explain how external factors can impact HR plans.

Exam Questions

Q1 Evaluate the advantages and disadvantages of internal and external recruitment for a retail organisation with 200 stores nationwide. [12 marks]

Q2 The HR department of an expanding business is carrying out a major HR planning exercise. Analyse how they could recruit, train and redeploy staff to match the business's new objectives. [12 marks]

Always be nice to HR staff, your future is in their hands...

Human resource planning is all about predicting what's going to happen in the future. Sometimes you get it right, and everything goes along swimmingly. Other times you get it wrong, and end up paying people to twiddle their thumbs.

Motivation and Job Design

For the past 150 years, industrial psychologists and sociologists have tried to figure out what motivates workers...

Motivated Employees get **More Done** than **Non-motivated Employees**

1) The value of motivation should not be **underestimated** — a motivated workforce is likely to be more **productive**, more aligned with **company objectives** and prepared to go **above and beyond** for the company.
2) Motivated workers are more **loyal**, which will decrease both **labour turnover** and **absences**, which reduces costs.
3) **Customer satisfaction** usually increases when a workforce feel **engaged** with what they are doing.
4) A company that **motivates** and **engages** its employees is a more attractive prospect for **future employees**. Companies with a **good reputation** will attract the **best employees** and gain a **competitive advantage**.
5) There are several different **motivational theories** — they each suggest different ways to motivate employees.

1) **Taylor** and **Scientific Management** — Concentrate on **Efficiency**

1) In the early 20th century, F.W. Taylor thought that workers were motivated by **money**. He believed workers would do the **minimum** amount of work if left to their own devices.
2) Taylor's goal was to figure out the **most efficient** way to do a job, and then make sure every single worker did it that way. Also, making sure that each task was being done by the **right worker**. This approach is called **scientific management**.
3) He favoured **division of labour** — breaking work down into a lot of **small repetitive tasks**, with managers taking **responsibility** for the workforce.
4) Taylor believed in paying workers according to the **quantity** they produced — the most **productive** workers got a **better rate**. He believed that financial incentives would **motivate** workers and raise **productivity**.
5) Increased productivity meant that **fewer workers** were needed — workers worried about losing their jobs.
6) There were other disadvantages, too — increased productivity could lead to a reduction in **quality**. **Supervisors** were needed to monitor efficiency and for quality control purposes.

Taylor's approach wouldn't work for modern businesses — it would be seen as **exploitation**. It also ignores the **demotivating** effect of doing very repetitive boring work. However, aspects of Taylor's theory have survived — **piece rate pay** is based on his ideas, and the **supervisor role** still exists.

2) **Maslow's Hierarchy of Needs** — people need the **Basics**

Maslow and Herzberg both believed that workers had needs which were specific to them as individuals.

Maslow said that people start by meeting the needs at the **bottom** of the pyramid. Once they've sorted out those needs, they can move on to the needs on the **next level** up.

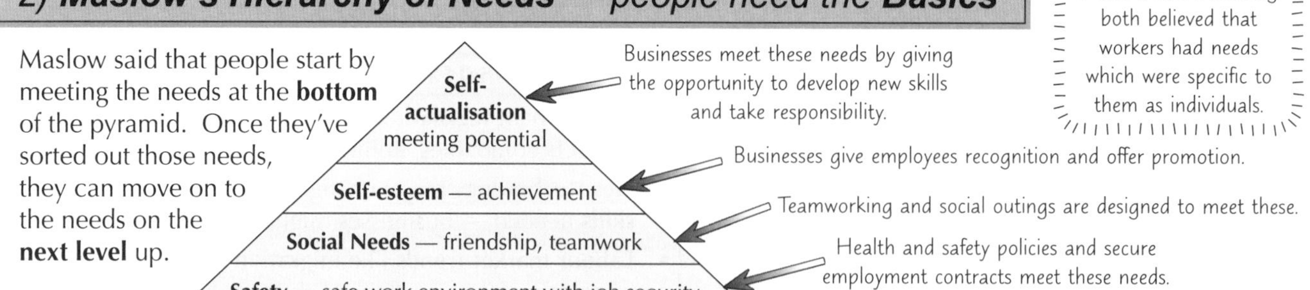

Maslow's theory is **appealing** as each of the five different needs have some **importance** to workers. However, it isn't always **obvious** which level an **individual** is at. Different workers may put their needs in a **different order**, e.g. some may value friendship and teamwork over achievement and meeting potential.

3) **Herzberg's Hygiene** and **Motivating** factors

In the 1950s and '60s, Frederick Herzberg interviewed accountants and engineers to find out what **motivated** and **satisfied** them at work. He identified **two groups of factors** which influenced the motivation of workers:

1) **Hygiene factors** are things like good **company policy**, **supervision**, **working conditions**, **pay**, and **relations** with fellow employees. They don't motivate as such, but if they **aren't good**, workers get **dissatisfied**.
2) **Motivating factors** are things like **interesting work**, personal **achievement**, **recognition** of achievement, and scope for more **responsibility** and personal **development**. These factors **do** positively motivate workers.

Herzberg's theory recognises that motivation comes from the **individuals' needs** and has influenced **motivational techniques** today — it provides clear solutions for businesses. However, it is often criticised for being based on a **small sample** of people and it doesn't consider that people have **different** hygiene and motivation needs.

Motivation and Job Design

Job Design outlines the way a job is Planned and Organised

1) **Job design** sets out the details of **what** is to be done and **how** it is to be done. It's **influenced** by **internal** and **external factors** that affect how the job can be carried out **effectively**.
2) The **day-to-day** tasks are the main **influence** on the **job design**. The things that need to be considered are: the **range** and **nature** of the tasks, the **way** and **order** tasks need to be completed, the **speed** the tasks need to be done, the **quality** required and the **number of people** required to complete the task.
3) External factors such as **new technology**, changes to **law** and **legislation**, **customer demand** and the availability of certain **skills** can all affect job design.

Hackman and Oldham — Job Design is Focused on the Person not the Job

1) **Taylor's scientific management** approach focused on **how** the job was done, whereas **Maslow's** and **Herzberg's** theories said that **more than money** was needed to motivate workers.
2) **Hackman** and **Oldham** thought that a job needed to be **designed** so that it would focus on the **person**, and the person would then be **motivated**.
3) Hackman and Oldham's model is broken down into **five key elements** of job design which lead to worker **motivation**, more worker **involvement**, higher **performance**, lower **staff turnover** and lower **absenteeism**.

Autonomy means giving workers the freedom to make their own decisions.

Job Characteristic	Impact of the characteristic on the workers	Effect on the workers
Skill variety Task identity Task significance	Makes work more meaningful for the workers	Motivation is improved Workers feel involved Quality of work is improved Workers are more satisfied with their work and are more committed to the business
Autonomy	Workers have more responsibility	
Feedback	Workers know how well they are performing and aim to improve	

- **Skill variety** — A wide variety of skills needed in a job can **motivate**. A lack of skill variety can demotivate.
- **Task identity** — Workers will feel **involved** if there is a clear task and they deal with it from start to finish.
- **Task significance** — If people think the job they are doing is **significant**, they will be motivated to do it well.
- **Autonomy** — Workers who make their **own decisions** will feel like their contribution is valued.
- **Feedback** — This tells the workers how they have **performed** and encourages them to do better.

4) Job design should constantly be adapted to meet the needs of the **business** and the **individuals**.
5) **Changing** job design has an **immediate** impact on **HR objectives**, as employees feel **engaged** and **involved**.
6) It can also have a less immediate effect on the overall **corporate objectives**, e.g. it can help to reduce the **costs** of the business, improve **productivity** of the workforce and improve **quality** of the product.

Practice Questions

Q1 Give three benefits of a motivated workforce.

Q2 Give a brief description of Taylor's views on motivation.

Q3 Give five factors that Herzberg would describe as 'hygiene factors'.

Q4 Write and describe the five job characteristics in the Hackman and Oldham model.

Exam Questions

Q1 Cheapos is a local supermarket chain that has a reputation for poor customer service. Analyse, with reference to Maslow's hierarchy, how Cheapos could motivate its workers to improve their customer service. [9 marks]

Q2 Use the Hackman and Oldham model to explain the effect of good job design on workers. [6 marks]

Design me a job where I sit and eat biscuits all day and I'm there...

Make sure you know the theories of motivation — the ideas might well come in handy for giving examples of how managers today can increase the motivation of their workers. You'll need to know about job design too.

Improving Motivation

Some businesses motivate their employees by offering financial incentives, others motivate their workers using non-financial methods. Personally I'm motivated by the thought of cheese and biscuits at the end of the day...

Payment Methods** can be used to **Reward** and **Motivate

There are several different ways a business can **pay** its employees:

Piece rate	Workers are paid per **unit produced**. They **don't** get a fixed salary and **aren't entitled** to sick pay, holiday pay or company pensions.
Salary Schemes	Workers are paid according to a given **time period**. This could be an **hourly rate**, a **weekly wage** or an **annual wage**.
Commission	Workers are paid a **bonus** on top of their salary — the bonus could be based on **sales** or **units produced**.
Performance-related pay	Workers are paid based on their **performance** or on the performance of the business. The amount is determined by both the **individual** and the **business meeting targets** — this is often done in annual **appraisals**.

1) **Piece rate** is used when the **quantity** produced can be measured easily — it can motivate workers to produce a **high quantity** of products. However, **quality** and **morale** can **suffer** and the manager will need to make sure some **quality control** measures are put in place. This is often used for **production/assembly line** workers.
2) Employees on **salary schemes** have to work a **minimum** number of hours and produce a certain amount of work. If they **don't** do the amount of work required, they will be expected to **work longer** until it is finished. This can **motivate** workers to do work quickly while not compromising on quality. The downside of salary schemes is that workers **can't** earn extra money by **working harder** and producing better **quality work**.
3) **Commission** is often used in **sales roles** such as in clothing stores and at car dealerships — workers are **rewarded** for selling certain products. It can increase **motivation** and **performance** of sales staff. However, it can also lead to **overselling**, and customers can feel like they are **overwhelmed** by staff whenever they enter the store. The business also doesn't know how much its **labour costs** will be each month.
4) **Performance-related pay** can be used to reward your **best workers**. Workers are motivated to meet their own **targets** and ensure the business meets its **objectives** — however, it can lead to **demoralisation** of staff if only certain people are getting increased pay when the **whole business** is doing well.
5) Employees may also get **fringe benefits**. These can include a **staff discount** for company products (common in retail, not so common in aircraft manufacturing...), employer contributions to employee **pensions**, private **medical insurance**, a company **car**, **profit-sharing** schemes or **shares** in the company.

Flexible Working** can help to motivate **Employees

1) Flexible working is when **working hours** and **patterns** are adapted to suit the **employees**.
2) Businesses offering flexible working are an **attractive prospect** to **highly skilled workers**. There are several types of flexible working, including:
   - **Flexi-time** — employees work **full-time hours**, but they can **decide** when to work, around fixed **core hours**. E.g. employees might have to work for 37 hours a week, but they only have to be in the office Mon-Fri between the hours of 10 am and 3 pm — the rest of their hours can be made up any time they like.
   - **Compressed hours** — employees work a set number of **hours** per week, but over **fewer days**.
   - **Annual hours** — employees work a certain number of **hours** over the **year**, but they choose when to work. E.g. employees with children might not work as much in the school holidays.
   - **Job-sharing** — **two people** share **one job**, e.g. working alternate weeks or splitting the week between them.
   - **Home working** — employees work from **home** instead of at the business premises.

Advantages of flexible working

1) Flexible working improves **motivation** so employee **productivity** should improve.
2) Flexible working helps employees with **children**.
3) Home working suits **families**, **disabled** workers and those who live in **remote** places.

Disadvantages of flexible working

1) It can be impractical for businesses that need to serve the **public** during normal working hours.
2) Home-workers may be easily **distracted** at home.
3) Job-sharing can lead to **confusion** over responsibilities and **unequal** workloads.

Improving Motivation

Non-Financial Motivation — Jobs are Designed to be more Satisfying

Lots of businesses today **design jobs** to be **motivating** (see p.90-91). There are **different ways** to do this:

See p.63 for more on quality circles.

1) **Job enlargement** gives the employee **more work** at the same level.
2) **Job enrichment** gives workers more **challenging** work, and the **training** they need to do it. It gives employees more **responsibility** for organising their work and solving problems.
3) **Empowerment** gives people **control** over their work, and a greater role in **decision-making** — **quality circles** let groups of workers from various departments meet to suggest **improvements** to productivity and quality.
4) **Teamworking** puts workers into **small teams** and lets them **organise** their own work — this can lead to **job enrichment** and **empowerment** as workers get a greater role in a variety of tasks.
5) Businesses can also motivate their employees by creating a **pleasant** working environment or providing **facilities** for the workers to use (e.g. free gym/sports facilities). These things can make workers feel as if the business is looking after them and will **motivate** the workers to do their **best work** for the business.

Organisational and Job Design affect the type of Motivation

1) **Organisational design** (see p.86) will influence the type of **payment method** a company chooses. E.g. a company with a **tall** structure might be more inclined to use piece rate or performance-related pay because there are lots of levels of authority to monitor the productivity and progress of the people below them.
2) The **size** of the business will also influence the payment methods chosen. E.g. a national supermarket chain might pay its shopfloor staff an **hourly rate** as it is difficult to distinguish one person's work from another.
3) Organisational design can also affect the non-financial motivation a company chooses. A business with a **flat** structure might **not** want to introduce **teamworking**, because **team leaders** introduce an **extra** level of **hierarchy**. They might try to motivate people through job **enlargement** or **enrichment** instead.
4) **Empowerment** is common in businesses with flat structures as **communication** is easier — this leads to staff feeling more motivated as they are being included in **decision-making**.
5) Businesses with **large numbers** of highly-skilled workers might put greater emphasis on non-financial motivation. **Highly-skilled workers** are more likely to respond to things like job **enrichment** and **empowerment** than they are to respond to financial incentives.
6) Non-financial incentives are a **long term** type of motivation — a company and its management invest a lot of time, money and effort into getting it right. If a business needs a job done **quickly** then it is much more likely to focus on **financial** incentives.

Practice Questions

Q1 Define the terms 'piece rate', 'commission', 'salary schemes' and 'performance-related pay'.

Q2 List three advantages and three disadvantages of flexible working.

Q3 Explain what is meant by the terms 'job enrichment' and 'job enlargement'.

Q4 Give five non-financial motivation techniques that businesses use.

Q5 Give a way in which the design of a business will affect the payment methods used.

Exam Questions

Q1 Colin is a checkout clerk in a supermarket, Jane is a travelling sales representative and Mike is a bricklayer. Say whether each person is likely to be paid by piece rate, hourly rate or commission, and explain why. [6 marks]

Q2 Analyse the effects of organisational design and job design on the type of motivation a business uses. [9 marks]

Q3 Analyse how the financial incentives of a multinational corporation might change as you move up the hierarchy. [9 marks]

Sadly I don't get paid on commission for all these gags...

Believe it or not, people aren't just in it for the money! Shocking, I know, but businesses also need to offer their workers some sort of non-financial motivation. Getting the balance right is what all businesses strive to achieve....

Improving Employer-Employee Relations

Communication is really important in business. I bet you never would've guessed that...

Employers and **Employees** need to **Cooperate** with each other

1) Employers and employees **need each other**. **Employers** need **hard-working staff** to contribute to the production of goods or a service that can be sold for a profit. **Employees** need a **secure income** to support themselves and their families.
2) However, there can be **conflict** between them. Employers would prefer to pay **lower wages** to keep **costs** down but employees want **higher wages** to improve their **standard of living**.

The two sides must **negotiate** to reach an **acceptable compromise** on wage rates, working conditions and terms of employment. **Failure** to reach agreement could lead to a **production stoppage**, and **both parties** would **suffer**.

A **successful** employer-employee relationship **maximises** the **cooperation** and **minimises** the potential for **conflict** between these two groups. It is built on a **culture of trust** between the two groups.

Communication between **Managers** and **Employees** is **Essential**

1) The purpose of communication is to pass on **information** and **ideas**.
2) Communication **within** the business is necessary for making **plans**, giving **instructions** and **motivating** staff. Managers need to communicate **goals** and **objectives** to staff so they know what they're meant to be aiming for.
3) For communication to be effective, the message that's **received** should be the **same** as the message that was **sent**.
4) Good communication is **clear** and **unambiguous**. If a manager arranges a conference call to start at 6 am but half the people who are suppose to be in the call think it starts at 6 pm, communication has obviously failed.
5) Effective communication is a **two-way thing**. Managers have to tell employees what they want them to **know**, and they also need to **listen** to what their employees have to say to them — employees will offer **new ideas** from a different **point of view**.
6) Good communication and relations make it easier for employees to accept **difficult decisions**. It can also help the **feedback** and **complaints** processes to run more smoothly.

Organisations need to **Overcome Barriers** to **Improve Communication**

There are several **barriers** that can prevent communication from being **effective**:

Attitudes — The receiver may **dislike** the sender or the receiver may be distracted.
Intermediaries — The **longer** the chain of communication, the more **mangled** the message becomes.
Language barriers — One word can mean **different things** in different cultures. **Jargon** can be confusing.
Sense of purpose — Staff who **don't understand why** they're being told something may ignore future messages.
Communication overload — If employees are **swamped** with messages, they won't be able to deal with them all.
Remoteness — It's easy to **misinterpret** the tone when you can't hear the speaker's voice (e.g. in letters or emails).
Group behaviour — Some employees might be **overbearing**, making others too **afraid** to speak up in meetings.

These barriers can be overcome by creating a **trusting relationship** between employers and employees.

1) Creating a more **democratic** management style allows everyone in the business to have a say in how things are run. This means that decisions are made when the **majority** of employees and employers agree on an issue. This **inclusiveness** makes employees feel more valued.
2) Making sure both parties recognise each others' **objectives** and **needs** can stop employees being told things they don't need to know or don't care about. It can **prevent** both parties feeling **overloaded** with information and **improve attitudes** within the business.
3) Changing **organisational structure** can help to reduce the number of intermediaries — **delayering** (see p.86) is a way in which businesses try to do this. A **flatter** organisational structure can help employees be more **involved** in decisions.
4) **Delegation** and **decentralisation** can also lead to more effective communication. **Empowering** employees can help reduce **negative** attitudes, give employees a **sense of purpose**, reduce a feeling of **remoteness** and eliminate **group behaviour**.

Betty soon began to regret telling her boss she was fluent in Japanese.

Improving Employer-Employee Relations

Good Employer-Employee Relations can Benefit Both Parties

1) Businesses with **good** employer-employee relations will get **more** from their employees than businesses with **poor relations**. Employees will also benefit from **maintaining** a good relationship with their employer.

Benefits to the employer	Benefits to the employee
The business will develop a **great reputation** among **prospective** employees, so it will attract the very best candidates during **recruitment**.	Employees will feel **involved** in the business which will give them a sense of **job security**.
If relations are good then **productivity** and **efficiency** are increased as new ideas and ways of working are picked up **quickly** by the employees. This allows the business to be more **competitive**.	If workers are more **productive** and **efficient** then the business will make **more money**. This increase in profit can be fed back into the workforce through **bonuses** or **pay increases**.
Getting the point of view of the employee is beneficial in making decisions. More **diverse** opinions will mean the business makes more **informed** decisions.	The **views** of the employee are considered during **decisions** so they will feel valued and motivated. This will increase their **job satisfaction**.
Good **communication** will mean that the objectives of the **employees** are more aligned with the objectives of the **business**.	Employees are able to communicate their **personal objectives** to the employer, which will help the employee **develop skills** and further their career.

2) **Employers** have to be careful not to have **too close** a relationship with their employees. Managers need to be able to keep some **control** over what's going on.
3) **Employers** need to make sure that they **aren't** employing workers just because they have a good relationship with them. They should expect the same **high standards** from every employee regardless of their relationship.

Each Employee has an Individual Relationship with their Employer

1) All employees of a company are treated as **individuals** for some purposes, such as employee appraisals. When **individual employees** negotiate with their employer about their own **working conditions**, it's known as **individual bargaining**.
2) **Individual bargaining** for **pay** means that employers can decide to pay an employee what they think he or she is **worth** to the firm. It might be **more** or **less** than other employees in the same role. This provides a financial **incentive** to the employee to work productively.
3) **Individual bargaining** is also used for things like **flexible working arrangements** — they're often based on the employee's **personal circumstances**, e.g. if an employee cares for young children or an elderly parent, the employer might allow that employee to work from home or work flexi-time (see p.92).

Practice Questions

Q1 Why is efficient communication between managers and employees essential?

Q2 Give seven barriers that can prevent communication being effective.

Q3 Give three benefits to the employer of a good employer-employee relationship.

Exam Questions

Q1 A publishing company is nationally considered to have a great relationship with its employees. Explain why this would make the business an attractive prospect for a prospective candidate. [6 marks]

Q2 Jenson & Hamilton Housing is a national estate agent. Discuss the barriers to communication that the estate agent could face and outline a plan that the business could use to overcome these barriers. [12 marks]

Employer-employee relations aren't just found in family businesses...

Good communication is incredibly important in business. Managers and staff have to communicate with each other to get the job done properly. The better the employer-employee relationship is, the easier communication will be.

Employee Representation

Obviously all businesses like their employees to do some work, but some like them to get more involved...

Employees** can be **Represented** in the **Decision Making Process

All businesses need ways of **communicating** with their workforce. They also need a way to **represent** the workforce in the decision-making process. The way that workers are represented will depend on many factors:

- **Organisational size** — in small businesses, employees can talk **directly** to managers about business decisions. In larger companies, employees need a **representative** to give them a **voice** at a higher level.
- **Organisational structure** — in wide and flat structures employees' views are **more likely** to be represented. In narrow and tall structures, communication can be **poor** and employees are **less likely** to be represented.
- **Leadership** and **management** — some businesses have a very **democratic** management style and so employee representation is **encouraged**. However some businesses (usually those adopting **hard HRM** — see p.83), do not like their employees to be involved in the decision-making process.
- **External factors** — the state of the **economy** can impact the extent to which employees are involved in decisions, e.g. in a **recession** the views of the employees might not be represented as the business is just trying to survive. **Legislation** can also dictate the extent to which employees are represented.

Works Councils** discuss **Work Issues

1) **Works councils** are committees made up of **employer** and **employee** representatives (usually elected).
2) They **meet regularly** to discuss **general work issues** e.g. training, new technology and methods of work.
3) The sharing of ideas and information in a relatively **relaxed** atmosphere does a lot to improve **relations**.
4) **Quality circles** (see p.63) are like works councils, but they only discuss **quality** issues. They meet regularly to discuss ways of improving quality. Quality circles include employees from **all levels** of the business.
5) In 1994, the EU brought in **European Works Councils** for businesses based in multiple European countries.

Trade Unions Negotiate** with **Employers** on behalf of **Employees

1) **Trade unions** act on behalf of **groups of employees** in the workforce when negotiating rates of **pay** and **working conditions** etc. with the employer.
2) By joining with others and belonging to a union, an employee **strengthens** their **bargaining power** in a way that wouldn't be possible if they tried to bargain as an **individual**.
3) Trade unions allow employers and workers to **communicate** with each other.
4) Trade unions give **advice** and **assistance** to **individual** employees who are having problems with their employer.

Trade unions take action in the workplace

1) Trade unions **negotiate** with employers on behalf of their members to secure fair rates of pay and/or productivity bonuses for their work.
2) Trade unions help negotiate reasonable **hours of work**, and **paid holiday** entitlement.
3) Trade unions help members get **safe** and civilized **working conditions**.
4) Trade unions help their members get greater **job security** with protection against **mistreatment**, **discrimination** and **unfair dismissal**.

If these negotiations don't work, trade unions may encourage workers to go on strike.

Trade unions take action at a national level

1) Trade unions can **put pressure on the Government** to bring in legislation that will serve the interests of the trade union members.
2) The **minimum wage** was introduced in **1998** by the Government after discussions with trade unions.
3) Trade unions pushed the Government to make **redundancy payments** compulsory.
4) Following demands from trade unions, the **Pension Protection Fund** was set up in April 2005 to protect the pensions of employees in private company pension schemes if their employer **goes bust**.

Trade unions take action in party politics

1) Many unions donate money to the **Labour Party** because they think its policies represent their interests.
2) In the 1970s and 80s, unions had a lot of **power** in the Labour Party. Since the **90s** they've had **less power**.

Employee Representation

Trade Unions *can influence the* ***Decisions*** *of the* ***Business***

1) When employers want to make **changes** to the **working practices** of the business (e.g. if the employer wants to reduce employees' contracted hours, or change the way it pays staff from an hourly wage to a piece rate, or vice versa), trade unions can help staff if they want to **resist** the change, e.g. by organising **strikes**.
2) Trade unions can also **facilitate change** by **liaising** between employers and union members, and communicating the **benefits** of the change in working practices to their members.
3) **Employees** are more likely to be **open** to change if union representatives are involved in decisions, because they **trust** trade unions to protect their interests, but may **not** trust their employers to do the same.
4) Trade unions stand up for employees' rights if employers want to make **redundancies**. They can negotiate with employers to persuade them to make **fewer** employees redundant, or negotiate better **redundancy payouts**.
5) If employers are planning changes that might **adversely affect** the current workforce, trade unions try to **prevent** these changes from taking place. E.g. if employers want to take on **cheaper** staff, current employees' wages could be **driven down**. A trade union would try to **stop** the recruitment of cheaper workers from going ahead.
6) If current staff are **overworked**, trade unions can try to convince employers to take on **more staff**.
7) Employers can **benefit** from trade unions too — if the business is **profitable**, its good news for **both** the employers and the employees, so it's in the interests of the trade unions to help the business achieve its objectives.
8) Trade union reps can share their **knowledge** about **employment law**, **health and safety**, etc. with the employer.

Employee Representation *has* ***Advantages*** *and* ***Disadvantages***

Employers and employees need to **cooperate** with each other to maintain a successful working relationship.

Advantages of employee representation

1) It's often more **effective** to approach an organisation as a group. Groups have a bigger **influence** and can be more **forceful**.
2) **Collective bargaining** can help achieve **long-term aims** because employers may sign **contracts** which lock them into **agreements**.
3) It can be helpful for management to have a **small representative group** of workers to negotiate with rather than consulting every individual.
4) Senior management get a **direct insight** into the concerns of the workforce.

Disadvantages of employee representation

1) Employee representation can lead to **industrial action**. This can take the form of deliberately decreased **productivity** or **strike** action.
2) Strike action can **get out of hand** or turn **violent**.
3) Industrial action leads to **lost profits**.
4) The majority vote within a trade union may **overrule** the demands of the individual. The individual is then **denied** the **opportunity** to represent themselves as they might want to.
5) Industrial action can **undermine the trust** between employer and employee. A **breakdown** in communication will damage the **relationship**.

Practice Questions

Q1 What is a works council?

Q2 What do trade unions do for their members?

Q3 Give two examples of ways that trade unions have influenced Government policy.

Q4 How can unions influence employment levels in a company?

Q5 Give three disadvantages of employee representation.

Exam Questions

Q1 Snapdragon Ltd. is a medium-sized clothes retailer employing 600 people in 10 stores across the country. To what extent is trade union membership beneficial to the staff and to the business? [25 marks]

Q2 Sarah works at a large company with a tall and narrow structure. She is not a member of a trade union. Evaluate how Sarah could best raise concerns with her employers. [12 marks]

Trade unions be representin' the employees, yo...

You have to know how employee representation is done, why it's good, and what problems can arise from it. You also should learn the influences employee representation has on the decision making of a business.

Mission, Objectives and Strategy

You'll be familiar with the idea of a business's mission and objectives — but see p.3-5 if you need a recap. You need to know a bit more about them though — like what influences them and how they link to a business's strategy.

Mission and Objectives are Influenced by Internal and External Factors

1) The **mission** of a business is its **overall purpose**. It's influenced by what the **owners** want the business to **achieve**, their **personal values** and **beliefs**, and what **market opportunities** there are.
2) The **objectives** of a business are the **goals** it sets in order to **achieve** its mission. **Corporate objectives** are the goals of the business **as a whole**, whereas **functional objectives** are the objectives of each **department** or **function** (e.g. marketing, finance, etc.), set to help achieve the corporate objectives.
3) Objectives can be set for **profit**, **growth**, **survival**, **cash flow** and **social/ethical** performance.
4) When setting objectives, there are many **factors** that may **influence** a business's decisions. **Internal factors** are important, as well as adapting to meet the demands of a **changing environment**, for example:

- **Ownership:** The **form** of the business and whether it's **for-profit** or **non-profit** (see p.8-11) will have a big effect on its objectives. Sole traders can pretty much **do what they like**, whereas limited companies have **directors** and **shareholders** to answer to.
- **Short-termism:** Shareholders can demand a **quick return** on their investment, which leads to **short-term objectives** to increase profit that don't necessarily **benefit** the business in the **long term**.
- **Internal environment:** The **size**, **culture** and **resources** of the business will affect its objectives — as will the **views** of the **leaders** or **management** (especially on issues such as **ethics** or **social responsibility**).
- **External environment:** **Political**, **legal**, **economic**, **social**, **technological** and **environmental factors**, as well as **competition**, influence a business's objectives. For example:

1) Changes in the **economy** will affect whether a business aims to **increase profits** or focuses on **survival**.
2) Consumer interest in **environmental issues** might influence a business's decision to set an objective to **minimise pollution**.

Strategies are Plans for Achieving Objectives

1) A **strategy** is a medium to long-term **plan of action** developed to achieve a business's **objectives**. A business's **corporate strategy** is based on achieving its **corporate objectives**.
2) A strategy can only be put into place once an organisation has **outlined** its aims and objectives. Businesses need to decide **what** they want to achieve before they can work out **how** to achieve it.
3) All businesses need to have a strategy. In **small firms**, these plans may not be **formally** written down. Strategies can simply be a **sequence** of business decisions made over time with the aim of reaching a particular **goal**, e.g. expanding into a new market segment.

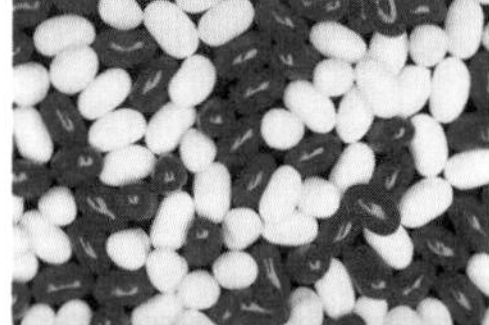

No, I said TACTICS.

4) In **larger firms**, strategy is usually more **clearly defined** because it will influence the plans of **individual departments**, such as marketing and HR.
5) **Tactics** are **short-term plans** for implementing strategy, so are more focused on **day-to-day activities**.

Functional Decision Making is based on Strategic Decision Making

1) Businesses make **strategic decisions** — they decide on **strategies** that will help the business to achieve its **corporate objectives**. Strategic decisions are **long-term**, **high-risk** decisions that determine the overall direction of the business.
2) **Functional decisions** are decisions made in **individual departments**. Departmental managers make decisions in order to **implement the overall strategy** — so they're based on the **strategic decisions** of the business. Functional decisions tend to be more **short-term** and **lower risk** than strategic decisions.

E.g. a business might have an **objective** to increase sales by 5% in one year. To do this, the business makes a **strategic decision** to expand its production capacity, so the HR department makes a **functional decision** to recruit more people.

Mission, Objectives and Strategy

Businesses use **SWOT Analysis** to make decisions about their **Future**

1) A **SWOT analysis** is a four-factor model that details the **strengths**, **weaknesses**, **opportunities** and **threats** facing a business — this helps managers to make strategic decisions.
2) The **strengths** and **weaknesses** of each department are **internal** factors that the business **can influence** (there's lots on **internal analysis** in Section 8).
3) The **opportunities** and **threats** are **beyond the control** of the business. The business has to **understand** them in order to react appropriately (there's lots on **external analysis** in Section 9).
4) **External factors** that might pose opportunities or threats include political, legal, economic, social, technological and environmental factors and competitor behaviour.

Strengths
Weaknesses
Opportunities
Threats

Example: Beasel's Tea Room is a small **tea shop** in a town-centre location. In 2014, they won an **award** in a local newspaper for "the best toasted teacake in the county". The tea shop only seats **22 customers**, but the owners have decided not to move to bigger premises because their current **location**, on a main shopping street, attracts **passing trade**. Instead, the manager has suggested that they start selling **takeaway** drinks and cakes to take advantage of their popularity. The owners are concerned about reports that a big **coffee shop chain** is planning to open a branch close to the tea shop, as they don't think they will be able to **compete** on price and may **lose business**.

Strengths: Good reputation, good location, good quality products.
Weaknesses: Small premises, cannot compete on price with chain stores.
Opportunities: Selling cakes and drinks to take away could increase their market size.
Threats: Possibility of a new competitor with lower prices.

SWOT analysis helps businesses to **Plan Strategies**

1) **SWOT analysis** is a very useful tool in developing **strategy** (see p.178-179 for more on **strategic planning**). It considers the business's **individual circumstances**, and is done in a **factual** and **objective** way.
2) In planning strategy, managers will focus on **opportunities** that build on the business's **strengths**, on **converting weaknesses** into **strengths** and on **managing threats**.
3) One advantage of SWOT analysis is that it can easily be **redone** to take into account **changing conditions** (e.g. a changing economy or unforeseen events such as floods). This means that a business can **adapt** its strategy using the new SWOT analysis.
4) SWOT analysis also lets the business know where it has a **competitive advantage** over its rivals — the business can change its **strategy** to focus on these elements.

Practice Questions

Q1 Give three internal factors and three external factors that could influence a business's objectives.

Q2 What is a strategy?

Q3 What does SWOT stand for?

Exam Question

Q1 A sandwich shop has carried out SWOT analysis and come up with the following information:
Strength — it is the only place in town that sells freshly-made sandwiches. Weakness — it is located down a dark alleyway. Opportunity — a new call centre with 100 employees is opening nearby. Threat — a local restaurant is introducing a low price lunch menu.
Evaluate how the sandwich shop could use this analysis in planning its strategy. [12 marks]

Time to SWOT up on your objectives and strategy...

That was a nice gentle start to strategy — but there's lots more to come. If you want a bit of extra practice, think about a local business and do a SWOT analysis for it (just at home — they might not appreciate it if you waltz in and start pointing out their weaknesses). Personally, I have a bit of a weakness for Hugh Jackman, but that can't be helped...

Financial Analysis — Balance Sheets

Businesses have different ways of reporting their financial information — balance sheets and income statements can be analysed to assess their performance. Luckily, that's what this section is all about. Read on to find out more...

Balance Sheets are lists of Assets and Liabilities

1) Balance sheets are a **snapshot** of a firm's finances at a **fixed point in time**.
2) They show the value of all the business' **assets** (the things that belong to the business, including cash in the bank) and all its **liabilities** (the money the business owes). They also show the value of all the **capital** (the money invested in the business), and the source of that capital (e.g. loans, shares or retained profits) — so they show where the money's **come from** as well as what's being **done** with it.
3) The '**net assets**' value (the total fixed and current assets minus total current and non-current (long-term) liabilities — see next page) is **always the same** as the '**total equity**' value — the total of all the money that's been put into the business. That's why they're called balance sheets — they **balance**.

Sally soon realised that balancing isn't as easy as it looks.

Interpreting balance sheets — Here's How It All Looks

ABC Company Ltd
Balance Sheet as at 30 March 2014

Premises			£100000
Machines			£10000
Vehicles			£15000
Total non-current assets			£125000
Inventories (stock)		£20000	
Receivables (debtors)		£10000	
Cash in the bank		£5000	
Total current assets		£35000	
Payables (creditors)	(£20000)		
Overdraft	(£2000)		
Dividends	(£10000)		
Unpaid tax	(£1000)		
Total current liabilities		(£33000)	
Net current assets			£2000
Non-current liabilities (long-term loans)			(£55000)
Net assets			£72000
Share capital			£60000
Reserves			£12000
Total equity (shareholders' funds)			£72000

Balance sheets show the financial state of affairs on one particular day.

Raw materials and finished products — things the business has spent money on, but not sold yet.

The value of non-current assets includes depreciation (see p.103) — it's what they're worth now, not when the business bought them.

Value of products sold but not paid for yet. Money owed to the business. See p.101.

Money owed by the business. See p.101.

Brackets mean a negative number.

Dividends (see p.10) not yet paid to shareholders.

Net current assets = current assets – current liabilities

This is the working capital available to pay for day to day spending. See p.102.

Net assets = net current assets + non-current assets – non-current liabilities.

These two figures ALWAYS balance.

The figure for reserves takes into account depreciation — depreciation is taken into account in 'net assets', so if it wasn't included here, the figures wouldn't balance.

Financial Analysis — Balance Sheets

Assets are things the Business Owns

1) Businesses can use **capital** to buy **assets** that will generate more revenue in the future — this is **investment**.
2) Assets (like machinery and stock) provide a **financial benefit** to the business, so they're given a monetary value on the balance sheet. Assets can be classified as **non-current assets** (fixed assets) or **current assets**.
3) **Non-current assets** are assets that the business is likely to keep for **more than a year**, e.g. property, land, production equipment, desks and computers. The '**total non-current assets**' value on the balance sheet is the **combined value** of all the business' non-current assets.
4) Non-current assets often **lose value** over time, so they're worth less every year. This is **depreciation** (see p.103). Businesses should factor in depreciation to give a **realistic** value of their non-current assets on the balance sheet.
5) **Current assets** are assets that the business is likely to exchange for cash **within the accounting year**, before the next balance sheet is made. All the current assets are added together to give the '**total current assets**' value on the balance sheet.

> Current assets include **receivables** (money owed to the business by other companies and individuals) and **inventories** (or **stock** — products, or materials that will be used to make products, that will be sold to **customers**).

6) The business' **current and non-current assets** are added together, then current and non-current liabilities (see below) are deducted to give the figure for '**net assets**' on the balance sheet.

Liabilities are Debts the Business Owes

1) **Current liabilities** are **debts** which need to be paid off within a year. They include **overdrafts**, **taxes** due to be paid, **payables** (money owed to **creditors**) and **dividends** due to be paid to shareholders. **Total current liabilities** are **deducted** from total fixed and current assets to give the value of 'assets employed'.
2) **Non-current liabilities** are debts that the business will pay off over several years, e.g. mortgages and loans.

Bad Debts are debts that debtors Won't Ever Pay

1) **Ideally**, every debt owed by debtors to the business would be paid. **Unfortunately**, the **real world** isn't like that. Most debts get paid eventually, but some debtors **default** on their payments — they **don't pay up**.
2) Debts which don't get paid are called "**bad debts**". These bad debts **can't** be included on the balance sheet as an **asset** — because the business isn't going to get money for them.
3) The business **writes off** these bad debts, and puts them as an **expense** on the profit and loss account. This shows that the business has **lost money**.
4) It's important to be **realistic** about bad debts. The business shouldn't be **over-optimistic** and report debts as **assets** when they're unlikely to ever be paid. On the other hand, they shouldn't be **too cautious** and write debts off as **bad debts** when they could make the debtors pay up.

Practice Questions

Q1 What do brackets mean on a balance sheet?

Q2 What are assets? What are liabilities?

Q3 What's the difference between current and non-current assets?

Exam Questions

Q1 Which of these values would always be negative on a balance sheet?
A inventories B receivables C overdraft D share capital [1 mark]

Q2 Describe what the non-current assets of a bakery might be. [4 marks]

I'm a bit of a liability really...

If your balance sheet doesn't balance, something's gone horribly wrong. However, you won't have to actually draw up a balance sheet in the exam, so that's one less thing to worry about for now. There's more detail on all the different bits of a balance sheet over the next couple of pages, so get yourself a cup of tea and a biscuit, read on and enjoy.

Financial Analysis — Balance Sheets

Now it's time to go into a bit more detail about some of those bits on the balance sheet.

Working Capital is the Finance available for Day-To-Day Spending

1) **Working capital** is the amount of **cash** (and **assets** that can be easily turned into cash) that the business has available to pay its **day-to-day debts**. The more working capital a business has, the more **liquid** (able to pay its short-term debts) it is. See p.108 for liquidity ratios.
2) Working capital is the same as **net current assets** on the balance sheet — the amount left over when you subtract **current liabilities** (e.g. overdraft, payables and tax due to be paid) from **current assets** (i.e. cash, receivables and stock):

Working capital = current assets – current liabilities

3) Businesses **can't survive** if they don't have enough working capital. As well as generating sales, the business must make sure it **collects money** quickly to get **cash** to pay its liabilities. They need to make sure that they don't **tie up** too much of their working capital as inventories or receivables — businesses **can't** use these to pay their current liabilities until they're turned into **cash**.

Businesses need Enough Cash but Not Too Much

1) Businesses need **just enough** cash to pay short-term debts. They shouldn't have too much cash, because spare cash is great at **paying off debts**, but lousy at **earning money** for the business.
2) Businesses with a **long cash-flow cycle** (see p.72) need more cash, as they have to **wait** for money to come in.
3) To make money, the business needs **non-current assets** that make sales possible (e.g. machinery that produces products).
4) **Inflation** increases the costs of wages and buying/holding stock, so firms need more cash when inflation is high.
5) When a business **expands**, it needs more cash to avoid **overtrading**. Overtrading means producing so much that the business can't afford to pay its **suppliers** until it gets paid by its **customers**.

Businesses also need finance for Capital Expenditure

1) **Fixed capital** (or **capital expenditure**) means money used to buy **non-current assets** (fixed assets). These are things used over and over again to produce goods or services for sale — e.g. **factories** and **equipment**.
2) Businesses need capital expenditure to **start up**, to **grow** and to **replace** worn out equipment. They must **set aside** enough **money** to stop **non-current assets** from **wearing out**, and then they can **decide** how much **money** to invest in **growth**. This is called **allocating capital expenditure**.
3) You'll find **capital expenditure** on the balance sheet (see p.100) as **non-current assets**.

Debtors (Receivables) and Stock (Inventories) must be Controlled

1) A business needs to control its **debtors** (people who owe money to the firm). It's important that businesses make sure that their debtors pay them **on time**.
2) A company might sell millions of pounds worth of goods, but if it doesn't make sure that **payment** has been received, there'll be **no money coming in**. That means that the business is **no better off** in terms of cash flow than if it had sold nothing at all.
3) The business still has to **pay** wages, loan repayments, etc. whether its debtors have paid up or not, so businesses have to control debtors to **survive**.

Karen and Rita spent many a long hour in the debtor control room.

1) A business needs to hold suitable volumes of **stock** (raw materials and unsold products) to allow it to satisfy the demands of the market.
2) A business holding **too little stock** will **lose sales** as it won't be able to supply enough goods to the market to meet demand.
3) A business with **too much stock** has money tied up in stock instead of **working** for the company. It would be better to use the money to pay debts or wages, or invest it in new projects.
4) Businesses **predict** what the **demand** for their products will be in order to make sure that they have a suitable level of stock.

Financial Analysis — Balance Sheets

Stock is Valued at Cost or at Net Realisable Value — whichever's Lower

1) Accounting conventions say that stock values must be **realisable**. The **net realisable value** is the amount the company could get by **selling** the stock right now in its **current state** (rather than after it's been used to make a finished product).
2) The **realisable value** might be **lower** than the **cost value** (the amount the business **paid** for the stock). Or the net realisable value might be **higher** than its original cost price, if demand for the materials has increased since the business bought them — this often happens in businesses like **jewellery manufacturers**, as the price of gold and precious stones fluctuates and might go up after the business has bought them.
3) The company must record the stock value in its accounts as the **lower** value out of **cost** or **net realisable value**.

Example: A computer business buys **300 microprocessors** at **£100 each** to use in the production of laptop computers, so the **total cost** is **£30 000**. Later, the business updates the specification of the laptops and **can't use** the microprocessors it originally bought, so it has to sell them. In the meantime, **technology** has **moved on** and there are more advanced, faster microprocessors on the market. There's **little demand** for the old microprocessors, and the business would only be able to sell the old stock for **£40 each** (**£12 000** altogether). The business has to record the value of the stock as **£12 000** in its accounts, rather than the **£30 000** it originally paid.

Assets Depreciate — they Lose Value over Time

1) Most assets **lose value** over time — the **longer** the business has them, the **less** they're **worth**. E.g. if a business has been using a piece of machinery for six months, it won't be worth as much as it was when it was new, even if it's still in good condition.
2) Assets lose their value for three main reasons — they suffer **wear and tear**, they may **break down**, and they become **old fashioned** when new models or inventions come onto the market.
3) The **drop in value** of a business asset over time is called **depreciation**.
4) Although most assets depreciate, sometimes it can work the other way round and assets can **increase** in value. E.g. **property** can increase in value over time because property prices tend to rise.

Derek wondered if this meant the factory wouldn't increase in value after all.

Accounts reflect the Depreciation of assets

1) Businesses **calculate depreciation** each year to make sure that an asset's **value** on the **balance sheet** is a **true reflection** of what the business would get from **selling** it.
2) Building depreciation into each year's accounts **avoids** the fall in value hitting **all at once** when the business **sells** the asset. Spreading out the cost of the depreciation over several years is a truer reflection of the situation and allows the business to make **comparisons** between financial years more easily.

E.g. by depreciating a piece of machinery over 10 years, a business can take a tenth of the **fall in value** of the equipment (the difference between what the asset cost to buy and what managers think they'll be able to sell it for when they finish using it) into account each year. Without depreciating the asset, the business would be **understating its costs** (and therefore overstating its profits) for each year until it got rid of the asset, which would then show up as a **huge cost** on the accounts.

3) The **amount lost** through depreciation is recorded on the **income statement** (see p.105) as an **expense**. It's unusual because it isn't a cash expense — it's a recognition of the money that's been put into the asset that the business can't ever get back.

Financial Analysis — Balance Sheets

OK, now you're clued up on balance sheets, it's time to think about how to use them to assess financial performance.

Balance Sheets show the Short-Term Financial Status of the Company

> The <u>liquidity</u> of an <u>asset</u> is how easy it is to turn it into cash and spend it. <u>Cash</u> is the most liquid asset, followed by <u>receivables</u>, <u>inventories</u> and <u>short-term</u> investments.

1) The balance sheet shows you how much the business is **worth**.
2) **Working capital** (net current assets) is the amount of money the business has available in the short term. It's calculated by subtracting **current liabilities** from **current assets**. See p.102 for more on working capital.
3) **Suppliers** are particularly interested in **working capital** and **liquidity**. They can look at the balance sheet to see how **liquid** the firm's assets are, as well as how much working capital the firm has. The more liquid the assets, the better the firm will be at **paying bills**. This helps them decide whether to offer the business supplies on **credit**, and how much credit to offer.
4) The balance sheet shows **sources of capital**. Ideally, **long-term loans** or **mortgages** are used to finance the purchase of fixed assets. A well managed business wouldn't borrow too much through **short-term overdrafts**, because overdrafts are an expensive way of borrowing.
5) This short-term information can help the business assess its internal **strengths** and **weaknesses**. For example, if the business has a large amount of **working capital**, they could **invest** this money in new equipment or use it to **pay off** some loans.

By Comparing Balance Sheets you can see Long-Term Trends

1) Comparing this year's balance sheet to previous years' accounts lets you pick out **trends** in company finances and evaluate the **financial performance** of the company. Looking at the "bottom line" over several years shows how the business is **changing**.
2) A **quick increase** in **non-current assets** indicates that the company has invested in property or machinery. This means that the company is investing in a **growth strategy**, which may increase its profit over the medium term — useful information for shareholders and potential shareholders, who want to see more profit.
3) Increases in **reserves** also suggest an increase in **profits** — good news for shareholders.
4) Looking at several balance sheets together also shows **trends** in how the business has **raised** its **capital**. It's risky to suddenly start **borrowing** a lot, in case interest rates rise. A company with a high value of loan capital and a relatively low value of share capital or reserves would be in trouble if the Bank of England put **interest rates** up.
5) Businesses can use long-term trends to identify their **strengths** and **weaknesses** too. If the **non-current liabilities** (i.e. long-term debts) have increased, the business might want to try and **reduce** its borrowing in the future.

Practice Questions

Q1 How do you calculate working capital?

Q2 What does 'net realisable value' mean?

Q3 What is depreciation?

Q4 Why do businesses calculate the depreciation of their assets each year?

Q5 Why would suppliers be interested in a business's balance sheet?

Exam Questions

Q1 The balance sheet for Joanne's salon shows £400 inventories (stock), £50 receivables (debtors), £150 cash and current liabilities of £120. Evaluate the short-term financial position of Joanne's business. [6 marks]

Q2 Explain why it is important for a business to control its debtors. [6 marks]

All this revision's making me feel a bit unbalanced...

There's loads to learn over the last few pages. It's all about balance — you don't want too much working capital, but on the other hand you don't want too little. The same goes for stock. Then there are debtors to chase up, and depreciation to take into account too. And then you have to walk the dog, empty the bins and make me a cake.

Financial Analysis — Income Statements

An income statement is a way of reporting profit or loss over a certain period of time (usually a year). It's a summary that shareholders and potential investors can use to assess the company's performance.

Income Statements show Revenue and Expenses

1) The income statement (also known as a profit and loss account) shows how much money has been **coming into the company** (**revenue**) and how much has been **going out** (**expenses**).
2) Revenue is **sales income** from selling goods and services. This includes **cash payments** and sales on **credit**. Expenses include the cost of **raw materials**, **production** costs, **marketing** costs, **wages** etc.
3) These figures can be used in **assessing** a company's **financial performance** — e.g. if **revenue** has **increased** by **more than** the rate of **inflation** (see p.126) since the business published its last income statement, it's often a sign that the company is **healthy**.
4) PLCs (public limited companies) have to **publish** their accounts so that they're available to **anyone** who wants to look at them — that includes shareholders, potential shareholders and competitors.

Income Statements cover a period of Time

1) Income statements should cover one whole accounting year. An income statement that covers **less than 12 months** can be **misleading**. High street retailers can generate **half their annual revenue** in the lead-up to **Christmas** — an income statement ignoring this period won't give an **accurate picture**.
2) Income statements can also contain the **previous year's data**, for **easy comparison**, to see what's **changed**. Some companies provide the previous five years' data. It's useful for spotting **trends** in revenue, expenses and profits, and helps whoever's looking at the accounts to see what kind of a **financial position** the business is in.

Income Statements show Different Measures of Profit

On page 70, you saw that there are **different measures** of **profit**.
Each measure shows **different things** about the company's finances.

1) **Gross profit** is **revenue** minus the **cost of sales**.
2) **Operating profit** is **revenue** minus the **cost of sales** minus **operating expenses** (or **gross profit** minus **operating expenses**).
3) **Profit before tax** takes into account any **profit** or **loss** from **one-off events**, and **other expenses** such as **finance costs**.
4) **Profit after tax** (also called **profit for the year**) is what's left after corporation tax has been paid.
5) **Retained profit** is what's left from profit after tax, once **share dividends** have been paid to shareholders.

These measures can be used to Assess Financial Performance

1) **Gross profit** shows the money being made from actually **making** and **selling** products. If gross profit is **low**, **managers** need to look at ways of **reducing the cost** of making the product, or **increasing the selling price**.
2) **Operating profit** shows the money made from **'normal' business operations**. If **operating profit** is significantly **lower** than **gross profit**, it could show that the company's **operating expenses** are a **weak area**. Managers should take steps to **reduce** these expenses, e.g. by reducing **marketing costs**. However, the operating profit could reflect a big **investment** in **people**, **premises**, etc. **Banks** and **investors** will look at this figure to assess the **risk** of lending to or investing in the business.
3) Comparing **profit before tax** to **operating profit** shows if **income** or **expenses** are coming from **other activities** (e.g. selling or buying a building), rather than 'normal' activities (e.g. making and selling goods), which may **not** continue in the future.
4) **Profit after tax** tells you if the company is **profitable** or not — **shareholders** and **potential investors** will look at this figure to assess investments.
5) **Retained profit** shows how much **internal finance** the company has available to **invest**, which shows how strong its **growth potential** is.

Financial Analysis — Income Statements

*Here's what an **Income Statement** looks like*

Here's a **simplified** version of an income statement. Sometimes the costs and expenses will be **broken down** into different categories, but I've lumped them all together so you can see what's going on.

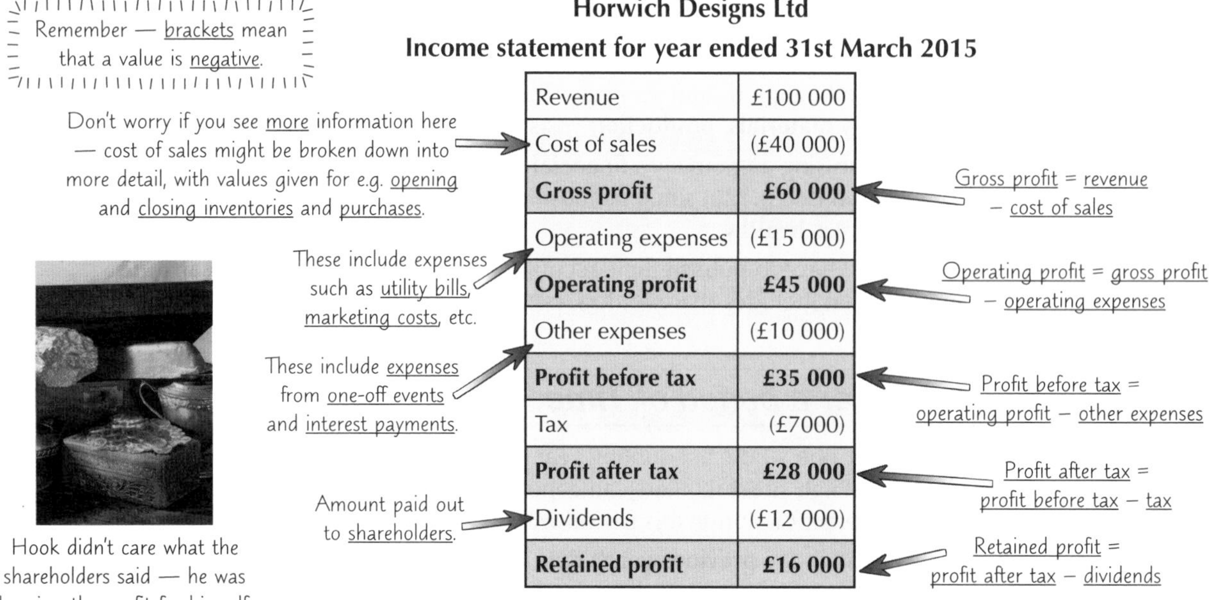

Horwich Designs Ltd

Income statement for year ended 31st March 2015

Revenue	£100 000
Cost of sales	(£40 000)
Gross profit	**£60 000**
Operating expenses	(£15 000)
Operating profit	**£45 000**
Other expenses	(£10 000)
Profit before tax	**£35 000**
Tax	(£7000)
Profit after tax	**£28 000**
Dividends	(£12 000)
Retained profit	**£16 000**

Hook didn't care what the shareholders said — he was keeping the profit for himself.

*Businesses can **Choose** what to do with their **Profits***

Businesses can use their **profits** in **two** main ways:

- they can pay **dividends** to shareholders,
- they can keep the profit in the business as **retained profit**.

1) **Shareholders** usually want companies to pay **high dividends** so that they get a **good return** on their investment. If companies **don't** pay dividends, or pay very **low** dividends, existing shareholders might **sell** their shares.
2) **Retaining profit** allows the business to **spend** on things that are likely to **increase** their profits in the future — e.g. buying **fixed assets** like machinery, business premises, etc. This allows the business to **increase production**, which could lead to **increased revenue** and **profits** in the future.
3) Companies usually try to find a **balance** between dividends and retained profit — they pay a proportion of their profit to their **shareholders** and **reinvest** the rest in the business to fund **growth**.

Practice Questions

Q1 What does an income statement show?

Q2 Why can income statements that cover less than 12 months be misleading?

Q3 What is retained profit?

Q4 How can investors use income statements to assess financial performance?

Q5 Give two examples of things a business can do with its profits.

Answer on p.201.

Exam Question

Q1 In the year ending 31st March 2015, a haulage company had an annual revenue of £1 500 000 and the cost of sales was £500 000. Operating expenses were £250 000, other expenses were £100 000 and the company paid £130 000 in tax. It then paid out £250 000 in dividends to its shareholders.
Draw up an income statement for this company, including values for gross profit, operating profit, profits before and after tax and retained profit. Do you think the company has had a successful financial year? Justify your answer. [16 marks]

I'd definitely spend all my profits on ice cream...

Income statements might look a little confusing, but if you need to complete one, work down from the revenue and subtract all the different expenses to find the different profits. Make sure you know how to interpret them too.

Financial Analysis — Value and Limitations

Having just spent 7 pages telling you all about financial analysis, it's time to think about how useful it is.

Financial Analysis is Useful for Decision-Making

1) **Analysis** of the balance sheet and income statement can be really useful for **comparing** a business's current performance to its **competitors' performance**, and to its own performance in the **past**, to identify **trends** in the business's financial performance.
2) The analysis can help managers to make **decisions** based on the company's **financial strengths** and **weaknesses**. For example, they might decide to **reduce dividends** and retain more of their profits to invest in the business if the analysis shows that the business's growth has been slow.
3) **Potential investors** and **lenders** can use the analysis to **decide** if they want to **invest in** or **lend to** the business.

Financial analysis Doesn't Cover anything Non-Numerical

1) Financial analysis **only** takes into account **financial data**. This is **useful** for **potential investors**, but it **ignores** a lot of **qualitative** (non-numerical) **data** that potential investors should also consider.
2) **Internal factors** that **don't appear** in the analysis include the **quality** of staff and products, the company's **market share**, future **sales targets**, **productivity** levels, the firm's impact on the **environment** and **customer satisfaction** (see pages 114-117).
3) **External factors** like the **economic** or **market** environment aren't reflected in the analysis either. It doesn't tell you anything about what a **competitor** might do next, or what legislation the government might pass. The development of **technology**, or potential changes to the **location** of the business (e.g. a new rail link) don't appear either. You'd need to analyse all these **external factors** to see how they might affect the business.

The Balance Sheet and Income Statement don't tell you Everything

1) The **balance sheet** is a statement about one point in the **past**, which may not help predict the **future**.
2) The balance sheet doesn't give any clues about the **market** or the **economy** that the business is trading in.
3) Balance sheets value some intangible assets (e.g. a brand recently purchased by the company), but they don't value intangible assets like **staff skill**, **staff motivation** or **management experience**.
4) If bad debts are included in the balance sheet as an asset, the analysis will be misleading — see p.101.

1) The **income statement** is useful for assessing the performance of the company, but it isn't the whole story.
2) It doesn't include any information about **external factors** such as **market demand**, which would be useful in forecasting **future revenue** and **profit**.
3) It doesn't include any information about **internal factors** such as staff morale, which would be useful in determining **productivity** and therefore **profitability**.
4) In times of **inflation**, the income statement isn't so useful, because inflationary rises in price distort the true value of revenue.
5) The income statement can be **deliberately distorted**, by bringing forward sales from the next trading period and including them as part of this trading period.
6) It's best to look at the income statement and the balance sheet **together** to assess a business's finances.

Practice Questions

Q1 Give an example of why financial analysis is useful to a business.

Q2 Give two examples of non-numerical external factors that affect businesses but aren't taken into account in their financial analysis.

Exam Question

Q1 Explain why you shouldn't rely solely on financial analysis to predict a company's future performance. [8 marks]

Financial analysis never tells me anything — I can't get it to say a word...

You might think some of the stuff on this page is obvious, but it's funny how your mind can go blank in an exam as soon as you get a question like 'Why shouldn't shareholders rely solely on financial analysis to make investment decisions?'

Financial Analysis — Ratios

Ratios turn financial data from balance sheets and income statements into easy-to-understand numbers. You can use them to compare companies to each other and to assess a company's performance over time.

Liquidity Ratios show How Much Money is available to Pay The Bills

1) A firm without enough **working capital** (see p.102) has poor **liquidity**. It can't **use** its assets to **pay** for things when it needs them.
2) The **liquidity** of an asset is how easily it can be turned into **cash** and used to **buy** things. **Cash** is **very** liquid, **non-current assets** such as **factories** are **not liquid**, and **stocks** (**inventories**) and money owed by **debtors** (**receivables**) are in between.
3) A business that doesn't have enough **current assets** to pay its liabilities when they are due is **insolvent**. It either has to quickly find the money to pay them, give up and **cease trading**, or go into **liquidation**.
4) **Liquidity** can be **improved** by decreasing stock levels, speeding up collection of debts owed to the business, or slowing down payments to creditors (e.g. suppliers).
5) A **liquidity ratio** shows how **solvent** a business is (how able it is to pay its debts). The main liquidity ratio you need to know is the **current ratio**.

Current Ratio = Current Assets ÷ Current Liabilities

1) The **current ratio** compares **current assets** to current liabilities.

$$\text{Current ratio} = \frac{\text{current assets}}{\text{current liabilities}}$$

The current ratio is also called the working capital ratio.

For example, a business with **£30 000** of **current assets** and **£32 000** of **current liabilities** has a current ratio of: $\frac{£30\,000}{£32\,000}$ = **0.9375** (this means that for **£1** of **liabilities**, the company only has **£0.9375** (or 93.75p) of **assets**, which isn't great, as it means there **aren't enough assets** to cover the **liabilities**).

You could write this in ratio form as 0.9375:1 — see p.192 for more on writing ratios.

2) In reality, a business probably couldn't **sell off** all its stock. It'd also need **additional capital** to **replace** stocks — the current ratio should be **higher** than 1 to take account of this. 1.5 or 2 is considered ideal.
3) A value much below 1.5 suggests a **liquidity problem** and that it might struggle to meet its current liabilities. See above for **ways** that a company can **improve** its **liquidity**.

Return on Capital Employed (ROCE) is a Profitability Ratio

1) A **profitability ratio** shows **profit margin**. The most important profitability ratio is the **return on capital employed** (**ROCE**). It's considered to be the best way of analysing profitability and is expressed as a **percentage**, calculated by:

There are other profit margins on p.71.

$$\text{Return on Capital Employed (\%)} = \frac{\text{operating profit}}{\text{total equity + non-current liabilities}} \times 100$$

The operating profit is on the income statement, and the total equity and non-current liabilities are on the balance sheet.

total equity + non-current liabilities = capital employed

2) The **ROCE** tells you how much money is **made** by the business, compared to how much money's been **put into** the business. The **higher** the ROCE, the **better**.
3) It's important to **compare** the ROCE with the Bank of England **interest rate** at the time, because this tells investors whether they'd be better off putting their money in the **bank**.
4) ROCE can be **improved** by **paying off debt** to reduce non-current liabilities, or by making the business more **efficient** to **increase operating profit**.
5) ROCE is just one measure of **return on investment** (see p.68). Another important one is the **average rate of return** (see p.138).

Financial Analysis — Ratios

Efficiency or *Performance Ratios* show how *Efficiently* the firm is working

1) Efficiency ratios show managers and shareholders **how well** the business is using its **resources**.
2) There are **three** important efficiency ratios you need to know — **inventory turnover** ratio (stock turnover ratio), **payables days** ratio (creditor days ratio) and **receivables days** ratio (debtor days ratio). They show how efficiently the business is using its **assets** and how well managers are controlling **stock**, **creditors** and **debtors**.

1) Inventory Turnover Ratio = Cost of Sales ÷ Cost of Average Stock Held

1) The inventory turnover ratio (stock turnover ratio) compares the **cost** of all the **sales** a business makes over the year to the **cost of the average stock** held.
2) You need to know the **cost price** of everything the business has **sold**, i.e. what the products cost the firm to make. **Stock** is valued at **cost price**, so you need **sales** at cost price too. You'll find **cost of sales** on the **income statement** and **stock held** on the **balance sheet**.

$$\text{Inventory Turnover} = \frac{\text{cost of sales}}{\text{cost of average stock held}}$$

You might see 'cost of sales' written as 'cost of goods sold' instead.

For example, if a business's **sales** cost **£160 000** and its **average stock held** costs **£8000**, it has an **inventory turnover** of $\frac{£160\,000}{£8000}$ = **20** (as a **ratio**, this would be 20 : 1).

Mabel much preferred apple turnover ratios to inventory turnover ratios.

3) This ratio tells you **how many times** during the year the business **sold all its stock** — so the business above sold its stock **20 times**. A fruit and veg stall might sell their **entire stock every day**, which would give a stock turnover ratio of **365**. A property developer who took **4 months** to do up and sell each house would have a ratio of **3**. Businesses operating **JIT production** have a **very high** ratio.
4) When you analyse this ratio, you need to judge if the business has **enough stock** to **fulfil orders**, but **not too much stock** to be **efficient**. Holding twice the stock needed might not be an efficient use of funds. The ideal turnover ratio depends on the type of the business, but companies generally aim for a higher value than in previous years or compared to their rivals.
5) The inventory turnover ratio can be improved by **holding less stock**, or **increasing sales**. Easier said than done...
6) **Aged stock analysis** lets managers make sure that old stock gets sold before it becomes **obsolete** and **unsaleable**. It lists all stock in **age order**, so the manager can **discount** old stock and cut down orders for slow-selling stock.

2) Payables Days Ratio = Payables ÷ Cost of Sales × 365

1) The payables days ratio (creditor days ratio) compares the **amount** the business **owes** to its **creditors** to the **cost** of all the **sales** a business makes over the year:

$$\text{Payables Days} = \frac{\text{payables}}{\text{cost of sales}} \times 365$$

'Payables' is a current liability on the balance sheet and 'cost of sales' is on the income statement.

For example, a business with **payables** of **£300** and **sales** that **cost £7000**, has a **payables days ratio** of $\frac{£300}{£7000} \times 365$ = **15.64 days**.

2) This is the number of days the firm takes to **pay** for goods it buys on credit from **suppliers**.
3) You can establish a **trend** over a period of time and use this trend to analyse the efficiency of the firm. For instance, if the trend is upwards it may suggest the firm is getting into **difficulties paying** its suppliers. This might be OK, but if the suppliers get the hump and decide they want to be paid **now**, it's a **problem**.
4) A business can also use this ratio to **maximise** its **cash flow**. So if the business above had an agreed credit period of **30 days**, it could take up to **2 weeks longer** to pay its debts, as it currently takes only 15.64 days.

Financial Analysis — Ratios

3) **Receivables Days Ratio** = Receivables ÷ Sales Revenue × 365

1) The receivables days ratio (debtor days ratio) compares the **amount owed** to a business by its **debtors** to the **total sales revenue** for the year:

$$\text{Receivables Days} = \frac{\text{receivables}}{\text{sales revenue}} \times 365$$

You'll find 'receivables' on the balance sheet as a current asset and 'sales revenue' is on the income statement.

For example, a business with **receivables** of **£1500** and **sales revenue** of **£50 000** has a **receivables days ratio** of $\frac{£1500}{£50\,000} \times 365 =$ **10.95 days**.

2) 'Receivables days' is the number of days that the business has to **wait to be paid** for goods it supplies on credit.
3) It's best to have **low** receivables days, because it helps with **cash flow** and **working capital**. What makes a good receivables days ratio depends on the type of business. **Retailers** tend to get paid **straight away** unless they offer credit on items such as TVs or fridges. **Medium size businesses** usually take **70-90 days** to get invoices paid.
4) You can **compare** receivables days ratios with previous months or years to look for **trends**. An **upward trend** may be because the business has offered **longer credit terms** to attract more customers. However, if it isn't monitored, the business may be heading for **cash flow problems**.
5) **Aged receivables analysis** lets managers **control receivables days**. Unpaid accounts are listed in order of how long they've been unpaid. The ones that are **most overdue** are **targeted** first for repayment.
6) **Inventory turnover** and **receivables days** are measures of **activity** — they tell you how **effectively** a business is using its **resources** to generate **revenue**.

Practice Questions

Q1 How do you work out the current ratio?

Q2 What does ROCE show?

Q3 What does the inventory turnover ratio show?

Q4 Which would have the higher inventory turnover ratio, a Porsche dealership or a shoe shop?

Q5 What's the difference between the payables days ratio and the receivables days ratio?

Exam Questions

Answers to Q1 and Q3 a) and b) are on p.201.

Q1 What is the return on capital employed of a business that has an operating profit of £50 000, total equity of £130 000 and non-current liabilities of £30 000?
A 61.54% B 16.67% C 31.25% D 20% [1 mark]

Q2 A medium-sized company is owed £7000 by its trade customers and has sales revenue of £20 000 over the year. Using receivables days analysis, evaluate how well the company controls its debtors. [6 marks]

Q3 The table below shows some financial information about a shop that sells skiwear.

Current assets	£40 000
Cost of sales	£120 000
Current liabilities	£50 000
Cost of average stock held	£80 000

a) Calculate the current ratio. [2 marks]
b) Calculate the inventory turnover ratio. [2 marks]
c) Use your results to evaluate the financial position of the company, and suggest ways in which it could improve its current position. [12 marks]

Oh look, what a lot of "lovely" ratios...

Being totally honest, these ratios are a bit of a pain in the backside. It's easy to get them mixed up, so make sure you know which one to use when. You have to be able to interpret them too — so make sure you know what the figures tell you about financial performance. Have a look at Section 15 if your Maths skills are a little bit rusty.

Financial Analysis — Gearing

If you were worried that there weren't enough financial ratios, never fear — there's still one more incredibly exciting ratio to go. Well, maybe not 'incredibly exciting' as such, but it does have an interesting name — gearing.

Gearing shows *Where* a business gets its *Capital* from

1) **Gearing** is another really important ratio. It shows **potential investors** where a business's finance has come from, i.e. what **proportion** of its finance comes from **non-current liabilities** (long-term debt), rather than **share capital** or **reserves** (equity).
2) Gearing is calculated using information from the lower part of a **balance sheet** (see p.100) — the part that shows where the money comes from. To work out the gearing, divide the amount of finance that comes from **non-current liabilities** by the **total amount** of finance in the company (from loans, shares and reserves):

$$\text{Gearing (\%)} = \frac{\text{non-current liabilities}}{\text{total equity} + \text{non-current liabilities}} \times 100$$

See p.101 for more on non-current liabilities.

3) A gearing **above 50%** shows that **more than half** of a business's finance comes from **long-term debt** — the business is **high-geared**. A gearing of **25%-50%** is fairly **standard** — **some** of its finance comes from long-term debt, but not too much. A gearing of **below 25%** shows it is **low-geared**, because **less than a quarter** of the finance comes from long-term debt.

Gearing shows how *Vulnerable* a business is to *Changes* in *Interest Rates*

1) The more the business is **borrowing**, the harder they'll be hit by a rise in interest rates. How much **borrowing** a business can do depends on its profitability and the value of its **assets** — the more assets the business can offer as **security**, the more money it will be able to borrow.
2) Gearing is a crude **risk assessment** that an investor can use to help decide whether to buy shares in the company. The more the firm borrows, the **more interest** it will have to pay — this may affect **profits** and the **dividend** paid to shareholders. The more the firm borrows, the more **risk** there is that the investor won't get much dividend.

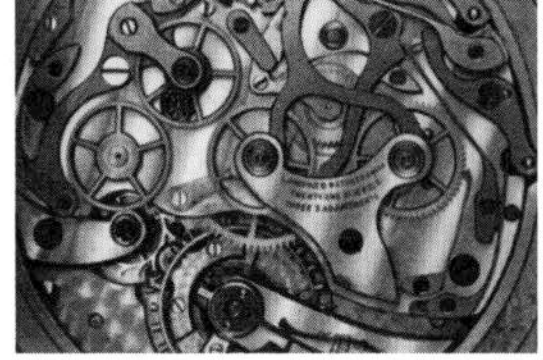
Looks pretty high geared to me.

Example

A firm has gearing of 11% — it's **low-geared**.
- This tells you that **most** long-term funds come from **shareholders**, not borrowing.
- This could be a sign that the firm is **risk averse** — it doesn't want to run the risk of spending too much money on interest payments.
- Because the firm doesn't have to spend its profits on interest payments, it can **withstand** a **fall** in profits more easily than a highly geared firm, since the firm can easily choose to **reduce** dividend payments to shareholders, unlike loan repayments, which have to be made.

Example

Another firm has gearing of 72% — it's **high-geared**.
- This tells you that **most** long-term funds come from **borrowing**.
- It's obvious that the firm is willing to take **risks** — if profits fall, or interest rates rise, the business still has to keep up with the **loan repayments** or it could **lose** the **assets** the loans are secured on (e.g. business premises).
- The company may be high-geared in order to fund **growth** (see next page), or because its directors don't want outside shareholders to **own** a large part of the business, and so they prefer to borrow money rather than sell shares.

Financial Analysis — Gearing

High Gearing has **Risks** and **Rewards** for **Businesses**

High gearing can be **risky**, but some businesses are willing to take these risks because of the **potential rewards**:

Rewards of high gearing for businesses

1) One benefit of **borrowing** money for the business is extra **funds** for expansion. Ideally, the loan is invested in projects or technology which **increase profits** by more than enough to pay off the loan repayments. **High gearing** can be attractive during a **growth phase**. A firm that's trying to become the market leader, and has growing profits along with a strong product portfolio, may decide to borrow heavily in order to **fund expansion** and gain a **competitive advantage**. This will **increase** the firm's **gearing**. During times of **growth**, there is plenty of **profit** even after they've paid the loan interest and repayments, so high gearing can be good for the business.
2) When interest rates are very **low**, high gearing is less risky because interest payments are lower.

Risks of high gearing for businesses

1) The **risk** to the business of borrowing money is that it might not be able to afford the **repayments** — it might not make enough profit to pay back the **loan** and **interest**.
2) Taking out loans can be **risky** even when interest rates are low, because they might **go up** later and the business will still be committed to making the **repayments**.

High Gearing has **Risks** and **Rewards** for **Investors** too

1) The reward (of investing money in the business) for the **lender** or **shareholder** is **interest** for lenders or a share **dividend** for shareholders (often paid out twice a year). Shareholders can also sell their shares at a **profit** if the share price goes up. Since high gearing can lead to high profits for businesses, shareholders might expect to see **large dividends** and a **big increase** in the share price compared to a low-geared company.
2) The **risk** to the **shareholder** of high gearing is that the business may **fail** if it can't afford to keep up with loan repayments. When a business goes into **liquidation**, lenders will probably get the money they're owed, but the shareholders could lose most or all of the money they've invested in the business.

Practice Questions

Q1 What is the formula used to calculate gearing?

Q2 What's meant by "high gearing"?

Q3 Changes to a business lead it to become high-geared. How could this affect shareholders?

Q4 Give one risk and one possible reward for a business of being high-geared.

Exam Questions

Q1 Calculate the gearing for a plumbing company that has non-current liabilities of £20 000 and total equity of £30 000. [3 marks]

Answer to Q1 on p.201.

Q2 Explain the risks of investing in a business which has high gearing. [6 marks]

Q3 An interior design company's gearing has increased from 48% to 54% in the last year, during a period when the economy was stable. To what extent do you think that this will benefit the company? [12 marks]

Low gearing is also helpful when driving uphill...

More ratios — good old AQA sure knows what makes A-level students happy. You can probably guess what I'm going to say — learn what gearing is for, and be prepared to use it in the exam. Exam questions might ask for a specific ratio analysis, or you might get marks for using ratios if you're asked to assess a business's financial position.

Value and Limitations of Ratios

Looking at ratios is a good way of assessing a company's financial performance, but it does have some limitations too.

***Ratio Analysis** can be very **Useful**...*

1) **Ratios** are a really good way of looking at a business's **performance** over a period of time — they can be used to spot **trends**, and to identify the **financial strengths** and **weaknesses** of the business.
2) However, these trends need to take account of **variable factors** — things which change over time, such as **inflation**, accounting procedures, the business activities of the firm and the market environment.
3) Managers can use ratio analysis to help with **decision making** — e.g. if their payables days ratio is low, they might negotiate a **longer credit period** which will **improve** the business's **cash flow**.
4) **Potential investors** can use the ratios to help them decide if they want to **invest** in the business — they may choose **not** to invest in a **high-geared business** if they think it is too risky.
5) It's also useful to **compare** ratios with **other businesses**, either in the same industry or in different industries. Ratios provide a more **meaningful** comparison when looking at **different-sized** businesses (which may have very different **profits**).

*... but it has its **Limitations***

All financial **ratios** compare figures from the **balance sheet** or **income statement**, and give you a raw **number** as an answer.

Ratios don't take account of any **non-numerical factors**, so they don't provide an absolute means of assessing a company's financial health. They have several **limitations**:

1) **Internal strengths**, such as the quality of staff, don't appear in the figures, so they won't come up in ratios.
2) **External factors**, such as the **economic** or **market** environment, aren't reflected in the figures. When the market's very **competitive**, or the economy's in a **downturn**, it's OK for ratios to suffer a bit.
3) **Future changes** such as technological advances or changes in interest rates can't be predicted by the figures, so they won't show up in the ratios.
4) Ratios only contain information about the **past** and **present**. A business which has **just started** investing for growth will have lousy ratios until the investment **pays off** — that doesn't mean it's not worth investing in.

Example of how ratio analysis can't predict changes in external factors

- Harry is interested in **investing** in XYZ Ltd. **Ratio analysis** indicates that XYZ is **performing strongly** and gives a **good rate of return** for the investor, so he decides to **buy 1000 shares**.
- Later that day, Harry talks to Sarah, who says **new EU health and safety legislation** will **ban XYZ** from making any more of its products from next year onwards. XYZ Ltd must now either **diversify** into another product/service or **close**.
- Harry doesn't feel so clever about his investment now. XYZ Ltd will need **time** and **money** to **reinvest** in a new production line so **profits will be very scarce** for the next few months. Worse still, XYZ Ltd may go **bankrupt** and he'd have shares with **no value at all**. What a nightmare.

Practice Questions

Q1 Why might comparing financial ratios to another business be more useful than comparing profits?

Q2 Give an example of an internal business strength that isn't allowed for in ratio analysis.

Exam Questions

Q1 Explain two factors that should be taken into account when comparing financial ratios for different years. [8 marks]

Q2 Ratio analysis gives information about the past and present.
Analyse the value of ratio analysis in predicting future performance. [12 marks]

Limitations of ratios — well, they can't do cartwheels for starters...

It's not possible to make 100% solid conclusions from ratio analysis alone. You need to use other data from several sources alongside ratios. It's important to consider the market that the business is trading in, and what its competitors are doing. Bear in mind that using data from the past isn't always a great way to predict the future — stuff changes.

Analysing Overall Performance

Looking at financial data is a good way of analysing a company's position — but there are many other factors that need to be taken into consideration to judge how well it's doing all round.

Non-Financial Data shows Strengths and Weaknesses in Other Areas

1) A company needs to assess its **strengths** and **weaknesses** using both **quantitative** (numerical) and **qualitative** (non-numerical) data. This is an important part of **SWOT analysis** (see p.99).
2) Analysing **non-financial data** allows a company to consider other **internal factors** (besides financial performance) that can combine to give them a **competitive advantage.** They'll look at a number of **performance measures** to see how they're doing.
3) Data is collected from each **department**, e.g. **marketing**, **human resources** (HR) and **operations**. **Performance measures** include things like:

Marketing

- Calculations of **market share, market growth** and **sales growth** (see pages 26 and 28).
- **Portfolio analysis** (see p.42) — the **products** a company has, what stage they're at in their **life cycle** (see p.44) and their **perceived** and **actual quality**.

Human Resources

- Calculations of **labour productivity**, **labour turnover**, **labour retention**, **employee costs as a percentage of turnover** and **labour cost per unit** (see p.84-85).
- An assessment of **staff skills** and **qualifications**, as well as HR plans for **training** and **recruitment** — to see if these are matched to the needs of the business. **Staff morale** and methods of **motivation** may also be assessed.

Operations

- Calculations of **capacity** and **capacity utilisation**, **unit costs** and **fixed/variable costs** (see p.56-57 and p.6).
- The **age** and **condition** of any **machinery**, the operations **processes** used, etc.

4) When **analysing** the data, managers need to **ask questions** and **make judgements**. For example, if **labour productivity** has gone **down**, they need to find out **why**. If **capacity utilisation** is nearly at **100%**, they'll need to think about how the business could **expand**.
5) Managers also need to analyse how well the business is doing **overall**. For example:
   - How well are **resources** being allocated between departments?
   - Do the **organisational structure** and **culture** support the company's activities?
   - How good is the company's **image**?

Businesses can Compare their data to Other Businesses

1) Businesses can **compare** their data with data from **similar businesses** — this allows them to compare their performance with that of their **competitors**, and see where they need to **improve** (or what they're doing **better** than their rivals).
2) Making comparisons puts a business's data in **context**. For example, if its **sales growth** is **low** but a competitor's sales growth is similarly **low**, managers would be **less concerned** about the business's performance than if the competitor's sales growth was much **higher**.
3) One way of making comparisons is by **benchmarking** (see p.156). Benchmarking means looking at **successful** businesses and identifying what they do **well**, then trying to **apply** their strengths to your business. It can be done by looking at **data** (e.g. unit costs) or by looking at the **processes** they use.
4) For example, if a rival business's **productivity** is much **higher**, a business can look at what their rival does **differently** and try to **adopt** their methods.
5) The benchmark business needs to be **comparable**, so their methods will be **relevant** — for example, a **fruit juice company** could compare its **capacity utilisation** to a **fizzy drinks company** and see if there are any **methods** it can **copy** to increase its capacity utilisation. The companies are **similar** enough to compare.

Analysing Overall Performance

Businesses can look at their data Over Time

1) **Data analysis** needs to be **repeated** at regular intervals to allow a business to see how things are **changing**.
2) Analysis of both financial and non-financial data can be helpful to show **trends** in performance. A trend is a **general pattern** in the data values over a period of time.
3) Analysing data over time allows the business to assess its **long-term performance**, as well as its **short-term performance** — it needs to consider whether the data shows that there is a **permanent trend**, or just a **temporary change**. The business will need to take this into account when developing its **strategy**.
4) A business should try to **predict future trends** by **extrapolating** the data (see p.32). This will help the business to see how likely it is that it will meet its **objectives**.
5) However, it can be **difficult** to **forecast future trends** as there are lots of **external factors** that are out of the business's control — e.g. changes in the **economy** or **government legislation**, **competitors' actions**, etc. This means there is a lot of **uncertainty** about the future.

Core Competences are Unique Features that make a business Competitive

1) **Core competences** are the **capabilities** of a business that are **unique** to that business and give it a **competitive advantage** over its rivals. They are capabilities that rivals do not have.

The idea of core competences was developed by Prahalad and Hamel in 1990.

2) They can be **any feature** that makes a business **different** — a specific piece of **technology** that allows a firm to produce items in a different way, **specialist staff training**, an **innovative production process**, an **understanding** of their customer base, etc. They can also be a **combination** of different features, or the way they work **together**.
3) It's easy to get **confused** over what's a core competence and what's not. Features that are **important** to a business but are a **standard expectation** of that type of business are **not** core competences — for example, good **customer service** is expected in a hotel, so it's **not** a core competence, as other hotels can easily offer the **same thing**.
4) Core competences are **fundamental** to the success of the business and should allow the business to **compete** in different **areas**. For example, WeightWatchers® started off as **meetings** and **support groups** — this **understanding** of how **support** helped people lose weight allowed the business to expand into **food products**, **recipe books**, **magazines** and even **electronic items**.
5) Core competences are **hard** for competitors to **copy**, which makes the business more **competitive**. They should also offer **benefits** to the consumer, so that consumers will **choose** the product over others.
6) A business should be able to **change** its core competences to meet the **changing demands** of its **market** (especially in rapidly-changing areas, such as **technology**). This will allow the business to **grow** and maintain its **competitive advantage**.
7) A business will **focus** on its core competences when developing its **strategy** (see p.178).

Unfortunately, navigation wasn't one of Captain Keith's core competences.

Practice Questions

Q1 Give an example of marketing, HR and operational data that could be considered when analysing performance.

Q2 Give two reasons why a business might compare its data with data from other businesses.

Q3 Why might businesses want to look at their data over time?

Q4 What are core competences?

Exam Questions

Q1 A company provides distance learning courses for business qualifications. Analyse how making comparisons with similar businesses could help the company to identify its strengths and weaknesses. [9 marks]

Q2 To what extent do you think it is important for a business to identify its core competences? [12 marks]

I'd give my overall performance a solid 8 out of 10...

Core competences are a bit tricky to get your head round — especially if they're made up of more than one factor. Try and think of a couple of core competences for yourself, and explain how they make the business successful. Then put on your favourite song and have a little sing and dance — trust me, it'll do you good.

Methods of Assessing Performance

There are a couple of methods of assessing the performance of a business that you need to know — Kaplan and Norton's Balanced Scorecard model and Elkington's Triple Bottom Line model. What a mouthful.

The **Balanced Scorecard Model** gives a **Balanced View**

1) **Kaplan and Norton's Balanced Scorecard model** is used to **assess business performance** and in **developing**, **implementing** and **monitoring strategy**.
2) It uses both **financial** and **non-financial data**, including measures of **efficiency** and **effectiveness**, and links them to the overall **strategy** and **vision** of the business.
3) It looks at four different **perspectives** (covered below). For each one, managers need to consider the **objectives**, **measures**, **targets** and **initiatives** that are **key** to the **success** of their strategy (these are sometimes shown on the model, but the one below is just a **simplified** version).
4) This process involves asking **questions**, choosing **measures** of performance based on the company's **key success factors**, setting **targets**, then coming up with **ideas** on how to achieve them.
5) Managers need to be able to **balance** these different perspectives — **improvements** in one area cannot be made at the **expense** of improvements in another. However, improvements in one area will often have a **positive impact** on another area.
6) The model is **valuable** as it treats the business as a number of **dependent**, rather than independent, **functions** — this means that all **departments** need to **consider** how their actions will **impact** on others.
7) It is a **balance** between the needs of different **stakeholders** (see p.24-25), both **internal** and **external**.
8) However, there can be **problems** when implementing this model — there's a possibility of **information overload**, potential **conflict** if one target contradicts another and **difficulty** putting the initiatives into place.

There are **Four Different Perspectives** to consider

The model looks at the business from **four different perspectives**.
The **analysis** for each one is tailored to the **strategy** and **vision** of the business.

Financial
Vision and Strategy
Customer
Internal Business Process
Learning and Growth

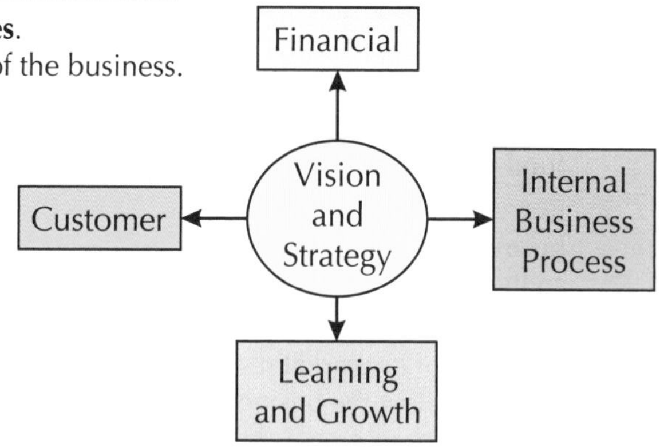

The Financial Perspective

Question: "how do we create **value** for **shareholders**?"

- **Objective**: e.g. increase profitability
- **Measures**: e.g. ROCE, (see p.108), sales growth, etc.
- **Target**: e.g. increase ROCE by 3%
- **Initiatives**: e.g. promotional campaigns, increase efficiency of production methods, etc.

The Internal Business Process Perspective

Question: "how can we improve our **processes**?"

- **Objective**: e.g. improve efficiency
- **Measures**: e.g. capacity utilisation, unit cost, productivity, etc.
- **Target**: e.g. increase labour productivity by 15%
- **Initiatives**: e.g. try different production methods, introduce new technology, etc.

The Learning and Growth Perspective

Question: "how can we continue to **grow** and **improve**?"

- **Objective**: e.g. increase employee development
- **Measures**: e.g. labour retention, amount of staff development, etc.
- **Target**: e.g. increase labour retention by 10%
- **Initiatives**: e.g. staff training and development, changing organisational design, etc.

The Customer Perspective

Question: "what do our **customers** value about us?"

- **Objectives**: e.g. improve customer loyalty, attract new customers
- **Measures**: e.g. market share, number of new customers, brand loyalty
- **Target**: e.g. increase number of new customers by 5%
- **Initiatives**: e.g. speed up delivery times, improve quality of product, etc.

Methods of Assessing Performance

Elkington's Triple Bottom Line Model measures Sustainability

1) **Elkington's Triple Bottom Line model** is used to measure a business's performance in relation to three **overlapping** areas — **profit**, **people** and **planet**.

- **Profit**: the 'traditional' financial or economic value created by the company.
- **Impact on People**: a company's social values and the way it treats its employees and the local community.
- **Impact on the Planet**: a company's environmental values and impact on the environment.

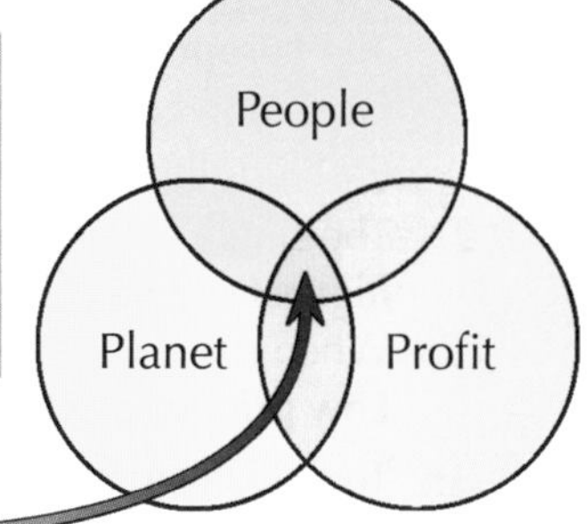

The **overlapping** area in the centre of the diagram (where all three circles overlap) is the area of **sustainability** — this is the **ideal balance** between social, environmental and financial performance.

2) Performance in each of these three areas is **assessed** and **reported** back to stakeholders. This is known as **triple bottom line reporting**.
3) The idea is that businesses are **responsible** to **all** their **stakeholders**, and to the **planet**. A business can only be **sustainable** if it **balances financial performance** with its **impact** on **people** and the **planet**.

Businesses set Objectives linked to each of the Three Areas

1) To **implement** the triple bottom line model, a business sets **objectives for performance** in each of the three areas. For example, it may aim to **reduce** its **carbon footprint** by 20%, or to pay all its staff the **living wage** or more (see p.121).
2) These objectives can be used by managers to guide **strategic planning** (see p.178-179), and to monitor the strategy's **effectiveness**.
3) The business will choose a set of **measures** to assess its performance. The values of these measures can be **judged** against **pre-set targets** or by **comparing** them to the **values** for other businesses. However, it can be more **difficult** to measure the impact of the business on **people** or the **planet** than it is to measure financial performance. Some businesses now produce **environmental** and **sustainability reports**.

No, that's an elk.

4) By **assessing** its performance in these three areas, the business is more likely to **consider** its actions in each area, and alter its **behaviour** or **culture** if necessary. If **corporate social responsibility** is important to a business (see p.133), it can use the model to help it to achieve its **social** or **environmental objectives**.
5) This model is a good way of assessing **overall** performance, as it takes into account the fact that businesses might have **other objectives** than just increasing their **profit**.

Practice Questions

Q1 What are the four different perspectives managers need to consider when using Kaplan and Norton's Balanced Scorecard model?

Q2 Give one advantage and one disadvantage of using Kaplan and Norton's Balanced Scorecard model.

Q3 What are the three areas of performance measured by Elkington's Triple Bottom Line model?

Q4 Give one difficulty in using Elkington's Triple Bottom Line model to measure the performance of a business.

Exam Questions

Q1 A delivery company has a fleet of 12 vans that it uses to deliver parcels across the UK. Analyse how the company could use the triple bottom line model to set objectives and assess its performance. [12 marks]

Q2 To what extent does Kaplan and Norton's Balanced Scorecard model assist businesses in their operational effectiveness? [25 marks]

Combine the rings to summon Captain Planet...

Sorry if that reference was lost on you — it's from a 90s TV show with a really cool theme tune (which I'll now be singing all day...). Anyway, make sure you know the details of both models and how they can be used to assess the overall performance of a business. Remember, there's more to performance than just meeting the financial objectives.

Business and the Legal Environment

The UK is a member of the EU — a union of 28 independent countries, with a population of over 500 million (bigger than the US and Japan put together). The UK's membership of the EU affects its laws in a big way.

The EU is a **Single Market** — **Trade** between member states is **Easy**

1) The **European Single Market** means there are very few **trade barriers** between EU member states. Firms don't pay **tax** when they **import** goods from other EU countries, so the EU provides easy **export** opportunities for UK firms.
2) The single market **smooths out price differences** between member states. **Producers** can look for the **highest selling price** within the EU, and consumers can look for the **lowest purchase price** within the EU. When the price in part of the EU is **high**, producers **flood** that area with their product, driving **down** prices. **Low prices** attract **more buyers** to the market, pushing prices **up**.
3) The EU **customs union** means the **same customs duties** apply to all goods entering the EU — it doesn't matter which non-member country they come from, or which EU country they're going to.
4) There's **freedom of movement** within the EU for all **raw materials**, **finished goods** and **workers**. EU citizens can **work** in any country in the EU and businesses have the **opportunity to expand** into other EU countries.
5) There are **common policies** on **product regulation** as well — such as how food should be **labelled**, or how much **energy** appliances can consume. Businesses have to take these regulations into account when making **functional decisions** such as **designing products** and **packaging** — e.g. the R&D department shouldn't spend time developing a powerful vacuum cleaner as the EU **banned** vacuum cleaners of more than 1600 watts in 2014.

A common law or policy is one that's the same in all EU countries.

There are **Laws** about **Competition**...

1) **Fair competition** means companies are motivated to provide **good quality products** for **reasonable prices**. If they don't, customers will simply go **elsewhere**. Competition also encourages companies to **innovate** and develop **new products**, as well as providing customers with **choice** by **product differentiation** (see p.146).
2) In the UK, the **Competition Act 1998** sets out the laws on competition and what constitutes unfair business practices. It's the job of the **Competition and Markets Authority (CMA)** to prevent companies breaking competition laws. **EU competition law** also regulates competition across the EU. Companies breaking the laws can be given **big fines** or even be criminally prosecuted.
3) Businesses need to understand competition laws so they **don't break them** and also so they can watch out for **competitors breaking them** — they'd want to report them so the authorities could **investigate**.
4) **Competition law** means that, amongst other things:

- Businesses can't conspire to **fix prices** — where an agreement is made to keep the price of a product above a fixed amount. E.g. in the early 2000s a number of sportswear retailers were fined millions for fixing prices of football shirts.
- Businesses can't conspire with competitors to **limit production** so that higher prices can be charged due to a **shortage**.
- Businesses can't **divide up the market** to avoid having to compete. E.g. one company agrees to sell only in Europe if another agrees to sell only in Asia.

... and about **Abusing** a **Dominant Position**

1) Businesses have a **dominant position** if they have a market share of **at least 50%**.
2) Some **laws** to stop businesses **abusing** this position are:

- Dominant businesses can't demand '**exclusivity**' — that wholesalers or retailers **only** buy from them.
- They can't demand that retailers must buy a **second type of product** in order to buy the popular product they actually want (known as **tying**).
- Businesses can't sell goods at a **loss** to force smaller competitors **out of the market** (**predatory pricing**).

3) A **monopoly** is when one business has **complete control** over the market. There's **no competition** and if customers **need** the product they have to pay **whatever price** the monopoly sets. The CMA can **prevent** monopolies from occurring by stopping **takeovers** and **mergers** — this will affect the **strategy** of a business, as they will have to use **other methods** of growth to expand their business.

Business and the Legal Environment

The **Law** protects the **Community** and the **Environment**

1) Industries which release waste into the **water** or **land** are regulated by the **Environment Agency**. Businesses have to ensure their **production processes** don't cause **unnecessary pollution**, or risk **heavy fines**.
2) Industrial processes which only release pollution into the **air** are regulated by **local authorities**. Businesses must get **authorisation** from the local council before carrying out processes which create **smoke** or make **noise**. **Environmental health officers** can force factories to **stop making noise** at night if it's disturbing **local residents**.
3) Here are some examples of specific laws and directives that affect businesses:
   - The EU directive on **Waste Electrical and Electronic Equipment (WEEE)** forces businesses to increase **recycling** of waste electrical and electronic equipment, much of which previously ended up in landfill sites. Since August 2005, manufacturers have had **increased responsibility** for ensuring that goods such as computers, TVs and VCRs are **recycled** once they've come to the end of their useful life.
   - The **Landfill Tax** was introduced in 1996 to **reduce the amount of waste** being dumped into **landfill** sites.
   - The **EU Packaging Waste Directive** forces businesses to increase the recycling of packaging. There are **targets** for the percentage of wood, paper, glass and plastic that must be **recycled**.
   - The **Climate Change Act** requires UK PLCs to report their **greenhouse gas emissions** in their annual reports. The idea is that if these are made **public**, companies are more likely to try to **reduce** them.
4) Businesses must factor in the **cost** of complying with these laws in any **decisions** they make. Decisions about the **materials** or **processes** used might also be influenced by environmental laws.
5) Some businesses are able to turn these **restrictions** into **unique selling points** of their products — e.g. by being the most **environmentally friendly** business in the market.

The **Law** protects **Customers** and **Consumers**

Certain laws protect customers and consumers — these laws affect the **functional decisions** made by different departments. E.g. the R&D, manufacturing and marketing departments need to bear the laws in mind when **developing**, **making** and **marketing** products.

- The **Trade Descriptions Act (1968)** ensures that businesses don't **mislead** consumers with **false descriptions** on **packaging** or **advertising materials**.
- The **Sale of Goods Act (1979)**, the **Sale and Supply of Goods Act (1994)**, and the **Sale and Supply of Goods to Consumers Regulations (2002)** set out the **rights** of customers. These laws mean that goods must be **fit for their purpose** and of **satisfactory quality**.
- The **Consumer Protection Act (1987)** says that **new consumer goods** must be **safe**. There are also other, **more specific regulations**, e.g. sofa and chair cushions must be made of **fire resistant** materials.
- The **Data Protection Act (1998)** prevents the **misuse of data**. Amongst other things, it stops businesses **holding onto customer data** that they don't need and stops them from **changing** or **destroying data**.

Practice Questions

Q1 What is the European Single Market?

Q2 Give three ways that a company might break competition laws.

Q3 Why does the Competition and Markets Authority aim to prevent monopolies?

Q4 Give three examples of laws that protect consumers.

Exam Questions

Vint-Age is a manufacturer of retro radios.

Q1 Analyse how Vint-Age may be affected by the UK's membership of the EU. [12 marks]

Q2 To what extent do you think that manufacturers such as Vint-Age need to consider their environmental impact when making business decisions? Justify your answer. [16 marks]

I fought the law and the law took my profits and stopped me from trading...

Most businesses comply with the law but, sadly, there'll always be some firms who try to get away with cheating customers and selling dangerous tat. The law's there to make sure that firms obey the rules or face the consequences.

Employment Law

Employment laws aim to make things fairer for workers and stop employers taking advantage of their employees.

Labour Laws control what rights Employees have

1) An employee has a legal right to **fair treatment** while at work, and also while looking for employment.
2) The **Equality Act 2010 protects** employees from **discrimination** based on age, gender, race, religion, disability, pregnancy, etc. These things are known as '**protected characteristics**'.
3) This Act **simplified** things by **replacing** several previous anti-discrimination acts, such as the **Race Relations Act (1976)** and the **Sex Discrimination Act (1975)**. It reflects the content of the **EU's Equal Treatment Directive**.
4) There are **two types** of discrimination — **direct** and **indirect**:

- **Direct discrimination** is treating someone **less favourably** because they have a protected characteristic, e.g. not employing someone because of a **disability**, or paying women **less** than men doing the **same job**.
- **Indirect discrimination** is when everyone is **treated the same** but it has a **worse effect** on one group of people than on others. E.g. a rule that employees must **not wear head coverings** could be indirect discrimination against some **religions**.

5) Employers have to make '**reasonable adjustments**' for workers with **disabilities**, such as installing wheelchair ramps.
6) **Parents** can ask to **work flexibly** (see p.92), and employers can only refuse for a **good business reason**. **Men** with young children who are **refused** flexible working could claim that it is **direct sex discrimination** if **women** with young children have had flexible working requests **approved**.

Discrimination Laws affect All Aspects of businesses

Recruitment

- Employers aren't allowed to **state** in job adverts that candidates must be a particular age, race, gender, etc. They can't use **discriminatory language**, e.g. advertising for a "waitress" excludes men.
- Businesses are only allowed to advertise for someone of a specific age, gender, etc. if it's a **genuine requirement** of the job — e.g. a female toilet attendant for ladies' toilets.
- Businesses have to make **decisions** about who to employ without discriminating. They have to be able to **justify** why they gave a job to a particular candidate, in case an unsuccessful candidate takes them to a **tribunal** (see below).
- **Avoiding discrimination** when recruiting means that businesses will recruit a more **diverse workforce**. This means they'll have a wider range of **skills**, **talents** and **experiences** to draw upon.

Pay

- Businesses have to give male and female employees the **same pay** for work of **equal value**. They're entitled to the same **benefits** too (e.g. a company car).
- Not paying fairly can result in a fall in the **quality of work** and poor **staff retention**, as well as having to pay **compensation** and **legal fees** if taken to tribunals.

Promotions and Redundancies

- Discrimination laws mean that everyone should have the **same opportunity** to get **promoted**. For example, businesses can't just **promote older people** because they think **young people** are more likely to change jobs.
- If businesses need to make **redundancies**, they can't **deliberately select** staff who are older, disabled, etc.

Employment Tribunals can settle Disputes

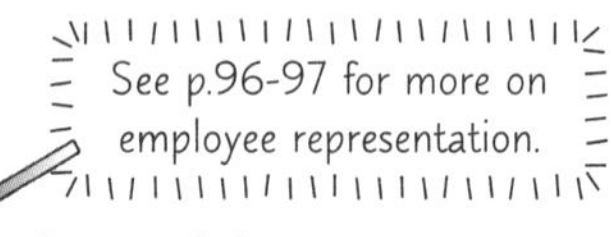

1) If employees feel that they've been treated **unfairly** by their employers they can make a claim to a **tribunal**.
2) At a tribunal, representatives of the employer and the employee put forward their cases, and a **tribunal judge** (or sometimes a tribunal panel) decides who's in the right.
3) The employer might have to pay **compensation** or give the employee their job back in an **unfair dismissal** case.

Employment Law

Employers have to pay staff at least the **Minimum Wage**

1) The **National Minimum Wage** was introduced in 1999 to prevent employees from being paid unfairly low wages.
2) The minimum wage **rises** every year. From **1st October 2015**, it's £6.70 per hour for people aged 21 or over, £5.30 per hour for people aged 18-20, and £3.87 for 16 and 17 year olds. **Apprentices** get at least £3.30 per hour. In July 2015 the government announced a **National Living Wage** of £7.20 an hour for over-25s, starting from April 2016. This will replace the minimum wage for people aged 25 or over.

The National Living Wage is **controversial** because it's **lower** than the **independently calculated** living wage. Some employers **voluntarily** pay employees the independently calculated living wage — this can **increase motivation**, **reduce absenteeism** and allows the company to market themselves as an **ethical employer**.

3) Employers who don't pay their staff enough have to **reimburse** their staff with the total amount that they've been underpaid and can also be 'named and shamed', **fined** up to **£20 000** or even prosecuted.

An **Employment Contract** sets out the **Conditions** of **Employment**

1) A contract of employment is a **legally-binding** agreement between the employer and the employee about what the **duties** and **rights** of the employee and the employer are, including hours, salary, etc.
2) Employees are entitled to receive a **written statement** of employment within **two months** of starting work.
3) There are some **responsibilities** that are **common** to all employers and employees, for example:

- Employees have the right to a **safe** working environment. The **Health and Safety at Work Act (1974)** states that the employer must ensure the working environment is **safe** (e.g. electrical equipment, moving machinery, etc. must be safe). Under the **Control of Substances Hazardous to Health Regulations 2002** (COSHH), businesses also have to protect employees from the risks of any **hazardous substances**.
- Employees are entitled to paid holiday. In April 2009, the **European Working Time Directive** gave full-time workers the right to **28 days** of **paid holiday** per year, including bank holidays.
- Employees have the right to **paid maternity** and **paternity** leave, although usually not on full pay. For many years, **mums** got up to 39 weeks paid leave and 13 more weeks unpaid, and **dads** got 2 weeks of paid paternity leave. However, new laws mean much of a mother's leave can be **shared** with the father.
- Employees have to **attend work** when they're supposed to, and be **on time**.
- Employees must be willing to carry out any **reasonable task** that's asked of them.

The **State Pension Age** is **Rising**

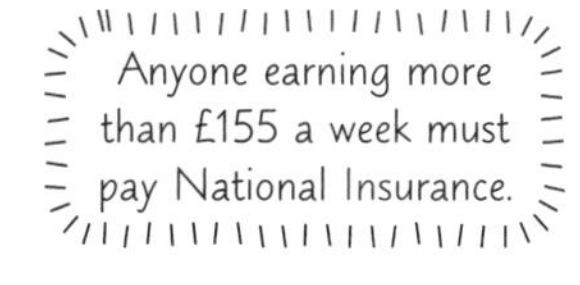

1) The **State Pension** means that everyone has some money to live on in their old age. **How much** you get depends on **how many years** you've paid **National Insurance** for.
2) For years men have been able to claim state pension from 65 and women from 60, but because people are **living longer**, the age is being **increased gradually**. Due to sexual equality, by 2018 it'll be 65 for women too, then it'll rise to 68 for both men and women.
3) A new law means that employers must **enrol most employees** in a **workplace pension** and pay into it.

Practice Questions

Q1 What's the purpose of the Equality Act (2010)?

Q2 State and explain the two different types of discrimination.

Q3 How does the Health and Safety at Work Act protect employees?

Exam Questions

Q1 Analyse how discrimination laws can impact HR decisions on recruitment, wages and redundancies. [12 marks]

Q2 To what extent do you agree that employment contracts benefit the employee more than the employer? [16 marks]

Can tribunals settle disputes about whose turn it is to make the tea...

Businesses have to take all these laws into account when making decisions. For example, an employer may try to save money by only recruiting under 18s, as they have a lower minimum wage. However, if an older applicant takes the employer to a tribunal and they're found guilty of age discrimination, they might have to fork out loads of money.

Business and the Political Environment

A government policy is a plan of action to make a change — here we'll look at policies affecting businesses.

Government Policies** encourage **Enterprise

1) The UK government encourages entrepreneurs to set up businesses because enterprise benefits the **economy** — new businesses **increase productivity** and create **new jobs**. The government is especially keen to promote enterprise in areas that need economic **regeneration** — this provides lots of **opportunities** for new businesses.
2) Some **strategies** for this are described in the **Business Enterprise policy**:
   - **Government schemes** allow enterprises to borrow money at **low interest rates** and encourage **private investment** in businesses, e.g. the Angel CoFund. The **Enterprise Investment Scheme** is a government scheme that offers tax incentives to people who invest in small businesses.
   - To make it easier for **small** businesses to succeed, they don't have to pay **business rates** and an **Employment Allowance** means their **National Insurance contributions bill** is reduced by £2000.
   - The **Great Business website** has been launched to **advise people** on setting up and running a businesses.
   - The government is backing **initiatives** to encourage **young entrepreneurs**, e.g. the '**Tenner Challenge**', which gives young people £10 to start a business and see how much **profit** they can make in a month.

*Many industries need **Regulation***

1) In the 1980s many state-owned firms were sold into the private sector to **improve efficiency** and make a **profit**. Examples include **British Telecom**, **British Gas**, **British Steel**, and the **water** companies.
2) Some industries are **natural monopolies** — for example, you wouldn't have several sets of rail tracks from one city to another, or several sets of water pipes and sewer pipes. When **privatising** a natural monopoly like the **railways** or **water**, the government needs to build in **regulations** to prevent the new owners from **exploiting** their position and raising prices or cutting quality.

Example: In 1989 the UK government **privatised** the ten **regional water authorities** in England and Wales by **selling assets** such as reservoirs. E.g. the water authority responsible for providing water and sewerage services to the north east of England was **taken over by** Northumbrian Water Limited.

Ofwat was created to **regulate** the industry and is mainly responsible for **setting limits** on how much companies can **charge** for water. Also, the **Drinking Water Inspectorate** was set up to **monitor** drinking water safety and quality. The **Water Industry Act 1991** sets out **laws** about the duties of the water companies and about what water can and cannot contain, etc.

3) There are lots of **regulated industries**, and the regulations affect the **decision making** of all the businesses operating in that industry. E.g. HR decisions on the number of employees needed at a residential home for the elderly would be influenced by the **Care Quality Commission**.

***Infrastructure** is **Vital** to businesses*

1) The UK's **infrastructure** is made up of **physical things**, such as the **transport** network (e.g. roads, railways and ports) and **pipes** and **wires** that allow water, energy and information to move about.
2) Improvements in infrastructure are **good for the economy** as they make businesses more **productive**, e.g. by allowing people, goods and raw materials to **move about** quickly, as well as making **data transfer** through the broadband network quicker. In the short term, infrastructure improvements provide **jobs** too, e.g. in constructing roads.
3) In the UK it's mainly the **private sector** that looks after the infrastructure, but the government has **overall policies**, laid out in its annual **National Infrastructure Plan**, about what the priorities are.
4) The government also **provides money** for projects. In addition to **state funding**, the government encourages **private investment** in infrastructure projects. E.g. the **UK Guarantees scheme** means that private lenders will definitely get **repaid** if the project they're investing in fails, so there's no **risk** for them.

In 2015 the government promised £8 million to provide **charge points** at key locations across the UK for **plug-in vehicles**. These vehicles have **really low emissions**, so encouraging people to use them helps **reduce greenhouse gases**, which is in line with what the **Climate Change Act 2008** says the government has to do.

Business and the Political Environment

Government policies aim to **Protect the Environment**

1) The UK is part of the **EU's 'Emissions Trading System'**. This gives **greenhouse gas emissions allowances** to businesses such as oil refineries, power stations, airlines and many manufacturers — e.g. producers of metal, glass and paper. Companies can **trade** their allowances, giving companies an **incentive** to choose greener processes. If a company doesn't need all their allowance, they can **sell** some to a business that has run out.
2) The government also has some '**green subsidy schemes**'. For example, the **Renewable Heat Incentive** pays businesses that use **renewable energy** to heat their buildings.
3) The government and the EU **fund organisations** that encourage more efficient use of raw materials, such as the **Waste and Resources Action Programme** (**WRAP**). WRAP works with businesses to achieve a '**circular economy**' which keeps resources in use for as **long as possible**.
   As well as protecting the **environment**, it helps businesses **save money**. For example:

   > Through a **WRAP initiative**, Britvic™ launched **Robinsons Squash'd®** in 2014. These are **ultra-concentrated** tiny bottles of squash. **Less packaging** means **less environmental impact** and also reduces transportation costs.

4) The **Environment Agency** is sponsored by the government to protect and improve the environment. One of its responsibilities is to **regulate businesses** that release pollutants into water or land.
5) Businesses breaking laws will be **fined** or **prosecuted** (see p.119 for more on how **environmental laws** and **EU directives** affect business decisions). As well as operating within the law, businesses can use government initiatives to help them implement strategies to reduce their environmental impact. This can also help them to cut costs and appeal to consumers.

Political Changes can make **International Trade** easier or harder

1) **Tariffs** (import taxes) **discourage** international trade. **Removing** or **reducing** tariffs between countries provides **opportunities** for business by making international trade **easier** and **cheaper**.
   Since the **World Trade Organisation** was set up in 1995 to encourage international trade, the proportion of imports worldwide that are **tariff-free** has risen greatly.
2) **Quotas** are trade restrictions set by governments that put **limits** on **imports** or **exports**. Countries sometimes use import quotas as a way of trying to **protect** their own economies and jobs — this is called a **protectionist policy** (see p.129). Sometimes two or more countries sign a free trade agreement which **removes** (or **reduces** the number of) quotas between them to **encourage** international trade, e.g. the EU and Chile entered into a free trade agreement in 2002.
3) Since the **UK** joined the **European Union** in 1973, British **exports** to EU countries have **increased** because there are **no quotas** or **tariffs** within the EU. **Imports** from other EU countries to Britain have also **increased**. EU countries also **manufacture** to increasingly **common standards**, which makes trade more **straightforward**.
4) **Trade embargoes ban trade** with a particular country. E.g. the USA has had an embargo against Cuba since 1962 (although in 2015 the US Government began to consider lifting or relaxing it). Less extreme are **sanctions** — these are imposed for various reasons, e.g. sanctions have been placed on **Syria** by the EU and USA because of its government's **violent repressive regime**.

These political changes affect decisions about the countries a business trades with.

Practice Questions

Q1 Give three ways in which the UK government encourages enterprise.

Q2 Give an example of a regulated industry.

Q3 What is infrastructure? Give two advantages of improving it.

Q4 What are tariffs and quotas?

Exam Question

Q1 Skoob's is a new business which manufactures an innovative range of tents. To what extent do you think it is necessary for Skoob's business decisions to be influenced by government policy? Justify your answer. [24 marks]

I always thought an embargo was some kind of embarrassing illness...

You've probably gathered that the government has a lot of policies. And a lot of them are relevant to businesses. Some policies cause businesses a headache, e.g. rules on packaging and disposal, but some policies help businesses, e.g. by reducing business rates for small businesses so that they can grow more easily (which also helps the economy).

Business and the Economy

There are different ways to measure the size and growth of a country's economy.

GDP indicates the Size of a Nation's Economy

1) **GDP (gross domestic product)** is the **total market value** of **goods** and **services** produced **within** a nation over a period of time (usually a year).

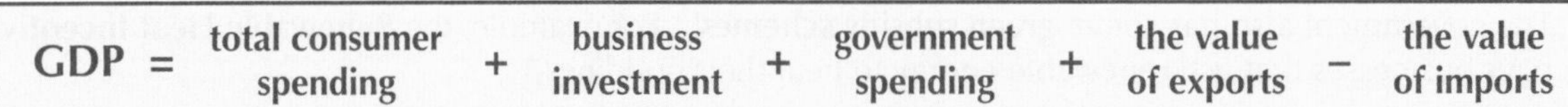

GDP = **total consumer spending** + **business investment** + **government spending** + **the value of exports** − **the value of imports**

2) GDP is used to measure the **economic performance** of a country, an area such as the EU, or the whole world.
3) It is calculated in **real terms**, i.e. it is adjusted so that **inflation** is ignored.

Economic Growth is the Increase in Size of a nation's Economy

1) Economic growth is an **increase** in a nation's production of **goods** and **services**.
2) It's measured as the **rate of increase in GDP**.
3) Economic growth means the same thing as "an increase in **economic activity**" — growth means there's **more demand** in the economy and **more output** to meet that demand.

Economic Growth is determined by Resources and Productivity

1) The **growth potential** of an economy depends on the **amount** and **quality** of economic **resources** available — e.g. labour and fixed assets.

Quantity and quality of labour	• **Quantity** of labour depends on **population size and age.** A problem facing the UK is its **ageing population.** The proportion of people above retirement age is **increasing** and many need **government support.** This means that fewer resources are available to **support economic growth.** • The **quality** of labour is the level of **education and training** that workers have reached. **High quality** labour enables an economy to **grow faster.** • India has the **largest youth population** in the world. It is believed that its economy could **rise dramatically** if they invest in the **education** and **health** of their young people.
Investment	• **Investment** increases the amount of **productive assets** (machinery etc. used for production). For the **value of productive assets to grow**, the **level of investment** in productive assets has to be **greater** than the amount of **depreciation** (the amount by which machines wear out) during the year.

2) Economic growth also depends on **productivity** — how hard the nation is willing or able to work.
3) **Governments** can encourage **short-term** growth by cutting taxes and interest rates (see p.14). This encourages **businesses** to **borrow** money and **invest** it in production. It also encourages **consumers** to **borrow** money and **spend it** on goods, which increases **demand** in the economy.

Economic Growth has Mainly Positive Effects for Businesses

1) On the whole, **growth** in GDP means **higher revenues** and higher **profitability** for **businesses**.
2) Economic growth gives the potential for **economies of scale** (see p.148).
3) Sustained growth increases **confidence** and helps businesses **plan** for the future.
4) Economic growth affects the type of **strategic decisions** that a business makes. In periods of **sustained** growth senior managers might decide to **expand** the business, launch **new products** or try to break into **new markets**.
5) On the down side, fast growth may cause **shortages** of raw materials and skilled labour.
6) Worse still, if growth is **too fast**, it's usually followed by a **recession** — a general **slowdown in economic activity**.

Business and the Economy

Rapid Growth is usually followed by Recession

Very high rates of growth are usually followed by **recession**, so governments try to keep growth at a **sustainable level**. **Fiscal policy** and **monetary policy** are two ways that they do this — see pages 128-129.

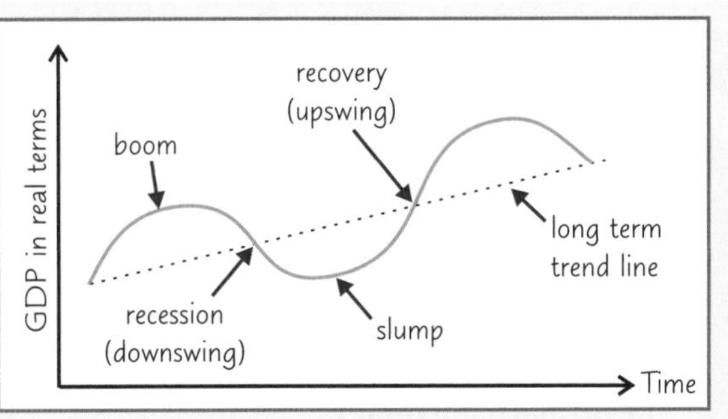

1) In a **boom**, GDP is high. As production reaches **maximum capacity**, there are **shortages**, and price increases. Shortages of skilled labour mean **wages rise**.
2) In a **recession**, incomes start to go down, and **demand** goes down. Business **confidence** is reduced.
3) In a **slump**, GDP is at a **low**. Businesses close factories and there are a lot of **redundancies**. **Unemployment** is **high**. A lot of businesses become **insolvent** or go **bankrupt**.
4) In a **recovery** or upswing period, **production increases**, and **employment** increases. People have more money to spend.
5) How much a business is **affected** by this cycle depends on the **income elasticity of demand** of its products (see page 37). Businesses selling **income elastic** goods such as luxury holidays find that demand shoots **up** in a **recovery**, and dives **down** in a **recession**. Firms selling **income inelastic** goods such as staple foods **aren't affected** all that much by these changes.

Income elasticity of demand = extent to which demand depends on customer income.

Businesses deal with Changes in Economic Activity Locally and Globally

The state of the economy, whether local or global, influences the **decisions** that businesses make:

1) During **booms**, businesses can **raise prices**. This **increases profitability**, and it **slows down demand** a bit.
2) In a long-lasting boom, businesses **invest** in **production** facilities to increase capacity. They may come out with **new products** to take advantage of increased consumer income.
3) During **recessions**, businesses may make workers **redundant** to **save wage costs** and **increase capacity utilisation** (see p.56-57).
4) During a **local recession**, businesses can **market** their goods elsewhere in the country — a local shop could market online. In a **national recession**, businesses can **market** their products **overseas**.
5) When a national recession or slump lasts a long time, some businesses choose to **relocate** abroad.
6) In general, **global upswings** provide growth opportunities for **everyone**, and **global recessions** are bad for **everyone**.

Practice Questions

Q1 What is economic growth and how is it measured?

Q2 What happens to production during a time of growth?

Exam Question

Q1 A business makes expensive robotic toys.
Use the graph and table to analyse whether extending its factory and investing in additional specialist machinery will increase profits in the long term. [20 marks]

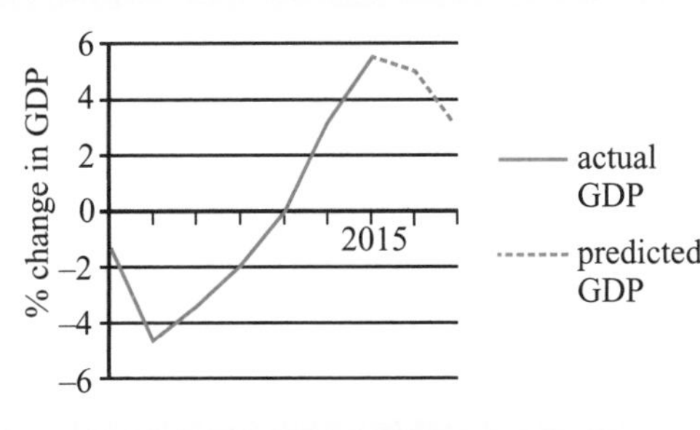

Year	2013	2014	2015
Sales (£million)	3.87	5.28	8.31

In 2008 the global economy was receding, these days it's my hairline...

Growth in the national economy is a good thing for businesses. The problems start when growth is too fast — production can't keep up, and a pleasant period of growth swings round into an unpleasant recession. Learn the ups and downs of the economy, and learn a couple of things that firms do to cope with them on a local and global scale.

Inflation and Exchange Rates

Here are two more delectable pages on how the economy affects businesses. Enjoy.

Inflation** is an **Increase** in the **Price** of **Goods** and **Services

1) The **Consumer Price Index** measures UK inflation — it tracks the prices of hundreds of goods and services that an average household would buy. There are **two types** of inflation:

Demand-pull inflation

High inflation can be caused by **too much demand** (more than the economy can supply). It happens when there's an **increase** in **disposable income** so people buy more and companies **can't supply goods** quickly enough and **increase** their **prices**. This is **demand-pull** inflation. **Excess demand** when the economy is near its full capacity is called **overheating**. **Demand-pull inflation** can actually make **profit margins** go **up**. Businesses can put up prices in response to **high demand** without their **costs** going up by as much.

Cost-push inflation

Rises in inflation can be due to **rising costs** pushing up **prices** — this is **cost-push** inflation. **Wage rises** can make prices go up — especially if productivity isn't rising. **Cost-push inflation** can make **profit margins** go **down** if businesses decide not to put up their prices.

2) When inflation is **high**, spending goes **up** temporarily — people rush to buy more before prices go up even more. If **wages** don't go up in line with inflation, however, spending goes **down** as people can afford less.
3) **Expectations** of inflation can make inflation worse. A business which expects its **suppliers** to put their prices up will put its **own** prices up to cover increased costs. Employees' expectations of rising prices makes them demand **higher wages**, so prices go up. This is the **wage-price spiral** — it's a big cause of cost-push inflation.
4) When **inflation** in the UK is **high**, it makes UK **exports** expensive abroad. UK businesses become **less competitive** globally. When inflation in the UK is **low**, UK businesses have a **competitive advantage** globally.
5) Inflation that's **too high** is bad for the economy. The Bank of England aims to keep the inflation rate within a **target range** set by the government — they do this by changing **interest rates**. See page 13 for more on interest rates and how they affect demand.

Inflation** affects **Business Strategy

1) Companies producing **premium goods** are the **most** likely to be **affected** by inflation because if customers have less to spend they start to look at **cheaper** alternative **products**. Manufacturers of premium products can react by **reducing prices** (although they have to be careful not to reduce them so far that the product loses its premium image) or by investing heavily in **advertising**.
2) Periods of high inflation can be a **good time** for firms to **expand** — if **interest rates** are **lower** than the rate of **inflation** it's **cheap** for them to **borrow money** to invest in **new premises** or **machinery**. The **interest** they'd earn on their savings would be **less** than the amount prices would have gone up by in the same time, so it makes sense to **spend** rather than save. However, the Bank of England often **raises** interest rates in times of high inflation to encourage saving, so businesses don't always benefit from high inflation.

   Firms compare **UK** and **foreign** interest rates. When the UK interest rate is high or volatile (fluctuating wildly), firms tend to expand into **other countries** with low, stable interest rates, as it's **cheaper** to borrow money there to invest in expansion.

3) It's harder for businesses to **plan** when inflation is **high**. They need **stable prices** in order to be able to make **accurate sales forecasts**.

Deflation** is a **Decrease** in the **Price** of **Goods** and **Services

1) **Deflation** is the **opposite** of inflation — it's when there's **not enough demand** so companies **reduce** their **prices**.
2) Deflation causes a **fall** in **productivity** because companies won't keep endlessly supplying the market with goods that nobody wants. **Lower productivity** usually means firms don't need as many workers — so deflation often leads to a **rise** in **unemployment**. This makes **demand drop** further and causes firms to **lower prices** even more.

Inflation and Exchange Rates

Exchange Rate is the *Value* of *One Currency* in terms of *Another Currency*

1) Exchange rates affect the amount of **foreign trade**.

- When the exchange rate is **high** (e.g. **more euros** to the **pound**), UK **exports** are relatively **expensive** abroad and **imports** into the UK are relatively **cheap** to buy. A **strong pound** is **bad** for UK exporters because their goods aren't competitively priced abroad.
- When the exchange rate is **low** (e.g. **fewer euros** to the **pound**), UK **exports** are relatively **cheap** for other countries (which is **good** for UK **exporters**) and **imports** into the UK are relatively **expensive** to buy.

2) A **strong pound** and **cheaper imports** mean **lower costs** for UK businesses importing raw materials from abroad, but they're **bad news** for UK manufacturers who **export goods**.
3) When a rise in the value of the pound is predicted, a business might decide to move its **production** abroad. A business can also consider **importing** their **raw materials**.
4) **Cheaper exports** should lead to increased **demand** and therefore higher **output**.

"Today's exchange rate is two sheep to the goat."

Make sure you can Convert *between* Currencies

Exam questions might ask you to use an **exchange rate** to **convert** between **two currencies**.

Example: Using an exchange rate of €1.41 to £1:

Convert €320 into pounds.	Divide: €320 ÷ 1.41 = **£226.95**
Convert £47 into euros.	Multiply: £47 × 1.41 = **€66.27**

Round your answer to 2 decimal places.

Check that your answers are sensible. The number of euros will always be higher than the equivalent number of pounds.

Exchange Rate Fluctuations create *Uncertainty*

Example: A UK manufacturer agrees a contract to sell to France, and agrees to be paid in **euros**. After the deal is made, the pound rises in value against the euro. The euro payment in the contract is now worth **fewer pounds** than before, so the UK manufacturer makes **less profit** from the contract than predicted.

Let's say that the UK manufacturer insists on being paid in **pounds** instead. When the pound rises in value, the goods are more expensive in euro terms for the French firm. They put the **selling price** up to compensate. The increase in price reduces **demand** for the goods, and there may be **less revenue** than predicted.

Some manufacturers that are based in the UK and **export to the EU** may consider **relocating** to **euro zone** countries (where the currency is the euro), so that their **costs** are in euros — the **same currency** their **customers pay in**. They may also decide to **pay UK suppliers** in euros.

Practice Questions

Q1 What is demand-pull inflation?

Q2 What type of goods are most likely to be affected by inflation? Why is this?

Q3 Is a strong pound good or bad for UK exporters? Why is this?

Q4 If 1 Australian Dollar = £0.49, convert £80 into Australian Dollars.

Answer on p.201.

Exam Question

Q1 A UK business imports components from South Korea and exports the finished products to Germany. The pound is forecast to strengthen against both the South Korean won and the euro. To what extent do you think this will influence the business decisions of the company? Justify your answer. [16 marks]

Changing interest rates — that's why we add daft stuff to our books...

The economy is pretty complicated and all sorts of things are interlinked — try to get your head around what inflation, deflation and changing exchange rates mean for a businesses. Exam questions often give you data and ask you to use it to 'analyse' why something may have happened. To get top marks you must use the figures to support your analysis.

Government Policy and the Economy

More government policies... hurray! OK, even if you're not as enthusiastic as me, you've still got to learn this stuff.

Government Policies *influence the* **Economy**

The government tries to keep the economy under control — two methods it uses are **fiscal policy** and **monetary policy**. **Taxation** is a major part of fiscal policy, so you'd best learn about that first.

Taxation Rates *affect* **Economic Activity**

1) **Individuals** are taxed on their **income**. **High** tax rates for individuals reduce consumers' **disposable income**, so people tend to **spend less** — this is bad news for businesses because it's likely to **reduce** their **turnover**. **Low** tax rates encourage people to spend, so businesses make **bigger profits**.
2) Businesses are taxed on their **profits** — sole traders and partnerships pay **income tax**, and limited companies pay **corporation tax**. These taxes are **direct taxes**. **High** tax rates for **businesses** mean that their **net profits** (after-tax profits) are **reduced**.
3) Businesses also pay **business rate** tax based on the **value** of their **premises**. The rate is the same all over the country. However, because **property values** are generally **higher** in the **South** than in the North, **businesses** in the South generally end up **paying more**. This can **reduce** their **competitiveness**.
4) Businesses want to **minimise** costs, so tax rates affect their **decisions** — e.g. where to **locate** themselves and whether to **hire** or **buy** vehicles.

Multinationals (p.162) often strategically locate their operations to countries with low tax rates — this can be controversial as many people see it as the company dodging taxes.

5) There are also **indirect taxes on spending**, e.g. VAT, taxes on pollution, tobacco and alcohol.
6) **High** tax rates **discourage** individuals from **spending**, and businesses from **expanding**. Increasing income tax **reduces spending power**, **cuts demand** and **lowers economic activity**.
7) **Reducing taxes** or giving businesses **subsidies** (financial assistance) encourages businesses to expand.
8) The effect of a tax cut or tax rise depends on the **income elasticity** of the good or service. Rises in income tax hit **luxury goods** (e.g. expensive kitchen appliances) harder than **staple goods** (e.g. petrol or bread).

Fiscal Policy *changes* **Taxes** *and* **Spending**

1) **Fiscal policy** does **two** things — it sets **tax rates** and the amount of **government spending**.
2) **Raising taxes** reduces spending in the economy, and cutting taxes increases it. **Low rates of tax** give businesses more profit, and **encourage business activity** like expansion and new start-ups.
   - It's fairly easy to predict the effects of a change in **direct taxation**. Raising **income tax** reduces consumer spending, and raising **business taxes** reduces economic output.
   - **Indirect taxation** is a bit harder to predict. In the **short term**, an **increase** in VAT tends to cause **inflation**, because the **higher tax** means that goods and services **cost more**. In the **longer term**, a rise in VAT **decreases** consumer spending, and **prices** have to **fall** to meet the **drop** in **demand**, so it causes **deflation**.
3) **Government spending** on social services, health, education etc. also pumps more money into the economy.
   - Changing government expenditure on **welfare benefits** has a **quick** impact on the economy, because people who receive benefits will instantly have more (or less) money available to spend.
   - Government spending on **infrastructure** such as roads has a **slower** effect on the economy.
4) **Fiscal policy** is really about the **balance** between tax and spending. The Chancellor of the Exchequer decides what the balance is going to be in the yearly Budget.

Fiscal Policy	When it's done	How it's done	Change in government borrowing	The effect it has
Expansionary fiscal policy	Economic slowdown / high unemployment	Cutting taxes and/or raising spending	Government **borrowing increases** (or government **surplus decreases**)	**Demand** for goods and services **increases**
Contractionary fiscal policy	Production at 100% capacity / risk of high inflation	Raising taxes and/or cutting spending	Government **borrowing decreases** (or government **surplus increases**)	**Demand** for goods and services **decreases**

5) Expansionary fiscal policy helps to **lower unemployment**. **Cutting taxes** gives people **more to spend** and increased **consumption** boosts **production** and creates **jobs**. It can cause **inflation** though, so it needs to be monitored.
6) Contractionary fiscal policy does the **opposite**. It's used to '**rein in**' economic growth to a sustainable level.

Government Policy and the Economy

Monetary Policy controls the *Interest Rate*

New monetary policy — chocolate coins... and lots of them.

1) Monetary policy means **tweaking the interest rate** (see p.15) to control **inflation** and **exchange rates** (see p.126-127).
2) When **interest rates** are **high**, **foreign investors** want to **save money** in **UK** banks. To do this, they **buy British pounds**, which boosts demand for the currency and makes the **exchange rate go up**, affecting **imports** and **exports**. When **interest rates** are **low**, investors prefer to invest abroad, so they **sell** their pounds and the **exchange rate falls**.
3) Interest rates are set by the Bank of England, **not** by the government — but the **Bank of England Monetary Policy Committee** bears the **government's fiscal policy** in mind when it makes its decisions.
4) Monetary policy aims to:

   1) Control **inflation**.
   2) Control the overall rate of **economic growth**.
   3) Manage **unemployment** levels (e.g. if interest rates are **low**, people have **more money** to spend and **increased demand** leads to a **rise in production** so **more workers** are needed).
   4) Influence **foreign exchange rates**.

The government must balance Open Trade *with* Protectionism

1) **Protectionism** is when a government protects **domestic businesses** and **jobs** from foreign competition by giving them **subsidies**, while imposing **tariffs** and **quotas** on imported products.
2) **Open** or **free trade** is when imports and exports are **not restricted**. The World Trade Organisation (WTO) (see p.123) regulates trade between member countries (almost all countries are members).
3) The **EU's Common Agricultural Policy** is an example of **protectionism**. It aims to keep farmers in business through things like **subsidies** and **guaranteed minimum prices**, as well as ensuring the EU has a **secure food supply**. It imposes **tariffs** on many imported products.
4) Open trade and protectionism have their **pros** and **cons**:

	Advantages	Disadvantages
Protectionism	Countries develop a variety of **new industries**, adding **local jobs** and **boosting economic growth**. Allows **small businesses** to grow as they don't have to **compete** with **multinationals**.	Prices of imported goods **rise** due to **decreased supply** — prices of domestic goods **rise** without a change in quality as there is **less competition**. If you **restrict** a country's trading in your country, they might **restrict your trading** in theirs.
Open Trade	Countries **specialise** in what they're good at. Countries benefit from **economies of scale**. **More choice** and **lower prices** for consumers. **Developing countries** can export goods and increase their **living standards**.	**Fewer local jobs** as multinationals expand **abroad**. Employee **skills** are concentrated around **certain jobs**. Some countries may use **sweatshops** and **child labour** to keep their costs down to **compete** internationally.

Practice Questions

Q1 What do fiscal policy and monetary policy do?

Q2 If the government raises taxes on individuals, how are businesses affected?

Q3 Give two advantages and two disadvantages of open trade.

Exam Question

Q1 Explain one way that an increase in the Bank of England's interest rate could affect a furniture retailer. [5 marks]

Political change — what's left over from government spending...

Getting the right balance between open trade and protectionism is a tricky balancing act for governments. Too much protectionism and global markets become unstable, too little and your domestic markets are at risk from competition.

The Global Economy

There have always been trade links across the world, but now it's like we're all living in one village — the global village...

Globalisation is the increase in how **Interconnected** the **World** is

1) **Globalisation** has resulted in businesses operating in **lots of countries** across the world. They can be **based** anywhere, and can **buy** from and **sell** to any country.
2) Globalisation allows businesses to make **strategic decisions** about where to get **raw materials** from, as well as where to **manufacture products** (e.g. in countries with cheaper labour).
3) Access to a **worldwide market** means businesses can benefit from **economies of scale** (see p.148), making them even more **competitive**.
4) There's more on the **opportunities** for businesses in international markets on pages 158-159.

Globalisation has **Rapidly Increased** during **Recent Decades**

There are several **reasons** for increased globalisation:

- The **internet** allows businesses to communicate between countries very quickly and cheaply. It also allows jobs to be **outsourced** across the world. E.g. if a business needs software developing, they can go to an **online staffing market** and find someone to do it, maybe in India where **labour costs** are lower.
- There's been a shift from **separate national finance markets** towards a **global finance market**, meaning it's easy to move **money** securely around the world.
- Giant **cargo ships** make it cheaper to **transport goods** around the world.
- Cheap, fast **air travel** means **goods** and **people** can move around the world easily for work.
- EU citizens can work in any other **EU country** without restrictions.
- There is **increased free trade** because of reduced tariffs, often due to the WTO (see p.123). There are various **trade blocs**, e.g. the EU and APEC (Asia-Pacific Economic Cooperation), in which the member countries have few or no trade barriers between them.

The number of **Global Brands** is **Increasing**

Huge multinational **brands** like McDonalds and Coca-Cola® can be found almost **anywhere** in the world. Some reasons for their increase are:

1) **International broadcasting** allows people to watch **television programmes** from different countries. This can create **international demand** for items in many countries. US brands like Levi's® and Coca-Cola® became popular in developing countries like India and China partly because they advertised on popular TV channels like MTV.
2) The **internet** also allows companies to market and sell their products internationally. Businesses can **sell** their products **internationally** but avoid the **expense** of setting up in foreign countries by advertising their products on **foreign websites** and offering **overseas shipping**. This allows them to create a global brand but avoids the **risks** that come with setting up a business abroad.

Businesses look for **Opportunities** in **Emerging Economies**

1) **Emerging economies** are **developing countries** with **fast growing**, but **not yet** fully developed economies. **China**, **India**, **Brazil** and **Russia** are four of the most significant emerging economies.
2) Emerging economies are a **good opportunity** for businesses as they offer **good returns** due to their **rapid growth**. **Labour** is usually **cheaper** in these countries too.
3) As jobs are created, people **move out of poverty** and a new **middle class** is formed. People are eager to spend money on **luxuries** they've never been able to afford before, creating lots of **economic activity**.
4) However, they are more **risky investments** as they're **less stable** — there might be sudden **political changes**, **currency fluctuations** or **infrastructure problems**.

The Global Economy

India and *China* are *Important* for *UK Businesses*...

1) China has removed its **protectionist barriers** to international trade and became a **member** of the WTO in 2001. This has provided UK businesses with more **opportunities** to **export** their products to China.
2) As **India's income** has increased, its **imports** have also increased, also providing **opportunities** for UK businesses.
3) China and India have very **large populations**, so they are both **huge markets** that can be very **profitable** for UK businesses if they manage to create **demand** for their products there.
4) Recent **economic growth** has produced many **millionaires** and even **billionaires** in China and India, so there's a lot of potential for UK companies selling **luxury products** to be very successful there.
5) UK businesses can **reduce** their **costs** by **outsourcing manufacturing** to emerging economies, or by having their **call centres** in them. E.g. average annual call centre salaries in the UK are about **£18 000**, compared with around **£2000** in India, so using Indian call centres can drastically reduce a business's costs and enable it to keep its **prices low** and stay **competitive**.

... but there are some *Difficulties*

1) Despite the recent economic growth, many people in China are still **very poor**. Although China has one of the world's largest economies in terms of GDP, its **GDP per person** is **below average**. In India around **25%** of people are **below** the **poverty line**. This means that the **number** of **potential customers** for any product is **reduced**.
2) The **Indian government** has put **restrictions** on **foreign businesses** investing in Indian companies. This trade barrier makes it **more difficult** for UK businesses to break into the Indian market.
3) **Language** and **cultural barriers** can prevent UK businesses from trading with India and China. These barriers are particularly difficult to overcome in **China** — in India more people speak **English**, and the **culture** is more similar to UK culture because it's a former British colony.
4) Emerging economies use **different currencies** to the UK, so UK businesses are **vulnerable** to changes in currency values (see p.127). A **strong pound** makes **British exports more expensive** abroad, which would **reduce demand** for products from UK companies in India and China.

India's trade barriers made Paul's job much more difficult.

Practice Questions

Q1 What is globalisation?

Q2 Give three reasons for the increase in globalisation.

Q3 What are the benefits for businesses in investing in emerging economies? Why is it risky?

Q4 Describe the benefits of marketing goods to China.

Exam Question

Q1 A washing machine manufacturer is considering launching products in a developing country. Some data about this country is given in the table below. Do you think that this country is a good market for the manufacturer to target? Justify your answer.

Year	2012	2013	2014	2015
GDP % growth	5.9	10.9	13.7	13.8
Exchange rate *developing country's unit of currency : £*	3.50	3.80	3.90	4.20

[20 marks]

Global economic powers are OK, but I'd still prefer super powers...

It's pretty strange to think that a few years ago India and China weren't very big players economy-wise, and now they're taking the world by storm. Makes you wonder which countries will be "global economic powers" in another few years. Anyway, no time for wondering, best get all this stuff learned and then have a choccy biccy. Yum.

Business and the Social Environment

Social concerns affect business — not the 'what shall I wear to the party' type of social concerns though.

Demographic Changes affect decision making

1) **Demographic changes** are changes in the **structure** of the UK **population** over time in terms of things like **age**, **sex** and **race** changes.
2) These changes create both **opportunities** and **threats**. E.g. the UK population is **ageing** (see p.16), this is:

A **threat** — the proportion of people **available to work** (those aged 16-65) is **falling**. If businesses **can't find** enough **workers** to fill all their vacancies, it'll make growth **difficult**.

An **opportunity** — the **market size** for firms such as private healthcare providers will **increase**. Retired people often **travel** a lot — so it's good news for **holiday companies** too.

3) Demographic changes often influence a business's **decision-making**. These changes include things like:

- **More working parents** will boost the workforce, but businesses might need to provide **flexible contracts**.
- An **increase in single-occupancy households** increases the demand for **smaller houses** and for food packaged in **smaller amounts**.
- An **increase in senior citizens** might prompt a business (e.g. a cinema or a hairdressers) to offer **special rates** during weekdays, when other people are working.

4) Changes in **consumer lifestyle** and **buying behaviour** also lead to firms needing to **alter** their strategic plans.

- Consumers now use the **internet** to **research** products before buying them. Companies often send products to relevant **bloggers** to review online. This gives them **cheap, long-lasting promotion**.
- An increase in **online social networking** means this is an important means of **promotion**.
- Customers increasingly **buy things online** but are too busy to **wait in** for deliveries. So some companies use **delivery services** which drop off parcels at **convenient locations** (e.g. petrol stations) from which the customer collects them. To stay **competitive**, a business might need to consider offering this.
- Increased use of **tablets** and **smartphones** means not everyone wants **physical products**. E.g. the Camping and Caravanning Club offers a cheaper '**online membership**'. Members get access to the magazines online, rather than receiving printed copies. This **saves** the business and the customer **money** and **reduces environmental impact**.

Urbanisation and Migration affect strategic decisions

1) **Urbanisation** is an **increase** in the **proportion** of the population living in **cities**. It happened a long time ago in the UK, but it is happening now at a **fast rate** in **emerging economies**, such as Brazil.
2) This trend provides **opportunities** for companies:

- There are **new markets** with **concentrated demand** — businesses might focus on their **distribution networks** in these areas at the expense of their **wider distribution network**.
- **Infrastructure**, **housing** and **communication technology** will be needed, so there will be lots of **opportunities** for new and existing businesses to **expand** into these industries.
- People have access to a **higher level of education**, so the workforce becomes **more skilled** — businesses might **move certain departments** (e.g. finance) to these areas to take advantage of the **labour supply**.

3) **Migration** is the **movement** of the population from **one area or country to another**. There are currently **more** people moving **into** the UK than moving **out** of the UK.
4) Migration affects businesses because:

- When there is a **shortage of labour**, businesses **struggle** to grow. Migrants can help some businesses overcome labour shortages and allow them to **expand** into new and current markets.
- Migrants can create **demand** for **certain products** which creates **new markets** for businesses to move into, e.g. a mobile phone operator might offer cheaper international calls to **expand** its **market share**.
- However, if too many skilled people **emigrate** from a country, it can cause a '**brain drain**'. Businesses in that country will **struggle** to get skilled workers which, in the worst case, will force them to **shut down**.

Business and the Social Environment

***Environmental** issues affect business strategy*

1) Customers, investors and the government can put **pressure** on businesses to be more **environmentally friendly** — businesses need to respond or they **risk damaging** their **brand loyalty** (see p.48).
2) Businesses can choose to do **environmental audits** — these **compare** the firm's activities with those required by **legislation** and with the company's **objectives**. The outcomes can be used in **strategic planning**.
3) Businesses might decide to hire **environmental consultants** to check that they have **complied with legislation**. This will please **customers** as the business is seen to be **conscious** of its **environmental impact** — it will also please **investors** as the business is protected from **hefty fines**.
4) The government makes businesses analyse their **energy usage** and **emissions** through schemes like the **Energy Savings Opportunity Scheme** (ESOS). This forces businesses to consider the **environmental impact** when they are making **strategic decisions**.

CSR** — Making the **World** a **Better Place

1) **Corporate Social Responsibility** (CSR) is the idea that a company should go **above and beyond** what is required by **law** to help **society**, its workforce's **quality of life** and the **environment**.
2) The public are **more aware** of what companies do now than they were in the past. Companies face **pressure** to act responsibly — consumers are likely to **boycott** their goods if they don't, or simply buy from a **competitor** who they think is **more ethical**.
3) CSR has become part of **business culture** — how people **expect** things to be done in business. Companies, especially larger ones, now **publicise** how they **benefit** the environment and society.
4) Some examples of CSR initiatives are:

- **Barclays** have a two year partnership with **Teach First** (a charity aiming to recruit and train high quality teachers to teach in low income areas).
- **Marks and Spencer** work to ensure their suppliers' employees have **good working conditions**. They agree **standards** with suppliers, **visit** them regularly and **work with them** to improve conditions.
- **McDonald's Planet Champion Programme** trains employees to find ways of reducing the **environmental impact** of the company. McDonald's also runs daily **litter picking patrols**, as well as employing full time '**litter champions**' in some city centres.

*CSR **Costs Money** but has **Advantages***

1) CSR should be **integrated** into a company's **operations** and **strategy** — ignoring it can lead to **long-term damage** to **profits** and **reputation**, as customers will choose more socially responsible companies.
2) Businesses implementing CSR can gain a **competitive advantage**:

- It improves **brand loyalty** and attracts **new customers** through **positive publicity** — although the public may be **sceptical** and think it's just a **PR stunt**.
- People will choose to work for firms with **good CSR records** over firms with bad ones — this means that the business will attract more **talented** applicants.
- **Employee morale** will **improve** and they will be **more motivated** to work for and stay with the company.

3) However, CSR can have its **downsides**:

- CSR has **costs**, which **shareholders** may see as a **misuse of funds** (see p.134). This can lead to them **withdrawing their investment**, or **pressuring firms** to stop their CSR activities.
- The costs may be **passed on to customers**. Most customers are prepared to pay **more** for 'socially responsible' products — however if the market is **price-sensitive** (e.g. during a recession), sales will fall.
- The expectation of CSR puts **small businesses** at a disadvantage. They are less likely to have **funds** to spare for CSR projects, or to be able to **employ** someone to organise their CSR activities.

Business and the Social Environment

Stakeholders and Shareholders don't always agree on CSR

1) Traditionally, the **decision-making process** put the **needs** of **shareholders first**, which meant that the business was concerned with its **profits** above all else.
2) Now it's considered normal for businesses to **balance** the **other stakeholders'** needs with those of the **shareholders** during the decision-making process. See p.24.
3) **Corporate social responsibility** goes even further. It makes the **general public** a stakeholder and expects the business to **actively improve things** for everyone.
4) Making a **profit** is still **key** — the **survival** of the business is in the **interests** of stakeholders such as employees, suppliers and customers. In reality though, it can be **hard** to take into account the needs of **all** stakeholders:

- If a company has promised to **invest** in a **local school** for the next **5 years** but its **profits fall** sharply, it has to decide which is more important — keeping **shareholders happy** or **behaving ethically**.
- Some large companies, such as Starbucks®, have been criticised in the media for **avoiding** paying **corporate tax** in the UK. They haven't done anything illegal — they've just **exploited loopholes** to **increase profits**. However, **public protests** have led to them **volunteering** to pay a meaningful amount of tax.

Carroll's Pyramid of CSR shows what Society Expects from a business

1) Carroll said that businesses have **four types** of **CSR responsibilities**. He arranged them in a **pyramid**, with each **layer** resting on the one below. The layers **shouldn't** be separated — the pyramid should be treated as a **whole**.
2) The model can be used to **analyse business decisions** and to assess whether they are made out of **necessity** (economic and legal responsibilities) or in a **voluntary** capacity (ethical and philanthropic responsibilities).

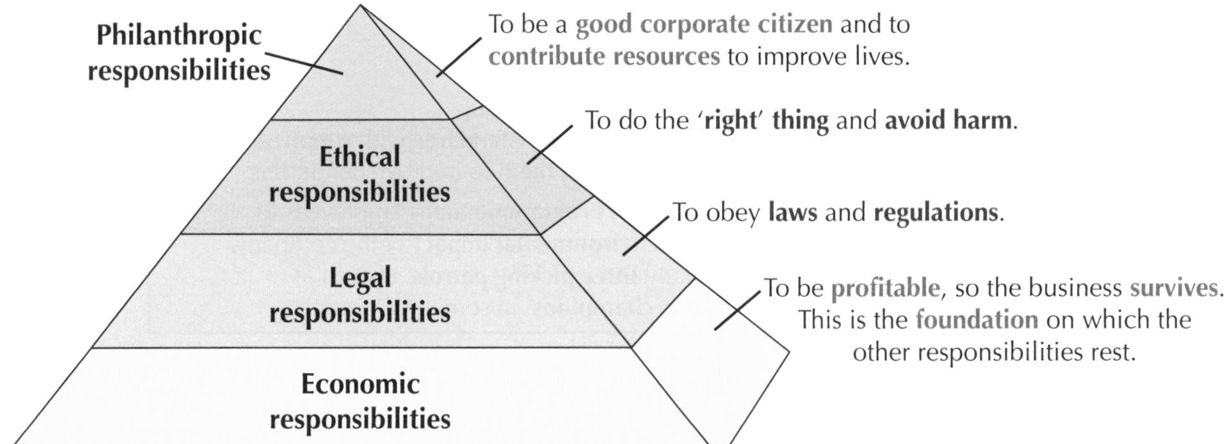

Practice Questions

Q1 Give an example of a demographic change which may affect companies.

Q2 Give two impacts of increased urbanisation.

Q3 What is CSR? Give three advantages of it for businesses.

Q4 What are the four layers of Carroll's corporate social responsibility pyramid.

Exam Questions

Q1 Analyse the possible influences on the level of CSR commitment of a medium-sized company. [9 marks]

Q2 A supermarket chain is aiming to increase its market share. To what extent should urbanisation and migration influence their strategic decisions? Justify your answer. [16 marks]

CSR — just a new TV crime series....

Corporate social responsibility has become far more important over the last few decades — lots of consumers worry about how the products they buy were made and how companies they buy from are run. On any big company's website, you'll find proud tales of how they look after the environment and all the CSR initiatives that they're part of.

Business and the Technological Environment

Stomp, stomp, stomp. That's the march of technology coming.

New Technology** creates **Opportunities** and **Threats

1) Businesses need to **monitor** the constant flow of **new** and **updated technology** to look for opportunities to **grow**, **innovate** or **improve functional areas** of the business.
2) Businesses need to decide which **opportunities** are **worth pursuing** and which are **too risky**. Here are some example of opportunities businesses can take:

- **New products** — businesses need to decide whether to **develop products** with a new technology or not. E.g. smartphone manufacturers may need to decide whether to put a new type of battery into a new phone.
- **Improving processes** — using new technology in processes can improve the business's **efficiency** and **productivity**, giving it an **advantage** over its competitors.
- **Mass customisation** (see p.65) — improvements to technology might mean that a business can adopt mass customisation — this can **decrease costs** and **increase revenue**.
- **Reduced barriers to entry** (see p.136) — new technology can make it **easier** for businesses to move into **new markets** — e.g. the development of ebooks means that businesses don't need a way of printing books.
- **E-commerce** — businesses are able to reach a **wider market** and **sell products** 24 hours a day.

3) Businesses need to **assess the threats** before making an **investment** into new technology. The main threat is from even **newer technology** being brought out **before** you've made your **money back** on the investment.
4) There is also a threat from **competitors** as new technology reduces the barriers to entry for **everyone** — businesses need to be wary of **new businesses** taking some of their **market share**.
5) The **growth of e-commerce** means that customers are relying much less on **physical shops**. This could mean that businesses **close stores**, leading to job **losses**.

See p.167 for more on e-commerce.

6) Businesses that rely **too heavily** on **digital technology** will experience **decreased productivity** every time something **breaks down** — if this happens on a **regular basis**, it could put the business in **financial trouble**.

***New Technology** can impact **Different Areas** of the business*

1) Businesses can adopt new **Enterprise Resource Planning** (**ERP**) software (page 167) to keep track of data from **all departments** in one place. E.g. if a manager in the **production department** wants to know some **financial figures** they can look on the software rather than having to consult the **finance department**. This type of software can **increase efficiency** — however, it can lead to people **making decisions** without consulting the right people, which can have **negative impacts** on the business.

2) Instead of monitoring stock levels at **individual sites**, businesses can use **stock control systems** (see p.64) to monitor stock levels from a **central location**. This can **reduce costs** and **increase sales** as stock is moved to where it's **needed most**. However, the needs of **individual sites** can often be **overlooked**.

3) Adopting new technology like **Computer Aided Design** and **3D printing** (see p.60) during manufacturing can **reduce costs** and **improve efficiency**. However, it can be expensive to **train staff** or **employ experts**.

Practice Questions

Q1 Give five opportunities that new technology can give businesses.

Q2 Describe two ways that changes to technology can impact a company's manufacturing department.

Exam Questions

Q1 To what extent will growth of e-commerce impact strategic decisions made by a multinational company? [9 marks]

Q2 VCP Ltd is a sportswear manufacturer. Analyse how technological change may improve the competitiveness of VCP Ltd. [9 marks]

Have you been threatened by new technology? Call Jim's Solicitors now...

Businesses need to be careful that they don't miss out on opportunities to adopt key technology at the right time — a few bad decisions and competitors will gain so much of an advantage that it could be curtains for the company...

Business and the Competitive Environment

Michael Porter came up with a model that businesses could use to analyse the level of competition in an industry. As Prof Porter is considered to be the leading authority on competitiveness, he's probably worth listening to.

Porter's **Five Forces Model** shows **Influences** on an industry

1) Porter's **Five Forces model** shows an industry being influenced by **five competitive forces**.
2) It analyses the state of the market and helps managers of existing businesses to figure out the **best strategy** to gain a **competitive advantage** — it is a **decision-making** tool.
3) It can show potential market entrants how **profitable** the market is likely to be and whether it is worth getting into — and if it is, where best to **position** themselves.

1) Barriers to Entry — how Easy it is for New Firms to enter the market

1) New entrants to the market will want to compete by selling similar products — it's in the **interests** of existing firms in the market to make it **hard** for new firms to get in.
2) **High start-up costs** (e.g. **expensive equipment**) might deter new firms from entering the market.

Strategies to raise barriers to entry:

- **Patents** or **trademarks** (see p.157) can be used to make it harder for new entrants to sell similar products.
- Established businesses may take control of **distribution channels**. This is known as '**forward vertical integration**' (see p.152). It makes the channel **unavailable** to new entrants and makes the market less attractive. E.g. an outdoor clothing manufacturer which **buys out** or **merges** with an outdoor clothing retailer.
- Threatening new entrants with a **price war**. Large existing businesses are likely to be benefitting from **economies of scale**, so can undercut the prices of new entrants (**predatory pricing**). However, selling goods at a loss to force competitors out of the market is against **EU competition law**.

2) Buyer Power — buyers want products at as Low a Price as possible

1) **Buyers** have **more power** when there are **few buyers** and many sellers.
2) Buyers have **more power** when products are **standardised** — it's easier for firms to charge a premium price for differentiated goods and services.
3) A supplier's **main customer** can **negotiate special deals** and lower prices.

Remember, this applies to business customers, wholesalers and retailers, as well as the general public.

Strategies to influence buyer power:

- A company might **buy the supplier out** — this is '**backwards vertical integration**' (see p.152), e.g. a burger chain which buys a beef farm.
- Similar businesses could come together to form a **buying group**. They'll be buying **bigger volumes** so will be able to demand a **better deal** and so increase their profits. Buying groups help **smaller businesses compete** with large businesses.

3) Supplier power — suppliers want to get as High a Price as possible

1) **Suppliers** have **more power** when there are **few suppliers** and lots of firms buying from them.
2) If it costs customers to **switch suppliers**, then this gives suppliers more power.

Strategies to influence supplier power:

- Businesses can try to tie buyers into **long-term contracts** to make it harder for them to switch suppliers. E.g. mobile phone companies often have **2-year contracts** and lock handsets to their network.
- Suppliers can use **forward integration** to gain power — e.g. by setting up their own **retail outlets** or **buying** the retailers they supply to.
- Businesses could **develop new products** and protect them with **patents** to gain supplier power. They'll be the **only ones** selling the product, so will be able to charge a **premium** if it's a hit.

Business and the Competitive Environment

4) Threat of Substitutes — how likely consumers are to Buy an Alternative

1) The **willingness** of customers to **substitute** is a factor affecting competitiveness.
2) Relative **price** and **quality** are important — buyers are unlikely to change to a poor value product.
3) For **undifferentiated products**, e.g. washing powder, the threat is higher than for **unique products**.

Strategies to reduce the threat of substitutes:

- Businesses can make it **expensive** or **difficult** for customers to switch to a substitute (although they have to be careful not to annoy them). E.g. if you buy a Kindle™ from amazon®, you'll usually buy amazon® products to read on it as it's tricky to convert other products to the correct format.
- Customers are often **loyal to a brand** that they perceive as better. If companies can **differentiate** their product and create **brand loyalty**, they'll reduce the threat of substitutes.
- Businesses can **identify** a group of customers whose **needs** aren't quite being met and market a product designed to meet their needs **exactly**, e.g. environmentally-conscious disposable nappy users. There **won't** be any substitutes for them to buy (until other businesses notice anyway).

5) Rivalry within the industry — how much Competition there is

1) Rivalry is **intense** in a market with lots of **equally-sized competitors**.
2) Industries with **high fixed costs** are **very competitive**, e.g. parcel delivery companies which have invested in vehicles. Firms have to sell **a lot** to even cover their fixed costs. So in competitive environments, they **cut prices** to **raise demand**. Even if they're not making a **profit**, it's often hard for them to get out of the market as their expensive equipment is hard to sell on — this **increases rivalry** even more.
3) Industries producing **standardised** goods (e.g. steel, milk, flour) have **intense** rivalry.
4) Rivalry is also **intense** in **young industries** where competitors are following **growth strategies**.

Strategies to reduce the effects of rivalry:

- Some businesses try to make it **easy** for customers to switch between standardised goods. E.g. it's a **hassle** to **switch bank accounts** no matter what incentives are offered so your new bank often handles the process of switching direct debits for you.
- Businesses with a **bigger promotional budget** might do better in markets with intense rivalry.

Practice Questions

Q1 What are the five forces in Porter's Five Forces model?

Q2 How could a business raise entry barriers to a market?

Q3 What strategies might businesses adopt to improve their power as buyers and as sellers?

Q4 What type of industries have the strongest rivalry?

Exam Questions

Q1 A children's clothing manufacturer buys a high-street shop to sell its products from.
What is this an example of?

A Backward vertical integration
B Forward vertical integration
C Horizontal integration
D Product differentiation

[1 mark]

Q2 A manufacturer is entering the pet food market.
Analyse how Porter's Five Forces Model could help it to devise a strategy to maximise its profits. [25 marks]

Porter conveniently ignores the force of gravity...

... which isn't a luxury most of us have. Darn pesky gravity, making things fall down. Anyway, the Five Forces model is a rather useful tool to analyse the market and see where threats and opportunities are. Porter also came up with three generic strategies which are on page 146 — there's a lovely strategic matrix too. That'll give you a reason to go on.

Assessing Investments

Investment appraisal helps businesses decide what projects to invest in, in order to get the best, fastest, least risky return for their money.

Investment *decisions must balance* ***Risk*** *and* ***Return***

1) Businesses often need to **invest** in order to achieve their **objectives** — e.g. if a firm's objective is to **increase sales** by 25% over three years, they'll need to invest in extra **staff** and **machinery** so that they can make the extra products they hope to sell.
2) Any situation where you have to **spend** money in the hope of **making** money in the future is **risky**, because there's always the possibility that you **won't** make as much money as you expect. Businesses like the **risks** to be **low** and the **return** (the profit on the investment) to be **high**.
3) When companies are making strategic **decisions** about how to **invest** their money (whether to launch a new product, take on more staff, relocate their call centre, etc.) they gather as much **data** as possible so that they can work out the **risk** and **reward** involved.
4) There are **two** main **questions** that businesses try to answer to enable them to make good investment decisions:
   - **how long** will it take to get back the money that they spend?
   - how much **profit** will they get from the investment?
5) There are **three main methods** that businesses can use to help them **answer** these questions and decide whether investments are a good idea: **average rate of return** (see below), **payback period calculation** (p.139), and **net present value calculation** (p.141).
6) These **investment appraisal methods** assess how much **profit** a project is going to make, and how **fast** the money will come in. The **faster** money comes in, the **less** risk in the long run.
7) All of the methods are **useful**, but they're only as good as the **data** used to calculate them.

Average Rate of Return *(ARR) compares* ***Net Return*** *with* ***Investment***

1) **Average rate of return** (ARR — sometimes called Accounting Rate of Return) compares the **net return** with the level of investment. The net return is the **income** of the project minus **costs**, including the investment.
2) The higher the ARR, the more **favourable** the project will appear.
3) ARR is expressed as a **percentage** and calculated by: → $\frac{\text{Average Net Return}}{\text{Investment}} \times 100$

Example:

	Investment	Yr 1	Yr 2	Yr 3	Yr 4	Yr 5
Project A — net cash flow	(£10m)	£4m	£5m	£6m	£7m	£5m
Project B — net cash flow	(£8m)	£3m	£3m	£4m	£6m	£6m

Numbers in brackets are negative. E.g. (£10m) means –£10m.

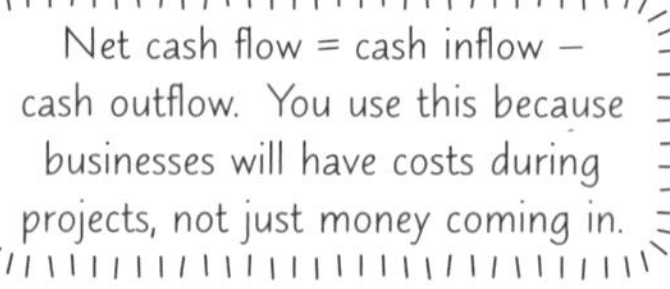
Net cash flow = cash inflow – cash outflow. You use this because businesses will have costs during projects, not just money coming in.

Net return (in £m) of **Project A** = –10 + 4 + 5 + 6 + 7 + 5 = **£17m**

Average net return = £17m ÷ 5 years = **£3.4m**

The investment was £10m, so **ARR** = $\frac{£3.4\text{m}}{£10\text{m}} \times 100 = 34\%$

Net return (in £m) of **Project B** = –8 + 3 + 3 + 4 + 6 + 6 = **£14m**

Average net return = £14m ÷ 5 years = **£2.8m**

The investment was £8m, so **ARR** = $\frac{£2.8\text{m}}{£8\text{m}} \times 100 = 35\%$

So managers would probably choose **Project B** because it has a higher ARR, but only just...

The pirate accountants were very fond of the average rate of return.

Assessing Investments

Payback measures the Length of Time it takes to Get Your Money Back

1) The **payback period** is the time it takes for a project to make enough money to pay back the **initial investment**.
2) The **formula** for calculating the payback period is: $\frac{\textbf{Amount invested}}{\textbf{Annual net return}}$

   For example, a £2 million project that has an **annual net return prediction** of £250 000 will reach payback in £2 million ÷ £0.25 million = 8 years.
3) Managers **compare** the payback periods of different projects so that they can choose which project to go ahead with — managers usually want to get their money back as soon as possible, so they prefer a **short payback period**.

There are Advantages and Disadvantages to ARR and Payback

Calculating the **ARR** and **payback period** can both be helpful, but they have **drawbacks** too:

	Advantages	Disadvantages
Average Rate of Return	• It's **easy** to **calculate** and **understand**. • It takes account of all the project's **cash flows** — i.e. it doesn't stop counting cash flow after a certain point, like payback period calculation does.	• It ignores the **timing** of the **cash flows** — e.g. a company might put more value on money that they get **sooner** rather than later. • It ignores the **time value** of money (see p.140).
Payback Period	• It's **easy** to calculate and understand. • It's very good for **high tech** projects (technology tends to become **obsolete** fairly quickly, so businesses need to be sure that they'll get their initial investment back before the products **stop** generating a return) or any project that might not provide **long-term** returns.	• It **ignores cash flow** after payback. E.g. two projects (project A and project B) might both have a payback period of three years. Project A will continue to provide a return of £20 000 a year after the payback period, while project B won't provide any more return after its payback period. Project A is clearly the **better investment**, but payback period calculation **doesn't** take this into account. • It **ignores** the **time value** of money.

Practice Questions

Q1 What are the two questions that businesses ask about potential investments?

Q2 Give the formula for the following: a) average rate of return b) payback period

Q3 Give two advantages of the average rate of return calculation.

Q4 Give two disadvantages of the payback period calculation.

Q5 What does ARR take into account that the payback period calculation doesn't?

Exam Questions

Answers on p.201.

Q1 A business is investing in a new product. The initial investment is £200 000. The product will generate a revenue of £320 000 over 8 years, with total costs of £40 000. Calculate the average rate of return on the investment. [3 marks]

Q2 Priya owns a doughnut shop. She's thinking of buying a new doughnut-making machine, costing £11 000. She estimates that it will generate a net return of £3000 per year. Calculate the payback period for the new machine. [2 marks]

'Revenge of the Business students: It's Payback Time'...

Arrrrr, there's nothing quite like a good average rate of return. Investment appraisal techniques are really useful for businesses, and they could come in quite handy in your Business exam if you get a question on them. So stick with it until it's all practically tattooed on your brain, and then turn over for... more on assessing investments (sorry).

Assessing Investments

Well, I know how much fun you had on the last two pages about assessing investments, so here's two more for you.

The **Future Value** *of cash inflow depends on* **Risk** *and* **Opportunity Cost**

Risk and **opportunity cost** both **increase** the longer you have to wait for money, which means that it's **worth less**. This is called the **time value of money**. If someone offers you £100 cash-in-hand now or £100 in one year's time, you'd be best off taking it **now**, because:

1) There's a **risk** that the person would never pay you the £100 after a year had gone by.
2) In a year's time the money would be worth less due to **inflation** — a general rise in prices over time. You wouldn't be able to buy as much with that £100 as you could today.
3) There's an **opportunity cost** — if you had the money now you could **invest** it instead of **waiting** for it. A high interest account would beat the rate of inflation and the £100 plus interest that you'd end up with in a year's time would be worth **more** than the £100 in your hand today, and much more than the £100 would be worth to you in a year.

Example: A bank might offer **3% interest**.
- If you put in **£100**, you'll have **£103** after a year.
- If you put in **£97.09**, you'll have **£100** after a year.

So, if you assume that you'd get an interest rate of **3%** if you invested the money today, **£100** paid to you at the **end of the year** would be worth the same as being paid **£97.09 today**.
This idea is explained in more detail below.

A payment after a year or two, or three, is **always worth less** than the **same payment** made to you **today**.

Discounting *adjusts the value of* **Future Cash Inflows** *to their* **Present Value**

1) **Discounting** is the process of **adjusting the value of money** received in the **future** to its **present value**. It's done so that investors can **compare like with like** when they look at the cash inflows they'll receive from projects. £4 million this year **isn't the same** as £4 million in five years' time, and it's not wise to **pretend** that it is the same.
2) **Discounting** can be seen as the **opposite** of **calculating interest**. It's done by **multiplying** the amount of money by a **discount factor**. This discount factor is like the opposite of a bank interest rate. Discount factors are **always less than 1**, because the value of money in the future is always less than its value now.

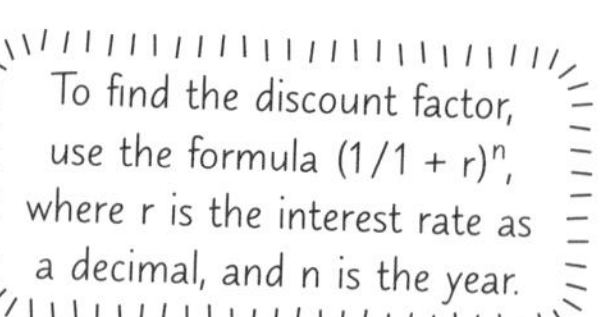

3) **Discount factors** depend on what the **interest rate** is predicted to be. **High** interest rates mean that the future payments have to be **discounted a lot** to give the correct present values. This is so that the present value represents the **opportunity cost** of not investing the money in the **bank** where it would earn a nice **high interest rate**.

Year	0	1	2	3	4	5
Discount Factor for 5% interest	1	0.952	0.907	0.864	0.823	0.784
Present Value of £1000	£1000	£952	£907	£864	£823	£784

Year 1 discount factor = 1/1.05 = 0.952. Year 2 discount factor = $(1/1.05)^2$ = 0.907.
Year 3 discount factor = $(1/1.05)^3$ = 0.864.

Present value of £1000.

4) As you might expect, when **interest rates** are predicted to be **low**, the future cash inflow doesn't need to be discounted so much. There's **less** opportunity cost.

Assessing Investments

Net Present Value is used to Calculate **Return**

1) **Discounted cash flow** (DCF) is an investment appraisal tool that uses the **net present value** (**NPV**) to calculate the **return** of the project.
2) **Net present value** is the **value** of the project assuming all future returns are **discounted** to what they would be worth if you had them **now**, which is **always** less than their face value (because of inflation and lost interest).
3) If you end up with a **negative NPV**, that means that the business could get a better return by putting their money into a **savings account** rather than going ahead with the project. Businesses will usually only go ahead with projects with a **positive NPV** — projects that are going to **make them money**.
4) The **downsides** of discounted cash flow are that it's a bit **hard to calculate**, and that it's difficult for businesses to work out what the **discount factor** ought to be, because they don't know what the bank interest rates are going to be in the future. The **longer** the project is set to last, the **harder** it is to predict the discount factor.

Here's an **Example** of **Discounted Cash Flow**

Project A has an initial investment of **£10m**, and **project B** has an initial investment of **£8m**.
The **expected rate of interest** is **10%**. The discount factors are given in the table below.

Project A	Net Cash Flow	Discount Factor (10%)	Present Value
Year 1	£4m	0.909	£4m × 0.909 = £3 636 000
Year 2	£5m	0.826	£5m × 0.826 = £4 130 000
Year 3	£6m	0.751	£6m × 0.751 = £4 506 000
Year 4	£7m	0.683	£7m × 0.683 = £4 781 000
Year 5	£5m	0.621	£5m × 0.621 = £3 105 000
Total Present Value of Net Cash Flows			£20 158 000
Net Present Value (Total minus Investment)			£20 158 000 – £10m = **£10 158 000**
Return ((Net Present Value ÷ Investment) × 100)			(£10 158 000 ÷ £10m) × 100 = **101.6%**
Project B	**Net Cash Flow**	**Discount Factor (10%)**	**Present Value**
Year 1	£3m	0.909	£3m × 0.909 = £2 727 000
Year 2	£3m	0.826	£3m × 0.826 = £2 478 000
Year 3	£4m	0.751	£4m × 0.751 = £3 004 000
Year 4	£6m	0.683	£6m × 0.683 = £4 098 000
Year 5	£6m	0.621	£6m × 0.621 = £3 726 000
Total Present Value of Net Cash Flows			£16 033 000
Net Present Value (Total minus Investment)			£16 033 000 – £8m = **£8 033 000**
Return ((Net Present Value ÷ Investment) × 100)			(£8 033 000 ÷ £8m) × 100 = **100.4%**

Net cash flow = cash inflow – cash outflow.

The return gives a percentage, so that two different projects can be compared more easily.

Working out the NPVs shows that **both** projects are **worthwhile**, because both have a **positive NPV**.
The **return** on both projects is **more** than 100% — so they more than **double** the investment.
Project A gives a **slightly better** return than **project B**.

Practice Questions

Q1 How do you calculate the net present value of a net cash flow?

Q2 What does it mean if a project has a negative net present value?

Exam Question

Q1 Explain the benefits of finding the net present value. [4 marks]

Discounts? Brilliant — I love a bargain...

Another tricky couple of pages here. Over halfway through the section though, so try to summon up the energy to learn these two pages, and then there's just two more to go. Discounting future income is a bit of a weird concept to get your head around at first, but it really makes sense for businesses to do it, so keep going over it until you're sure you've got it.

Investment Decisions

The last few pages have covered techniques that analyse the numbers involved in an investment. But there are loads of other, non-numerical factors to consider too.

Non-Numerical, Qualitative** factors affect **Investment Decisions

The **investment decisions** made by managers are based upon a range of numerical data and **quantitative** methods. But managers must also put the decisions into a **qualitative** context, based on **internal** factors and market **uncertainty**.

Business Objectives and Strategy can Influence Investment Decisions

- An investment appraisal recommended purely on **financial data** may not fit in with the **objectives** of a firm. Many businesses will only make an investment if the project will help them **achieve** their objectives.
- For example, a business that aims to produce **low cost products** for a large mass market (e.g. teaspoons) would be **unlikely** to invest as much in **research and development** as a high-end technology business.
- **Human resources** investment takes away from short-term profit, so a firm with the objective of **maximising** profit for shareholder dividends would be unlikely to invest too highly in staff development. On the other hand, a business which aims to produce **high quality**, high-tech products would invest in **skilled staff.**

Corporate Image can Influence Investment Decisions

- **Good corporate image** brings **customer goodwill** and **loyalty** in the long term, and the firm may consider this more important than **short-term rate of return** on investment. Investment decisions that create **bad publicity** and **damage** customer loyalty will damage profits in the **long term.**
- A firm with a green, **environmentally friendly** image would avoid investments that would damage the environment. Some firms incorporate **environmental costs** into their investment appraisals.

Phil had spent all morning perfecting his corporate image.

Industrial Relations can Influence Investment Decisions

- Investments which result in a **loss of jobs** may be turned down, even if they show a good rate of return.
- **Loss of jobs** affects **staff morale**. Cost of **redundancy payments** should be factored into the decision. Trade unions may **strike** over job losses, which would affect **productivity**. **Corporate image** may also be damaged.

*There's **Always Risk** and **Uncertainty** involved in **Investments***

1) Businesses can use all the investment appraisal methods on the last few pages, but that **doesn't** mean that a **new project** will necessarily be successful just because they expect it to be — there's **always** a **risk** involved in investing in a new project.
2) All investment appraisal methods are based on **predictions** about how much **income** they can generate from investments. It's very **difficult** to **accurately** predict what's going to happen in the future, so businesses **can't** always **rely** on their predictions. E.g. a business might work out that the **payback period** of a machine is four years, based on a predicted income from the investment of £8000 a year — but the investment could end up only generating £3000 a year, so their payback period calculation would be **completely wrong**.
3) Market environments are always **uncertain**. Circumstances might change **unexpectedly**, and this could have a negative impact on the business. **Exchange rates** may alter, **sales** may decrease, **customers' tastes** may change, **competitors** may become stronger, the **cost** of **raw materials** may increase, etc.
4) Any change in the **circumstances** that businesses based their investment **predictions** on can mean that their predictions are **no longer valid**. E.g. if a business works out the net present value based on an interest rate of 6%, but the interest rate actually goes up to 9%, their net present value results will be **inaccurate**.
5) Every firm has a **different attitude** to **risk** — some firms are happy to take **big risks** that might lead to **big financial rewards**, but other firms prefer to **play it safe** and go for **less risky** investments.
6) It's often a good idea to have a set of **investment criteria** — conditions that need to be **met** for an investment to be **approved**. These could include anything, such as expected **return**, **job** creation, or **environmental** targets.

Investment Decisions

Sensitivity Analysis tests Assumptions that decisions are based on

1) Most decisions rely on certain **assumptions** about future events. For example, an **investment decision** might be based on the assumption that the **price** of raw materials will increase by **8%** over the next three years, and that **sales revenue** will increase by **3%** each year. All the assumptions put together makes a **scenario** for the future called the **base case**.
2) **Sensitivity analysis** looks at the base case and **considers** what would happen if you **alter** the assumptions, for instance if the price of raw materials increases by **10%** or **15%** instead.
3) The most simple method analyses factors **one at a time**. Analysing more than one factor at a time can be very **complicated**, but can be done with specialist **software**.
4) A business can use this information to **evaluate** the **risk** of an investment — if they could cope with raw materials going up in price by 10% but not by 15%, they need to decide whether it's worth the risk, or if they could take **extra measures** to reduce the risk.

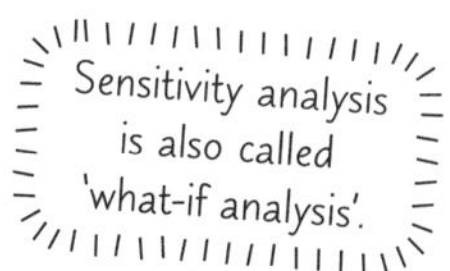

Example

The owner of a music shop is considering **investing** in larger premises. Her **research** suggests that **operating** in the new premises will cost **10% more** than the current premises, and that **passing trade** will **increase** by **3%**. She decides to use **sensitivity analysis** on these two factors.

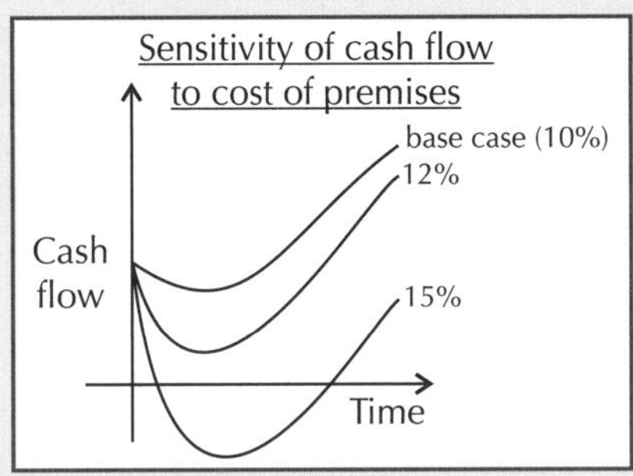

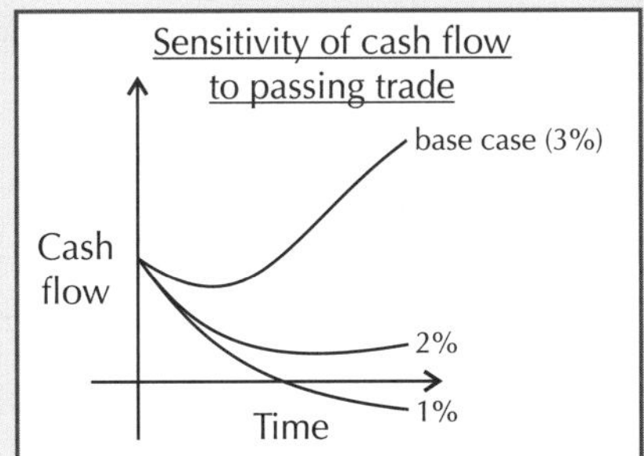

- The top graph shows that if the cost of operating in the new premises is **12%** more, it isn't that different to the **base case**. But if it costs **15%** more, then the shop will have a significantly **reduced** cash flow, even going **negative** for a period.
- The bottom graph shows that having a **2%** increase in passing trade has a **big effect** on the cash flow compared to the base case, and having a **1%** increase leads to a negative cash flow.
- The owner of the shop could decide that the **risk** is too great, and not invest in the premises. Or she could decide that it is worth the risk, but only with **precautions**. For example, she could **negotiate** with the estate agent and energy suppliers to prevent the cost of premises from increasing too much, and make the shop front more **appealing** to keep passing trade at a suitable level.

Practice Questions

Q1 How can industrial relations influence investment decisions?

Q2 Why can't businesses rely completely on their predictions?

Q3 What are 'investment criteria'?

Q4 What is a base case?

Q5 How does sensitivity analysis work?

Exam Question

Q1 Analyse the value of sensitivity analysis in investment decisions. [9 marks]

My take on sensitivity analysis is to call my boss names and see if he cries...

The stuff on these pages is pretty important in business. A company doesn't just launch straight into an investment with no considerations — it'll want to look at all the different risks and uncertainties and figure out if the investment is worth it. And you've reached the end of this section. Bravo — treat yourself to a little rest. Have a biscuit, or a cuppa (or both...).

Marketing Strategies

North. No, west. OK, how about north-west? Oh, that's not what you mean by choosing strategic direction. Whoops.

Strategic Direction is guided by the Marketing Strategy

1) **Strategic direction** is the **general path** a business takes, based on its **mission** and **achieving its objectives**.
2) The strategic direction influences how a **business's strategy develops** and affects **all areas** of the business.
3) **Key factors** in setting strategic direction are the choices of **which markets** to compete in, **what products** to offer and **which direction** the business should **grow** in.

Marketing Strategy decides on Markets and Products

The **markets** that a business plans to compete in and the **products** it plans to offer are influenced by **market research** and **analysis** as well as **internal skills** and **resources**. Here are some **important factors** that influence these choices:

Markets

- **Type of product** — the products that a business offers will impact its **choice of market**. Certain products are more suited to **B2B** markets than **B2C** markets (see p.28), **niche** markets than **mass** markets, etc.
- **Level of competition** — businesses will favour markets where there is a **low level of competition**. They will also prefer to compete in **growing markets** rather than **saturated markets**.
- **External factors** — e.g. **political**, **social**, or **economic factors** could create opportunities in certain markets.
- **Internal resources** — e.g. if a business only has a **small production facility**, it might be more inclined to choose to compete in **niche markets** rather than **mass markets**.
- **Attitude to risk** — businesses that take **big risks** are more likely to compete in **new** and **unknown markets**.

Products

- **Research and development** (R&D) — a company with a **strong** R&D department can develop **new**, **innovative** products to sell (see p.154-155).
- **Competitors** — businesses need to **react** to the actions of rival companies. If a competitor has launched a new, successful product, they might choose to **develop** a **similar product** in order to compete.
- **Technology** — changes in technology could affect the **products**. A company making TVs will need to develop **smart TVs** to keep up with the rest of the market.
- **Finances** — businesses that have **healthy finances** and **working capital** can afford to spend more money **developing new products**.
- **External factors** — just like the **choice of market**, products are influenced by different external factors, like social, economic or environmental factors.

There are Different Options for Strategic Growth

A chap called Igor Ansoff came up with **four** different **strategies** that a business can use to **grow**. These strategies set the **direction** for business growth and strategy development.

1) **Market penetration** means trying to **increase** your **market share** in your **existing market**. E.g. if a company makes washing powder and currently has a 25% market share, it might try to achieve a 30% market share using **sales promotions**, **pricing strategies** and **advertising**. This strategy works best in a **growth market**. It **doesn't work well** in **saturated markets**, where demand for the product has stopped growing.
2) **New product development** is selling **new products** in your **existing markets**. It's best when the market has good **growth potential** and the business has high market share, strong R&D and a good **competitive advantage**.
3) **Market development** (or **market extension**) is selling **existing products** to **new markets**. It can be done through **repositioning** — this means that a business focuses on a **different segment of the market**. They need to **research** the target market segment and work out how they can **adapt** their product or promotion to suit the needs of a different set of consumers. This might involve creating a **new advertising campaign** or **promotion** which **targets** a different audience. Businesses can also target different market segments by using **new channels of distribution**, e.g. using **e-commerce** to sell **directly to consumers** rather than selling through a **retailer** or **agent**.
4) **Market development** can also be done by **expanding** into new geographical markets to exploit the same market segment (e.g. in a different country — see p.158-159).
5) **Diversification** means selling **new products** to **new markets**. Diversification is a **very risky** strategy, as it involves moving into markets that the business may have **no experience** of. It's used when a business really needs to reduce their dependence on a **limited product range** or if **high profits** are likely, which **reduces** the **risk**.

Marketing Strategies

Ansoff's Matrix is used to decide on a *Growth Strategy*

1) **Ansoff's matrix** is a tool for comparing the **level of risk** involved with the different growth strategies. It helps **managers** to decide on a direction for **strategic growth**.
2) The **advantage** of Ansoff's matrix is that it doesn't just lay out potential strategies for growth — it also forces managers to think about the **expected risks** of moving in a certain direction.
3) One **disadvantage** of the matrix is that it fails to show that **market development** and **diversification** strategies also tend to require **significant change** in the **day-to-day workings** of the company.
4) **Product development** is less risky than diversification, but it works best for firms that already have a strong **competitive advantage**.
5) **Market penetration** is the **least risky** strategy of all — so **most firms** opt for this approach to start with.
6) Some people believe that Ansoff's matrix **oversimplifies** the **options** available for growth. For example, **diversification** doesn't have to be **completely unrelated** to what the business does currently. It might be a **safe option** to diversify by moving into your **supplier's business**, as you know there's a **guaranteed market** for that product.

Markets \ Products	Existing	New
Existing	Market penetration	Product development
New	Market development or extension	Diversification

Increasing Risk (down) — Increasing Risk (across)

Example: KFC® International Market Development

KFC®'s expansion from the USA market to the UK market is an example of **market development**. KFC® began operating in the USA in 1952 and extended their market by opening an outlet in Preston, UK in 1965. This was the **first American fast food chain** to open in the UK. There are now over 750 outlets across the UK and Ireland. These outlets were run as a **franchise** by an **independent company**, KFC GB Ltd, until it was bought by PepsiCo in 1986.

Ansoff's matrix shows that KFC®'s market development strategy is the result of taking an **existing product**, their fast food business model, and developing it in a **new market**, the UK. This is a **safer** option than **diversification**, particularly since the UK had no other fast food chains in 1965 so there was **no competition**.

Practice Questions

Q1 Give two internal and two external factors that affect marketing strategies.

Q2 What does a market penetration strategy involve?

Q3 What is diversification?

Q4 What are the four areas of Ansoff's matrix?

Exam Questions

Q1 Which of these is the least risky growth strategy?
A market penetration B product development C market development D diversification [1 mark]

Q2 A company is considering developing a new product to sell in their existing market.
Explain the advantages and disadvantages of new product development as a growth strategy. [6 marks]

Q3 Organoats is a company that makes organic porridge. They currently just sell plain porridge oats, which are selling well. By considering the Ansoff matrix, analyse the different marketing strategies the company could implement in order to grow. [16 marks]

Ansoff's Matrix — bet Keanu wouldn't want to star in that one...

Marketing strategies probably won't save the world but they can be pretty useful for businesses who want to plan for the future. And knowing about them won't help you win the war against intelligent robotic lifeforms or help you escape from virtual reality but they just might come in useful when you're sitting your A-level Business exams.

Positioning Strategies

Positioning is all about where you place your brand and products in relation to others — see p.39 for a reminder.

Positioning Strategy is an important Strategic Choice

1) **Strategic positioning** means choosing how to **compete** with the other businesses in the market. A business's **positioning strategy** is part of the marketing strategy — the choice influences the **general direction** a business **develops in** and affects **all areas** of the business.
2) **Different positioning strategies** work for **different companies**. It is important to choose the right strategy — it should play to the company's **strengths** and give them a **competitive advantage**. The wrong positioning strategy can be **disastrous** — **value** products with too **high** a price and **luxury** products with too **low** a price will **fail**.
3) The positioning strategy chosen will be **affected** by a number of things. The **product** itself will be very important, as will the state of the **economy**. The company's **image** and **resources**, along with its **mission**, are important too.

Businesses want to have a Competitive Advantage

1) If a business has a **competitive advantage**, customers see an **advantage** to buying **its products** compared to its **competitors' products** — competitive advantages are often gained through a firm's **core competences** (p.115).
2) Porter identified **two types** of **competitive advantage**:

Cost advantage

1) A business can get a **competitive advantage** by selling a similar **product** at a lower cost than its rivals.
2) **Low-cost airlines** like EasyJet and Ryanair use a "no frills" strategy to keep their costs at a **minimum** — they use cheaper airports like Luton and cut out travel agents' fees by using online booking.

Differentiation advantage

1) Selling **better products** at the same or a slightly higher price creates a **competitive advantage**.
2) Offering a product that consumers see as **different** from competitors' products can make consumers think it's **better**. This is called **product differentiation**.

3) Having a **competitive advantage** is great for a company — they'll either sell a **high volume** of products at a **low price** and make a **large profit**, or they'll be able to sell enough products at a **high price** to make a **large profit**.
4) A competitive advantage can also build **brand loyalty** — customers **associate** the particular advantage with the **brand**, which makes them **more likely** to choose that brand in the future.
5) However, **holding on** to your competitive advantage can be **tricky**. Maintaining **low cost production** might be difficult. **Competitors** can **lower** their **prices** or **copy** your **unique features**. **Consumer tastes** can change, and a changing **economy** can alter the demand for luxury or value products. Businesses need to continuously monitor both **internal** and **external factors** in order to **keep** their advantage.

Porter suggested Three Generic Strategies to Gain Advantage

These three strategies are **competitive strategies** based on the strengths of **low costs** and **differentiation**.

Cost Leadership

1) **Cost leadership** strategy calls for the **lowest cost of production** for a given level of quality. **Big firms** with **large** and **efficient production facilities**, benefiting from **economies of scale**, can use this strategy.
2) In a **price war**, the firm can maintain profitability while the competition suffers losses. If prices **decline**, the firm can stay profitable because of its **low costs**.

Differentiation

1) **Differentiation** strategy requires a product with **unique attributes** which consumers value, so that they **perceive** it to be **better** than rival products. Unique products allow businesses to charge **premium prices**.
2) Businesses that are **innovative**, have **strong branding** and offer **quality products** can benefit from this strategy.
3) Risks include **imitation** by competitors and **changes** in **consumer tastes**.

Focus

1) **Focus** strategy concentrates on **niche market segments** to achieve **either** cost advantage or differentiation.
2) This strategy suits firms with **fewer resources** who can target markets with specific needs. A firm using this strategy usually has **loyal customers**, making it very hard for other firms to compete.

Positioning Strategies

Porter's **Strategic Matrix** helps decide on a **Competitive Strategy**

1) Porter's **strategic matrix** helps a business choose its **positioning strategy** based on its **competitive advantage** and its **market scope**. A business can place itself in a particular section depending on whether it's aimed at a **broad** or **narrow market** (also known as a niche market, see p.39), and whether it offers **cheaper** products than competitors or **unique**, **quality** products.
2) For example, in the jewellery market, Accessorize sells products to a broad market at relatively low prices, so it would be placed in the **cost leadership** section of the matrix. Tiffany & Co. sells high-quality products at premium prices, focusing on a narrow market, so it would fit into the **differentiation and focus** section.

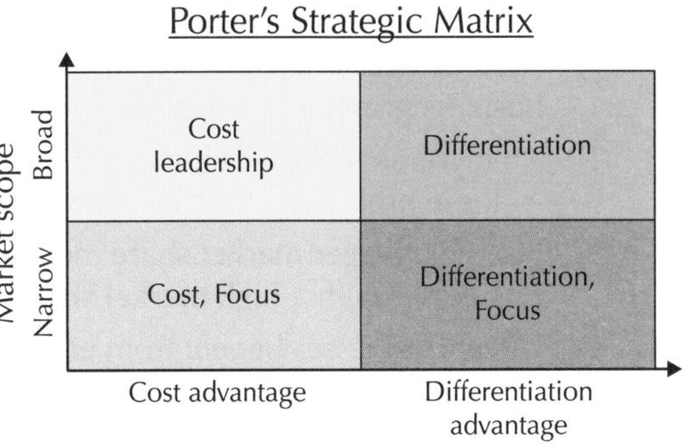

Bowman's Strategic Clock shows **Pricing** and **Differentiation Strategies**

1) **Bowman's strategic clock** shows different **positioning strategies** based on different combinations of **price** (from low to high) and **perceived added value** or **benefits** (also from low to high). It shows that some positioning strategies are likely to be **more successful** than others.
2) It can be used to analyse the **competitive position** of a company. It's **similar** to Porter's strategic matrix above, but goes into a bit more **detail**.
3) Position 1 corresponds to a strategy of low price products with low added value — this will only be successful if the products sell in a **high volume**.
4) Position 2 corresponds to the **cost leadership** section of **Porter's strategic matrix**.
5) Position 3 is the **hybrid** area — **modest prices** with a relatively **high** perceived added value.
6) Position 4 corresponds to the **differentiation** section of Porter's strategic matrix, and position 5 corresponds to the **differentiation and focus** section.
7) Positions 6-8 (the grey area) combine a **high price** with fairly **low** perceived added value. Unless a company has a **monopoly** (see p.15), if it adopts these positioning strategies it will ultimately **fail**.

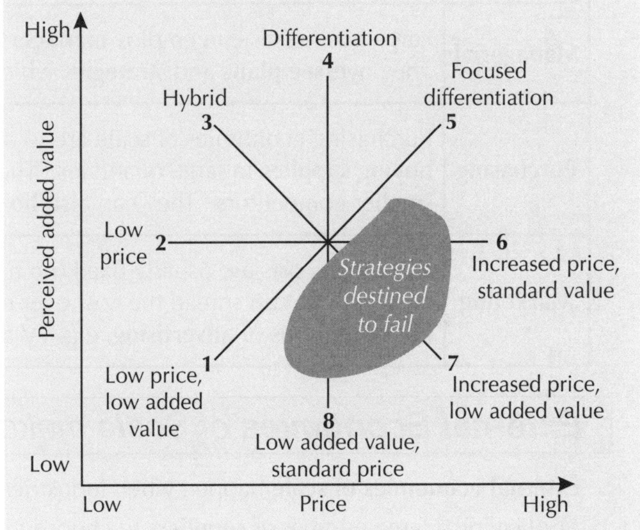

Practice Questions

Q1 Explain one way a company could lose its competitive advantage.

Q2 Describe Porter's generic strategies.

Q3 What are the four areas on Porter's strategic matrix?

Q4 Where is the hybrid position located on Bowman's strategic clock?

Exam Question

Q1 The Norfolk Wales ice cream company sells luxury organic ice cream. To what extent do you agree that the company has chosen a 'differentiation' positioning strategy? [12 marks]

What time is it Mr Bowman — time for your strategy to fail...

I know, I know — it's a bit of a weird clock that only goes up to 8 o'clock. And they might as well have labelled that grey area between 6 and 8 as 'DOOM' or 'WARNING: HERE BE MONSTERS'. But other than that, it's OK really. 3, 4 and 5 are the only ones with funny names, so if you learn them, you'll be laughing all the way to the exam.

Business Growth

A business might pursue a strategy of growth so that it can reap the rewards that come with being a bigger business...

Large Businesses are More Stable than Small Businesses

1) Business **size** is usually measured by **revenue**, **profit**, **market share**, **number of employees** or **assets**. When a business **grows** it means these measures are increasing — growth can be **organic** or **external** (see p.150-153).
2) An increase in **sales volume** and **revenue** will likely mean bigger **profits** for the business — these profits can then be **reinvested** back into the business to **stimulate more growth**.
3) Having a **bigger market share** means that the business has more **influence** over the market. Businesses with a **high market share** can use their influence to **control prices**.
4) Larger businesses benefit from **economies of scale** and **economies of scope** which means **lower unit costs**.
5) Bigger businesses often have a **range of products** or **services**, so they can cope better if the **market changes**.

Economies of Scale mean bigger is Cheaper

Economies of scale mean that as the scale of production **increases**, the **cost** of producing **each item** (the unit cost) **decreases**. **Internal** economies of scale increase efficiency **within** a firm, and there are several different types:

Technical	Technical economies of scale are related to **production**. Production methods for **large volumes** are often more **efficient**. Large businesses can afford to buy better, more advanced **machinery**, which might mean they need **fewer staff**, and **wage costs** will **fall**.
Managerial	Large businesses can employ **managers** with **specialist skills** to manage specific departments. They **oversee plans** and **strategies** which can result in work being done more **quickly** and **efficiently**.
Purchasing	Purchasing economies of scale are to do with **discounts**. Big businesses can negotiate discounts when buying **supplies** in large quantities. They can get bigger discounts and longer **credit periods** than their smaller competitors. They can also **borrow money** at lower rates of interest than small businesses.
Marketing	Marketing costs are usually **fixed** (no matter how many units are sold), so a business with a **large output** can spread the cost over more units. A **large** business can also afford more **effective** forms of **advertising**, e.g. TV adverts.

External Economies of Scale make a Whole Industry or Area more efficient

External economies of scale happen when industries are concentrated in **small geographical areas**.

1) Having a large number of **suppliers** to choose from gives **economies of scale**. Locating near lots of suppliers means firms can **easily negotiate** with a **range of suppliers**, which tends to **increase quality** and **reduce prices**.
2) A good skilled local **labour supply** makes an industry **more efficient**. This is most important in industries where training is **expensive** or takes a long time. For example, **software development** firms in California's "Silicon Valley" know that plenty of people who are **qualified** to fill their vacancies already live **within driving distance**.

The Experience Curve — the More you do something, the Better you get

As a business **grows** and increases its **sales volume**, it will begin to **produce more** products. Workers will get **more experienced** and **more efficient** at making the products, which will cause the **cost per unit** to decrease.

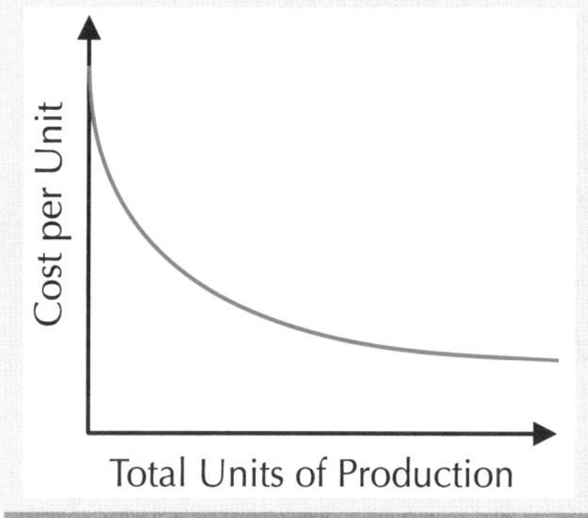

1) In general, the **production** of any **goods** or **services** will follow the experience curve. As the **total units produced** by a business **increases**, the **cost per unit decreases** at a **constant rate** — e.g. if the total units produced doubles, the cost per unit might decrease by 20%.
2) The main reason for this effect is that as workers get more **practice** and **experience** at making the products, they become **more productive**.
3) **Efficiency increases** as **total units produced increases** — workers develop better ways to make the product, including wasting **fewer materials**, taking **less time** and becoming better at using **technology** and **machines**.

Business Growth

Economies of Scope mean More Variety is Cheaper

1) **Economies of scope** arise when a business produces **multiple products** instead of specialising in one.
2) It's **cheaper** for **one business** to produce **many products** than it is for **many businesses** to produce **one product** each.
3) A business that already has **people** and an **infrastructure** in place will be **more efficient** at producing an additional product than a new business, specialising in only that product, will be. They are able to **expand** the **production department** without having to expand **other departments** in the business, so **unit costs decrease**.
4) Existing businesses are also able to benefit from **brand loyalty** (see p.26) — people already know the company's brand, so they are more likely to buy other products that they make.
5) Economies of scope allow businesses to charge **lower prices** due to **lower unit costs**. This gives them a **competitive advantage** over other businesses and can force rivals out of the market.

Diseconomies of Scale — being bigger can be Bad News, too

1) **Diseconomies of scale** make **unit costs increase** as the scale of production increases. They happen because large firms are **harder to manage** than small ones.
2) It's important to keep all departments working towards the **same objectives**. **Poor coordination** makes a business **less efficient**. In a big firm, it's hard to **coordinate** activities between different departments.
3) **Communication** is harder in a big business. It can be **slow** and **difficult** to get messages to the right people, especially when there are **long chains of command**. The **amount** of information circulating in a business can increase at a faster rate than the business is actually growing.
4) It can be hard to **motivate** people in a large firm. In a **small** firm, managers are in **close contact** with staff, and it's easier for people to feel like they **belong** and that they're working towards the same aims. When people **don't feel they belong**, and that there's **no point** to what they're doing, they get **demotivated**.
5) Diseconomies of scale are caused by problems with management. Strong **leadership**, **delegation** and **decentralisation** (see p.87) can all help **prevent diseconomies** of scale and keep costs down.

Businesses may become Smaller — this is called Retrenchment

1) **Retrenchment** may be necessary in order for a business to remain **profitable**. The need for retrenchment is often due to **diseconomies of scale**, **declining markets**, **economic recession** or **improved competitor performance**.
2) **Retrenchment** means that the business will have to **downsize** in some areas. This can be achieved by:
    - **Cutting jobs** — if **sales** are decreasing, a business will need to **decrease** its **wage bill** by cutting jobs.
    - **Reducing output** — if a business is selling **fewer units** it has to **reduce** its **output** and **capacity**.
    - **Withdrawing from markets** — businesses might choose to **stop selling products** in **less profitable markets**.
    - **Splitting the business up (demerging)** — it's easier to **manage** and **control** a smaller business, so a large business might **split up** into several smaller ones and focus on making each one **profitable**.
3) Retrenchment affects **workers** — if it is done in lots of **little steps** over a **long time**, then workers may not be too badly affected. However, if a business has to **retrench quickly** (e.g. during a recession), the impact on workers is **significant** — it can lead to **decreased productivity** which might make the problem even worse.

Practice questions

Q1 Outline three benefits of growth to a business.

Q2 Give two internal and two external economies of scale.

Q3 What is retrenchment?

Exam Questions

Q1 Explain the advantages of economies of scale for a manufacturing business. [5 marks]

Q2 A retail business is growing rapidly. Analyse the possible benefits and drawbacks of this growth. [12 marks]

Tea and retrenchments will be served at the end of this section...

Make sure you can tell your economies from your diseconomies and your scale from your scope when you're learning this stuff. You can even put the experience curve into practice — the more business you revise, the better you'll get at it.

Business Growth — Organic

If a business is a success and demand for its products is high, it may decide to implement an organic growth strategy.

Organic Growth is when a business Grows From Within

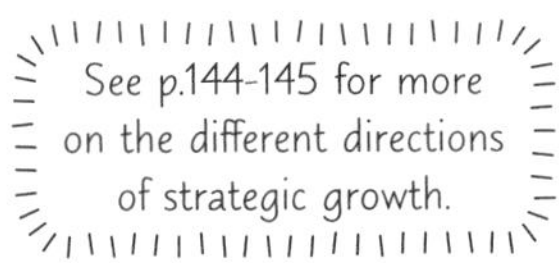

1) Expansion from within a business is known as **organic growth** (or internal growth) — a business can come up with **strategies** to sell more products, make new products, increase market share, expand into new markets, etc. in order to **grow**.
2) Businesses that grow organically are often able to **finance** their growth (increased capacity, new premises, more staff, etc.) by **reinvesting profits** into the business.
3) Businesses find it easiest to grow organically when the **markets** they are in are **growing quickly** and when they are **outperforming** their competitors, enabling them to increase their **market share**.
4) Organic growth is **slower** and **more gradual** than **external growth** (i.e. mergers and takeovers — see p.152), which means that it's easier for the company to **adapt** to growth.

Advantages of Organic Growth over External Growth	Disadvantages of Organic Growth compared to External Growth
• Can maintain current **management style**, **culture** and **ethics** of the business. • **Less risk** as it's expanding what the business is good at and it's usually **financed using profits**. • It's easy for the business to **manage** internal growth and **control** how much the business will grow. • Less disruptive changes mean that workers' **efficiency**, **productivity** and **morale** remain high.	• It can take a **long time** to grow a business internally and it can take a while for the business to **adapt to big changes** in the market. • **Market size** isn't affected by organic growth. If the **market isn't growing**, the business is **restricted** to increasing its **market share** or finding a **new market** to sell products to. • Businesses might miss out on **opportunities** for more **ambitious growth** if they only grow internally.

Growing in Size brings its Own Problems

1) Large companies can suffer from **diseconomies of scale** (see p.149) — any further growth will result in them **losing money** and the only solution may be **retrenchment**.
2) Growing companies find it more difficult to **manage cash flow** — they need to **invest** in **infrastructure** and **assets** but also have enough cash available for the **day-to-day expenses** of the business.
3) Fast growth increases the risk of **overtrading** — increased **demand** means the business needs to buy more **raw materials** and employ more **people**. This **reduces** the amount of **working capital** available to pay the bills, and the business runs the risk that they'll go bust before they have the chance to get paid by their customers.
4) When a company grows in size it will often change from a **private limited company (Ltd)** to a **public limited company (PLC)**. This can make running the company more complicated:
   - The **original owners** lose some control to new **shareholders** which can affect strategy (see p.188).
   - Becoming a **PLC** can make managers more **short-termist** as shareholders seek a **quick return** on investment through **dividend** payments.
   - Once a company becomes a **PLC**, it's more open to being **taken over**. Anyone with enough money could buy enough of its shares to take a **controlling interest**.
5) Businesses have to avoid growing so much that they **dominate** their market and become a **monopoly** (see p.15) — companies can be penalised by the **Competition and Markets Authority (CMA)** if they **damage competition** in a market.
6) Business owners may choose to **restrict** growth or **retrench** for the following reasons:
   - They may want to **maintain the culture** of a small business.
   - The business will become more **complicated** to manage as it gets bigger.
   - Growth requires the business to **secure additional financial resources**, which can be complicated.
   - They may not want to put too much **strain** on their **cash flow** position.

Being bigger was very bad news for Jerry — his wife banned him from eating pies.

Business Growth — Organic

Greiner's Model of Growth describes different Phases of Growth over Time

The Greiner Model shows that each **phase of growth** is followed by a **crisis**.

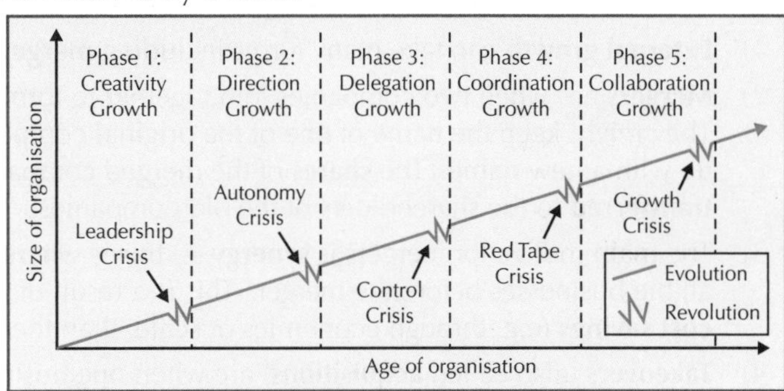

Phase 1 — Creativity → Leadership Crisis

When a business is starting up it is often **very creative** and everyone in the business can **share ideas** easily. Once the business gets to a certain size, there is a need for **strong leadership** to give the company **direction** and **structure**.

Phase 2 — Direction → Autonomy Crisis

Leaders set up a formal **organisational structure** with defined **departments** and **roles**. As employees become **more experienced** they will want **more say** in decisions, and the business will be **too big** for **senior managers** to **manage everything**. So more **autonomy** through **delegation** is needed.

Phase 3 — Delegation → Control Crisis

More **power** and **responsibility** is **delegated** down to middle-managers and the organisational structure may become **decentralised**. Leaders may try to regain some **control** in order to have a more **coordinated business** that is **optimising** its use of the **resources** available.

Phase 4 — Coordination → Red Tape Crisis

As **control is regained** by senior managers, certain decisions become more **centralised** and **new procedures** to **coordinate** different areas of the business are implemented. However, there can be **too many procedures**, which will **decrease efficiency** as people are constantly **waiting for decisions** to be **made** and **approved**.

Phase 5 — Collaboration → Growth Crisis

To continue growing, some **formal procedures** are replaced by **collaboration** between departments and teams. More focus is put on **communication** and **information management** (see p.171). At this point the company might **struggle** to **grow internally** and may have to consider **external growth** (see p.152).

Franchising allows established businesses to Grow Quickly

1) A **franchise** is an **agreement** (contract) which allows a new business to use the **business idea**, **name** and **reputation** of an **established business**.
2) The **franchisor** is the established business which is willing to **sell**, or **license**, its idea, name and reputation. The **franchisee** is the business which **buys** into the franchise. They usually pay the franchisor an **initial fee**, plus **ongoing payments** — usually a **percentage** of their **revenue** or **profit**.
3) Franchising allows the franchisor to **grow quickly** as most of the **costs** and **risks** are taken on by the franchisee. For example, through franchising, SUBWAY® **increased** the number of its fast-food restaurants in the UK & Ireland from **100** in 2002 to **over 2000** by 2015.
4) Franchising can have **some risks** for the **franchisor**. If just one of their franchisees has **poor standards** and gets a **bad reputation**, then it will affect the reputation and profits of the franchisor.

Practice questions

Q1 Give three advantages and three disadvantages of organic growth.

Q2 According to the Greiner Model, what are the five phases of growth?

Q3 What is franchising?

Exam Questions

Q1 Stu's Soda Co. is a fast-growing new business that brews and sells fizzy drinks. By referring to Greiner's Model of Growth, analyse the potential problems that the business might face as it grows. [9 marks]

Q2 Analyse the reasons why a fast-food restaurant might want to restrict the growth of the business. [12 marks]

Organic Growth is better for the environment but 100% more expensive...

"To grow or not to grow?" That's the question all businesses need to ask themselves. You should learn the pros and cons of organic growth and know the phases of Greiner's model as well as the hairs on your knuckles... just me then?

Business Growth — External

Businesses can also grow externally — an external growth strategy often means working with other businesses.

External Growth can help Businesses to Grow Quickly

1) **External growth** can take many forms including **mergers**, **takeovers** and **ventures**.
2) **Mergers** are when two companies join together to form one company. They might keep the name of one of the original companies, or come up with a new name. The **shares** of the merged company are **transferred** to the shareholders of the old companies.

Demergers are the opposite of mergers — they're when a business splits into parts. This is an example of retrenchment (see p.149).

3) The main motive for mergers is **synergy** — this is where the business after the merger is **more profitable** than all the businesses before the merger. This is a result of the **merged business** generating **more revenue** or **cost savings** (e.g. through economies of scale) than the **independent businesses** could between them.
4) **Takeovers** (also called **acquisitions**) are when one business buys enough shares in another so that it has **more than 50%** of the total shares. This is called a **controlling interest**, and it means the buyer will **always win** in a vote of all shareholders. Takeovers can be **agreed** or **hostile**:

- **Hostile takeovers** occur when one **public limited company (PLC)** buys a **majority** of the shares in **another** PLC against the will of the directors of that company. It can do this because the PLC shares are **traded** on the stock exchange and **anyone** can buy them. The company will encourage existing shareholders to sell them the shares by offering a **premium** — an extra payment on top of the value of the shares.
- **Agreed takeovers** happen when shareholders or other types of owners such as sole traders (see p.9) **agree** that they'll sell the business to someone else. This is usually because the owners believe it would benefit the **survival** of the business.

5) **Ventures** are **small businesses** or **projects** that are set up by **existing businesses** in the hope of making a **profit**. They are often set up to try and **meet needs** that are not being met in the **current market**. If **more than one** business invests then it is called a **joint venture**.
6) In a joint venture, businesses **share their resources** but there is **no change of ownership** for the businesses involved. When the joint venture is **terminated**, bills are paid off, profits are shared and the businesses remain **separate**.
7) A joint venture can be a good way to set up a **new business** if you don't have the **capital** to do it yourself — it can also be a good way for businesses to **access markets** in **different countries**.
8) A venture often involves a lot of **risk** to the business setting it up — a joint venture is often **preferable** because the **risk can be spread** among the businesses involved.

External Growth can be Horizontal, Vertical or Conglomerate

1) **Horizontal integration** happens when a firm combines with another firm in the **same industry** at the **same stage** of the production process (e.g. two suppliers). It's a very **common** type of takeover or merger. It **reduces** the **competition** in the market — for example, the Morrisons supermarket chain bought out Safeway to extend its branch network and reduce competition.
2) **Vertical integration** occurs when a firm combines with another firm in the **same industry** but at a **different stage** of the **production process**, e.g. a retailer taking over a manufacturer or distributor.
3) Vertical integration can be **forward** or **backward**.

- **Forward vertical integration** is when a business combines with another business that is **further on** in the production process. For example, a manufacturer merging with the **outlets** where its products are sold gives the manufacturer **direct access** to the retail market and they can then **control** what is sold and exclude competitors' products.
- **Backward vertical integration** is when a business combines with another business at an **earlier stage** of the production process. For example, a retailer taking over its suppliers allows them to **control production** of their supplies so they can be sure that supplies won't be **disrupted**.

4) **Conglomerate mergers** are between **unrelated** firms — they aren't competitors of each other, and they aren't each other's supplier or customer. **Pure conglomerate mergers** are between totally unrelated firms. **Product extension mergers** are between firms making **related products** (e.g. hairbrushes and hairspray). **Geographic market extension mergers** are between firms in the same industry, but competing in **different geographic markets**.

Business Growth — External

External Growth Methods are used to *Gain Resources*

External growth is **much quicker** than organic growth and can rapidly increase the **capacity**, **workforce**, **technology**, **skills** and **assets** available to a business. It can also increase the **market share** of the business, which will **directly increase sales**. The **reasons** and **motives** for growth will **influence** the type of **external growth** a business chooses.

1) Some businesses want to **diversify**, so they **combine** with an **existing business** operating in the market they want to **enter**. They **gain** from the **experience** of those employed by the business they combine with.
2) Businesses can **reduce** the amount of **competition** they face through **takeovers** or **mergers** with companies that **operate in the same market**.
3) Businesses who want to move into **another country** will often combine with companies who already **operate** and have **established infrastructure** in that country.
4) Companies in the same industry may combine so that they can benefit from **economies of scale** and **economies of scope** (see p.148-149).
5) In the car industry, companies such as Ford, Peugeot, BMW and General Motors have bought out car manufacturers overseas. They can **switch production** from country to country where **labour costs** may be lower but the **expertise** already exists.
6) If businesses **lack** certain **technology** or **expertise** needed to develop **new products** and **processes**, they might consider combining with a business that **already has** the technology and expertise required.

External Growth can be a *Risky Strategy*

1) There can be **tensions** between the staff of merged businesses as they try to **establish** their **status** in the new organisation. It will also take **time** for staff to **learn** new procedures — which may lead to **poor customer service**.
2) Some parts of the new organisation may need to be **sold off** or **closed**. This could mean additional **redundancy costs**, which will **reduce profitability**.
3) Businesses involved in mergers and joint ventures may have **different objectives** and **cultures**. This could lead to **clashes on important issues** and **inefficiency** which may result in **diseconomies of scale**.
4) When one business buys another, it takes on all the **liabilities** of the other business — this could include things like **compensation claims** for long-term disabilities suffered by **ex-employees** of the other business.
5) The **Competition and Markets Authority** investigates whether a proposed merger will **restrict competition** in the marketplace. If this is found to be the case the government can **stop** the merger from taking place or place **restrictions** on it. The finance used to **plan** the merger would then be **wasted**.
6) If a takeover is part of a **diversification strategy** (see p.144), the purchasing business will have **limited experience** in the new industry and it will take time to **learn** how it works. Mistakes would **reduce profitability**.
7) When companies **expand overseas** they should consider the **different laws**, **languages** and **cultures** of the host country. Just because a growth strategy is **successful in one country** doesn't mean it'll be **successful in another**.

Practice Questions

Q1 What's the difference between a takeover and a merger?

Q2 Explain what a joint venture is.

Q3 Define the terms 'horizontal integration', 'vertical integration' and 'conglomerate merger'.

Q4 Give four reasons why a business might base its growth strategy on external growth.

Exam Question

Q1 In 2009 Deutsche Telekom owned T-Mobile UK and Orange SA owned Orange UK. They announced that they were going to merge T-mobile UK and Orange UK in a joint venture to form EE. Analyse the possible benefits and drawbacks of this joint venture for both Deutsche Telekom and Orange SA. [24 marks]

External Growth Strategy: Seek immediate medical advice...

There are quite a few different terms to learn on these pages — mergers, ventures, horizontal integration, vertical integration... Try not to get too bogged down with it all — all the terms are quite descriptive, so you'll probably find they're not too hard to remember once you get going. Just don't have nightmares about hostile takeovers.

Innovation

Businesses need to come up with new ideas if they want to stay ahead of the competition...

Innovation comes in the form of New Ideas, Products and Processes

1) Innovation means thinking of a **new idea** and putting it into **action**. This could be in the form of a **new product** or a **new process**.

   Product Innovation — making **new** goods/services or **improving** existing ones. E.g. car manufacturers are constantly innovating **new features** to put on their latest models.

   Process Innovation — putting in place new or improved **production** and **delivery methods**. E.g. in 2007, amazon® introduced amazon Prime to the UK, which provides unlimited **one-day delivery** for an **annual fee**.

2) New ideas can come from **anywhere** in the business, but many businesses have a **Research and Development** (R&D) department that drives innovation.
3) Businesses are always looking for ways to innovate as it can help them to stay ahead of **competition**, expand their **markets** and increase their **market share**.
4) The **pressure to innovate** is greater in some industries than others — e.g. in the technology industry businesses need to constantly innovate **new products** or they will **fall behind** their competitors.

Innovation can be Risky but is often the best way to make Big Profits

Some industries are particularly **fast moving** and need to **constantly** develop new products. However, **innovation** can have **benefits** and **drawbacks** for a business:

Benefits of Innovation	Drawbacks of Innovation
• Businesses can initially charge **higher prices** for innovative products and services before their **competitors** bring **similar products** to market. • Being innovative can be good for a firm's **reputation** — if they've been the **first to launch** exciting **new products** in the past, people will naturally be **interested** in their **future products**. • Innovations in **processes** can help **add value** to existing products and services. • Businesses with lots of innovative products can take advantage of **economies of scope** (see p.149).	• Innovation can be a **very costly** and **time consuming** process — businesses risk running out of money if they **invest too much** into R&D and don't get the products to market **quickly enough**. • Businesses can end up **wasting resources** by developing something customers **don't want**. • Businesses might not be able to produce the new product on a **large scale** at a **low enough cost** — there is no guaranteed **return on investment**. • Businesses risk ruining their reputation if the innovative product is **poor quality**.

Innovation affects Functional Areas of the business

FINANCE R&D for innovative products is **expensive**, so the finance department might need to raise extra **working capital** to pay for it. For more about ways of raising finance, see pages 80-81.

OPERATIONS Innovation in **production methods** might mean that the **operations department** has to set some of its budget aside to spend on **expensive new machinery**. They will also need to organise **training** for employees to get them **up to speed** with the **new methods**.

MARKETING The amount of **market research** a company does is **increased** when researching a new idea — the **risks** and **costs** are **high**, so they need to be sure customers want or need the product. Innovative products require changes to the **marketing mix**. E.g. marketing might use a different **pricing strategy** (usually skimming — see p.46) for an innovative product. **Promotional activity** increases too — there's often a lot of **PR** (public relations) activity when a new product is launched.

HUMAN RESOURCES Innovation can mean there's a change in **staffing needs** — if a company suddenly decides to focus heavily on R&D they might need more **skilled staff**. HR also needs to make sure that the business has the right **culture** for innovation to thrive. In a culture where staff are **scared** of the consequences of **failing**, workers are unlikely to want to take risks. HR needs to find ways of **encouraging** employees to take **risks**, e.g. by **rewarding** people who try **new things**.

Innovation

New Product Development (NPD) has Six Stages from Idea to Launch

The **Research and Development** department can turn **raw ideas** gathered through **market research** into **innovative** new products using the **new product development** process.

1) Idea

The business comes up with **new ideas**, explores and **develops existing ideas** or **modifies competitors' ideas**. New ideas can come from **brainstorming** in a group, from **employee suggestions** or from **R&D department meetings**. New ideas are also discovered through **market research** finding out what consumers want, or from customers submitting requests to a firm. Businesses can sometimes also use **already patented ideas** (for a fee).

2) Analysis and Screening

The business wants to see if the product can be produced and sold at a **profit**. All aspects of the idea are investigated — whether there's a **potential market** for it or not, based on market research, whether the **technology** and **resources** exist to develop it, whether a **competitor** has an existing patent on a similar idea. At this stage, a **prototype** may be made to see what the product will be like.

3) Development

The **R&D department** develop a **working prototype**. They test it **scientifically**, and tweak the design to make the **functional** design (how it works) and **aesthetic** design (how it looks, feels — or smells and tastes if it's a food) as good as possible. This is the real "meat" of research and development.

4) Value Analysis

The business tries to make the product good **value** for money. This means balancing the **function**, **features** and **appearance** of a product with the cost of **making**, **warehousing** and **distributing** it — the goal is to make a product that is **good value** for both **business** and **consumer**.

5) Test Marketing

This is where the marketing department gets involved again.

The business sometimes sells the new product in a **limited geographical area**, and then analyses **consumer feedback** on the product, price and packaging. This allows **modifications** to be made before a wider launch.

6) Launch

A successful launch requires **enough stock** of the product to be distributed across the market. It also needs an effective **promotional campaign** in place to **inform** retailers and consumers about the product and **persuade** them to buy it.

The new product launch certainly went with a bang.

Practice Questions

Q1 What is the difference between product innovation and process innovation?

Q2 Give two reasons why innovation is risky.

Q3 Give two ways that innovation can involve the marketing department of a business.

Q4 Outline the six stages of new product development.

Exam Question

Q1 Evaluate the need for, and risks of, innovation in a digital technology firm. [20 marks]

R&D — not to be confused with R&B, which can also be fast-moving...

Hey, all those amazing new products have to come from somewhere. Just think, there are research and development eggheads beavering away as we speak, to come up with something utterly amazing that we'll all rush out to buy.

Innovation

As well as the work of the Research and Development department, there are other ways that businesses can innovate.

Kaizen can be a **Continuous** form of **Innovation**

See p.63 for more on kaizen.

1) The **kaizen** approach to innovation is by encouraging employees to improve the **way they work** and the **processes** they use all the time. Over a long period of time these small kaizen changes can **add up** and lead to **innovation**.
2) Another important part of kaizen is to give workers some control over **decision making**. Whenever there's a problem, workers are encouraged to ask '**why?**' until they get to the root of the problem. This creates a **working environment** in which **innovation** can thrive.
3) The **benefits** of using kaizen to drive innovation are that the company doesn't have to spend lots of **time** and **money** on research and development, and the processes become **more efficient** all the time.
4) However there are many **downsides** to only relying on kaizen for innovation. For example, the kaizen approach probably **won't** lead to **innovative new products** as workers aren't really encouraged to think about the **wants** and **needs** of the customer.
5) The kaizen mindset also means that workers are focused on making **small changes** to their **own job** rather than thinking about **big changes** they could be making to the **whole process** — this means that big innovation leaps are rare.

Some businesses **Encourage Employees** to become **Intrapreneurs**

1) **Intrapreneurship** is when employees **within a business** are encouraged to **solve a problem** by coming up with **innovative new ideas**.
2) Businesses allow intrapreneurs to take risks and experiment with lots of different ideas until they find the **most productive** and **effective** way to complete a task — their solution can then be implemented across the **whole department** or **company**.
3) An advantage of intrapreneurship is that it is done **alongside** the intrapreneur's regular role, so the company isn't **wasting money** employing someone just to try new things. Even if the intrapreneur **doesn't find a solution** to the problem, they will still have **produced some work** along the way.

Examples of intrapreneurial innovation

- Intrapreneurship can lead to **innovation** of the **technology** used by the company. For example, in a publishing company, an intrapreneur might investigate different publishing **software** in order to find the most efficient type for making a book — this software could then be implemented across the whole editing department.
- Intrapreneurs can also come up with **innovative goods and services** during their experiments and research. E.g. Google™ allows its workers time to be **creative** and work on **personal projects** — one of the biggest successes to come out of this is Gmail™.

Benchmarking Learns from **Other Businesses**

1) Benchmarking studies **other businesses** with excellent **quality standards**, and aims to innovate by **adopting the same methods**. Companies can sometimes do this by joining **benchmarking groups**, where firms agree to **share information** about their way of doing things.
2) Businesses can **benchmark internally** — they can study activities in efficient departments and use what they learn to **innovate processes** in other departments.
3) It's also possible to benchmark across **different industries** — e.g. in 2010, Tesco introduced **Click+Collect** to their **UK supermarkets**, which let customers **order online** and pick their groceries up **at the store** without having to **leave their car**. This was benchmarking of the popular **drive-though service** offered at **fast-food restaurants**.
4) Benchmarking tends to **motivate** staff. It's more encouraging to **introduce** a process or a product that you've already seen working **successfully** somewhere else than it is to introduce something **unknown**.
5) Another advantage is that it provides **early warnings** to businesses about **technology** or **methods** that might allow their competitors to **overtake** them.
6) A downside to benchmarking is that it won't directly lead to **new products** — **competitor products** are likely to be protected by a **patent** or **copyright** (see next page) and you need to be careful what ideas you take from them.
7) Another downside is that **processes** can't always be transferred between different **corporate cultures** — what works for one company might not be **suitable** for another company with a **different culture**.

Innovation

Original **Ideas** are business **Assets** that can be **Protected** by law

Businesses and individuals who produce **original work** and earn an income through it need to **protect their ideas** from being copied by others. This is known as protecting the **intellectual property** of a business or individual and it can be done in several ways, depending on what is being protected:

1) A patent is a way of registering and protecting a new invention

- If you have a new invention, you can apply for a **patent** from the **Patent Office** (a government agency that checks that an invention is unique and original enough to be issued a patent). You can get patents for your **product** and the **method** for producing it. No one else can copy it unless you give them a **licence** — and you can **charge** for the licence.
- Patents allow businesses to maintain the **unique features** of their products for as long as the patent lasts. They do not have to worry about **competitors copying** their exact invention.
- The more **general** a patent is the better — if a patent is **very specific** then it is very **easy** for **competitors** to tweak the invention and get around the protection that a patent offers.

2) Trademarks (™) protect logos, slogans, etc.

- If you want to protect your business's **name**, **logo** or **slogan**, you can register it as a **trademark** (™) so that nobody else can use it.
- For example, the McDonald's golden arches logo is the **intellectual property** of McDonald's International Property Company Ltd and it can't be used by any other company. McDonald's promote a certain **brand image** — if the logo was used by other companies, McDonald's **reputation** might be damaged. McDonald's might also lose **profits** if consumers went to another restaurant by mistake because it had the same logo.
- It can be **difficult** to register some slogans as a trademark — especially those that **don't include** the **company's name**. McDonald's were able to trademark the slogan "I'm lovin' it" because of its distinctiveness (they might have been less successful if they'd tried to trademark the phrase "I love it").

3) Copyright gives protection to written work and music

- It's **illegal** to reproduce other people's work without their permission.
- Authors and musicians or their publishers receive **royalties** (payment) every time their work is published or played on the radio.
- Any **original writing, music, video, images** and **photos** are **automatically protected** under UK copyright laws.

Copyright only protects against some things... karate protects against everything.

Practice Questions

Q1 How can a kaizen approach to work lead to innovation?

Q2 Give two advantages of intrapreneurship.

Q3 What is benchmarking?

Q4 What are the advantages of a business applying for patents for its products?

Exam Questions

Q1 Which of these would prevent another business from copying your logo?
A benchmarking B copyright C a patent D a trademark [1 mark]

Q2 Paul Newby wants to innovate the processes of his business by benchmarking against similar firms. Explain the benefits of doing this, as well as some of the problems he might encounter. [9 marks]

Q3 Snack4now is an online retailer that makes and delivers snacks to homes and offices. Analyse the effects that adopting a culture of kaizen and intrapreneurship will have on Snack4now's innovation. [16 marks]

Benchmarking — the defence method favoured by lazy footballers...

Kaizen, intrapreneurship and benchmarking allow businesses to become more innovative without investing loads of money into research and development. Companies need to be careful when they're benchmarking though — certain processes and products will be protected under patent laws so they'll have to ask permission if they want to copy them.

Entering International Markets

Businesses can gain advantages through targeting, operating in and trading with international markets.

International Markets offer businesses Growth Opportunities

Moving into international markets is called internationalisation.

1) Businesses can **increase** their market size by **selling existing products** in **new countries** (this is a **market development strategy**, see p.144) — the **bigger the market**, the **more** they're likely to sell and the higher their **revenue** will be. E.g. Tesco have nearly saturated the UK market, but they can still **increase** the size of their market by **targeting other countries**.
2) Businesses can **extend** the **life cycle** (see p.44) of their products by launching them in **new countries** as the product enters **maturity** in its home market. This is common with cars — businesses can sell models that are **old-fashioned** in the UK to **developing countries** like India.
3) Businesses can **reduce costs** by getting their **raw materials** from countries with the **cheapest** prices. Businesses can also buy **components** from **overseas** countries at cheap prices and then put the **final product** together in the UK — this is called **global sourcing**.
4) **Operating** in **developing countries** with **low wage rates** can also reduce costs (e.g. by relocating factories).
5) If the UK economy is in **recession**, businesses can secure revenue by trading in international markets — e.g. by **exporting** to a **growing economy**.

Many factors affect the Attractiveness of International Markets

1) Size of the Market

- Countries with **large populations** and **developing markets** (such as China and Brazil) can be attractive prospects for businesses as **markets** will be **bigger** there. However, they also need to consider the **population demographics** when assessing the **size** of the market — e.g. a pharmaceutical company might specifically **target** countries with **ageing populations**.
- The **wealth** of the population will also affect the size of a business's **potential market**. For example, a designer clothing company is more likely to open outlets in Switzerland where wages are **generally high** than in Bangladesh where wages are **generally low**.
- The availability of **technology** can also affect the size of the market — e.g. internet streaming services such as Netflix won't enter countries where the **internet isn't readily available** or **connection speeds are low**.

2) Political and Economic Factors

- Businesses entering **international markets** need to take into account the **laws** in the country they are entering — **employment**, **environmental** and **tax laws** can all affect the **profitability** of a business.
- Businesses also need to consider **political controls on trade** through **tariffs** and **quotas** (see p.123).
- Businesses would prefer to enter a country with a **stable political environment** — if there is **political unrest** in a country, a business might **wait** until the problem is **resolved** before entering the country.
- Fluctuations in **exchange rates** (see p.127) make the cost of international trade **unpredictable**, so it's difficult for businesses to accurately **forecast** revenue and profits.

3) Cultural, Ethical and Environmental Factors

- Businesses will find it **easier** to trade with countries with **similar cultures** and **languages** to the one that they already operate in. It's more difficult to **trade** with countries when there are **language** and **cultural barriers**.
- Cheap labour can make certain countries attractive for businesses, however businesses need to be careful that they are not **exploiting workers** — this is very **unethical**, and can lead to consumers **boycotting** the company if its unethical practices come to light.
- Businesses might take into account the **damage** that their activities might do to the **environment**. Getting **raw materials** from abroad is often **cheaper**, but **transporting** them from one country to another causes lots of **pollution**. **Distributing** finished products to other countries also causes **pollution**.
- Businesses can **exploit** the lack of **environmental restrictions** in other countries to gain **cheap resources**, e.g. through deforestation. However, **ethical companies** will choose a more **sustainable source**.
- Countries that have **fewer restrictions** on the buying and selling of **certain products** can be appealing to some businesses. For example, **weapons manufacturers** can make money by selling **missiles** and other **weapons** abroad, but selling weapons to countries that are seen as a **security threat** is unethical.

Entering International Markets

Methods of **Entering International Markets** have different amounts of **Risk**

Importing and Exporting

- Businesses can easily enter **international markets** by **importing** or **exporting** goods and services. This means **buying from** or **selling to** companies and consumers in **other countries.**
- Businesses **importing** from other countries will benefit from **greater variety** and **cheaper prices.** Businesses **exporting** to other countries will benefit from an **increased market size.**
- However, putting the **infrastructure** in place for **importing** or **exporting** can be **expensive** — these costs will **decrease the value added** unless the **price** of the product is **increased.**

Licensing

- Businesses can also get **foreign firms** to produce their products **under licence** (e.g. another firm makes the product, but the **original company's name** is on the product) — this is known as **licensing.**
- An advantage of this method is that the **business benefits** from the **infrastructure** foreign firms already have in place — they can **make money** without having to do very much work and with a very **low amount of risk.**

Alliances

- Businesses can join forces with similar companies **abroad**, combining **local knowledge** with a product that has already proved **successful** in their own country — this is called an **alliance.**
- Alliances can **spread out** the **costs** and **risks** and help businesses **overcome trade barriers** (see p.160).
- The **main drawback** is that the business **loses some control** over their venture into that country.

Direct Investment

- **Direct investment** is when a business **takes over** or **merges** with a business in a **different country.**
- The **main benefit** of this is that it allows the business to **enter markets quickly** and already have an **instant share of the market.** The business doesn't need to invest in establishing its **name** and **reputation** in the new country.
- Direct investment can also **reduce the risk of failure** — the business benefits from the **knowledge** and **experience** of the **local market** and **culture** provided by the business it joins with.

Entering International Markets can **Impact** all areas of the business

Internationalisation can affect the decisions and activities of **different departments** within the business.

1) HR may start recruiting people who can **speak multiple languages** so they can **communicate more effectively** within the **business** and with their **customers** — they might also have to help current employees **relocate** abroad.
2) The finance department will have to put methods in place for dealing with **fluctuating exchange rates** as goods are bought and sold in **different currencies.**
3) Marketing may have to split into separate **international** and **national departments** as products will be **priced** and **promoted differently** depending on the country they are being marketed in.

Practice Questions

Q1 Give five reasons why a business might enter an international market.

Q2 What political and economic factors could affect a business's decision to expand into a country?

Q3 Give four methods of entering international markets.

Q4 What effect could entering a new international market have on the marketing department of a business?

Exam Questions

Q1 Analyse the external factors affecting a mobile phone operator starting to enter African markets. [9 marks]

Q2 The Golden Spud Company is a fast-food restaurant, specialising in jacket potatoes, based in the UK. Evaluate the different methods they could use to enter the French market. [20 marks]

If only you could form an alliance before entering your exam...

You'll need to learn the reasons and methods for businesses entering international markets. Then it's the same old story of learning the factors affecting their strategy and thinking about the knock-on effects to functional areas of the business.

Locating Abroad

Firms can locate some or all of their business abroad in order to gain advantages when trading or producing goods.

Producing Abroad *can be a way of* ***Cutting Costs*** *or* ***Increasing Revenue***

1) Locating abroad can reduce costs

- One of the main reasons why companies choose to move **production** overseas is that they can often pay **foreign workers** much **lower wages** than they would have to pay their UK employees. Some companies have been accused of not paying foreign workers enough to live on — this is **unethical**.
- The cost of **land** and **office space** also tends to be **cheaper** overseas, especially in emerging markets. **Utilities** like water and electricity might also be cheaper abroad.

2) Locating abroad is a way of targeting new international markets

- Locating a firm close to the overseas market makes it easier to spot **local market trends**.
- The company is able to absorb more **local knowledge**, which means it's less likely to make **expensive marketing errors** and it might even spot new market **niches**.
- Locating close to a **new international market** will also make **distribution** of products to the market **easier** and **decrease** the company's **distribution costs** to that market.

3) Locating abroad helps companies avoid trade barriers

- Some countries create **trade barriers** in order to **protect** domestic companies from **foreign competition**. These barriers might be things like **taxes** or **restrictions** on sales of goods from abroad.
- Locating part of a business **within** a country with trade barriers helps companies **get round** these penalties.
- Trade barriers can protect **domestic** industries from international competition, causing them to become **inefficient**. This could mean that a **foreign** company that locates in a country with trade barriers will have a **competitive advantage**, because it's likely to be more efficient.

4) Locating abroad has been made easier by improved transport and communication links

- The **price** and **availability** of **air travel** means it's **easy** for people to **travel** between overseas locations.
- Trading overseas has also been made easier because countries with **emerging markets** are **investing** heavily in **infrastructure**. This means that they have better **road and rail networks** and **ports** than they had in the past.
- Doing business overseas has also been made easier by **technological** developments. Businesses can communicate internationally by **email** and **video-conferencing** — so people don't have to leave the UK.

Offshoring *means* ***Moving*** *parts of a business to* ***Cheaper Countries***

1) Many businesses locate some of their **departments**, such as their call centres or payment processing departments, **overseas** — this is called **offshoring**.
2) The countries that firms move to most often are **China**, **India**, **Malaysia**, **Mexico** and **Indonesia** — these countries all offer much **cheaper labour** than the UK.
3) Although offshoring is a good way to **cut costs**, it's not always good for a company's **image**. The **media** and **trade unions** often criticise companies for **UK job losses** caused by offshoring.

Staff loved the new off-shore department.

Re-shoring is when a business moves departments back to its country of origin

- Some businesses are **moving departments back** to the UK in reaction to changing **customer attitudes**.
- Customers are **more aware** of a business's overseas activities than they used to be — businesses that are seen to **treat overseas staff poorly** will get a **bad reputation** and face a **backlash** from their customers.
- Re-shoring allows a business to **improve the quality** of its products and processes as **manufacturing** is easier to **monitor** and **control** if everything is made in the same country.
- Re-shoring also means that **distribution** to the home market is **cheaper** and **more efficient** as products don't have to be shipped all over the world — businesses can offer a **better delivery service** to their customers.
- Sometimes the **low wages** of overseas labour are still **too appealing** for companies — however, as the **wage gap** between UK workers and oversees workers **decreases**, more and more companies will begin to **re-shore**.

Locating Abroad

Certain countries can offer **Benefits** to **Specific Departments**

1) As a result of offshoring, some countries have become **specialised** in providing certain skills or services.
2) Countries that **specialise** in particular areas will attract lots of business from **overseas companies**. This creates a **competitive environment** in that country which can lead to even **cheaper prices** and **better services** being offered.

- **India** specialises in **communications** (e.g. call centres) and **IT services**, so they can offer competitive **prices** and a pool of suitably **trained workers**. Businesses might choose to take advantage of this by moving their **customer service department** to India.
- **China** and **Brazil** have lots of **cheap** and **skilled labour** — some businesses have moved their **manufacturing departments** to these countries to take advantage of this. Their products are made for relatively **low labour costs** but often to quite a **low standard** as they focus on volume rather than quality.
- **China** also attracts lots of **Research & Development** departments as they relocate to be closer to the manufacturing department and to take advantage of the **skilled low-cost labour** and **infrastructure**.
- The **Philippines** has a lot of **young university graduates** with very **strong work ethics** and very good **digital communication infrastructure**. Some businesses have begun moving their **IT departments** to the Philippines to benefit from the **people** and **technology** that they already have in place.

3) Countries that offer specialised services do run into **problems**. Workers may lose **motivation** as the majority of **available jobs** are in the **same industry**, or the size of the industry may lead to **diseconomies of scale**. There's also a risk that **another country** will find a way of providing the skills or service even **more efficiently**.

Locating Abroad has **Non-Financial Benefits** and **Costs** to a business

1) **Non-financial benefits** and **costs** are the **positive** and **negative impacts** a business has on the **outside world**. These benefits and costs don't have a **direct impact** on the business's **profits** but they can affect its **reputation**.
2) Before making any **decisions** about locating abroad, businesses need to consider the **impact** that they are going to have on the country they are **moving into**.
3) The non-financial benefits of locating abroad are that the company will create **new jobs** in that country, which can increase people's **income** and **standard of living**. Companies also **invest** in the host country by paying for factories, roads, etc. to be built, and by paying **taxes** to the local government.
4) However there are **non-financial costs** of locating abroad too — it will lead to a **loss of jobs** and **investment** in the original country. It can also have negative impacts on the country they're moving into — **overseas workers** can be **exploited** if they aren't protected by **employment laws** and there may be a **rise in pollution**.
5) Although it can be difficult to put an **exact financial value** on these costs and benefits, companies should still **weigh up** the impact that these issues have on their **reputation** before making any decisions.

Practice Questions

Q1 Describe four advantages of locating abroad.

Q2 Explain the terms 'offshoring' and 're-shoring'.

Q3 Give two advantages of offshoring your IT department to a country that specialises in IT services.

Q4 Outline the non-financial costs of relocating a business abroad on the country you're leaving.

Exam Questions

Q1 Ulverston Broadband Co. have a call centre based in India.
Analyse the reasons why they might choose to re-shore their call centre back to the UK. [9 marks]

Q2 Flimby Gadgets Ltd manufactures innovative digital gadgets and plans to relocate its manufacturing department to Brazil. Analyse the benefits and drawbacks of doing this. [16 marks]

Offshoring communication — sending messages in bottles...

I don't think it's that difficult to understand why companies might like to locate abroad. After all, who wouldn't rather stare out of the window at a sunny beach rather than at a rainy, grey town centre? Make sure you know the benefits that re-shoring can bring too — have you ever tried to get your hands on a decent pork pie or scotch egg in Brazil?

Multinationals

Multinationals are businesses that are based in more than one country. A bit like those annoying celebrities who have holiday homes in various exotic locations. Multinationals aren't quite as glamorous though I'm afraid.

Multinationals are located in More Than One Country

1) A **multinational company** is a business that has **branches** or **departments** in more than one country. Its **head office** will be based in **one country** and it will coordinate its **global activities** from there. It will also have **offices** or **factories** in **other countries** that offer services or produce goods.
2) Multinationals are able to utilise the **different locations** of their factories in order to **produce goods** in the most **cost-effective way** — this has increased the overall level of **international trade**.
3) Some of the largest multinationals now have **annual turnovers larger** than the **GDP** (gross domestic product — see p.124) of some countries. This means these businesses have a lot of **economic power**.

Multinationals can Benefit Developing Countries...

1) Multinationals **increase employment opportunities** for the populations of countries where they're based.
2) Multinationals **increase** the local **standard of living**. Although they get paid less than workers in developed countries, the employees of multinationals in developing countries often receive **better pay and conditions** than employees of **local companies** in the developing country.
3) **Inward investment** into the host country increases because multinationals **spend money** on building the **factories** and **infrastructure** (roads, etc.) that they need. This is called **foreign direct investment** (FDI).
4) Multinationals cause **economic growth** for each country they expand into. The GDP of the host country increases as a result of **additional spending** in the economy on things like **increased travel** into the area and **demand for hotel rooms** from visiting businesspeople.
5) Multinationals locating in developing countries will **pay taxes** to the **local government**. This results in increased **government income**, which might be spent on projects such as **schools** and **hospitals**. Payments by multinationals to local governments might include:
   - taxes on the **purchase of land**,
   - taxes on the **wages** of local employees,
   - taxes on **profits** they make,
   - taxes on products **exported** abroad.
6) **Ethical multinationals** try to benefit the countries they locate in by paying **fair wages** rather than exploiting workers — see below. This **increases costs**, but if businesses highlight the fact that they trade ethically then consumers may be willing to pay slightly higher prices for their products.

... but they can also Exploit Developing Countries

1) Some multinational businesses may **exploit developing countries** in order to **maximise** their **profits**.
2) Some multinationals base their production in countries with **low wages** to **reduce** their **costs**. They might set up **sweatshops** — factories where employees work long hours in difficult and sometimes dangerous conditions for minimal payment.
3) A multinational might locate in a country with **less strict employment laws** in order to reduce costs by employing **child labour**, making employees work **long shifts**, or not providing the correct **safety equipment**.
4) Multinationals sometimes sell **products** which **don't** quite **meet** EU or American **safety standards** to developing countries.

Confusing 'sweatshop' and 'sweetshop' when you're looking for a job could have disastrous consequences.

5) A multinational might extract large quantities of **unsustainable natural resources**, i.e. oil, gas or minerals. It might also fail to redevelop the landscape when there's no more to extract. In a developed country a company would be required to **minimise** its **environmental impact**, but in some developing countries, **environmental laws** are **less strict**, and multinationals might take advantage of this.
6) The **governments** of developing countries might **overlook unlawful behaviour** by multinational businesses because they **rely** on the **tax income** they generate, so they won't want the business to relocate away from their country.
7) Many multinational companies are increasingly committed to **Corporate Social Responsibility** (see p.133), so **exploitation** is **less common** than it used to be.

Multinationals

Multinationals also locate in **Developed Countries**

1) Developed countries often have **stable** and **growing economies** — this can be attractive for a multinational as there will be plenty of **potential customers** to sell their products to.
2) Instead of just **selling their products** in a developed country, multinationals often **set up factories** in them — this can help them to keep their **distribution costs low**.
3) **Producing** goods in the country where they're sold also helps companies to **avoid** some **taxes**.
4) Many global multinationals have **factories** and **distribution centres** in at least one country that is a member of the European Union (EU). This allows them to **sell** their products to all EU countries without having to pay **import tax**. For example, Toyota and Honda (both Japanese car manufacturers) have **factories** in the UK for **distribution** within the EU.

Multinationals are subject to **Political**, **Economic** and **Legal Restraints**

1) As multinational corporations operate in **many different countries**, each with its own **laws**, governments sometimes **coordinate** their approaches to **control** and **manage** the activities of multinationals.
2) The **European Union** has tried to **standardise employment laws** such as equal opportunities and health and safety standards to ensure that multinational corporations within the EU have to meet **minimum standards** wherever they locate. This is known as **harmonisation**.
3) Governments sometimes use **protectionist policies** like **tariffs** and **quotas** to protect their own economies (see p.123).
4) **Pressure groups** sometimes try to **influence government policy** on multinational organisations. They try to persuade governments to put **tighter controls** on how multinationals from one country operate in **other countries** (e.g. to stop multinationals from using child labour in foreign countries).

Not that kind of legal restraint...

5) **Transfer pricing** is when a multinational business buys and sells products between parts of the company based in **different countries** — it can make it very difficult for governments to **control** the **taxes** a multinational pays. Transfer pricing can be used to make all the **profits** appear to belong in a country with very **low tax rates**, which **reduces** the amount of **tax** a multinational pays. However, this might **conflict** with any **Corporate Social Responsibility** (CSR) code the business has.

Practice Questions

Q1 What is a multinational?

Q2 Give two possible benefits to the country that a multinational expands into.

Q3 State three ways in which multinationals might exploit developing countries.

Q4 Give two reasons why a multinational would locate in a developed country.

Q5 How can governments manage the activities of multinationals?

Exam Questions

Q1 Analyse the extent to which governments can control multinationals. [9 marks]

Q2 To what extent do you agree with the statement "multinationals locate their manufacturing plants in developing countries in order to increase employment levels and provide economic support for the countries through payment of taxes"? [16 marks]

Mini skirt, turtleneck, straw hat and sandals — I'm a bit of a multifashionable...

You've probably noticed that most location decisions for multinationals are based on one thing — money. You need to learn why companies locate parts of their business in developed or developing countries (it often comes down to saving money one way or another). You should also understand the benefits and drawbacks for the developing countries.

International Business Strategies

There are different strategies for managing international businesses. The choice of strategy will depend on how important it is for the business to reduce its costs and be able to adapt to the local market.

Multinationals can be difficult to **Manage Effectively**

This year's grand multinational was off to a chaotic start.

1) The **management strategies** needed to run a **multinational** are very **different** from those needed to run a **domestic business**.
2) Multinationals are very **complex** — different parts of the business are subject to the **laws**, **culture**, **economy** and **markets** of the country they operate in.

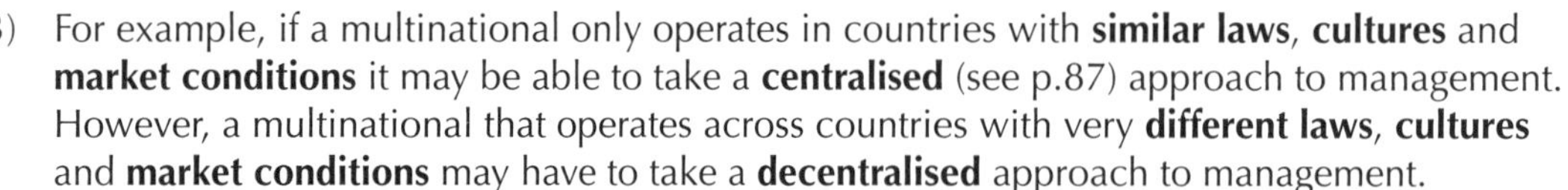

3) For example, if a multinational only operates in countries with **similar laws**, **cultures** and **market conditions** it may be able to take a **centralised** (see p.87) approach to management. However, a multinational that operates across countries with very **different laws**, **cultures** and **market conditions** may have to take a **decentralised** approach to management.

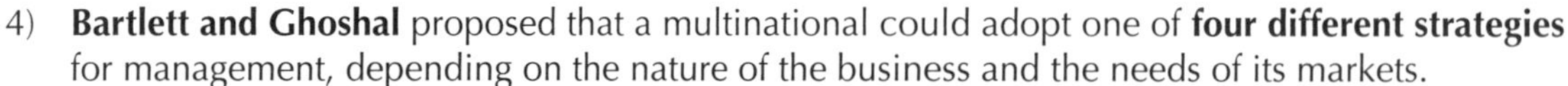

4) **Bartlett and Ghoshal** proposed that a multinational could adopt one of **four different strategies** for management, depending on the nature of the business and the needs of its markets.

Bartlett and **Ghoshal's International Business Strategies**

The **four international business strategies** outlined by Bartlett and Ghoshal are shown on the grid below. The level of pressure for **local responsiveness** (e.g. adapting products for different locations) and the level of pressure to **reduce costs** through **global coordination** can be used to help a business **decide on a strategy**.

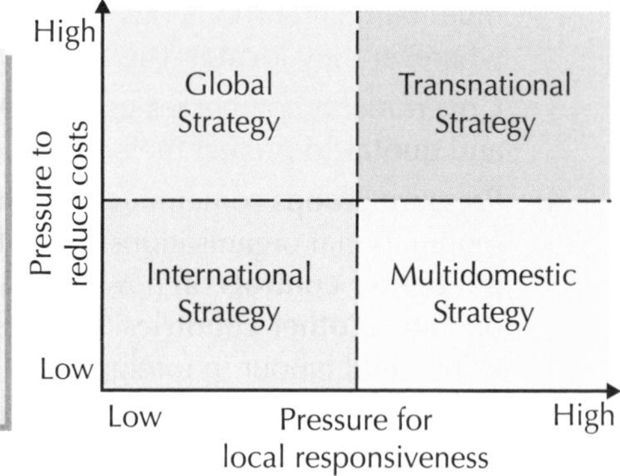

International Strategy

- If the **demands of markets** in other countries are **similar** to the demands of the home market, the pressure for local responsiveness is **low**. If pressure to **reduce costs** through global coordination is also **low**, then an **international strategy** is adopted.
- The business structure will remain very **centralised** with most of the **research**, **big decisions** and **development** being carried out at **head office**. These decisions can then be implemented in the parts of the business that are **located abroad**.

Multidomestic Strategy

- When the demands of the **different markets** are **very different** and there is **little pressure** to reduce costs through global coordination, a **multidomestic strategy** should be implemented.
- The business structure becomes **decentralised** and the business operates as if it were lots of **independent companies** each running itself. Most **decisions** are made **locally** to meet the **local needs**.
- **Different branches** of the business will **look** and **work differently** — products will be **adapted** and **promoted** to suit the **local markets**, and **knowledge won't be shared** between the separate branches.

Global Strategy

- A **global strategy** is used when the demands of the different markets are similar and global coordination of the business could **reduce its costs significantly**.
- The business structure will be **centralised** and it will **coordinate operations** across countries to take full advantage of **economies of scale**.
- Products will remain **standardised** and innovation and development will take place at a **central location**, with **knowledge** and **resources** being passed on to the **different branches**. A business may decide to only sell **specific products** in certain countries rather than its **full range**.

Transnational Strategy

- When pressure to reduce costs and meet local needs are **both high**, a **transnational strategy** is best.
- The focus of a transnational strategy is on **developing knowledge** and **ideas locally** and **sharing them globally** in order to benefit the **whole business**.
- The business structure will be a balance between centralisation and decentralisation, where the **responsibilities** passed down to each branch of the business are based on its **experience** and **capabilities**.

International Business Strategies

Management of Different Functions becomes more *Complex*

When a company becomes a multinational, its functional areas will need to change. This may result in them being **spread** across **different locations**, **increasing in size** or just adapting to **new challenges** facing the business.

FINANCE

1) If **finance** remains based at a **central location** then staff will have to adapt to work with **different currencies** and ensure that the different **branches** of the company have a **healthy cash flow**.
2) Trade laws **limit** the **amount of money** that multinationals can **take out** of a country's **economy** — finance will need to **comply** with the **trade laws** of the different countries.
3) They also need to know and understand the **tax laws** in different countries so that they can provide **detailed analysis** of **expansion opportunities** and point out any **risks** of planned expansions.
4) Due to the **complexity** of multinationals, **financial functions** might be spread across different locations. For example, the financial functions that apply to the **whole business** (e.g. making budgets, managing debts and managing assets) might be done at a **central location**, while **functions** that are specific to **certain branches** (e.g. purchasing and day-to-day cash flow) might be done at the **different branches**.

MARKETING

1) If products have been **adapted** to **meet the needs** of **local markets**, marketing will need to have different **campaigns** and **strategies** to **promote** the different products.
2) If products are **standardised**, then marketing may still need to adapt their **promotional message** to appeal to the different markets. E.g. in developed countries they might highlight the **ethical nature** of the product, whereas in **developing countries** they might emphasis the **functionality** of the product.
3) Depending on the **type of product** that a company sells, marketing campaigns may need to be adapted to take into account the different **advertisement laws** in a country.

OPERATIONS

1) If the business is producing **standardised global products**, the different **manufacturing facilities** will need to be **coordinated** — they will all need to work in the **same way** using the **same materials** and **machinery** in order to make products that are all up to a **consistent standard**.
2) If the products are being **adapted** for the different **local markets** then it's **less important** that the **manufacturing** facilities are **coordinated** — it's more important that each one runs **efficiently**, even if that means **independent facilities** using **different processes**.

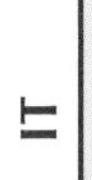

1) **IT functions** will often be carried out at **each branch** of the business in order to manage the **day-to-day** IT problems that are specific to that branch's **machines** and **IT systems**.
2) If the business is trying to adapt to **local markets**, **IT** might need to create, manage and update **several different websites** which may result in the department **expanding**.

Along with the difficulties faced within **each functional area**, multinationals will also face **culture clashes** and **language barriers** across the whole business. This will be a bigger problem if the business structure is **centralised** as they will need to think about how **decisions** will **affect** and **be communicated** to all the branches of the business.

Practice Questions

Q1 Why are multinationals harder to manage than domestic businesses?

Q2 According to Bartlett and Ghoshal when should businesses use an international strategy?

Q3 Explain the difference between a global strategy and a transnational strategy.

Q4 How might a company's marketing department be affected by the choice of international business strategy?

Exam Questions

Q1 A multinational cardboard box manufacturer operates in 28 different countries. Evaluate the four different strategies suggested by Bartlett and Ghoshal and suggest which one is best for this company. [16 marks]

Q2 Analyse the effects that a transnational strategy will have on the functional areas of a business. [9 marks]

Cooking and hoovering — yet another example of a multidomestic strategy...

Multinationals can be managed in a variety of ways — make sure you know the difference between international, multidomestic, global and transnational strategies. You'll also need to learn when businesses should use each strategy.

Use of Digital Technology

Digital technology is changing all the time and it is up to businesses to change with it. If businesses don't embrace digital technology, they risk missing out on great opportunities to grow their business.

Businesses face Pressure to Update their Digital Technology

1) New digital technology is constantly being **developed** and businesses must decide which developments will provide them with the **greatest return on investment** and which will have the **greatest impact**.
2) If businesses make the **correct decisions** and adopt the **right technology** at the **right time**, they can **grow rapidly** and gain the **upper hand** on competitors.
3) However, if businesses make the **wrong decisions** or they are **too late** to take up new technology they may **lose ground** to their competitors and might never be able to gain that **market share** back.

Digital Technology can lead to Innovative New Products

1) The research and development department can incorporate **up-to-date digital technology** in new products — these **innovative products** have a chance to revolutionise the market and make the business a lot of money.
2) Digital technology can offer **small upgrades** to existing products to keep the business ahead of its competitors. For example, smartphones are always being **upgraded** to offer better cameras, more powerful processors and a wider variety of features — these small upgrades allow the business to **retain its market share**.
3) The internet allows businesses to **monitor updates** to digital technology on a **global scale**. E.g. an R&D department in the UK might see an invention in Japan and find a way of incorporating it in their own product.

Disadvantages of Digital Technology for Innovation

- It is often **very expensive** to develop new products that are based on **new digital technology** — if these products never make it to market then the business has **wasted a lot of money**.
- New technology hasn't always been **fully tested**, so if a business chooses to use it in their product they are running the risk of their product having **lots of bugs** and **not working properly**.
- Problems with digital technology can be **difficult to diagnose**, customers can get **frustrated** with a company if they can't get products to work properly.
- Businesses run the risk of the new technology not catching on. E.g. Sony® brought out their first **MiniDisc player** in 1992 but it was **too expensive** and never really sold very well.

Digital Technology can make the Production Process more Efficient

1) New technology can lead to changes in the way that **products are made** — this can result in positive changes, e.g. **better quality products**, **increased capacity** (see p.56) and **increased efficiency**.
2) Businesses need to **weigh up** whether the expense of implementing new digital technology in the **production process** is actually going to be **profitable** in the **long-term**.
3) It can take a **long time** to apply new technology to the process — by the time you've implemented it and got the process **running efficiently** again, there may be **better technology** available.
4) To use new technology efficiently, staff often require some **specialised skills** — they will need to be **retrained** so that they have the skills required to interact with the new technology. This means that efficiency will fall until staff are properly **up to speed** with the **new processes**.
5) If a business introduces **too much** new technology to their production process, staff will become **overwhelmed** and **resistant** to the **changes**.

Examples of Digital Technology in Production

- The introduction of **3D printing** means that businesses are able to produce **prototypes** of their new products **quickly** and **cheaply** — it's also much easier to tweak aspects of the product than it was previously.
- Developments in software have made it easier to keep track of **inventory** and **deliveries** from suppliers, which allows the production process to run much more smoothly and efficiently.
- The introduction of **more machines** has resulted in business shifting away from **labour-intensive production**. This saves the business a lot of money in **wages** but can have a **negative impact** on the **company's reputation** and the **workers' morale**.

Use of Digital Technology

Digital Technology has given businesses New Opportunities

1) **Improvements** in digital technology have allowed businesses to gather **big data** (see p.34-35) — they can **collect it** using **social media**, **loyalty cards**, **etc**. or they can **buy it** from other businesses.
2) Big data can then be **analysed** using computers and specially designed **digital software** to spot correlations and trends — this analytical process is know as **data mining**.
3) Data mining can make sense of big data and supply **useful information** on **customers** and **competitors** to the **functional areas** of the business. For example, the R&D department can use this information to develop new products, the marketing department can use it to inform decisions about the marketing mix (see p.40) and the finance department can use the information when making cash-flow forecasts (see p.72-73).

E-commerce provides lots of new opportunities for businesses

1) Improvements in digital technology have resulted in **e-commerce** becoming the primary way for some businesses to **trade goods and services**. This means that businesses don't need to invest as much money in **stores** as they can reach a much **bigger customer base** through a **website**.
2) The growth of e-commerce has given businesses **greater access** to **international markets** — businesses can translate their website into **different languages** and offer **worldwide delivery** in order to expand their markets.
3) **Manufacturers** can use their **own website** or **online market places** to sell **directly to consumers** rather than selling through an **agent** or **retailer** — this allows them to keep **all** of the **revenue** for themselves.
4) Companies such as amazon® **keep track** of the **online order history** of their customers. This allows them to **make personal recommendations** to customers that they know will be interested.
5) Business are able to **interact more directly** with their customers through **social media**. This means that businesses can regularly update customers about **improvements** to their goods and services.
6) Businesses are able to deal with **customer complaints** more **efficiently** by switching from **telephone services** to **live online assistance** — this means that **a customer service assistant** can deal with **many customers** at once.
7) However, customers also have access to this technology — they are able to look up **reviews** of a **product** and find **prices** of **similar products** within seconds. This means that the **products** and **prices** a business offers have to be **genuinely competitive**. E.g. they can't gain an advantage by being the only DIY shop in town.

Enterprise Resource Planning (ERP) can benefit every department

1) Enterprise Resource Planning is **business management software** that allows a business to **monitor activities** in **every department** through the **collection** and **interpretation** of data.
2) It can help the **HR department** to track the **work rates** of staff to see who needs **extra training** or when **productivity drops** — e.g. in a supermarket, managers can monitor the scan speed of their checkout operators.
3) The **finance department** might use data from previous infrastructure changes to budget for upcoming changes.
4) It helps the **marketing department** to keep track of how well their promotional products are selling and to **compare sales** before and after **promotion**.
5) It can be used to track **stock levels**, **distribution networks** and **productivity** in order to see how well the **operations department** is functioning and if any improvements are needed.

Practice Questions

Q1 Give two disadvantages of using brand new technology in new products.

Q2 Give two examples of how the production department of a business can use new technology to improve efficiency.

Q3 What is data mining?

Q4 How can ERP benefit the functional areas of a business?

Exam Question

Q1 Analyse the advantages and disadvantages of using digital technology to advertise and sell products. [9 marks]

Digital technology has more uses than annoying celebrities on Twitter...

You need to understand the value of digital technology to a business and know how all departments can benefit from adopting and updating their technology. You should also consider the risks to departments of too much technology.

Causes of Change

Businesses need to keep an eye out for change and the things that cause it. Doing this helps them to act before they end up in trouble, or allows them to adapt various aspects of the business to make the change work to their advantage.

Change can be caused by Internal and External Factors

When the business environment changes, managers must **change** the way the business is run to suit the new **circumstances**. They might change **staffing levels**, **location** and **product range** or they might start **spending** more on **research and development**, staff **training** and **new machinery**. There are **internal factors** (within the business) and **external factors** (outside the business) that cause firms to make changes:

Internal Factors

- A change in **leadership/management** often leads to further changes. If the director of a company leaves or is replaced, the new director may have different ideas about how the business should be run, which could lead to changes in the **organisational culture** or **structure** of the business.
- **Better than expected performance** could lead to a decision to expand the business, in order to take advantage of the increased profits. **Poor financial performance** may lead to changes such as **retrenchment** (see p.149), i.e. cutting down or reorganising in order to save money.
- If there are **changes** to the **staff**, it could mean that the business no longer has the required **skills** and further changes need to be made. The company might go through **recruitment** or **retraining**, or **outsource** their work.
- **Business growth** can lead to other changes. For example, a business expanding into **international markets** may have to adapt its **product range** to match the needs of customers in other countries.
- The **type** of business can influence the amount of change. For example, if a business is **innovative**, it may keep coming up with **better methods** of doing things, so the business may **continually change** to use these new methods. More **traditional companies** might prefer to stick to the old, **tried** and **tested methods**.

External Factors

- The availability of **new technology** can cause change. Businesses might change their production methods if new technology means production can be **faster** or **cheaper**. New technology can also lead to **shorter product life cycles** (see p.44-45) — companies have to **change** and **update** their products **frequently** if they want to **stay ahead** of the competition.
- If consumer **tastes** change, the business might need to alter its **product range** to fit in with changing demand.
- If the **economy slows**, people will have **less disposable income**, so product prices may need **reducing**.
- Changes in the **law** can affect the way businesses are run — e.g. government restrictions on pollution may force businesses to alter their **methods of production** or change to a **local supplier**.
- Changes in the **ethical views** and **social awareness** of customers may result in companies purchasing ethically sourced products from fair trade suppliers.
- Changes in **competition** can result in a business losing a lot of its **market share** for particular products — they may need to act to **regain** their market share or **prevent** further losses.

Changes are Vital for a Thriving Business

1) Although change can **create uncertainty** amongst employees and can be **disruptive** to a business, it is **necessary** if the business wants to **grow** and **stay competitive**.
2) Making changes within a business can allow it to take advantage of **new**, **effective** ideas, possibly saving **time** and **money** in the process.
3) People within the business will naturally **resist** change (see p.172) — however, the **advantage** a business gains from implementing a change will often **outweigh** the **disruption caused**.
4) Businesses may be **forced** to change in order to **survive** in a ever-changing market. The **rate** at which technology advances is **speeding up**, so change becomes more and more **essential**. For example, in the car manufacturing industry it is necessary for businesses to be **constantly developing** up-to-date technology for their cars.
5) Without change, a company may **fall behind** its competitors, which could eventually lead to **insolvency** (see p.68).

Graeme was resistant to change — it was the 1992 FA cup final for the tenth night running.

Causes of Change

Change can be Incremental, Disruptive or somewhere In Between

Incremental change is gradual

It's usually the result of a **strategic plan** being put in place, and often attempts to minimise disruption. Managers decide a **timescale** for the necessary changes and then **timetable strategies** for achieving them (e.g. training, closures, product development, promotional activities and all that sort of thing).

Disruptive change is sudden

Disruptive change forces firms to suddenly do things in a different way to usual. They may have to **close or sell off subsidiary companies**, spend heavily on **promotions** to raise customer confidence or **totally restructure** the way the firm's organised.

For example, Coca-Cola® had to change their US recipe after the colouring used was linked to cancer in rodents.

When you think of disruptive change, you usually think of a **negative event** that makes customers suddenly go elsewhere. However, it's also possible for **customer demand** to **increase** and force the company to expand even though it wasn't planning to.

Changes in the **law** can be **incremental** or **disruptive**. Sometimes, the government gives **plenty of notice** that they're going to change the law, so that businesses can **plan ahead** and put a strategy in place. Sometimes governments change the law **suddenly**, e.g. in response to a health scare.

Force Field Analysis is used to analyse Forces For and Against Change

1) **Kurt Lewin** developed a concept called **Force Field Analysis** to help understand **change** in different situations.
2) A **diagram** is drawn (see right) to show the **plan**, the forces **supporting** the plan, and the forces **opposing** the plan.
3) After the forces are written down they are **numbered** to show how significant they are, from 1 (least) to 5 (most).
4) The numbers are added up to show the **total force** for and against the plan.
5) The **analysis** can be used to help decide whether the plan should **go ahead**. Alternatively, it can help managers work out how forces could be **strengthened** or **weakened**.

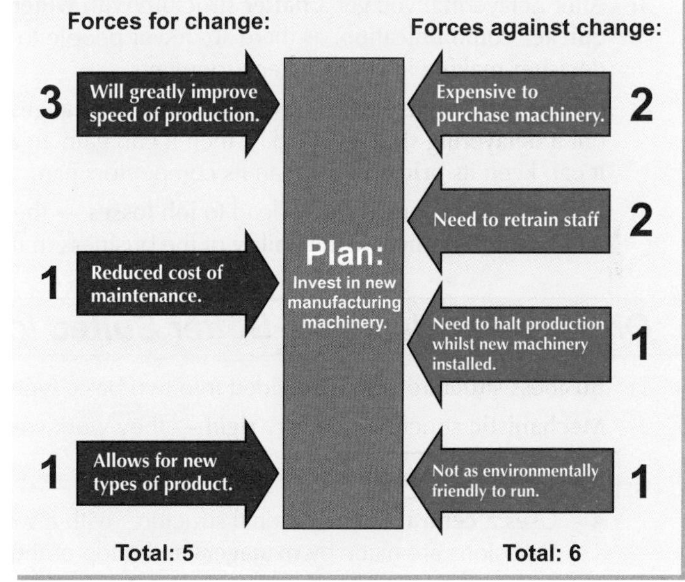

Practice Questions

Q1 Give two examples of internal and external causes of change.

Q2 Give an example of a disruptive change.

Q3 Draw an example force field analysis diagram for a hotel that wishes to build an extension with 20 new rooms.

Exam Question

Q1 A food and soft-drink manufacturer has been growing over time to become one of the UK's leading food and drink producers. To what extent is it inevitable that the business will need to make changes as time goes on? [25 marks]

Accidentally getting your hair dyed green, a classic disruptive change...

Change is a fact of life, and a fact of business too. In general, people prefer stability — change is stressful, and the bigger the change, the more stressful it is. Without change though, things start going to pot — the business could become unprofitable, get into trouble with the law or lose out to competitors. It may never be able to recover.

Managing Change

Change management isn't about the guys who sit in those little money booths in the arcade — it's all about how businesses can adapt to external and internal change. As you'll see, it's important for businesses to be flexible.

Flexible Businesses are able to Restructure frequently

See pages 86-87 for more on organisational design.

1) Changing the **organisational structure** of a business is known as **restructuring**.
2) Businesses that are able to restructure **quickly** and **efficiently** can adapt their structure in order to keep up with changes in the **external environment** or to implement **new strategy**.
3) The main reason for restructuring is to **maximise** the **efficiency** of **decision-making**, **communication** and **division of tasks** in the business's current situation. Restructuring can also **reduce costs**, which makes the business **more competitive**.
4) Businesses might **decentralise** in **fast-changing environments** to give more **power** and **flexibility** to different departments or sites. E.g. in fashion chains, each **store manager** (rather than head office) might be allowed to choose the stock for their store, because they know what **fashions** the customers in their particular store are likely to be interested in.
5) Having a **flexible organisational structure** is also important in times of **hardship**, e.g. during a recession. Business may need to **quickly** switch to a **centralised structure** as even **small decisions** can become very important to the **success** of the business.

The staff were really embracing the concept of a flexible organisation.

Delayering improves Communication and reduces Costs

1) Delayering means **removing** parts of an organisation's hierarchy — usually a layer of middle-managers.
2) Businesses with flexible structures are able to delayer in order to **reduce** their **costs**, improve **communication** and give **more responsibility** to employees at lower levels of the hierarchy.
3) After delayering, you get a **flatter** structure with **wider** spans of control. Flatter structures usually have **quicker communication**, as there are fewer people to pass messages through. This can help with **decision-making** in **changing** environments.
4) Delayering can help a business to **respond to changes**, such as **difficult economic conditions**. If it can carry out a **delayering strategy** quickly, then it can gain an **advantage** over its **competitors** — by **cutting costs**, it can keep its **prices** lower than its competitors can.
5) However delayering can also lead to **job losses** — the business risks losing some vital **skills** and **experiences**, which could **reduce** the **flexibility** of the business in the future.

Organic Structures are Better Suited to Change than Mechanistic ones

1) Business structures can be divided into two basic types — **mechanistic** and **organic**.
2) **Mechanistic** structures are very **rigid** — they work well for businesses operating in a **stable** environment.

Mechanistic Structure

- Uses a **centralised**, traditional structure, with a well defined hierarchy of power. Decisions are made by **managers** at the top of the hierarchy.
- Uses a **tall structure**, so messages can take a **long time** to travel through the business.
- Suited to businesses that don't need to adapt to change very often. Departments are given tasks which don't vary much so it's easy to assign **resources** efficiently, but it can be **slow** to make **changes** within the business.
- Employees are **specialised** in certain tasks and tend to **work separately** on them. For example, each marketing employee may focus on a **specific market** rather than all of them looking at the whole market.

3) When **flexibility** is **important** to a business they may choose to have an **organic** structure.

Organic Structure

- Uses a **decentralised structure**, meaning employees get more say in **decision-making**.
- Uses a **flat structure**, which allows **fast communication** throughout the business.
- Best suited to an uncertain, **changing environment** as information can be acted upon **quickly**.
- Employees in an organic structure usually **work in teams** to complete tasks, rather than each person having a **strict single role**. These teams can be adapted to suit the situation.

Managing Change

Knowledge *and* ***Information Management*** *Increases* ***Flexibility***

1) **Knowledge** and **information management** refers to the **collection**, **organisation**, **distribution** and **application** of knowledge and information within a business.
2) Knowledge can be any **data** gathered by the business, as well as **procedures**, **workers' skills** and **individuals' expertise**. Knowledge can be stored and organised in **specifically designed databases** that allow anyone using them to quickly **sort** and **find** the information that they require.

The most useful data is directly **relevant**, **correct**, **up-to-date** and **easy** to **analyse**.

3) Businesses should try to get employees to **record** any **specialised knowledge** they have so that if **someone leaves**, the business will still be able to use the **knowledge** gathered from that **employee**.
4) A business can **improve** its **internal communications** by implementing **procedures** to collect and distribute knowledge effectively. For example, if staff share '**lessons learned**' at the end of a project, it allows others to **learn** about the difficulties faced, which should help them **avoid** the **same problems** in the future. A business may also try to **improve communications** within and between **sites** and **departments**, so that staff can contact individuals who have the required expertise **easily**.
5) Having a **wide range** of knowledge and information **easily accessible** by everyone in the business helps a business to be **flexible** and to **respond to change**. If people have information to hand, they can **quickly assess** the current position of the business and **decide** what action to take. It also makes it easier for staff to **change roles** and learn their new responsibilities quickly.
6) Data needs to be **maintained** and **updated** to make sure the most up-to-date information is accessible — large businesses will need to **employ people** just to deal with the day-to-day **management** of information.

Flexible Employment Contracts *help a business to* ***Manage Change***

1) Flexible employment contracts allow businesses to be more **flexible** themselves — so the business is more effective at **managing change**. For example, if a business has a lot of employees on **zero-hours contracts** (see p.54) it can easily cope with increases and decreases in demand.
2) A flexible workforce can be achieved through employing a mixture of **core workers** and **peripheral workers** (see p.65) — core workers can provide a **stable environment** for the change to take place and the peripheral workers can help with any **additional work** during the change.
3) A flexible business is also able to **outsource** some of its work in order to **manage change**. For example, if a business is updating the machinery in its manufacturing department, it might outsource some of the manufacturing while staff are **trained** and get up to speed with the **new processes**.
4) Employing people on flexible contracts can also make it easier for businesses to hold onto **valuable employees** and open up more **job opportunities** for **skilled applicants**. Businesses will then have a wider range of **skilled employees** when it comes to implementing change — they may not even need to **retrain people**.
5) Unfortunately, flexible contracts have **downsides**. Allowing people to work **flexi-time** (see p.92) could result in **poor communication** and **teamwork** between staff who work at **different times**. This could make it a lot **more difficult** to manage change effectively and businesses may need to put a **strategy in place** to deal with it.

Practice Questions

Q1 Give two ways in which a business can change its structure in order to react quicker in fast-moving environments.

Q2 Give two features of a mechanistic structure.

Q3 Give three ways that businesses can use employment contracts to become more flexible.

Exam Question

Q1 Staff at a call centre have recently been moved onto flexible contracts.
To what extent is this likely to affect the performance of the business? [12 marks]

It was 27 °C today, but apparently it's inappropriate to 'de-layer' in the office...

Make sure you learn the difference between mechanistic and organic business structures. Imagine mechanistic structures like a well-oiled machine — a traditional, inflexible system where employees all work on specific, separate tasks. Organic systems are flexible, flat and decentralised, with employees working together as a team.

Overcoming Barriers to Change

Unlike the 100 m hurdles at sports day, you can't just jump over barriers to change — you have to manage them...

Resistance** is the most common **Barrier to Change

1) In order to **manage change** effectively, businesses need to be able to **overcome barriers to change**.
2) Even with the **best plans** and **strategies**, businesses will face some barriers:

- **Organisational structure:** some structures can make it difficult to manage change — e.g. if the business has a **tall structure** it can be difficult to **communicate** the change and the reasons for it to the lower layers.
- **Resources:** businesses need to have the correct resources **in place** before making a change — e.g. a business shouldn't introduce **new machinery** until they employ someone who can **operate it**.
- **Poor management:** when managers are unable to **communicate** effectively and **engage** workers — this is usually the result of a **lack of trust** between the manager and the worker.
- **Passive resistance:** when people carry on with the **old ways** despite being aware of the **new needs** and being shown the **new processes**. Passive resistance is most common in **employees** and **suppliers**.
- **Active resistance:** when people **argue** against the change and **challenge motives** for the change. **Workers** can organise themselves through their **trade union** (see p.96) and **refuse** to carry out tasks. **Customers** can also show active resistance by refusing to make further **purchases** from the company.

3) Businesses need to be able to **communicate effectively** with groups of workers throughout the business. If workers feel **engaged** and are kept **up-to-date** with any changes, they are much **less likely** to resist them.
4) **Good planning** and **strategies** can help businesses to **avoid** some of the barriers to change. For example, a business may have to give staff **better training** before implementing the change.

***Kotter** and **Schlesinger's Four Reasons** for **Resistance** to change*

Managers need to consider which of the following reasons is **most relevant** to the **specific change** in their company.

1) Self-interest

- People are more concerned with their **own situation** rather than the success of the business — if they can't see how the change **directly benefits** them, they will **resist it**.
- People can't see that ultimately a **more successful** business may have **individual benefits** too.
- For example, **organisational change** through delayering may meet resistance from middle-managers who fear **loss of income** or **redundancy** — they can't see that a more successful business might create **new positions** for them even **higher up** the hierarchy.

2) Misunderstanding

- People also resist change when they don't **fully understand** what it means for them. They will usually think that they have **more to lose** than **gain** until they are told otherwise.
- **Poor communication** from management can lead to **incorrect information** being passed down to workers. This breeds **uncertainty** and **confusion** and will **increase anxiety** amongst employees.
- Businesses need to have a **high level of trust** between employees and managers to prevent misunderstandings.

3) Low tolerance of change

- People get used to **completing tasks** the way **they know** — they will resist change if they **fear** that they won't be able to develop the **news skills** required after the change. They may believe that they won't perform as well in the **new situation** and they will lose their **job security**.
- There may also be a **loyalty** to **existing relationships** and **methods** as these are **known** and **established** — e.g. workers may be **comfortable** in their current teams and not want to break up existing work groups.

4) Different assessments of the situation

- The **key stakeholders** may have **strong disagreements** over the reasons for change and therefore there may be an inability to accept the **need for change**.
- They may not be able to see the **advantages** brought about by the change — they may only see the **disadvantages** that the change will bring and everything that could **go wrong**.
- They may **agree** that a change is needed but think that they have a **better idea** of what to change.

Overcoming Barriers to Change

Kotter and Schlesinger's Six Ways of Overcoming Resistance to change

Once managers have identified the reason for resistance, they can try to **do something about it**.

1) **Education and communication**

Managers need to **raise awareness** of the reasons for change and how it will be carried out. The education process usually involves **discussions**, **presentations** and **reports** — they should clearly communicate the **reasons** behind the planned change and identify the **benefits** for the business and individuals.

2) **Participation and involvement**

Key stakeholders should be **involved** in the **design** and **implementation** of the change. If they **participate** in the decision-making process then they will feel more **engaged** and their ideas form part of the change — if people become **part of the process**, it'll be more **difficult** for them to resist the change.

3) **Facilitation and support**

Listening to the **concerns** of the workforce by holding **regular meetings** will help workers to adjust as they'll **feel supported** — it can also help the business to meet the needs of the workers. **Support groups** can help workers to overcome their **anxiety** about the changes. Businesses should also provide **training** for workers who will be required to gain **new skills**.

4) **Negotiation and agreement**

Giving stakeholders opportunities to **negotiate** and compromising over **key sticking points** can lead to full agreement over the proposed change. **Financial** or **non-financial incentives** may need to be offered by the business in order to obtain **full acceptance** of the change. If full agreement can't be made then **voluntary redundancy** or **early retirement** may be offered to employees who are resisting change.

5) **Manipulation and Co-option**

An employee who is resisting change may be given a **desirable role** in the decision-making process in order to gain their cooperation. This can be a **risky strategy** as these roles often give the worker **little power** and they can feel **tricked** into agreeing to change. Alternatively, a manager may **manipulate** the information regarding the change, e.g. they may **exaggerate** the extent of a financial crisis and state there is no other alternative. If it's found out that the manager has **manipulated information** they will have **lost the trust** of their workers.

6) **Explicit and implicit coercion**

As a last resort, in order to speed up the process, a person may be **threatened** to comply with the planned changes or face consequences. The consequences of resistance could be clearly stated or just implied. These could be **redundancies**, losing out on **promotion opportunities**, or transfers to other departments, etc.

Practice Questions

Q1 Describe two barriers to change for an organisation.

Q2 Outline Kotter and Schlesinger's four reasons for resistance to change.

Q3 Identify Kotter and Schlesinger's six ways of overcoming resistance to change.

Q4 Give one advantage and one disadvantage for using "Facilitation and Support" as a method to overcome resistance to change in an organisation.

Exam Questions

Q1 Discuss two ways of overcoming resistance to change in a multinational organisation. [6 marks]

Q2 A furniture manufacturing company plans to install new technology in order to improve productivity. Evaluate the strategies it should implement to overcome the likely resistance to change from workers. [16 marks]

Businesses need to overcome resistance or else there'll be friction...

There's loads to learn on these two pages — most of it thought up by those clever chaps Kotter and Schlesinger. Make sure you can identify all the barriers to change that businesses can face and give reasons why they come about. Then it's just a case of learning the six different ways that businesses can deal with any resistance that they might face.

Managing Organisational Culture

A company's organisational culture (or corporate culture) is based on the company's values and objectives.

Organisational Culture is the Way things are Done in a Business

1) **Organisational culture** is the way that people do things in a company, and the way that they expect things to be done. It's an important way to shape the **expectations** and **attitudes** of staff and managers.
2) Because organisational culture **affects staff behaviour** and how they make decisions, it has an effect on **planning**, **objective setting** and **strategy**.
3) Organisational culture is **created** and **reinforced** by company **rules**, **managerial attitudes**, **managerial behaviour** and **recruitment** policies that recruit people who "fit in".
4) Culture is often affected by the way in which employees are **rewarded**. For example, if an employee acts in an **unethical** manner, yet has **high sales**, rewarding them could lead to a culture valuing **short-term profits** over the **company's reputation**.
5) A company's culture can be **identified** by looking at its **heroes** (people who represent the company's values), the **stories** that are told repeatedly within the company, **symbols** that represent the company's values (like staff mottos and sayings), and the **ceremonies** that the business holds (such as office parties).

Organisational Culture can be Strong or Weak

Strong culture

Organisational culture is strong when employees **agree** with the **corporate values** of the company. Having a strong corporate culture has several advantages:

- Employees need **less supervision**, because their behaviour will naturally tend to fit in with the company's values.
- Staff are more **loyal** to the business, so **staff turnover** is lower.
- It increases employees' **motivation**, so they work more productively.

Weak culture

Weak culture is where the employees of a company **don't** share the company's values, and have to be **forced** to comply with them (e.g. through **company policies**).

There are Four Main Types of Organisational Culture

Organisational culture has a big impact on how companies handle change, and whether staff are **open** to change or **resistant** to it. In 1993, Charles Handy identified the following **four main types** of organisational culture:

1) Power culture

- **Power cultures** have a **centralised structure** where decision-making authority is limited to a **small number** of people — perhaps just **one person** in the **centre** (possibly the owner).
- Power cultures may begin to **struggle** if the business **grows** and cannot be run from the **centre**.
- Employees are likely to be **more resistant** to change, because they don't have the opportunity to give their **opinions** on what changes should and shouldn't be made.
- They might also be **resistant to changes** because they don't have enough **faith** in senior managers who they feel are **out of touch** with the day-to-day activities of the business.

2) Role culture

- **Role cultures** are common in **bureaucratic firms** where authority is defined by job title. **Decisions** come from **senior managers**, so employees don't have the **opportunity** to get involved in the **decision-making process**.
- Organisations with role cultures tend to have **poor communication** between departments so they **respond slowly** to change — this could result in them **losing out** to **competitors** in **new** or **expanding** markets where strategies need to be developed and implemented quickly.
- These organisations also tend to **avoid risk** for fear of failure which means that **change** is **quite rare**.
- Any changes that are brought in will meet **resistance** as employees are **not used** to doing things differently.

Managing Organisational Culture

3) Person culture

- **Person culture** is common in loose organisations of **individual workers**, usually **professional partnerships** such as solicitors, accountants, doctors, etc.
- The **objectives** of these firms will be defined by the **personal ambitions** of the individuals involved. The firms have to ensure that the individuals actually have **common goals**.
- **Decisions** are made **jointly**, so all employees are likely to be **comfortable** and **accepting** of any changes that are made because they have agreed to them.
- However, decisions on **change** can be **difficult** to make — individuals will often think about what is **best** for **themselves** rather than thinking about what is **best** for the **organisation**.

4) Task culture

- Organisations with a **task culture** place an emphasis on getting specific **tasks** done.
- Task culture gets **small teams** together to work on a project, then disbands them. There may be **conflict** between teams for **resources** and **budgets**. It can be confusing if a firm has too many **products** or **projects**.
- This culture supports **objectives** which are based around **products** (e.g. make Product X the market leader).
- Task cultures respond well to **management by objectives**, which translates corporate objectives into **specific targets** for each **department** and for each **individual employee**.
- Staff working in a company with a task culture are likely to think that change is normal because they are used to **changing teams** often and working with a variety of people. This means that they are likely to be **less resistant** to change in general.

There are many other types of **organisational cultures**. An example is **entrepreneurial culture**:

Entrepreneurial culture

- Employees are encouraged to look for **new ways** of bringing **revenue** into the company.
- **Change** is a big part of entrepreneurial culture, and **all employees** are responsible for coming up with ideas to **improve** how the business is run.
- If employees are encouraged to be **creative** and **innovative**, they are likely to be much more **open** to change, especially when changes are made based on their **suggestions**.

Vicky was brilliant at managing her change.

Other examples of organisational culture are **customer-focused** culture (which bases its values on customer **feedback** and **satisfaction**), **clan** culture (where the organisation acts more like a **family** with managers as **parent-figures**) and **market** culture (where the focus is on **competition** with **other organisations** and **between employees**).

Practice Questions

Q1 What is organisational culture?

Q2 Give three benefits of an organisation having a strong culture.

Q3 Describe a power culture.

Q4 Why can change be hard to implement in an organisation with a person culture?

Exam Questions

Q1 In which of the following cultures is change least likely to meet resistance from employees?

A weak culture B role culture C power culture D task culture [1 mark]

Q2 MindGadgitz are a company developing new household gadgets for sale to the public.
They have decided to change their organisational culture from a power culture to a task culture.
Analyse how the change may affect the performance of the company. [9 marks]

We always go bowling on Sundays — we have a strong roll culture...

This stuff on organisational culture's pretty interesting I reckon. Remember that the organisational culture of a business affects all sorts of things — from whether they take financial risks, to whether they have office parties. When you get a case study, look for clues about the culture of the business — it can tell you a lot about what's happening and why.

Managing Organisational Culture

Sorry old chap/chappette — there are another two pages of organisational culture...

***Corporate Culture** is **Important** for the **Stakeholders** of the business*

The **organisational culture** of a business affects stakeholders such as **staff**, **customers** and **shareholders**:

1) **Staff** — Culture affects the **motivation** of the employees. E.g. a **power culture** or **role culture** can **demotivate** creative staff who can see ways to **improve** things but don't have the **power** to put changes into practice.
2) **Customers** — Organisational culture affects **customers' loyalty** to a business. Businesses with a **customer-focused** culture are more likely to have customers loyal to the firm or their brands.
3) **Shareholders** — The level of **risk** that businesses take depends on their organisational culture. Shareholders might get **low returns** on their investment if they invest in a company with a **low-risk culture**, whereas investing in a company with a **high-risk culture** gives shareholders the possibility of **high returns**, but there's also the risk that they'll **lose money**.

*Managers might want to **Change** the **Organisational Culture***

There are **two** main reasons why the managers of a business might want to **change** the organisational culture:

1) The organisational culture of a business depends on the **preferences** of its **leaders**. When a new manager joins a business, they might change it to make it more **similar** to businesses they have worked in **before**. E.g. if a manager who is used to working in a business with a **role culture** starts working in a business with a **task culture**, they might **force** the business to adopt a role culture because that is what they are used to.
2) A business might change its culture in order to be more **competitive**. E.g. businesses with a **power culture** can be **slow** to spot ways to **save money**, or more **efficient** ways of working, so adopting an **entrepreneurial culture** where all the staff are constantly looking for ways to **improve** the business could make the business more **competitive**.

*Changes such as **Growth** can **Influence** organisational culture*

1) If a business **grows**, it might need to take on **new employees**. New employees may have different **expectations** and **aims**, which could influence the pre-existing culture.
2) A business's **growth** and **success** can lead to it becoming **more corporate**, with a more **rigid structure**. This can sway the business towards a **role culture**.
3) If a business becomes a **multinational**, its culture may be influenced by the culture of the country the business has entered. Companies can use **Hofstede's six dimensions of national culture** (see next page) to analyse the differences between the culture of each country.
4) The **amount** by which a culture is **affected by a change** depends on how **strong** the original culture was (see p.174), how well it was **reinforced** and whether employees **appreciate** its values.

Changing** the **Organisational Culture** can be **Difficult

1) Employees usually **resist** any kind of change (see p.172), including changes in **organisational culture**. Employees who have worked for the business for a **long time** are **especially likely** to resist changes to the **organisational culture**, because they'll think the way they've **always done** things is better.
2) Changing organisational culture means changing the **attitudes** and **behaviour** of staff, so it's much more **complicated** than changing things like pricing structure. E.g. the managers of a company might want to change from a **person culture** to a **task culture**, but splitting people up into **small teams** and giving them **a project** won't achieve anything if employees just want to work **individually** and in their own **interests**.
3) Changing the organisational culture can also be very **expensive**. It might involve changing the **office layout**, giving **extra training** to staff, devising **new processes**, changing the **company motto** on marketing material, etc. This means that businesses can't always **afford** to **change their culture** as much as they would like to.
4) The **HR department** plays a **big role** in changing the organisational culture of a business — they might need to change their **recruitment** and **induction procedures**, change their **payment and reward system**, etc.

Managing Organisational Culture

The **Dimensions of National Culture** show how cultural values **Differ**

1) **Geert Hofstede** used a large set of data collected from employees across **different countries** to identify **four areas** or '**dimensions**' of national culture. Since then, **two more dimensions** have been added, making a total of **six**.
2) Countries are **scored** on each of the **six dimensions** — these scores allow **businesses** to assess the **cultural differences** when dealing with businesses from **different countries** and plan for any **culture clashes**.

Power Distance
The extent that people accept that power and wealth is distributed **unequally**. Societies with **low power distance** expect **equality**, and societies with **high power distance** (such as Saudi Arabia) accept the **hierarchy** of power without argument. For example, in a country with **high** power distance you would be expected to follow your boss's orders **without question**.

Uncertainty Avoidance
The extent to which people attempt to **minimise uncertainty**. This can be done by **introducing rules** or regulations. People in societies with **low uncertainty avoidance** tend to be **open to change**.

Individualism vs. Collectivism
The extent to which people are expected to **look after themselves** rather than **support each other**. Societies with **high individualism** focus on **personal achievement** and **rights**, and people are expected to look after **themselves** and their **close family**. Collectivist societies, e.g. Pakistan, are made up of **large groups** (such as large extended families) where members are expected to **support** each other in return for **loyalty**.

Masculinity vs. Femininity
Masculine cultures are highly **competitive** and **powerful**, with **contrasting gender roles**. **Feminine** cultures focus on **caring** and **quality of life**. The higher the masculinity, the more focus there is on power and money.

Long-term Orientation
The higher the long-term orientation, the more the society looks to the **future** and accepts new ideas, rather than following **tradition**.

Sandra's new-fangled cultural-reality headset let her see in 6D.

Indulgence vs. Restraint
Indulgent societies allow their people to **satisfy** their desires and impulses, within reason. **Restrained** societies attempt to **regulate** the desires of their people.

3) Businesses can use this model to plan for **communication problems** when **trading** with international suppliers, **expanding** into other countries or during **mergers**, **takeovers** and **joint ventures** (see p.152) with businesses in other countries. It can also help businesses to foresee any **potential issues** when **entering international markets**.
4) The model is also handy for **multinationals** — it allows them to assess how **proposed changes** will affect their employees in **different countries**. They can then adjust the changes to **match the cultures** in different countries.

Practice Questions

Q1 Why is changing organisational culture difficult?

Q2 What are the six dimensions of national culture?

Q3 What is individualism?

Exam Question

Q1 A company has been slowly expanding over the last 20 years, increasing its market share to around 12%. The directors plan for the business to continue growing and to set up factories in different countries. To what extent might this affect the organisational culture of the business? [25 marks]

Organisational Culture Club — an 80s tribute band formed by executives...

Make sure you're confident with the six dimensions of national culture — you'll find them useful when you're writing longer answer questions. You also need to understand how businesses can use them when trading internationally.

Planning Strategy

It's not a great idea to just pluck a strategy out of thin air — there are loads of factors that need to be considered. Strategic planning is the process of analysing and evaluating these factors and working them into a great strategy.

*Businesses can go through a **Planning Process** to create a **Strategy***

A business's **strategy** is a **plan** for achieving its **corporate objectives**. For example, if a business's main objective is to grow, it needs a strategy for how it's going to go about growing. One way of deciding on strategy is to go through a **strategic planning process**.

The strategic planning process involves several stages:

- Senior managers set the long-term **corporate objectives** of the business based on its mission.
- They analyse the **internal** position of the business to identify **strengths** and **weaknesses**. They analyse the **external** environment to identify **opportunities** and **threats** (see below for more on analysis).
- They develop possible **strategies** to achieve the corporate objectives, **evaluate** each one and then select the strategy that best **fits** their business.
- They plan out how the strategy will be **implemented**. This will include an outline of **functional objectives** for each department, the resources needed, etc.
- They set up **processes** for **monitoring** and **evaluating** the strategy as it is being implemented.

The key information is written up in a **strategic plan**. This document clearly **defines** a business's corporate objectives and strategy, along with an outline of how the strategy will be **implemented** and **monitored** throughout the business.

Strategic plans are sometimes called 'corporate plans'.

Analysis** of **Internal** and **External Factors** influences a **Strategy

A business needs to look at **many** different **factors** to decide on a **strategy** that will work for it.

1) When **planning** a strategy, a business looks at **internal** factors to determine its **strengths** and **weaknesses**.
2) These can include many different things, such as the **skills** and **motivation** of the staff, the **quality** of the products, the business's **finances**, the **production capacity** and the **core competences**.
3) For example, if a business has the **capacity** for **increased production**, this would be a **strength** in enabling it to **grow**. Or if a business's **strength** is making **high quality** products, it could develop a strategy for building its **brand** around quality.
4) A business will also look at **external** factors to identify any **opportunities** and **threats**.
5) These can include **political**, **legal**, **economic**, **social**, **technological** and **environmental** factors and **competition**.
6) For example, the **growth** of internet shopping might provide an **opportunity** to **increase sales**, or it could be a **threat** to a business that only sells through **physical** channels.
7) There are helpful tools that a business can use to analyse the internal and external factors, such as **SWOT analysis** (p.99), **Porter's five forces** (p.136-137) and the **Balanced Scorecard Model** (p.116).

There's loads more detail on internal factors in Section 8, and on external factors in Section 9.

Risk** and **Feasibility** affect **Strategic Decision-Making

Strategic decisions are **long-term** and **high-risk** — a business needs to weigh up its strategic options carefully.

1) A business needs to assess **risk** and **feasibility** when selecting strategy.
2) A useful **tool** for assessing risk is **sensitivity analysis** (see p.143). This looks at each **assumption** that a strategy relies on, and predicts how well the strategy would still do if these assumptions **change**. For example, could the business cope if the increase in costs is greater than expected. Based on this analysis, the business will **assess** whether the strategy is **worth** the risk.
3) The business could also consider how different **stakeholders** would react to a strategy — they should consider how highly the stakeholder **maps** (see p.24 for more on **stakeholder mapping**).
4) **Feasibility** is also an important factor — the business needs access to the **resources** or **skills** necessary to implement the strategy.

Planning Strategy

Contingency Plans prepare for Out Of The Ordinary Events

1) Strategic planning can include **contingency planning** — outlining what to do if something **unexpected** happens.
2) Contingency planning can help a business **respond** to lots of different types of **crises**. For example, a **hostile takeover bid,** a **fire** that destroys a factory, **bad news** or **PR** in the media, a sudden **change in demand** for products, or **lost** or **corrupt data** caused by computer network problems.
3) Businesses **can't** plan for **every unforeseen event**. Some adverse events are hard to plan for. Contingency planning is very **expensive**, so it's not worthwhile to plan for every single thing that could possibly go wrong. Managers have to decide **how likely** a particular adverse event is to happen, and how **badly** it would damage the business if it did happen.
4) **Crisis management** is when an unexpected situation **occurs**, and a business has to respond.

- If managers haven't carried out **contingency planning** they're **not prepared**, so they have to make **snap decisions** about what to do. If they've done contingency planning then they've already decided what to do in that situation, which makes crisis management **much more straightforward**.
- Managers need to **act quickly** and **decisively** to **limit** the amount of **damage** caused. This is best achieved through **strong leadership**, e.g. an autocratic leader (see p.18).

Strategic Planning can Help and Hinder businesses

1) Strategic planning can be **helpful** because a strategic plan gives the business a **clear direction**. It can **communicate** exactly what the business is trying to achieve, so everyone works towards the same goals.
2) Strategic planning makes managers think about the **strengths** and **weaknesses** of the business, and its **external threats** and **opportunities**. This helps managers to spot opportunities that they might not have noticed, and to match strategy to the current situation.
3) However, strategic planning can **restrict** the business's **flexibility** — employees might think that they have to follow the plan even if the situation has **changed** since it was made, or if there's a **better way** of doing things. Also, the plan is based on **analysis**, which may be **inaccurate** — e.g. it's difficult to **predict** long-term trends.
4) Strategic planning is likely to be more **useful** for businesses operating in **stable** markets, rather than more **innovative** businesses that need to respond to change on a regular basis. An innovative business would be more suited to an **emergent strategy** (see page 187).

Practice Questions

Q1 Describe the steps involved in carrying out strategic planning.

Q2 Give two examples of information that could be included in a strategic plan.

Q3 Give three examples of internal factors that might influence a business's strategy.

Q4 Give three examples of external factors that might influence a business's strategy.

Q5 Give three examples of situations that a business might have a contingency plan for.

Exam Question

Q1 Do you think strategic planning is essential for all businesses? Justify your answer. [16 marks]

My contingency plan: hide in a cupboard and hope the problems go away...

These pages are pretty packed... And there you were, hoping for a gentle introduction to the section... There's a lot of important stuff here though, so it's definitely worth taking time to make sure you understand it all — maybe challenge yourself to list as many SWOT factors that influence strategy as you can. That sounds like a fun game, right...?

Implementing Strategy

Implementing strategy effectively is really important in business. I bet you never would've guessed that...

Implementing Strategy is putting strategy into Action

If a business has come up with a great **strategy**, it'll also need to come up with an effective way of putting it into **action**. There are a few things that need to be **considered**:

- A business might have to **make big changes** to implement their strategy. So the success of a strategy will depend on how well the business **manages change**.
- The business needs to **plan** and **organise** the **resources** they need — e.g. assign responsibilities to staff, organise training or recruitment, or budget time and finances.
- To effectively implement strategy, there are three main factors that a business needs to get right — **leadership**, **communication**, and **organisational structure**.

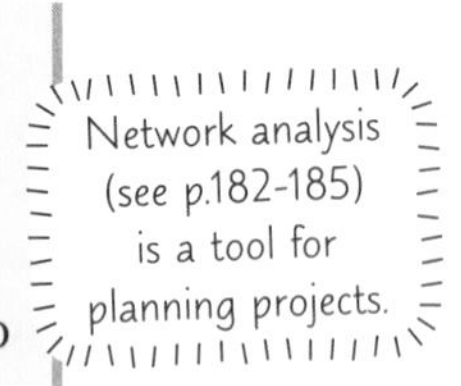

Leadership is important in Implementing Strategy

1) Implementing strategy often means a business makes **big changes**. For example, they might change teams around, bring in new technology, move to a new location or alter their product range.
2) A **good leader** can **take action** to make sure the changes go as smoothly as possible:

- A leader should take overall **responsibility** for management of strategic implementation, and **delegate** responsibilities for different elements where necessary.
- The leader should create a **clear** and **inspiring** vision that comes from the top and **sets an example** for everyone in the business.
- They can **motivate** everyone in the business to **engage** with the process. This can be done by creating a **positive** culture, for example by **rewarding** employees for hitting targets.
- Leadership is important in successfully **managing change** — this can be done with clear **communication**, lots of employee **involvement**, and a suitable **leadership style**.

Leaders are usually senior managers.

See p.173 for more on managing change.

3) In times of change, **authoritarian** leadership might make employees more **fearful** of change, and they might be more likely to resist it. **Laissez-faire** leadership can mean that employees don't have **confidence** that changes will work out well, so they won't be **supportive**. The most **suitable** forms of leadership for helping employees cope with change are the **paternalistic** and **democratic** styles. See p.18 for more detail on leadership styles.

Good Communications are vital in Implementing Strategy

1) The purpose of communication is to **clearly** pass on **information** and **ideas**, and to **motivate** people.
2) **Senior managers** need to communicate the **functional objectives** to department managers, and the business's **objectives** and **strategy** to all staff so that they know **what** the business is doing and **why**.
3) Different **departments** also need to communicate with **each other** in order to coordinate their activities.
4) Any employee affected by a strategy needs to be **told** how it's going to **change** their **role** or **responsibility**.
5) Communication is a **two-way process** — for instance, employees should inform their managers if there are any **issues** with implementing the strategy, and managers should respond to the feedback.

Example Part of a company's strategy is to have a big **publicity launch**.

- **Senior managers** need to **communicate** with **Marketing** and **Operations managers** to inform them of the **work** required from their departments.
- These departments will need to communicate with **HR** to **decide** on the best action to take — for instance, hire **more** people (as either permanent or temporary staff) or ask current employees to work **overtime**.
- **Finance** will also need to be involved, so that they can calculate **costs**, **cash flow**, etc.
- Every decision has **knock-on** effects, and they all need to be **considered** carefully and the outcomes communicated clearly.

Implementing Strategy

A **Business** needs an **Organisational Structure** that suits its **Strategy**

You've come across different types of organisational design (pages 86-87) and general structures (p.170) before. Here are **four specific types** of organisational structure a business can use. Depending on the strategy, a business may need to **change** its structure — e.g. by reorganising departments or creating new ones.

Functional Structures organise staff by **Department**

1) Businesses can be organised into several **departments**, which group jobs together by **function**.
2) The main four departments are **finance**, **marketing**, **operations** and **HR**, which are all run **separately**.
3) Each function can work in its own area of **expertise**, which can make **implementing strategy** simpler.
4) However, this could mean each department has its **own culture** and focuses on its own priorities. If communication between departments isn't good, it will be **hard** to **coordinate strategy**.

Product-based Structures organise staff by **Product**

1) In a business that produces **lots** of different **products**, each group of products can be run almost as a **separate business**. Each product division has its **own director**, **marketing** team, **finance** team, etc.
2) This would be an **ideal** structure for implementing certain **strategies** — for example, a business may want to grow the **market share** of one particular product, while keeping another product's market share steady.
3) But there may be **unnecessary duplication** of roles — e.g. instead of each division having its own research team, it might be more **efficient** to have just one research department for the whole company.

Regional Structures organise staff by **Geographical Location**

1) **Regional** structures are based on **location**. A business might have branches all over the country, which are grouped into **regional divisions** that run themselves.
2) A **global** company could have **headquarters** on each continent, which oversee **national divisions**. For example, an Asian HQ oversees the Japanese and Indian divisions.
3) A regional structure tends to suit a **market development strategy** where the business is expanding into **new geographical markets**. If there are **different market demands** in different locations, control can be **decentralised** so each division can run itself independently and adapt to local needs.

Matrix Structures can organise staff by a **Combination** of **Factors**

1) **Matrix** structures organise staff by **two different criteria**.
2) The diagram opposite shows a business organised by **project** and **function**. Each project team has workers from different functions. The red circle shows a **salesperson** working in **Project B** — they **report** to a Sales manager and the manager of Project B.

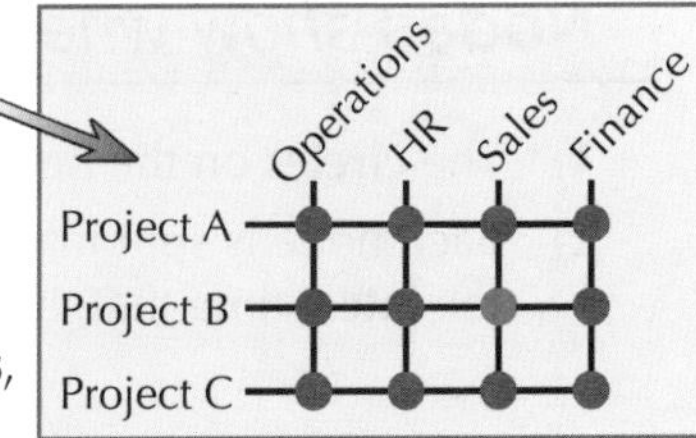

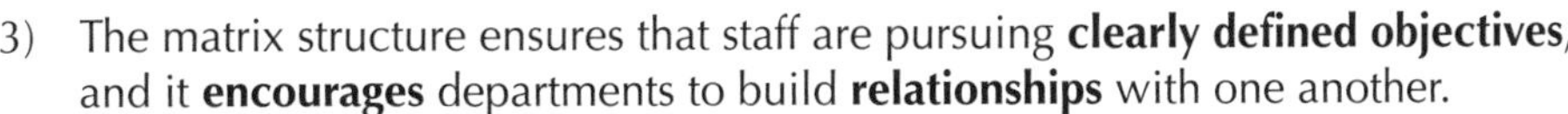
3) The matrix structure ensures that staff are pursuing **clearly defined objectives**, and it **encourages** departments to build **relationships** with one another.

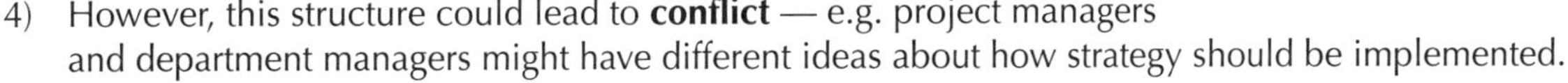
4) However, this structure could lead to **conflict** — e.g. project managers and department managers might have different ideas about how strategy should be implemented.

Practice Questions

Q1 Give three factors that are important in implementing strategy effectively.

Q2 Describe each of the following structures in a few sentences: a) functional
b) regional
c) product-based

Exam Question

Q1 To what extent is communication likely to be the most important factor in implementing strategy effectively? [25 marks]

Take me to your leader...

The key to all this is being able to say what is appropriate for a particular situation — there's no "one structure fits all", so a business needs to figure out which structure will be best for implementing their strategy. Not always easy...

Network Analysis

Network analysis is used to find the most time-efficient way of doing a complex project. It's a really handy tool for working out how best to organise resources and activities when implementing strategy.

Network Analysis works out the Quickest Way to Finish a Set Of Tasks

Network analysis identifies the most **efficient** and **cost-effective** way of completing a complex project — i.e. a project made up of a series of **activities**. Network analysis is sometimes called 'critical path analysis'.

1) The various activities which make up the project are **identified**, and the **order** or **sequence** that these activities must be performed in is worked out.
2) The **duration** (how long each activity will take) is **estimated**.
3) These **activities** are then arranged as a **network** or graph, showing the **whole project** from start to finish, and showing which tasks can be **performed** at the **same time**. For large, **complicated** projects made up of lots of activities, **computer programs** are used to construct the network.
4) The **shortest time** required to get from start to finish can then be identified. The sequence of tasks which have to be done one after another with **no gaps in between**, to get the project done as fast as possible, is called the **critical path**. Activities on the critical path are called **critical activities** — if they're delayed, the **whole project** is delayed.

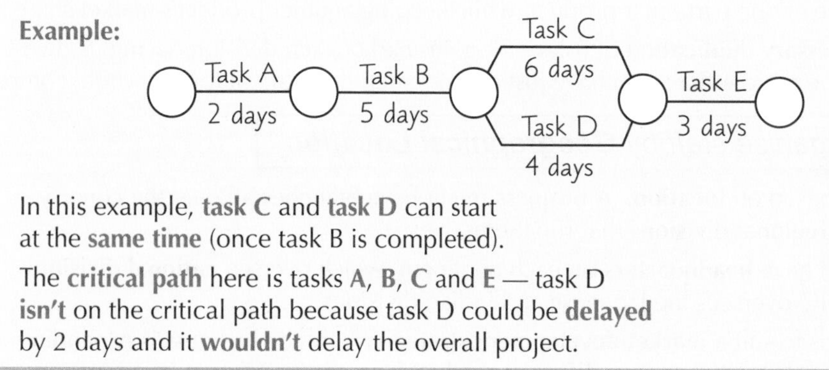

"Dearest, we really must get back to the path before we ruin our skirts. It's absolutely critical."

Nodes show when one task Must Finish and when the next task Can Start

1) The **circles** on the network are called **nodes** — they show where one activity **stops** and another activity **begins**.
2) Each node is split into **three** parts. The numbers inside each node show the **number** of the **node**, the **latest** time that the **previous** task can **finish**, and the **earliest** time that the **next** task can **start**:

- The **left** part of the node shows you which **number** node it is.
- The number in the **top right** is the **earliest start time** (EST — see next page) of the activity **following** the node. That's the **earliest** time from the beginning of the project that the activity can **start**, assuming that all the activities before it are completed in as short a time as possible.

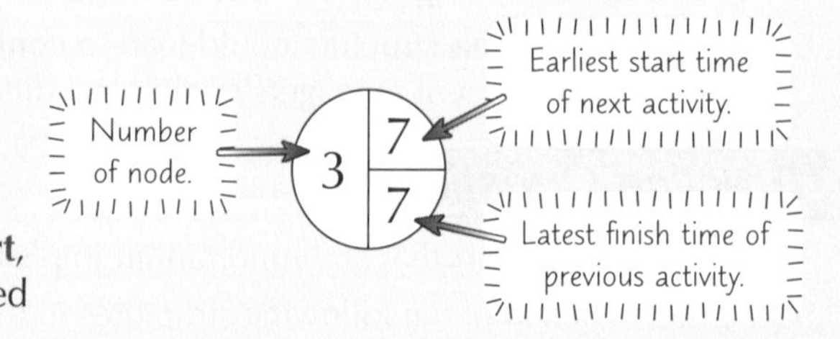

- The number in the **bottom right** of the node is the **latest finishing time** (LFT — see next page) of the activity immediately **before** the node (or the LFT of the activity with the longest duration if there's more than one activity going into the node). That's the **latest** time that the activity can **finish** without having the knock-on effect of making the whole project **late**.
- If the **EST** and the **LFT** are the **same**, then the node is on the **critical path**.

Network Analysis

Networks include Start Times, Finishing Times and Float Time

It's really important to know the **earliest** and **latest start** and **finishing times** for each activity so that you can make sure the whole project can be completed **on time** — if you **miss** the latest start time of an activity, there's **no way** you can finish the project on time (unless you can do individual activities **more quickly** than you predicted).

1) **EST** = **earliest start time** (in number of e.g. days, weeks, months) since the start of the project. An activity can't start until the activity before it has been completed — e.g. you can't ice a cake before it's baked. EST is worked out by **adding** the **duration** of the **previous activity** to its **EST**. The EST of the first activity is always 0.

   E.g. a business wants to trade internationally. Their strategy involves **opening** a new office (**1 month**), **hiring** new staff (**3 months**), **producing** the product (**6 months**) and **launching** the product in the new market (**2 months**). So, the **EST** (in months) of **producing** is: **0 + 1 + 3 = 4**.

2) **EFT** = **earliest finishing time**. It's the time that an activity will **finish** if it's **started** at the **earliest start time**. You can work out the EFT for an activity by **adding** its **duration** (in months here) to its **EST**.

   Using the same example, the **EFT** of **producing** is: **4 + 6 = 10**

   The EFT isn't shown on the nodes of a network.

3) **LFT** = **latest finishing time**. This is the **latest** time by which the activity can be completed without **holding up** the **completion** of the project. It's **calculated** by working **backwards** from the **final** node. The LFT of the final node is **equal** to the EST of the final node.
   To work out the LFT of the node before, you subtract the duration of the next activity from its LFT.

   If the business needs the product launched by the end of **month 12**, the **LFT** of **hiring** is: **12 – 2 – 6 = 4**

4) **LST** = **latest start time**. It's the **latest time** an activity can be **started** and still be **finished** by its **LFT**.
   To calculate LST, **subtract** the **duration** of the activity from its **LFT**.

   The **LST** of **hiring** in the example above is: **4 – 3 = 1**

   The LST isn't shown on the nodes of a network.

5) **Float time** is the **spare time** available for an activity. Only **non-critical** activities have **float time**.
   Total float is the length of **time** you can **delay** an activity without delaying the **completion** of the **project**.
   You can work it out by:

   total float = LFT – duration – EST

   There's an example of a network on the next page.

Practice Questions

Q1 What is meant by the "critical path"?

Q2 What do the three numbers inside each node show?

Q3 What do the initials EST and LST mean?

Q4 How do you calculate the latest finishing time of an activity?

Q5 Explain the term "total float time".

Exam Question

Q1 Explain how a critical path network is produced. [8 marks]

If you're here to study an online dance craze, that's 'net twerk analysis'...

To be honest, this does all sound a bit confusing. But there's an example on the next page which should make it a lot clearer. If you have a network to show the order of tasks in a project, you can figure out where there's some spare time. Remember that you work forwards to fill in the ESTs, and then backwards to fill in the LFTs.

Network Analysis

These are the last two pages on network analysis, so make the most of it — you'll miss it when it's gone...

Here's an **Example** of **Network Analysis**

A project is made up of **nine separate tasks** — A to I:

- **Task A** takes **4 days** to complete and can be done at the same time as **task G** (5 days).
- **Task B** (7 days) and **task C** (9 days) can be done at the **same time** once **task A** is finished.
- **Task D** (6 days) can start once **task B** is completed.
- **Task E** (5 days) can start once **task B** and **task C** have **both** finished.
  Task E can be done at the **same time** as **task D.**
- **Task F** (3 days) can start once **task D** and **task E** have both finished.
- **Task H** (7 days) can start once **task G** has finished.
- **Task I** (4 days) can start once **task F** and **task H** have both finished.

You can work out the **ESTs** of all the tasks by working **forwards** from the start of the project, and then work out the **LFTs** of the tasks by working **backwards** from the end of the project.

The network looks like this:

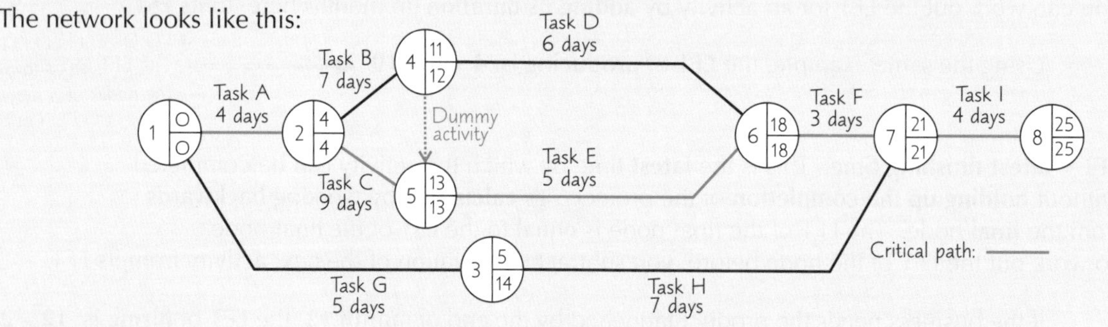

1) The **critical path** (in pink) is task **A**, then task **C**, task **E**, task **F** and finally task **I.**
   If you add up the time taken to do each task, it shows that the project can be completed in 4 + 9 + 5 + 3 + 4 = **25 days** in total. The LFT of task I in the final node is 25 days.
2) In each node on the **critical path**, the **EST** equals the **LFT**.
   For nodes that aren't on the critical path, the **EST** and **LFT** are **different**.
3) **Task B** and **task D** both have a **total float time** of 1 day, and **task G** and **task H** have a total float time of 9 days. These tasks are **non-critical activities** — if there is a **delay** in starting them, it's still possible to complete the project **on time**. E.g. if task G starts on day 5 instead of day 0, it will still be completed before its latest finishing time. If **critical tasks** start **late** or take **longer** than they're expected to, the project **can't** be completed on time.

There is a **dummy activity** between node 4 and node 5. A **dummy activity** is an **imaginary activity** — it just shows that one activity is **dependent** on another. In the example, the dummy activity shows that **task E can't start** until **task B** and **task C** have **both** finished. **Without** the dummy activity it would look as though **task E** was only dependent on **task C**, but having only **one node** between tasks B and C and tasks D and E would imply that **task D** was dependent on **both task B** and **task C**, instead of just **task B**.

Network Analysis can be used for **Time Management** of **Strategies**

1) Network analysis is used when **implementing** a **strategy** or **planning** a **complicated project**, such as the launch of a new product or building a new office block.
2) It allows companies to work out when they'll need **resources** to be **available**, e.g. that a certain **machine** will need to be **free** on Friday or that a **new office** is open and ready to use 15 months into a project.
3) In many cases, it's possible to **shorten** the **critical path** by allocating **additional resources** to an activity. For example, sewing buttons onto a batch of jumpers might be expected to take 5 days, but if the company hired extra machinists, it might be possible to reduce that to 3 days.
4) Some **resources** can be **switched** between activities — e.g. recruiters can be moved from hiring manual labour to hiring managers.
5) Network analysis also helps managers with **decision-making**. Knowing the **latest finish time** of a project makes it easier to decide when to launch an **ad campaign** or when to become a **public company**.

Network Analysis

Network Analysis has several Advantages

1) Network analysis identifies the **critical activities** (activities on the critical path), which need to be supervised closely, to make sure they meet their deadlines.
2) Resources can be transferred from activities with **float time** to **critical activities**, if needed. For example, people packing items could change roles to making them.
3) If different **functions** such as finance, operations, marketing and human resources can start work at the **earliest start time**, then this will make the implementation of **strategy** as speedy as possible. This saves on many **costs**, including the opportunity costs of not working on other projects.
4) Network analysis helps firms forecast their **cash flow** — it gives definite earliest start times when cash will need to be spent by different functions, which allows the firm to budget accurately.
5) Network analysis finds the **shortest time possible** for completing a complex project. This can give a competitive advantage. It's an important element of **time-based management** (see p.59).
6) It's an excellent **visual aid** to communications, because it shows at a glance which steps take place at the **same time**, and which have any **float time**.
7) Network analysis forces managers to think about the **activities** involved in a strategy. Without the **systematic approach** of network analysis, something might be forgotten.
8) Network analysis can be used to review progress on **individual tasks**, e.g. if a task overruns its float time you can see if it will delay the overall project or just the next activity.
9) If there are changes and modifications to the progress of the project, the network can be **amended** as the project goes on.

Professor "Biddy" Bidness preferred rhyme-based management.

Network Analysis has Disadvantages as well

1) Network analysis relies on **estimates** of how long each task will take. If these aren't accurate, the whole analysis will be wrong.
2) **Constructing** and **amending** the network will require a significant amount of **planning** and **time**.
3) Network analysis sets **tight deadlines**, especially for critical activities. It's tempting for employees to **cut corners** in the rush to meet deadlines, which means that **quality** can suffer.
4) Network analysis can't tell you anything about **costs** — or anything about **how good** the project is.

Practice Questions

Q1 What is a dummy activity?

Q2 Give two examples of projects that managers might use network analysis for.

Q3 Give two advantages to managers of using network analysis.

Q4 Give two disadvantages of network analysis.

Answers on p.202.

Exam Question

Q1 A project contains seven separate activities. Activity A must be completed first, and it has an estimated duration of eight days. Activities B, C and D can take place at the same time — B takes four days, C takes six days and D takes four days. E can only be started once B, C and D are completed and will take seven days. Once E is completed, F and G can take place at the same time — F takes three days and G takes five days.

a) Construct a network to show this data. [9 marks]

b) Find the critical path and state the minimum number of days the project will take to complete. [2 marks]

c) What are the float times for activities B and F? [2 marks]

You take the high road and I'll take the critical path...

Network analysis can seem a bit tricky, but don't be put off by a scary-looking network — just break it down and it'll seem a whole lot simpler. Don't forget to learn the advantages and disadvantages of network analysis too — they could easily come up in the exam. (You could say that one disadvantage is that you need to learn it for the exam...)

Difficulties with Implementing Strategy

It'd be nice if you could just come up with a strategy and then implement it, no hitches. Unfortunately, things aren't usually so simple. Problems can arise at any time, and have to be dealt with.

Strategic Decision-Making involves Risk and Uncertainty

When a business is **deciding** on a strategy, there are usually a large number of factors that have to be **considered**. The more factors there are to consider, the higher the number of potential **problems**.

1) Most strategies will have an element of **risk** involved — when you're trying to plan for the future there will always be **unknowns** that you can't account for. When managers are **making decisions** on strategy, they will need to consider how much risk is involved. However, it can be **difficult** to figure out exactly which parts of a strategy are risky.
2) It is also difficult for a business to judge the **feasibility** of a strategy. Managers need to have **information** about the resources, skills and time available. But even with this information, it can still be hard to **choose** between strategies.
3) The **external environment** is continually **changing**, but strategic decisions can **rely** too much on the **current** environment. This can make implementing the strategy **difficult** if the business faces **changes** from **external factors**.
4) The **internal environment** also **changes** — e.g. a business's resources might change unexpectedly, which can cause issues when trying to implement a strategy. Contingency plans (see p.179) should be included in the strategic decision-making **process**.
5) **Stakeholders** often want **different** things from a business — it's difficult to keep all groups happy all of the time. A business may have to take into account the views of a **group** of stakeholders in its decision-making, and be able to **justify** its **decisions** to other stakeholders.

It's important for a business to **think** about all the **potential problems** when **making decisions** about strategy — otherwise it might make things more difficult when it comes to **implementing** the strategy.

Implementing a strategy isn't Straightforward

There are many **difficulties** that a company needs to **overcome** to ensure the **success** of its strategy.

For example:

1) A lack of **resources** (e.g. money, skills, time) can make implementing a strategy **difficult**, especially if big changes are needed. **Heavy investment** can mean there is **less working capital** available for day-to-day activities.
2) Managers at all levels need to **understand** the strategy being implemented. If it isn't fully understood, this could lead to problems such as **miscommunication** or tasks being **assigned incorrectly**.
3) If managers **don't** provide strong, clear **leadership** and **communication** to manage the change, employees might **not embrace** the changes required.
4) A strategy may rely on **assumptions** about the **amount of resources** needed and the **length of time** tasks will take. **Accurate forecasting** can be very difficult, but any inaccuracies can cause problems.
5) **Changing the structure** of a company can cause difficulties — for example, if a company **delayers** (see p.170), then this will involve making redundancies. A structure change could also lead to a change in the **culture** of the business.
6) If a strategy sets out a **strict** path for the business, it may have difficulty implementing it in the future. A lack of **flexibility** in a strategy could mean that if the **environment** changes, the strategy will no longer be **relevant**.

Valerie's view of the new customer service strategy had taken a sudden downturn.

Difficulties with Implementing Strategy

There are **Issues** with **Planned Strategies**

Strategies can be described as **planned** or **emergent** (or somewhere in between). **Planned strategy**, as you can probably guess, is **planned out** before action is taken to **implement** it. This sounds sensible **in theory**, but planned strategy has its **disadvantages**.

1) **Planning** a strategy can **cost** a lot of **time** and **money**. It's easy to get caught up in trying to plan the **perfect** strategy, which is practically **impossible**.
2) A planned strategy will gradually become **out of date**. For instance, if strategy is planned every 5 years, then 3 years into the **implementation**, the **environment** could have **changed** a lot from the time of planning. It's difficult to **adapt** a planned strategy to a changing environment.
3) **Senior managers** who plan the strategy could be **out of touch** with what's really going on in the business.
4) Strategic planning could require the **input** of many people, each with a specific **skill set**. There is a chance that these people will only understand their own **contributions**, and not see the **bigger picture**.
5) A planned strategy could be **too detailed** and **theoretical** — the plan might not focus on how to implement the strategy **in practice**.
6) Managers can become too concerned with **analysing data** and making sure that everything is going **exactly** according to the plan. The strategy can become too **rigid**, which stops people being **creative** or **innovating**.
7) Senior managers who implement strategy could be **too busy** to fully **oversee** everything. If tasks are **delegated** down to people without authority, then things could be trickier to implement.

Emergent Strategies solve some of the **Problems** of **Planned Strategies**

Emergent strategy develops over time, as a business's actions lead to **patterns of behaviour**. Emergent strategy can be **adapted** as the business **learns** what works in the **current environment**. Following an emergent strategy can **solve** many of the **problems** that occur with a planned strategy.

1) **Emergent strategies** save a lot of **time** and **money** that would otherwise have been spent on strategic planning.
2) Emergent strategies stay **relevant**, because they can **adapt** to the **changing environment**.
3) A planned strategy relies on senior managers making a lot of the decisions. An emergent strategy is based more on the decisions of **junior- and middle-managers** — they will often have access to more **up-to-date information** about the business and its environment.
4) Junior- and middle-managers will be more **knowledgeable** about employees — e.g. who would be most **suitable** for different tasks or projects. Emergent strategies also give low-ranking employees a **chance** to **have a say** in some aspects of strategy, instead of all decisions being made by people at the top.

Alligators only occasionally implement an emergent strategy.

Emergent Strategies also have **Disadvantages**

Of course, not everything about **emergent strategies** is perfect — they have their **downsides** too.

1) With an **emergent strategy**, it might not be clear what the **end** goal is — a **planned strategy** is clearly working towards stated objectives.
2) If the strategy is constantly changing in the **lower ranks** of a company, those at the **top** might have **little idea** about what's going on in their business. This could lead to senior managers believing that the company is following a **particular direction**, but in **reality** it's going in a completely **different** direction.
3) It can be very difficult for **large companies** to implement an emergent strategy because the different parts of the business need to coordinate with each other. Emergent strategies work best in a company that has a flat organisational structure — **communication** is easier and **decisions** can be made more quickly.
4) Some organisations might be affected by certain **requirements** that don't allow for an emergent strategy. For example, the NHS will have a lot of its strategic decisions made for it by the **Government**.

Difficulties with Implementing Strategy

Strategic Drift happens when Strategy and Reality grow Apart

1) **Strategic drift** is what happens when **strategy** becomes **less and less suited** to the business's **environment**. It happens when a business's strategy **doesn't adapt** to keep up with **changes** in the **environment**.
2) Many different **factors** can cause strategic drift to happen. For example, new **technology**, changes in consumer **tastes** and **expectations**, and **legal**, **political** and **economic** factors. A business should **respond** to these changes, especially if **competitors** are benefiting from them.
3) Managers might react to poor results simply by **improving** the way the strategy is being **implemented**. If that doesn't work, managers may make **small alterations** to strategy, sticking mainly to what the business **knows** and does already. They may think it's too **risky** to introduce big changes, or there might be **resistance** to change, e.g. from employees, or managers worried about their own positions.
4) Small changes might work in the **short-term**, but as external change increases, **strategic drift** will **increase**. At this point, managers will be required to step out of their comfort zones to implement **big** strategic change — there will be lots of uncertainty as they try to decide what direction the business should go in. This **transformational change** will be needed for the business to survive.

Divorce Between Ownership and Control causes Conflicting Interests

1) In **small** firms, the **owner** often **manages** the firm on a day-to-day basis.
2) As a firm **grows**, the owner can raise finance by **selling shares**. The new shareholders become **part owners**, and the firm will be run by **directors**, who are appointed to **control** the business in the shareholders' interests.
3) This is known as the **divorce between ownership and control** — the owner(s) of the firm are **no longer** in day-to-day control. In large firms, much of the control will pass down to managers.
4) So there will be **different groups** with **ideas** and **influences** — e.g. the original owners, new shareholders, directors and managers might all have **different views** on **objectives** and **strategy**.

- **Corporate governance** describes the **power structure** of a business. It lays out how decisions should be made, the influence that different groups of stakeholders have on strategy, and the information that should be available to each group.
- When ownership and control are separate, a company could have internal and external **stakeholders** with many **different interests** competing for **influence** on strategy.
- For example, the **board of directors** might decide strategy, but shareholders appoint the board, so **shareholders** can also influence strategy by choosing board members who represent **their own interests**.
- **External stakeholders** can influence strategy by influencing **internal stakeholders**. For example, if a company has a lot of union members as employees, the **union** can call for strike action. Or if a **bank** funds a company, the bank can cut off funding and force the company to adopt a strategy that the bank prefers.
- Different groups of stakeholders **competing** for their own interests to be **represented** in a strategy can make it **difficult** to make **strategic decisions**.

Practice Questions

Q1 Give three examples for each of the following: a) difficulties in the strategic decision-making process,
b) difficulties in the implementation of strategy.

Q2 What is strategic drift?

Q3 How does divorce between ownership and control affect corporate governance?

Exam Question

Q1 Evaluate the advantages and disadvantages of following an emergent strategy. [20 marks]

In my divorce, I got the TV — but I lost ownership of the control...

It was dreadful. I had to get up and press buttons actually on the actual television set, can you believe. But then my armchair strategically drifted towards the telly, so I don't have to get up anymore. Look who's laughing now, Sandra.

Evaluating Strategy

Just one little page left now — and it's all about figuring out how well a strategy is working.

Strategies must be continually **Checked** and **Reviewed**

A business must **evaluate** whether its **strategy is working** — and whether it's on track to meet its overall objectives.

1) The managers who devise a strategy must **monitor** whether all parts of the firm are **meeting** their targets for implementing the **strategic changes**. They need to check that each **department** is **sticking** to its **timescale** and budgeted **resources**.
2) Plans include a series of deadlines by which certain **objectives** should be met. When each deadline is reached, **actual** performance should be measured against the **objectives** in the plan.
3) The **competitive environment** also needs to be monitored so that any **external factors** that could lead to **strategic drift** are **spotted** and **acted on**.
4) If **targets** or **objectives** are not being met, it's crucial to find out **why**. For example, it could be because a department isn't implementing the strategy **effectively**, or that a strategy is no longer **suitable** for the environment. **Action must be taken** to get back on track.

Businesses use **Various Techniques** to **Monitor** how the strategy is going

Businesses use **market analysis** and **management information systems** to measure the **performance** of the business and to monitor the progress of the strategy towards the business's objectives.

Market analysis shows if assumptions about the **market** are correct.

1) Firms use both primary and secondary **market research** to check how the strategy is proceeding.
2) They **audit sales levels**, concentrating particularly on the **target markets**. If there is a big **difference** between **expected** sales and **actual** sales, then the business will want to know why.

Management information systems provide most of the information.

1) **Management information systems** are computer systems that constantly **collect** and **process** routine departmental data, to give a picture of the **current state** of the business. One example of this is **Enterprise Resource Planning** (see p.167 for more). This data is used to see if the business is on course to meet its **objectives**.
2) Managers use **mathematical techniques** such as extrapolating trends to interpret the data.

Picture of the currant state.*

Practice Questions

Q1 Explain why a business needs to monitor its strategic performance.

Q2 Explain how management information systems can be used to monitor the progress of a strategy.

Exam Questions

Q1 Which of the following is not part of the process of evaluating strategic performance? [1 mark]

A Monitoring departmental targets.

B Measuring performance against objectives.

C Conducting network analysis.

D Monitoring the external environment.

Q2 A business plans a strategy for the next five years. To what extent do you agree that the strategy should only be evaluated at the end of the five-year period? [8 marks]

My strategy is so out of date, I get it evaluated on Antiques Roadshow...

This evaluating stuff is really important to a business — there's no point coming up with a brilliant strategy and then not checking it's working. And now all I've got left to say is 'Congrats!' for making it all the way to the end of the section.

*It's Wyoming, made of raisins... Obviously...

Maths Skills

There are loads of statistics involved in running a business, so you need to be able to understand what they all mean.

Businesses produce lots of **Statistics**

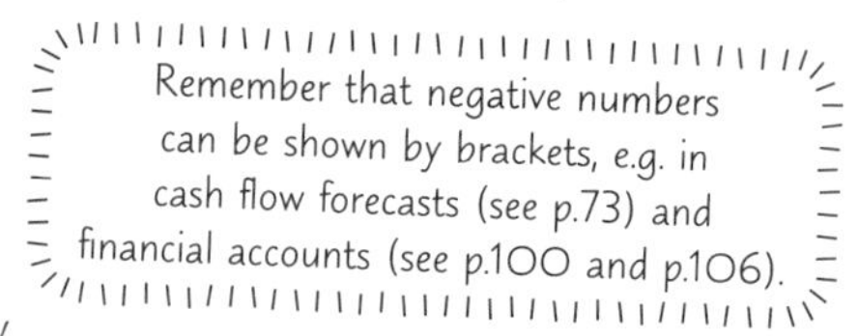

1) Businesses have a lot of **figures** — e.g. figures for sales, costs, revenues and profit, and market research data.
2) Businesses need to understand what their figures **mean** so that they know how well the business is **performing**, and can forecast how well it will perform in the **future**. In order to understand the data and be able to use it, they present it in a way that makes it **easy** to understand.

Diagrams make data **Easier** to **Understand**

1) **Pie charts** can be used to show **market share**. Each **1% share** is represented by a **3.6°** section of the pie (because there's 360° in a circle and 360 ÷ 100 = 3.6). Pie charts are **simple to use** and **easy** to **understand**. They can be created quickly using **spreadsheets**.

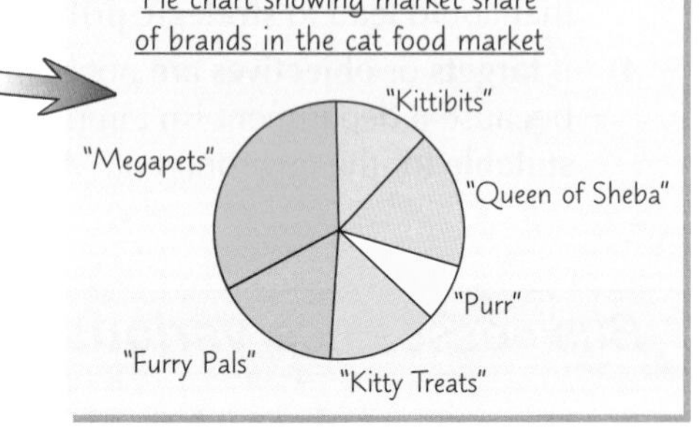

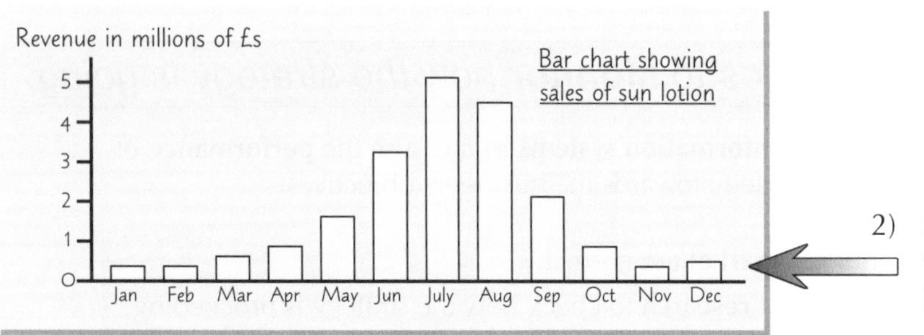

2) **Bar charts** show different values for a **single variable**. They're **easy** to **construct**, easy to **interpret** and they have **high visual impact**.
3) A **histogram** looks quite similar to a bar chart. However, in a histogram the **area** of each block is proportional to the value of the variable measured (not just the height), and there are no gaps between the blocks. So a histogram is different from a bar chart because the bars can vary in both **width** and **height**. Histograms are suitable for comparing variables with **large ranges**.
4) A **pictogram** is a bar chart or histogram where the bars are **pictures** — logos or images. Pictograms are often used in **corporate brochures** — e.g. Cadbury might use pictures of their choccie bars in their sales charts.
5) **Line graphs** plot one variable against another — e.g. sales against time (see p.32). **More than one line** can be shown to make comparisons — they should be in different colours to keep the graph easy to read.

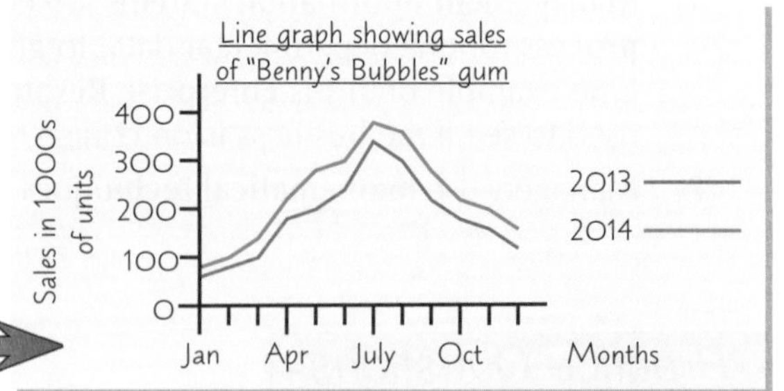

Diagrams can be **Misleading**

1) Graphs and charts can sometimes give a **false impression** of what is actually going on.
2) If the scales on a graph don't start at **zero**, it can be difficult to see what they show and the meaning can be distorted — e.g. the graph on the right seems to show that the profit has **tripled** between 2010 and 2013, but actually it has only gone up by **10%**.

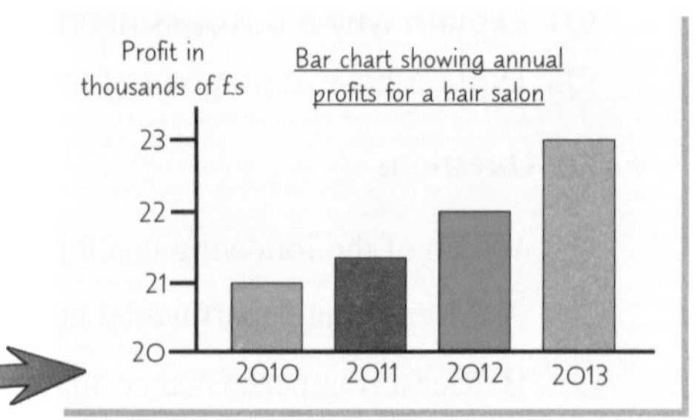

You need to be able to **Analyse Data** and **Graphs**

- As well as being able to read graphs and charts, you need to be able to **analyse** them.
- This means you need to be able to say what you think is the **important bit** of the chart — e.g. an upward trend in sales, or a big market share.
- You need to be able to say what you think is **causing** it, and what the potential **effects** might be — e.g. a **decrease** in market share might have been caused by the arrival of a new **competitor**, so the **marketing** budget will have to be **increased** to try to get the market share back.

Maths Skills

Data is clustered around an Average — Mean, Median or Mode

1) The **mean** is found by **adding together** all numbers in a data set and **dividing** the total by the **number of values** in the data set. Shops could calculate the mean spend per customer:

> **Example:** 5 customers spend £5.90, £27.97, £13.62, £24.95 and £78.81
>
> $$\textbf{Mean spend} = \frac{5.9 + 27.97 + 13.62 + 24.95 + 78.81}{5} = \frac{151.25}{5} = £30.25$$

2) The **median** is the **middle** value in a data set once all the values are put in **ascending order** — e.g. a business might rank all salespeople by the revenue they've generated over the past month, then identify the **median** and pay everyone above this position a bonus for good performance.
3) The **mode** is the **most common number** in a data set. E.g. Marks & Spencer might check the modal dress size when planning their shop displays so that the mannequins would reflect the most common body size among British women.
4) The **range** is the **difference** between the **largest** and the **smallest** in a group of numbers. It's not an average, but it's often used alongside averages.
5) A **confidence interval** is a range of values used to show the **uncertainty** of an **estimate**. E.g. if a business estimates sales of 2200 units, they might say that they are **95% confident** that the actual sales will be **between** 2000 and 2400. Luckily you don't have to calculate confidence intervals, you just need to know what they mean.

Confidence intervals are on p.34.

Index Numbers show Changes in data over time

1) **Index numbers** are a simple way of showing percentage changes in a set of data over time.
2) Businesses take a set of data showing revenue/profits etc. over a number of years, and make the earliest year the **base year** — the value for the base year is set as 100, and the figures for the following years are shown as a **percentage** of this figure. E.g. the table below shows the index numbers for revenue for an Italian restaurant:

Year	Total Revenue	Revenue Index (2010 = 100)
2010	£17 000	100
2011	£19 550	115
2012	£21 250	125
2013	£22 440	132
2014	£24 650	145

To work out the revenue index for any year, take the total revenue from that year, divide it by the total revenue in the base year and multiply it by 100, e.g. for 2013:

$$\frac{22\,440}{17\,000} \times 100 = 132$$

3) The main advantage of indexing is that it makes it easy to see trends within the business.

Rearrange Formulas to get them into the Form you Want

Sometimes you'll have to **rearrange** a formula before you put the numbers in. Rearrange so that the value you're trying to find is on one side of the formula, and everything else is on the other side.

> **Example:** A company selling novelty doorbells has fixed costs of £6000 and the variable cost per unit is £15. They have to sell 1500 units to break even. What is the selling price per unit?
>
> Use the formula: **Contribution per unit = selling price per unit – variable costs per unit**
>
> Rearrange to get the value you're looking for on its own:
>
> **Selling price per unit = contribution per unit + variable costs per unit**
>
> See p.78 for a reminder of the break-even formulas.
>
> But you don't know the contribution per unit, so you'll need another formula to work this out:
>
> $$\textbf{Break-even output} = \frac{\textbf{fixed costs}}{\textbf{contribution per unit}}$$
>
> Rearrange to get contribution per unit on its own: $\textbf{Contribution per unit} = \dfrac{\textbf{fixed costs}}{\textbf{break-even output}}$
>
> So: $\textbf{Selling price per unit} = \dfrac{\textbf{fixed costs}}{\textbf{break-even output}} + \textbf{variable costs per unit}$
>
> $= \dfrac{6000}{1500} + 15 = 4 + 15 = \mathbf{19}$. So each novelty doorbell must sell for **£19**.

Maths Skills

Businesses use **Percentage Changes** to **Analyse** Figures

1) Businesses work out **percentage** increases or decreases in figures like sales volume, revenue, profit and market share in order to see how performance is **progressing** over time. By looking at percentage changes over a number of months or years, they can see **trends** in the business's performance.

2) The **formula** for working out percentage change is:

$$\text{Percentage change} = \frac{\text{new figure} - \text{previous figure}}{\text{previous figure}} \times 100$$

E.g. if sales of hats have gone up from 9000 to 11 000, the percentage increase in sales is (11 000 – 9000) ÷ 9000 × 100 = 22.2%.

3) By rearranging the formula, you can **increase a figure** by a **percentage**:

$$\text{New figure} = \frac{\text{percentage change} \times \text{previous figure}}{100} + \text{previous figure}$$

E.g. if a business's profit was £40 000 in 2013 and it increased by 20% in 2014, then the 2014 profit was (20 × 40 000) ÷ 100 + 40 000 = 8000 + 40 000 = £48 000.

Related: 100 percentages that will restore your faith in humanity (#148 BLEW MY MIND)

Percentages, **Fractions** and **Ratios** are all **Related**

You could be given data about a company or a product in a few different ways, and you should be able to convert between them.

To get from **fractions to percentages**, times by 100. And to get from **percentages to fractions**, divide by 100 and simplify.

For example, if $\frac{1}{4}$ of a company's total revenue is profit, then $\frac{1}{4} \times 100 =$ **25%** of its total revenue is profit.

You can also convert from **fractions to ratios** — a ratio is a way of comparing one amount to another. Here, there is 1 part profit to 4 parts revenue, so the ratio of **total revenue to profit** is 4 : 1. This means that for every £4 of revenue, the company makes £1 of profit.

Example: During one year, the average number of employees at a company is 100, and 20 employees leave the company. Calculate the labour turnover as a percentage and as a fraction, and find the ratio of the number of employees leaving to the average number of employees.

$$\text{Labour Turnover (\%)} = \frac{\text{Number of staff leaving}}{\text{Average number of staff employed}} \times 100$$

See page 85 for more on labour turnover.

Labour Turnover (%) = $\frac{20}{100} \times 100 =$ **20%**, so labour turnover as a **fraction** is simply $\frac{20}{100} = \frac{1}{5}$.

The **ratio** of the number of employees leaving to the average number of employees is 20 : 100 or **1 : 5**.

Practice Questions

Q1 Why can graphs and charts sometimes be misleading?

Q2 Explain the difference between the "mean", "median" and "mode" of a set of data.

Q3 What do index numbers show?

Exam Questions

Q1 Discuss how statistics can hinder as well as help decision-making. [8 marks]

Answer on p.202.

Q2 Look back at the revenue table for the Italian restaurant on page 191. The restaurant owners now decide to take 2012 as their base year. Calculate the new revenue index for 2014. [2 marks]

Ladies and gentlemen, you have been warned — maths kills...

All this maths stuff can be very helpful, but it can also be biased. If you're given a table or graph as part of an exam question, watch out for things like how the axes are labelled, whether the axes start at zero, and whether important info is left out. Businesses often use graphs and charts to put their facts and figures in as good a light as possible.

The A-Level Exams

This page will get you familiar with how the A-level exams are set out, so there'll be no nasty surprises on the day.

A-Level Business has *Three Exam Papers*

1) A-level Business is made up of **three exams** — Paper 1 (Business 1), Paper 2 (Business 2) and Paper 3 (Business 3).
2) All three exams test the **whole A-level course** — that's **everything** in this book. They also test your **maths skills** — calculating and interpreting data crops up in different topics, and there are some more general maths skills you need as well (see section 15).
3) Each exam lasts for **2 hours** and is worth **100 marks**. Allowing for reading time, that means you need to achieve a **mark almost every minute**. Each paper counts for **33.333...%** of your A-level.
4) Each paper tests the same four **assessment objectives** (AOs). These are AO1 (**showing knowledge**), AO2 (**applying knowledge**), AO3 (**analysis**) and AO4 (**evaluation**) — there's more detail on each AO on the next page. The AOs have **different weightings** on each paper (see below).

At least 10% of the exam marks will be for maths skills.

Paper 1 has *Four Different Sections*

Paper 1 is made up of **four different sections** — Section A is worth **15 marks**, Section B is worth **35 marks** and Sections C and D are worth **25 marks each**. Each section is made up of different **types** of question.

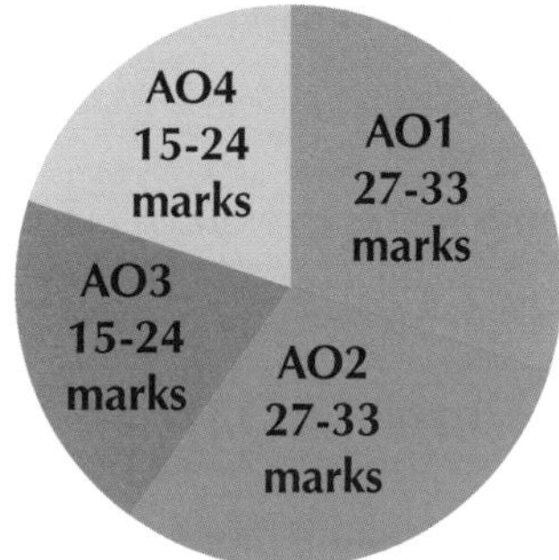

1) Section **A** is made up of **15 multiple choice questions**, worth **1 mark** each. There are 4 options to choose from for each question.
2) Section **B** is made up of **short-answer questions** that could be worth up to **9 marks** each. You'll need to **cover a few points** in these answers, or show a few steps of working in **calculation** questions.
3) In Sections **C** and **D**, you'll be given a **choice** of two questions — and you'll only have to answer **one** for each section. Each question is worth **25 marks**, so you'll have to write an **essay** to get all the marks.

Paper 2 has *Three Case Studies*

For Paper 2, you'll be given three mini **case studies** and asked **questions** about them (these are known as **data response questions**).

1) In each **case study**, you'll be given some **written information** or some **data** given in **graphs** and **tables** (e.g. costs or profits) — or a mix of both.
2) You'll be asked roughly **3 or 4 questions** on each case study, ranging from **short-answer questions** (worth around **3-4 marks**) to **extended-answer questions** (worth **16** or **20 marks**).
3) Some of the questions will involve **calculations** and **interpretation** based on the data you've been given.

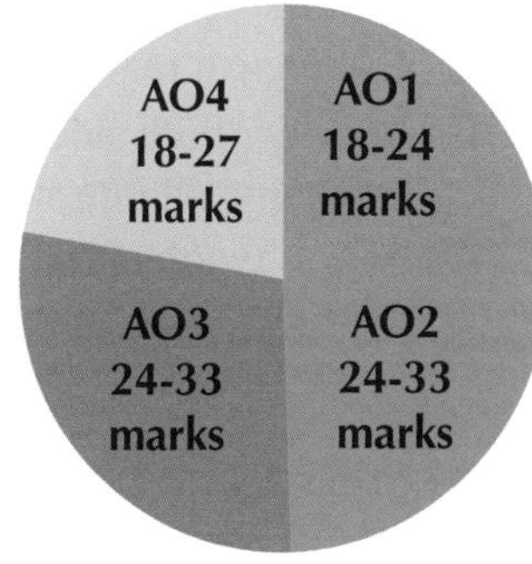

Paper 3 has *One Case Study*

For Paper 3, you'll be given one extended **case study** and asked **questions** about it.

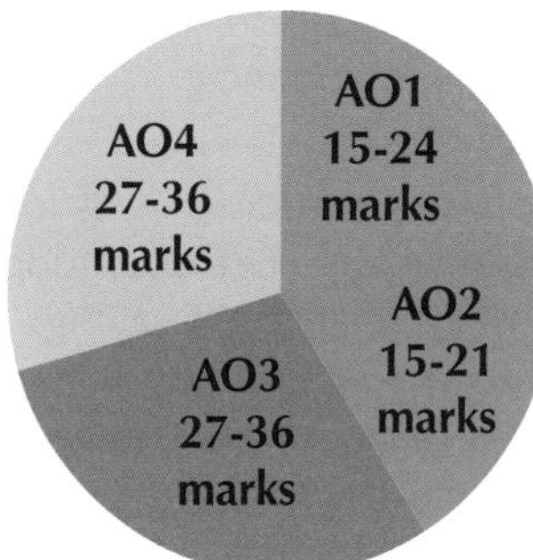

1) You'll be given a lot of information about a business, including **written information** and **data** for calculations.
2) You'll be asked about **6 questions** on the case study, ranging from **12 to 24 marks** each — they all require **longer answers**.
3) Even if the question doesn't ask you to do any **specific** calculations, you might need to do some calculations to **back up** your answer with **evidence**.

There are some **worked examples** of different types of question on pages 196-198.

Get Marks in Your A-Level Exams

These pages explain how the exams are marked. Basically, the marks are divided up into four different skills — AO1, AO2, AO3 and AO4. So to get all the marks, you need to demonstrate all the skills.

You get marks for **Showing Knowledge (AO1)** and **Applying Knowledge (AO2)**

AO1 and AO2 questions usually start with words like "**Describe**", "**Explain**" or "**Calculate**".

"**Describe**" questions ask you to say what something **shows** or **means**, "**explain**" means you have to **give reasons** for something and "**calculate**" means you have to **work something out**.

1) **AO1** marks are for **knowledge** of e.g. **terms, methods** and **theories**.
2) This means things like knowing the **proper definitions** for **business terms** (this is often what you're asked for in **multiple choice** questions).
3) For a multiple choice question, you'll get **1 mark** for AO1. For longer questions, you'll usually get between **2-5 marks** for AO1, whether the question is a **short-answer** one worth 4 marks, or an **extended-answer** one worth 16, 24 or 25 marks.

To make sure you get these marks, always give definitions of terms you're using, or formulas if you're doing a calculation.

1) **AO2** marks are for **application** — applying your knowledge to a situation. This means thinking about the **type of business** in the **question**, the product or service it's selling, and the type of market it's in.
2) Numerical **calculations** and **interpretation** are also awarded **application** marks.
3) AO2 is usually worth **2-3 marks**, but questions which want you to demonstrate AO2 will be expecting you to demonstrate **AO1** too, so they'll be worth between **3 and 6 marks** overall.

You'll get more marks when you **Analyse (AO3)** and **Evaluate (AO4)**

AO3 marks are for **analysis** — thinking about benefits, drawbacks, influences, effects and limitations.

Analysis questions often start with the word "**Analyse**".

1) Use your knowledge to **explain** your answer and give **reasons**.
2) If there's data, say what the figures **mean**, talk about what might have **caused** them and say what **effect** you think they will have on the business in the **future**.
3) Use **logical reasoning** to link **influences, actions** and their **effects** together.
4) Consider **both sides** of the **argument** — you can only get **limited** analysis **marks** by looking at **one side**.
5) AO3 is worth about **4-6 marks** — but the questions will expect you to demonstrate **AO1** and **AO2** (and maybe even **AO4**) as well. AO3 marks are usually given for **longer-answer** questions (worth **9**, **12**, **16** or **20 marks**).

Lucinda, Tarquin, Jemima and Angelica were experts at demonstrating AOs 1-4.

AO4 marks are for **evaluation** — using your **judgement**.

Evaluation questions usually start with words like "**Evaluate**", "**Justify**" or "**To what extent**".

1) **Weigh up** both sides of the argument — consider the **advantages** and **disadvantages** and say which **side** of the argument you think is **strongest**.
2) Make sure you **justify** your opinions — you should always give **evidence** to support your views.
3) Remember to consider **all** the factors involved when you're asked to consider the importance of a **particular factor**. This is essential when answering "**to what extent**" questions.
4) You don't always need a **definite** answer. You can point out that it **depends** on various factors — as long as you say **what the factors are**, and say **why** your answer would depend on those factors. Use your judgement to say what the **most important factors** are. The most important thing is to **justify** what you're saying.
5) AO4 is usually worth **7-10 marks**. It's tested in **extended-answer** questions (worth between **16** and **25 marks**) and you'll have to demonstrate **AOs 1-3** in these questions as well.

Get Marks in Your A-Level Exams

*Make sure you write **Clearly** and **Structure** your answers well*

1) You have to use the **right style** of writing and **arrange relevant information clearly** — write in **full sentences** and **link** your points together. Don't just write a list of bullet points. You need to use **specialist vocabulary** when it's appropriate, so it's well worth **learning** the **fancy terms** used in this book.
2) You have to write **neatly** enough for the examiner to be able to read it. You also need to use good **spelling**, **grammar** and **punctuation** to make your meaning **crystal clear**. Don't worry, you won't lose marks for spelling errors — but if your handwriting, grammar, spelling and punctuation are **so** far up the spout that the examiner **can't understand** what you've written, then it's a **problem**.
3) You won't get any marks for **written communication** — but you might **lose marks** if the examiner can't **read** or **understand** your writing.

Jotting down a quick plan will help with extended-answer questions or essay questions.

Dudley got no marks for his "Boston Matrix in Mime".

*The **Examiner** will try to show you **How Much to Write***

1) The examiner does try to help you by telling you how many **marks** each question is worth and by giving you an idea of how **much** you need to write. The **more lines** there are for an answer, the **more** you're expected to **write**.
2) Remember, you're aiming to score **a mark a minute** — so if a question is worth **5 marks**, you should spend about **5 minutes** on it.
3) Generally, if the question is worth **2 or 3 marks** then you just need to show your business **knowledge**. Give a **short answer** and move on quickly.
4) For a question worth **16 or more marks**, you need to show **analysis** and **evaluation**. You'll have to write much more for these questions. They usually expect you to make a **decision**, or have an **opinion** and be able to **justify** it. There's rarely a right or wrong answer to this sort of question, so just **convince** the examiner that your opinion is **valid** by **explaining** your reasons (based on your business knowledge).

*Don't forget to include **All** the **Skills** in **Extended-Answer Questions***

1) When you come up against a long question (worth, say, 16 marks), **don't jump** straight to the **evaluation** stage. The examiner will be looking for **evidence** of the **other skills**, too.
2) Remember, a question testing **AO4** will also be testing **AOs 1-3** — so you need to demonstrate **all** of the assessment objectives (see previous page).
3) So, if they ask you how a business can increase its profits, and you think it should either decrease its **operating expenses** or make some staff **redundant**, you need to:

    1) **Define** what is meant by operating expenses and redundancy (this will get you your **AO1** marks).
    2) Explain how operating expenses/redundancy are **relevant** to the type of **business** in the question (for **AO2** marks).
    3) Give the **advantages** and **disadvantages** of each method of increasing profits (for **AO3** marks).
    4) Finally, for the **AO4** marks, **weigh up** both sides of the argument and **decide** if the business should decrease its operating expenses or make some staff redundant (you might decide it needs to do both).

For an example of an extended answer, which demonstrates all the skills, see p.197-198.

It's exam time — let's get down to business...

These pages should take some of the surprise out of your exams. You don't need to know this upside down and back to front like you do the actual business stuff. What you do need to know is what the examiners actually want to see from you — not just that you know the facts, but also that you understand and can use what you've learnt.

Worked Exam Questions

Here's an example of the kind of case study and questions you might get in Paper 2 or Paper 3.

Crinkle Cakes Ltd

Crinkle Cakes Ltd is a business that makes cakes, set up by Janet Jones, who made cakes in her own kitchen to sell to family and friends. Over eight years, it has grown from a sole trader business to a medium-sized private limited company. Although Ms Jones still plays an important day-to-day role in the business, it is no longer based in her kitchen. The business now operates out of premises equipped with machinery which allows them to produce 50 cakes per hour. Crinkle Cakes employs 40 staff on both full-time and part-time contracts.

The business operates in a very competitive market which is dominated by two national bakeries. It also faces competition from a long-established local firm, which has an excellent reputation in the area. In order to ensure the long-term survival of the business, Crinkle Cakes needs to compete more effectively and achieve its objective of increasing both sales and market share. Money is tight though, since the machinery was obtained using a bank loan which is still being paid off.

Crinkle Cakes aims to sell its products in the big supermarkets, but so far has been unable to secure a deal to supply any of the major chains. The main reasons the supermarkets gave for not stocking Crinkle Cakes products were that they had a very narrow product range (selling only whole cakes rather than multi-pack slices or individual portions), and that their cakes were priced higher than competing bakeries.

The marketing manager has been looking at ways to expand the product range. He did some market research into the types of cakes consumers buy, and the results are displayed below (see Table 1). He also examined the prices of the cakes in their market. Crinkle Cakes had originally aimed to charge prices that could compete with the local competitor, but the reality is that Crinkle Cakes's prices are on average 10% higher than their local competitor's and approximately 30% higher than the national competitors'. The marketing manager wants to decrease the price of their cakes, but to do this the company will have to cut costs.

The operations manager has been looking at ways to cut costs. She has discovered that one problem is the rising cost of ingredients from their suppliers. Table 2 shows the expenditure budget and their actual expenditure for a typical month.

Table 1

Results from Market Research (Percentage of People Asked)

Product	Purchased weekly	Purchased monthly	Purchased rarely	Never purchased
Whole cakes	2	8	62	28
Multi-pack, e.g. slices	55	23	14	8
Individual portions	67	17	10	6

Table 2

Expenditure Budget

	Budget	Actual	Variance
Raw materials	£20k	£30k	£10k (A)
Staff costs	£50k	£48k	£2k (F)
Marketing	£5k	£8k	£3k (A)
Insurance & utility bills	£10k	£8k	£2k (F)
Other	£5k	£4k	£1k (F)

An ***Example Short Question and Answer*** to give you some tips:

Q1 Crinkle Cakes Ltd is a private limited company.
Explain **two** features of the legal structure of Crinkle Cakes Ltd. [4 marks]

Crinkle Cakes is owned by its shareholders, who have bought shares privately. The shares cannot be bought by the public and won't be quoted on a stock exchange.

The shareholders of Crinkle Cakes have limited liability, which means that they are not personally responsible for the debts of the business. The only money they can lose is the money they have invested in the company.

Other points that could have been made include the fact that Crinkle Cakes doesn't have a minimum share capital requirement and that a shareholder will need the agreement of other shareholders to sell their shares.

Worked Exam Questions

An **Example Extended Question and Answer** to give you some tips:

Q2 Crinkle Cakes Ltd are considering changing their marketing mix to make the business more competitive. To what extent do you think that the product is the most important element of the mix to change? [16 marks]

The marketing mix is all the factors a business has to take into account when marketing a product. This is more commonly referred to as "the seven Ps" of product, price, place, promotion, people, physical environment and process. In order to adapt a marketing mix it is necessary to examine each of these factors in turn.

There are a number of ways in which Crinkle Cakes could make changes to the product. At present they produce mainly whole cakes, which 28% of customers never buy according to the research findings in Table 1. This has meant that few supermarkets have shown a willingness to sell Crinkle Cakes' products. Based on this, one change would be to make a wider range of cake sizes. In addition to the whole cakes, they could introduce a multi-pack containing cake slices, aimed at families, and single-slice packs, perhaps aimed at single people or impulse buyers. This would increase the market segments they appeal to and increase the likelihood of sales to the big supermarkets. Another alteration that Crinkle Cakes could make to their products is to target niche markets (e.g. by making gluten-free products), which would reduce their competition and would mean that they could charge higher prices and still be competitive. However, this may require further market research.

Another element of the marketing mix is price. The case study states that Crinkle Cakes charges higher prices than its competitors, but that this is necessary because of costs, e.g. of ingredients. Table 2 shows that they are paying £10K per month more for their raw materials than budgeted, which will impact on costs and the prices they can charge. To be able to charge more competitive prices, Crinkle Cakes could cut costs, e.g. by negotiating a better deal with their supplier, or by changing suppliers. Lower prices would make the cakes more appealing to consumers and especially the big supermarkets. Or, instead of trying to reduce prices, the company could market the cakes as a luxury item (or aimed at a particular niche market) to justify the prices.

As far as place is concerned, Crinkle Cakes could take steps to get their products into the major supermarkets, which should be possible if they make the changes to the product size already discussed. Crinkle Cakes could also attempt to supply high-end bakeries if they decide to sell luxury cakes.

The case study does not give any detail about what promotion has taken place. The company could reposition their brand as a luxury cake company in order to differentiate themselves from their competitors. They could also consider promoting their products through a company website or social media to increase awareness and demand.

There is very little information in the case study about the people, physical environment and process of Crinkle Cakes, so it is not possible to recommend how to improve these factors.

In conclusion, adapting the product is very important to the continued success of Crinkle Cakes, but there are other factors that need to change too.

Margin notes:

- Stating knowledge is fine, but don't waste too much time on it
- AO1: Refers to, and defines, marketing mix
- AO2: Links knowledge about marketing mix to business in question
- Make use of information in the case study
- AO3: Identifies problems and suggests solutions
- Apply your suggestions to the business in question
- AO4: Evaluates the impact of changes to the product
- AO2: Links issue of price to business in question
- Make use of information in the case study
- AO3: Identifies problems and suggests solutions
- AO4: Evaluates the impact of changes to the price
- This is a little vague
- AO3: Links marketing decisions with actions
- Here you could refer to Table 2, which shows an adverse variance for marketing costs that could limit changes to promotion
- This is too brief
- AO4: Makes vague attempt at overall analysis

- This is a reasonably good answer and would get about **12 marks**. It considers a range of changes to the marketing mix and applies them to the business in the case study. This answer has been set out sensibly with a separate paragraph for each aspect of the marketing mix.
- However, it doesn't use the information given in Table 2 when talking about promotion, and the last three Ps have been skimmed over. Although there isn't much information in the case study, it would have been good to make **suggestions** on how to use these factors to increase competitiveness.
- The **conclusion** is poor and doesn't add anything to the answer. It doesn't really answer the question, and doesn't cover the 'to what extent' element of the question.

Worked Exam Questions

An **Essay Question and Answer** to give you some tips:

Q3 To what extent is product development a good choice of a marketing growth strategy for a multi-product business? [25 marks]

States knowledge but doesn't spend too long on it

AO1: Describes Ansoff's growth strategies

The main marketing growth strategies that a company should consider, as outlined by Ansoff, are market penetration, product development, market development and diversification. The multi-product business should assess all these options before deciding on the best course of action.

Comes up with an example business to help illustrate point

AO3: Suggests a potential problem and gives reasons why it might not matter

Could do with explaining how this links to the question.

Product development means a business tries to sell new products in the market it currently operates in. So for a cleaning product business, it would need to develop a new cleaning product to sell to its existing customers. This is a good strategy in a market with growth potential, but much less effective in a saturated market. This strategy also depends on the research and development department and their ability to produce innovative new products; however, as the business already offers a number of products, it can be assumed that developing a new one is within their capabilities. A multi-product business will also benefit from economies of scope. This is a good strategy to pursue if the business already has a high market share.

AO2: Links knowledge to business in question

Could do with recommending which option to take

AO4: Evaluates other factors and makes recommendation

Market penetration is when a business tries to increase its market share in the market it currently operates in. As the business has multiple products, its market share may vary for its different products. One product could have a high market share in its individual market, whereas another's market share might be quite low. The business must decide whether it wants to try to increase its market share for all its products, or just to focus on one or two. Before choosing this strategy, the business must consider the condition of its market. If the market is growing, then this is a good strategy, as demand is still growing. However, if the market is saturated, market penetration is not a good strategy for them, as they will struggle to increase their market share.

Could also evaluate the cost of this strategy

AO3: Considers other action that may be needed

Considers each strategy in turn

Explains how the company could pursue this strategy

Market development is when a business tries to sell to a new market or segment. This can be done by repositioning the products to appeal to different consumers, or by adapting the product slightly to meet different needs. To do this, a business needs to carry out market research and come up with a new marketing campaign. An example of market development is if the cleaning product company targeted the industrial sector of the market, rather than individual consumers.

AO4: Makes recommendation and justifies it

Finally, a business could consider diversification. Diversification is trying to sell a new product to a new market, and is the most risky and most expensive strategy, as the business probably won't have any knowledge or experience of the market they're moving into. The research and development team would need to develop a new product, taking into account their existing capabilities. Diversification is a good strategy when high profits are likely, or when a business does not want to rely too heavily on a limited range of products; however in the case of a multi-product business, this is probably not a concern, so diversification is unlikely to be the best strategy.

AO4: Good conclusion that answers the question with justification

Conclusion is related to the business in the question

In conclusion, product development is probably the best strategy for a multi-product business to take. The business already has a number of products, so adding another product to the range is a sensible and realistic option. However, they must take the state of the market, the economy and their own financial position into account before pursuing any strategic decision.

- This is a **pretty good** answer and would get you **most** of the marks. It **considers** all four of Ansoff's marketing growth strategies, and **examines** each one in context of the company.
- It has a clear **conclusion** which **answers the question** — with a **recommendation** as to which strategy is the best for this company (but also takes into account **other factors** that might influence the decision).

Answers to Numerical Questions

Section One

Page 7 — Exam Questions

Q1 Total costs = 23 + 54 = 77% of revenue ***[1 mark]***
So profit = 100 – 77 = 23% of revenue ***[1 mark]***
23% of £650 000 = £149 500 ***[1 mark]***

Q2 a)

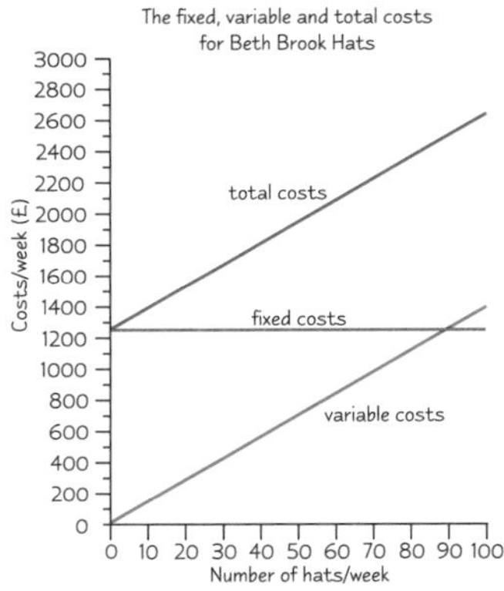

[6 marks available — 1 mark for each correct start/finish point of each line]

b) Costs at 60 hats per week
= fixed costs + variable costs ***[1 mark]***
= 1260 + (60 × 14) = £1260 + £840
= £2100 ***[1 mark]***
Revenue = selling price × quantity sold
= £50 × 60 = £3000 ***[1 mark]***
Profit = revenue – costs = £3000 – £2100
= £900 ***[1 mark]***

Section Two

Page 23 — Exam Question

Q1 a)

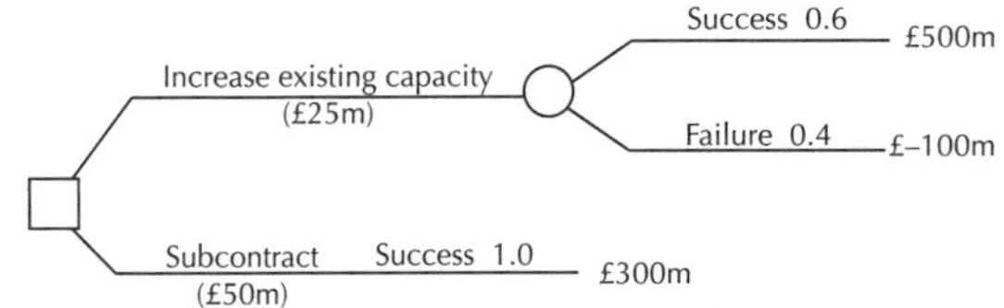

[4 marks available — 1 mark for two branches for the courses of action, 1 mark for the correct probabilities for increasing existing capacity, 1 mark for the correct pay-offs for increasing existing capacity, 1 mark for the correct probability and pay-off for subcontracting]

b) Expected value of increasing existing capacity:
(0.6 × 500m) + (0.4 × –100m) ***[1 mark]***
= 300m – 40m ***[1 mark]*** = £260m ***[1 mark]***
Net gain = £260m – £25m = £235m ***[1 mark]***
Expected value of subcontracting:
1.0 × 300m ***[1 mark]*** = £300m ***[1 mark]***
Net gain = £300m – £50m = £250m ***[1 mark]***
Based on the decision tree, the company should subcontract ***[1 mark]***

Section Three

Page 29 — Exam Questions

Q1 a) If they increase their 2013 sales by 10% they will sell:
(250 × 10%) + 250 = 275 units ***[1 mark]***
They actually sold 290 units in 2014 so they have met their objective. ***[1 mark]***

Page 33 — Exam Question

Q1 a)

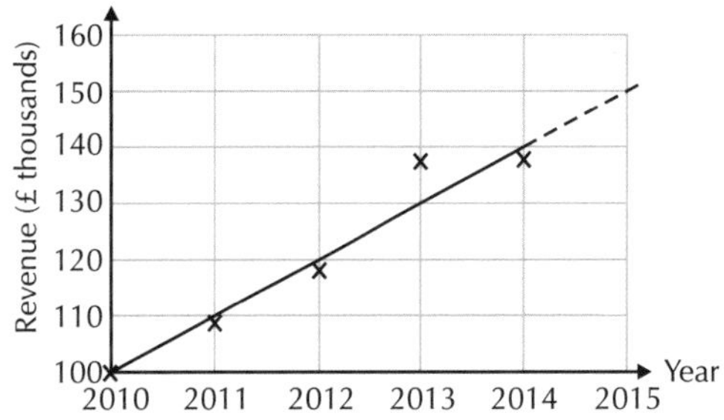

So in 2015 the estimated revenue is £150 000.

[3 marks available — 1 mark for drawing a line of best fit, 1 mark for extrapolating your line to 2015, 1 mark for reading the value from your graph correctly]

Page 37 — Exam Questions

Q1 The company's current revenue is
£1500 × 200 = £300 000 ***[1 mark]***

Price elasticity of demand

$$= \frac{\text{\% change in quantity demanded}}{\text{\% change in price}}$$ ***[1 mark]***

So, % change in quantity demanded
= price elasticity of demand × % change in price
= –0.7 × 15% = –10.5% ***[1 mark]***

The new price of a horse will be
£1500 + (£1500 × 15%) = £1725 ***[1 mark]***

100 – 10.5 = 89.5%
The company will sell
200 × 89.5% = 179 horses ***[1 mark]***

The company's new revenue will be
179 × £1725 = £308 775 ***[1 mark]***

Which is an increased revenue of
£308 775 – £300 000 = £8775 ***[1 mark]***

Answers to Numerical Questions

Section Four

Page 57 — Practice Questions

Q1 Capacity utilisation (%) = $\frac{\text{output}}{\text{capacity}} \times 100$

$= \frac{44}{64} \times 100 = 68.75\%$

Q3 Unit cost = $\frac{\text{total costs}}{\text{units output}} = \frac{£1719}{450} = £3.82$

Page 57 — Exam Question

Q1 a) Weekly capacity = 7 × 3 × 300
= 6300 ***[1 mark]***

Capacity utilisation (%) = $\frac{\text{output}}{\text{capacity}} \times 100$

$= \frac{2205}{6300} \times 100$ ***[1 mark]***

= 35% ***[1 mark]***

Page 59 — Practice Questions

Q1 Output per hour = 168 000 ÷ 35 = 4800 m^2

Labour productivity = $\frac{\text{output per period}}{\text{number of employees}}$

$= \frac{4800}{4}$

= 1200 m^2 per worker per hour

So the correct option is C.

Page 64 — Practice Questions

Q3 Re-order level = lead time × average daily usage + buffer stock level
= 5 × 9 + 7 = 52 units

Page 64 — Exam Question

Q1

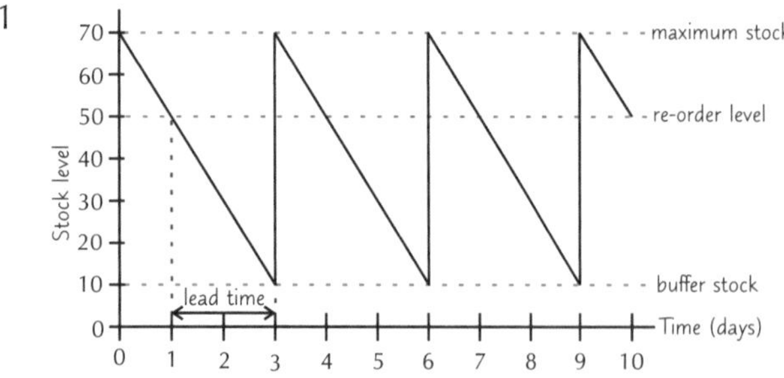

[4 marks available — 1 mark for the correct maximum and buffer stock, 1 mark for the correct reorder level, 1 mark for the correct lead time and 1 mark for the black line drawn correctly]

Section Five

Page 71 — Practice Questions

Q1 Percentage change in profit

$= \frac{\text{current year's profit} - \text{previous year's profit}}{\text{previous year's profit}} \times 100$

$= \frac{52\,000 - 50\,000}{50\,000} \times 100 = \frac{2000}{50\,000} \times 100 = 4\%$

Q2 Profit for the year = operating profit + other profit – net finance costs – tax
= £21 000 + £3000 – £2000 – £6000
= £16 000

Page 71 — Exam Questions

Q2 a) Operating profit = sales revenue – cost of sales – operating expenses
= gross profit – operating expenses ***[1 mark]***
= £750 000 – £250 000 = £500 000 ***[1 mark]***

Operating profit margin (%)

$= \frac{\text{operating profit}}{\text{sales revenue}} \times 100$ ***[1 mark]***

$= \frac{£500\,000}{£2\,000\,000} \times 100 = 25\%$ ***[1 mark]***

Page 73 — Practice Questions

Q3 Net cash flow = cash inflows – cash outflows
= £8000 – £9500 = (£1500)

Q4 Closing balance = opening balance + net cash flow
= £20 000 + (£7000) = £13 000

Page 75 — Practice Questions

Q2 Profit budget = income budget – expenditure budget
Rearranging gives:
Expenditure budget = income budget – profit budget
= £125 000 – £30 000 = £95 000

Page 77 — Practice Questions

Q2 Variance = £15 000 – £18 000 = £3000 (A)
so there is a £3000 adverse variance.

Page 77 — Exam Question

Q1 a)

	Feb cumulative variance	Mar budget	Mar actual	Mar variance	Mar cumulative variance
Revenue	£10k (A)	£110k	£120k	£10k (F)	£0
Wages	£9k (F)	£40k	£39k	£1k (F)	£10k (F)
Rent	£1k (A)	£10k	£11k	£1k (A)	£2k (A)
Other costs	£2k (A)	£5k	£5k	£0	£2k (A)
Total costs	£6k (F)	£55k	£55k	£0	£6k (F)

[10 marks available — 1 mark for each of the variances in red]

Answers to Numerical Questions

Page 79 — Exam Questions

Q2 Contribution per unit = selling price per unit – variable costs per unit ***[1 mark]***
= £13 – £5 = £8 ***[1 mark]***

Break-even output $= \dfrac{\text{fixed costs}}{\text{contribution per unit}}$ ***[1 mark]***

$= \dfrac{£1000}{£8}$ = 125 customers ***[1 mark]***

Section Six

Page 85 — Practice Questions

Q2 Labour cost per unit $= \dfrac{\text{labour costs}}{\text{units of output}}$

Labour costs = units of output × labour cost per unit
= 50 × £100 = £5000

Q4 Labour Turnover (%)

$= \dfrac{\text{number of staff leaving}}{\text{average number of staff employed}} \times 100$

$= \dfrac{18}{600} \times 100 = 3\%$

Section Eight

Page 106 — Exam Question

Q1 E.g.

Revenue	£1 500 000
Cost of sales	(£500 000)
Gross profit	**£1 000 000**
Operating expenses	(£250 000)
Operating profit	**£750 000**
Other expenses	(£100 000)
Profit before tax	**£650 000**
Tax	(£130 000)
Profit after tax	**£520 000**
Dividends	(£250 000)
Retained profit	**£270 000**

[16 marks available — 1 mark for correctly writing the revenue and expenses, 1 mark for naming the five measures of profit, 1 mark for ordering the five profits correctly, 1 mark for each correctly calculated profit, 8 marks for a suitable analysis]

Page 110 — Exam Questions

Q1 ROCE $= \dfrac{\text{operating profit}}{\text{total equity + non-current liabilities}} \times 100$

$= \dfrac{£50\,000}{£130\,000 + £30\,000} \times 100$

$= 31.25\%$

So answer C is correct ***[1 mark]***

Q3 a) Current ratio $= \dfrac{\text{current assets}}{\text{current liabilities}}$

$= \dfrac{£40\,000}{£50\,000}$ ***[1 mark]***

= 0.8 ***[1 mark]***

b) Inventory turnover

$= \dfrac{\text{cost of sales}}{\text{cost of average stock held}}$

$= \dfrac{£120\,000}{£80\,000}$ ***[1 mark]***

= 1.5 ***[1 mark]***

Page 112 — Exam Questions

Q1 Gearing (%)

$= \dfrac{\text{non-current liabilities}}{\text{total equity + non-current liabilities}} \times 100$

$= \dfrac{£20\,000}{£30\,000 + £20\,000} \times 100$ ***[1 mark]***

$= \dfrac{£20\,000}{£50\,000} \times 100$ ***[1 mark]***

= 0.4 × 100 = 40% ***[1 mark]***

Section Nine

Page 127 — Practice Questions

Q4 £0.49 = $1
80 ÷ 0.49 = 163.265..., so £80 = $163.27

Section Ten

Page 139 — Exam Questions

Q1 Overall net return = £320 000 – £40 000 – £200 000 = £80 000 ***[1 mark]***.

Average net return $= \dfrac{£80\,000}{8}$ = £10 000 ***[1 mark]***

ARR $= \dfrac{\text{average net return}}{\text{investment}} \times 100$

So ARR $= \dfrac{£10\,000}{£200\,000} \times 100$ = 5% ***[1 mark]***

Q2 Payback period $= \dfrac{\text{amount invested}}{\text{annual net return}} =$

$\dfrac{£11000}{£3000}$ = 3.67 years (or 3 years and 8 months).

[1 mark for working, 1 mark for answer]

Answers to Numerical Questions

Section Fourteen

Page 185 — Exam Question

Q1 a)

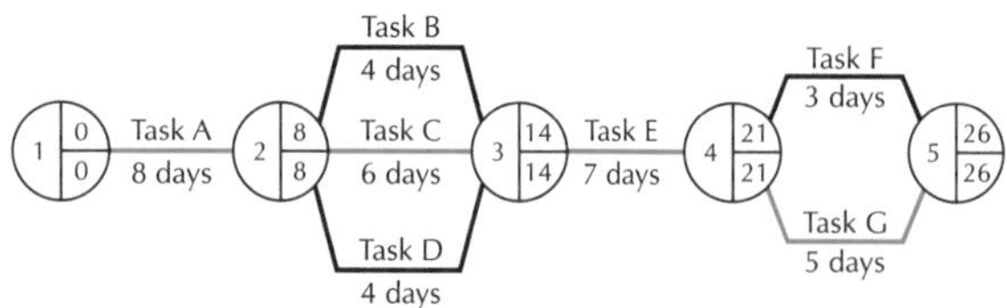

[9 marks available — 3 marks for putting (A), (B, C and D), (E), and (F and G) in the right order, or 2 marks for 1 error, or 1 mark for 2 errors. 1 mark for B, C and D as simultaneous, 1 mark for F and G as simultaneous. 1 mark per node (2, 3, 4 and 5) fully correct.]

b) ***[1 mark for the critical path (the thick pink line on the diagram), 1 mark for the total time — 26 days]***

c) Float times for B and F are both 2 days. ***[1 mark for each]***

Section Fifteen

Page 192 — Exam Questions

Q2 Divide revenue of 2014 by the revenue of the base year (2012) and multiply by 100:

$\frac{24650}{21250} \times 100$ ***[1 mark]*** = 116 ***[1 mark]***

Glossary

Ansoff's matrix Shows the strategies that a firm can use to expand, according to how risky they are.

asset Anything that a business owns.

balance sheet A snapshot of a firm's finances at a particular time.

barrier to entry An obstacle that makes it harder for companies to enter a market.

benchmarking Identifying how to improve your business by comparing its performance, products and processes against those of another firm.

big data A term used to describe the vast quantities of data that can be collected from various sources.

Blake Mouton grid A grid used to define managers according to how much they care about employees and about production.

Boston Matrix A matrix that compares a firm's products based on their market growth and market share.

Bowman's strategic clock Shows positioning strategies based on different combinations of price and perceived added value/benefits.

break-even analysis Identifies the point where a company's total revenues equal its total costs.

budget Forecasts future earnings and future spending.

capacity utilisation How much of its maximum capacity a business is using.

capital A company's wealth in the form of money or other assets.

capital expenditure Money used to buy fixed assets (also called fixed capital).

Carroll's Pyramid of CSR This is a diagram showing four elements of CSR as layers in a pyramid.

cash flow Money that moves in and out of a business over a set period of time.

centralisation A way to structure a business where all decisions come from a few key people.

channel of distribution The route a product takes from the producer to the consumer.

competitive advantage The way that a company offers customers better value than competitors do — generally either lower prices or more product features.

confidence interval A range in which you can say, with a certain level of confidence, that a value lies.

confidence level A percentage (often 95% or 99%) showing how confident you are that a value falls within a confidence interval.

Consumer Price Index This measures changes in prices of a sample of consumer goods and services. It measures inflation.

contingency plan A plan preparing for an event that's unlikely to happen, just in case it does.

contribution The difference between the selling price and the variable costs of a product.

core competence A unique feature of a business that gives it a competitive advantage.

corporate objective A goal of a business as a whole.

corporate social responsibility (CSR) A company's contribution to society.

correlation The relationship between two variables.

cost-push inflation When rising costs (e.g. for raw materials or labour) push up prices.

creditor Someone who a business owes money to.

critical path In network analysis, the series of activities that is critical in the timing of the overall project.

current ratio A liquidity ratio that compares current assets to current liabilities.

debt capital The capital raised by borrowing (also called loan capital).

debtor Someone who owes money to a business.

decentralisation A way to structure a business where decisions are shared across the company.

decision tree A method of analysing the expected pay-offs of different business decisions.

delayering Reducing the number of levels in the hierarchy of an organisation.

demand-pull inflation When a rise in disposable income means there's too much demand for too few goods, leading to businesses increasing prices.

demographic change A change in the structure of a population.

depreciation Loss of value over time — fixed assets often depreciate.

developed country A relatively rich country with a high GDP.

developing country A relatively poor country with a low GDP.

dimensions of national culture A model used to compare the differences in cultural values between different countries.

director A person responsible for running a company.

discrimination When one group of people is unfairly treated differently to others, e.g. due to race, age or gender.

diversification Selling new products to new markets.

Glossary

divorce between ownership and control When the owners of a company no longer have total control.

earliest start time (EST) In network analysis, the earliest time that an activity can possibly start.

economic growth The rate of increase in GDP.

economies of scale When the cost of producing each item decreases as the scale of production increases.

economies of scope When a single company can make two or more products more cheaply than they can be made by separate companies.

elasticity of demand Shows the relationship between changes in demand for a product and the change in another variable (such as price or income).

Elkington's Triple Bottom Line model A model that assesses performance by considering three overlapping areas: profit, people and planet.

embargo A ban on trade with particular countries.

emergent strategy A form of strategy that develops over time, based on experience and changes in the environment.

emerging economy A developing country with a fast growing, but not yet fully developed, economy.

employment tribunal A type of court which hears disputes between employers and employees.

equity capital The capital raised by selling shares.

ethical Morally and professionally acceptable.

exchange rate The value of one currency in terms of another, e.g. £1 = €1.36.

fiscal policy The government's method of adjusting tax rates and its spending to control the economy.

fixed asset An asset that a business keeps long-term or uses repeatedly — e.g. property, equipment, land, computers.

fixed cost A cost that stays the same — no matter how much or how little a firm produces.

flat structure An organisational structure that has few layers of management.

float time The amount of time a non-critical activity can be delayed without delaying the completion of the entire project.

force field analysis A technique used to analyse forces for and against change.

forecasting Trying to predict what will happen in the future.

franchising An agreement which allows one business to use the name, knowledge and processes of an established business.

functional objective An objective of an individual department or business function.

gearing The proportion of a business financed through debt rather than equity or reserves.

globalisation The increase in how interconnected the world is.

gross domestic product (GDP) The total market value of goods and services produced within a nation over a period of time (usually a year).

historical budget A budget based on previous budgets.

Human Resource Management (HRM) Looks after all the people-related aspects of a business — like recruitment and training.

income statement Statement showing how much money's gone into and out of a company over a period of time.

inflation An increase in the price of goods and services.

infrastructure The basic facilities such as roads, railways, power lines, water pipes and communication networks that allow society to function.

innovation Coming up with new ideas, products and processes.

insolvent Unable to pay debts.

interest rate The fee paid for borrowing.

inventory A business's entire stock.

inventory turnover ratio How many times a year a business sells and replaces all its stock.

just-in-time (JIT) production Manufacturing process that operates with very small amounts of stock.

kaizen A lean production method that involves encouraging everyone to constantly improve quality.

kanban The system used in JIT production that triggers repeat orders.

Kaplan and Norton's Balanced Scorecard model A model that assesses performance using four different perspectives: financial, internal business process, learning and growth, and customers.

labour retention The proportion of staff that stay at a company for a given period.

labour turnover The proportion of staff that leave a company during a given period.

latest finishing time (LFT) In network analysis, the latest time that an activity can finish without delaying the completion of the entire project.

lean production Techniques that aim to reduce waste to an absolute minimum (e.g. JIT production).

Glossary

liability A debt a business owes.

liquidity ratio A ratio that shows whether a business has enough liquid assets (e.g. money) to pay its short-term liabilities.

living wage The amount of money thought to be enough to allow an acceptable standard of living.

margin of safety The difference between break-even output and actual output.

market development (or market extension) Selling existing products to new markets.

marketing mix The seven Ps firms use to market their products — the four traditional Ps (price, product, promotion, place) and the three extra Ps (people, physical environment, process).

market mapping A graph that compares two aspects (e.g. quality and price) of different products or brands in a market.

market penetration Trying to increase market share in your existing market.

market share The percentage of sales in a market made by one firm or brand.

Maslow's Hierarchy of Needs A way of considering employees' needs in a job.

mass customisation This combines aspects of bespoke production with the low costs of mass production.

matrix structure A way of organising staff by two different criteria, e.g. into a combination of departments and teams.

merger Where two companies agree to join together into one business.

migration The movement of people from one place to another.

minimum wage The lowest amount that someone can legally be paid.

mission statement A written description of a company's corporate aims.

monetary policy The government's method of controlling inflation, exchange rates and the economy by adjusting interest rates.

monopoly When one business has complete control over the market. Lack of competition can lead to high prices and low quality.

multinational A business with its headquarters in one country and bases in other countries.

net realisable value The amount a company could get by selling its stock in its current state.

network analysis A method of calculating the most efficient order in which to carry out a series of activities.

new product development Selling new products to existing markets.

node A feature of networks that shows where activities start or finish.

objective A medium- to long-term target.

offshoring When a firm has one or several of its activities carried out abroad.

opportunity cost The idea that money or time spent doing one thing means missing out on doing something else.

organic growth When a business grows from within, also know as internal growth.

organisational culture The way things are done within a business, in relation to expectations, attitudes and how staff make decisions.

organisational design The structure or hierarchy of a company.

outsourcing When a firm has one or several of its activities carried out by another specialist company.

payable Money that a business owes.

payables days ratio The number of days it takes a firm to pay for goods bought on credit.

planned strategy A form of strategy that involves all strategic planning being done before it is implemented.

Porter's Five Forces Model A framework for analysing competition within an industry and judging how attractive the market is.

Porter's strategic matrix Identifies a competitive strategy, based on competitive advantage and market scope.

Porter's three generic strategies Three different strategies that can be used to gain a competitive advantage: cost leadership, differentiation and focus.

privatisation When state-owned firms are sold to private companies.

product A good or a service.

productivity The output per worker in a given time period.

profit The difference between total revenue and total costs.

protected characteristic The Equality Act 2010 makes it illegal to discriminate against people based on a protected characteristic, such as age, disability, pregnancy or religion.

protectionist policy A policy designed to protect domestic businesses from foreign competition, (e.g. by using subsidies, tariffs or quotas).

Glossary

quality assurance Measures that are introduced to the production process to ensure quality products.

quality circle A meeting of a group of employees to discuss quality.

quality control Checking goods as they are made to see if anything is wrong with them.

quota A limit on the quantity of a product that can be imported or produced.

re-shoring When a firm brings activities back to the country it is based in.

receivable Money owed to a business.

receivables days ratio The number of days a business has to wait to be paid for goods it supplies on credit.

recession A temporary decline in a country's economic activity.

regional structure A way of organising a business based on geographical location.

regulation Government rules that apply to all firms in a particular industry.

retrenchment When a business decreases in size.

return on capital employed (ROCE) Shows you how much money is made by the business compared to how much money's been put into the business.

return on investment (ROI) A calculation of how efficient an investment is.

revenue The value of sales (also called sales or turnover).

sanction A restriction on trade with a particular country.

scientific management A method of management that makes sure every worker is doing the right job for them and in the right way to improve efficiency.

shareholder A person that owns a share of a company.

single market The countries in a single market have few trade barriers between them. This means goods and labour can move freely within the single market.

sole trader A self-employed individual who trades under his or her own name, or under a suitable trading name.

stakeholder Anyone with an interest in a business, including workers, shareholders and customers.

strategic drift When a business's strategy doesn't adapt to changes in the environment.

strategy A medium to long-term plan for achieving a business's objectives.

SWOT analysis A method of assessing a business's current situation — it looks at the strengths, weaknesses, opportunities and threats facing the business.

tactics Short-term plans for implementing strategy.

takeover Where one firm buys over 50% of the shares of another firm, giving them a controlling interest.

tall structure An organisational structure that has many layers of management, with a strict hierarchy.

Tannenbaum Schmidt Continuum A scale used to define managers based on the style of their decision-making.

tariff A tax on imports or exports that is put in place to restrict trade.

time series analysis (TSA) Recording data over time to help identify trends.

total equity The total money that's been put into a business by shareholders.

total quality management (TQM) A system that involves the whole workforce having input into quality improvements.

trade bloc A group of countries with few trade barriers between them.

trade union A group that acts on behalf of a group of employees in negotiations with employers.

urbanisation An increase in the proportion of a population that lives in towns and cities.

variable cost A cost that varies, depending on how much business a firm does.

variance The difference between a budgeted figure and an actual figure.

venture capital High-risk investment in a business, in the form of share or loan capital.

wage-price spiral A cycle in which wage increases cause price increases, which then cause further wage increases, and so on.

working capital Money available for day-to-day spending.

World Trade Organisation (WTO) An international organisation which encourages trade between member countries. It deals with trade rules and negotiations.

zero-based budget A budget that is based on the specific spending plans for the year ahead.

Index

3D printing 60
7Ps 40-53

A

active resistance 172
added value 54
adverse variance 76
advertising 48, 49
aged receivables analysis 110
aged stock analysis 109
aims 3-5
alliances 159
analysing data 190
analysing overall performance 114, 115
annual general meetings 12
annual hours 92
Ansoff's matrix 145
assessment centres 88
assets 100-104, 108
authoritarian leadership 18
autocratic leadership 18
average rate of return (ARR) 138
averages 191

B

backwards vertical integration 136, 152
bad debts 101
Balanced Scorecard Model 116
balance sheets 100-104, 107
bank loans 81
Bank of England Monetary Policy Committee 129
bar charts 190
barriers to change 172
barriers to entry 136
Bartlett and Ghoshal 164
base cases 143
base years 191
benchmarking 114, 156
big data 35, 167
Blake Mouton grid 19
bloggers 132
booms 125
Boston Matrix 42
Bowman's strategic clock 147
brain drain 132
branding 48
brand loyalty 26, 146
break-even analysis 78, 79
budgets 74-77
  expenditure 74
  fixed 75
  income 74
buffer stock 64
business enterprise policies 122
business growth 148-153
business rates 128
buyer power 136
buying groups 136

C

capacity 56
capacity utilisation 56, 57
capital 69, 100-104
  employed 108
  expenditure 102
  value 10
capital-intensive 61
Carroll's Pyramid of CSR 134
cash cows 42
cash flow
  cycles 72, 73
  objectives 4, 68, 69
centralised structures 87
change
  causes of 168, 169
  demographic 16, 132
  management 170, 171
channels of distribution 50, 51
charities 8
circular economy 123
collective bargaining 97
collectivism 177
commission 92
communication 94, 95, 170, 171, 173, 180
competition 15, 118
Competition Act 118
Competition and Markets Authority (CMA) 118
competition law 118, 136
competitive advantage 115, 146, 147
competitive environment 136, 137
competitive pricing 47
compressed hours 92
computer-aided design (CAD) 60
computer-aided manufacturing (CAM) 60
computer technology 60
concentrated marketing 38
confidence intervals 34
confidence levels 34
conglomerate mergers 152
Consumer Price Index 126
consumer products 42
Consumer Protection Act 119
contingency plans 179
contractionary fiscal policy 128
contribution 78
convenience products 42
copyright 157
core competences 115
core workers 65
corporate governance 188
corporate image 142
corporate objectives 3, 98
corporate social responsibility (CSR) 133, 134
correlation 33
cost leadership 146, 147
cost of sales 70, 105, 106, 109
cost-push inflation 126
costs 6, 7, 14-17, 70, 78, 105, 106, 146
  fixed 6, 78
  objectives 54, 68, 69
  variable 6, 78
country club style 19
credit controllers 72
creditor days ratio 109
creditors 24, 72, 101, 109
critical path 182
crowdfunding 81
cultural barriers 131
currency conversions 127
current assets 100-102, 104, 108
current liabilities 100-104
current ratio 108
customer perspective 116

Index

D

debt factoring 72, 80
debtor days ratio 110
debtors 72, 101, 102, 108, 110
debts 101, 102
decentralised structures 87
decision-making 20-25, 98, 178
decision trees 22, 23
decline (product life cycle) 44
deflation 126
delayering 86, 170
delegation 86, 93, 94
demand-pull inflation 126
democratic leadership 18
demographics 16, 38, 132
dependability 54
depreciation 101, 103
development stage 44, 155
diagrams 190
differentiated marketing 38
differentiation strategies 146, 147
digital advertising 48
digital technology 34, 35, 60, 135, 166, 167
dimensions of national culture 177
direct discrimination 120
direct investment 159
direct mail 49
direct selling 49, 50
discounted cash flow (DCF) 141
discount factor 140
discounting 140
discrimination 120
diseconomies of scale 149
disruptive change 169
distribution channels 50, 51
diversification 144, 145
diversity (of workforce) 82
dividends 12, 13, 100, 101, 105, 106
divorce between ownership and control 188
dogs 42
dominant position 118
downsizing 57
dynamic pricing 47

E

economic growth 124
economic performance 124
economies of scale 136, 148
economies of scope 149
economy 124, 125
efficiency 54, 58-61
efficiency ratios 109
elasticity of demand 36, 37
Elkington's Triple Bottom Line model 117
embargoes 123
emergent strategies 187
emerging economies 130-132
Emissions Trading System 123
employee costs as a % of turnover 84
employee-employer relations 82, 94, 95
employee representation 96, 97
employment
- allowance 122
- contracts 121, 171
- laws 120

empowerment of employees 83, 93
Enterprise Investment Scheme 122
Enterprise Resource Planning (ERP) 135, 167, 189
entrepreneurial culture 175
entrepreneurs 122
Environment Agency 119, 123
environmental factors 16
environmental laws 123
environmentally friendly 16, 133
Equality Act 120
equity 111
ethical objectives 5
ethics 17, 21
EU Common Agricultural Policy 129
EU competition law 136
EU directives 119-121
European Single Market 118
European Union (EU) 123
exchange rates 127, 129
expansionary fiscal policies 128
expected value 22
expenses 105
experience curve 148
exporting goods 124, 127, 129, 158, 159
extension strategies 45
external recruitment 88
extrapolation 32, 33, 115

F

fair trade 17
favourable variance 76
feasibility of strategies 178
feminine cultures 177
financial objectives 68, 69
financial perspective 116
fiscal policy 128
fixed assets 100-102
fixed budgeting 75
fixed capital 102
fixed costs 6, 78
flexibility 54, 65, 66, 170, 171
flexible budgeting 75
flexible working 92
flexi-time 92
float time 183-185
focus strategy 146, 147
force field analysis 169
forecasting 32, 33, 115
forward vertical integration 136, 152
fractions 192
franchising 151
free trade 129, 130
free trade agreements 123
functional decisions 98
functional objectives 3, 98
functional structures 181
future value 140

G

GDP (gross domestic product) 124
gearing 111, 112
global finance market 130
globalisation 130
global recessions 125
global strategy 164
global upswings 125

Index

goods 2
government policies 122, 128
graphs 190
green subsidy schemes 123
Greiner's model of growth 151
gross profit 70, 71, 105, 106
group behaviour 94
growth
  business 148-153
  economic 124
  market 26, 28, 42
  sales 26, 28, 44
growth objectives 4

H

Hackman and Oldham 91
hard HRM 83
harmonisation 163
Herzberg 90
hierarchies 86
hierarchy of needs 90
histograms 190
historical budget 75
Hofstede's dimensions of national culture 177
home working 92
horizontal integration 152
Human Resource Management (HRM) 82, 83
human resources 82-97
  data 84, 85
  flow 84, 85, 88, 89
  objectives 82, 83
hygiene factors 90

I

implementing strategies 180, 181
importing 124, 159
impoverished style 19
income elasticity of demand 37
income statements 105-107
incremental changes 169
index numbers 191
indirect discrimination 120
indirect selling 50
individualism 177
indulgent societies 177
industrial action 97
industrial marketing 47
industrial relations 142
inflation 102, 105, 126, 129, 140
infrastructure 122
initial costs 22
innovation 54, 154-157
intangible benefits 43
interest rates 13, 15, 126, 129
intermediaries 50, 51, 94
internal business process perspective 116
internal recruitment 88
international business strategies 164, 165
internationalisation 158, 159
international markets 158, 159
international strategy 164
interpreting marketing data 32-35
interviews 88
intrapreneurship 156
introduction stage (product life cycle) 44
intuitive decision making 20
inventories 64, 101, 102, 108
inventory control charts 64
inventory turnover ratio 109
investment 101, 138-143
  criteria 142
  decisions 142

J

job-sharing 92
job design 90, 91
job enlargement 93
job enrichment 93
joint ventures 152
just-in-time (JIT) production 59, 64

K

kaizen 63, 156
kanban 59
Kaplan and Norton's Balanced Scorecard model 116
Kevin the koala 52
knowledge and information management 171
Kotter and Schlesinger 172-173

L

labour
  cost per unit 84
  -intensive 61
  productivity 58, 84
  retention 85
  supply 14
  turnover 85, 100, 192
laissez-faire leadership 18
language barriers 94
large-scale production 7
leaders 18
leading questions 31
lead time 64
lean production 55, 58, 59
learning and growth perspective 116
Lewin's force field analysis 169
liabilities 8, 10, 100-102, 104, 108, 111
licensing 159
life cycle 44, 45
limited liability 8, 10
line graphs 190
line of best fit 33
linked networks 66
liquidity 104, 108
  ratios 108
living wage 121
loans 81
locating abroad 160-161
long-term loans 104
long-term objectives 5
loss leaders 47

M

management decision making 20, 21
management information systems 189
managers 18, 19
managing change 170, 171
margins of safety 79

Index

market
  analysis 28, 29, 189
  capitalisation 10
  conditions 14
  development 45, 144, 145
  extension 144, 145
  growth 26, 28, 42
  mapping 29
  penetration 144, 145
  research 30, 31, 98, 190
  share 26, 28, 42
  size 26
marketing
  mix 40-53
  objectives 26, 27
  strategies 144-147
masculine cultures 177
Maslow's Hierarchy of Needs 90
mass customisation 65
mass markets 39
matrix structures 181
maturity (product life cycle) 44
mean (average) 191
mechanistic structures 170
median (average) 191
merchandising 49
mergers 152, 153, 159
Middle of the Road style 19
migration 132
minimum wage 121
mission 3-5, 21, 98, 144
mission statements 3
mode (average) 191
monetary policy 129
Monetary Policy Committee 129
monopolies 15, 118, 122, 147
mortgages 104
motivation (of employees) 90-93
multi-channel distribution 50
multidomestic strategies 164
multinationals 162-164
mutual organisations 8

N

National Infrastructure Plan 122
national living wage 121
national minimum wage 121
natural monopolies 122
net assets 100
net cash flow 138, 141
net current assets 102, 104
net gain 22
net present value (NPV) 141
net realisable value 103
net return 138
network analysis 182-185
new product development 144, 145, 155
niche markets 39, 144, 146, 147
non-profit businesses 8
non-strategic suppliers 67

O

objectives
  cash flow 4, 68, 69
  corporate 3, 98
  costs 68, 69
  ethical 5
  financial 68, 69
  functional 3, 98
  growth 4
  human resource 82, 83
  long-term 5
  marketing 26, 27
  operational 54, 55
  profit 4, 68, 69
  revenue 68, 69
  short-term 5, 98
  SMART 4
  social 5
  survival 4
off-the-job training 89
offshoring 160
oligopolies 15
on-the-job training 89
open trade 129
operating expenses 70, 71, 105, 106
operating profit 70, 71, 105, 106, 108
operational objectives 54, 55
opportunity costs 21, 64, 140
ordinary share capital 10
organic growth 150
organic structures 170
organisational charts 86
organisational culture 174-177
organisational design 86, 87, 93
organisational structures 86, 87, 170, 181
outsourcing 56, 65
overdrafts 72, 80, 104
overtrading 102, 150
ownership 98

P

passive resistance 172
patents 136, 157
paternalistic leadership 18
payables 101
payables days ratio 109
payback period 139
penetration pricing 46
pensions 121
people (marketing mix) 40, 52, 53
percentages 192
perfect competition 15
performance measures 114
performance-related pay 92
peripheral workers 65
personal objectives 3
personal selling 49
person culture 175
philanthropic responsibilities 134
physical environment (marketing mix) 40, 52, 53
pictograms 190
piece rates 92
pie charts 190
place (marketing mix) 40, 50, 51
planned strategies 187
population (marketing research) 34
Porter's Five Forces model 136, 137
Porter's strategic matrix 147
Porter's three generic strategies 146
positioning 38, 39
  strategies 146, 147
power culture 174
predatory pricing 27, 47, 118, 136

Index

price 40, 46, 47
  discrimination 47
  fixing 118
  skimming 46
  takers 7
  wars 136
price elasticity of demand 36
primary research 30
private limited companies (Ltd) 10-13
private sector 2, 8, 11
privatisation 122
process (marketing mix) 40, 52, 53
process innovation 154
produce or perish style 19
product-based structures 181
product 40, 42-45
  decline 44
  development 44, 45, 144, 145, 155
  differentiation 146, 147
  innovation 154
  introduction 44
  life cycle 44, 45
  maturity 44
  portfolios 42
production methods 55
productivity 58-61
profit 2, 6, 7
  after tax 105, 106
  before tax 105, 106
  for the year 70, 71
  gross 70, 71, 105, 106
  margins 71
  objectives 4, 68, 69
  operating 70, 71, 105, 106, 108
  retained 80, 105, 106
profitability 68, 71
  ratio 108
promotion (product) 40, 48, 49
protected characteristics 120
protectionism 123, 129
psychological pricing 47
public limited companies (PLC) 10-13, 105
public relations 49
public sector 2, 8, 11

Q

qualitative data 26, 30
qualitative factors 142
quality 54, 62, 63
  assurance 62
  circles 63, 96
  control 62
quantitative data 26, 30
question marks 42
quotas 123
quota samples 31

R

Race Relations Act 120
ratio analysis 113
rationalisation 57, 80
ratios 108-113, 192
re-order level 64
re-order quantity 64
re-shoring 160
realisable value 103
rearranging formulas 191
receivables 101, 102, 108, 110
receivables days ratio 110
recession 124, 125
recruitment 88
recycling 119
redeployment (of staff) 89
redundancies 89
regional structures 181
regulation 122
remoteness 94
repositioning 144
research 30
reserves 111
resistance to change 172, 173
responsibilities 134
restrained societies 177
retained profit 80, 105, 106
retrenchment 149
return on capital employed (ROCE) 108
return on investment 68, 108
revenue 6, 7, 105, 106
  objectives 68, 69
rewards 20
risks 20
rivalry 137
robotic engineering 60
role culture 174

S

salary schemes 92
sales
  acts 119
  growth 26-28
  value 26
  volume 26
samples 31, 34
sanctions 123
scientific decision making 20
scientific management 90
seasonality 14, 32
secondary research 30
segmentation 38
sensitivity analysis 143
services 2
Sex Discrimination Act 120
share capital 81, 111
shareholders 10-13, 24, 25, 134, 188
share price 13
shopping products 42
short-termism 98
short-term objectives 5, 98
simple random samples 31
slump 125
SMART objectives 4
social enterprises 8
social media 25, 26, 34, 38, 49, 88, 167
social objectives 5
soft HRM 83
sole traders 9, 11
sources of finance 80, 81
speciality products 42
speed of response 54
stakeholder mapping 24, 25
stakeholders 3, 24, 25, 134, 176, 178, 188
stars 42
state pension 121
statistics 190
stock 64, 101-103, 108
stock control 64
stock turnover ratio 109
storage costs 64
strategic decisions 98, 179

Index

strategic direction 144
strategic drift 188
strategic planning 178, 179
strategic suppliers 67
strategies 98, 99, 144-147
stratified samples 31
strong organisational culture 174
subcontracting 56, 65
supplier power 136
supply chains 65-67
survival objectives 4
sweatshops 162
SWOT analysis 99, 178

T

tactics 98
takeovers 152, 159
tangible benefits 43
Tannenbaum Schmidt Continuum 19
targeting 38, 39
tariffs 123, 129
task culture 175
taxation 128
Taylor 90
team style 19
teamworking 93
technology 17, 34, 35, 60, 135, 166, 167
test marketing 155
threat of substitutes 137
time-based management 59
time management 184
time series analysis 32
total equity 100, 108, 111
total quality management (TQM) 63
trade blocs 130
Trade Descriptions Act 119
trademarks 157
trade unions 96, 97
training 89
transfer pricing 163
transnational strategy 164
trends 32, 104, 115
tribunals 120

U

uncertainty 20, 142
under-utilisation 57
undifferentiated marketing 38
unique selling points (USP) 43, 62
unit cost 57, 148, 149
unlimited liability 8
urbanisation 132

V

value analysis 155
vampire slayers 25
variable costs 6, 78
variance 76, 77
VAT 128
venture capital 12, 81
ventures 152
vertical integration 152

W

wage-price spiral 126
wastage costs 64
weak organisational culture 174
what-if analysis 143
working capital 100, 102, 104, 108, 110
works councils 96
World Trade Organisation (WTO) 123, 129

Z

zero-based budgeting 75